STEPHEN HARPER

STEPHEN Harper

JOHN IBBITSON

SIGNAL

McCLELLAND
& STEWART

Signal is an imprint of McClelland & Stewart,
a division of Random House of Canada Limited,
a Penguin Random House Company

Signal and colophon are registered trademarks of McClelland & Stewart,
a division of Random House of Canada Limited,
a Penguin Random House Company

Library and Archives Canada Cataloguing in Publication is available upon request

Published simultaneously in the United States of America by
Signal/McClelland & Stewart, a division of Random House LLC,
a Penguin Random House Company, New York

Library of Congress Control Number is available upon request

ISBN: 978-0-7710-4703-9
ebook ISBN: 978-0-7710-4704-6

Typeset in Bodoni by M&S, Toronto
Printed and bound in the USA

McClelland & Stewart,
a division of Random House of Canada Limited,
a Penguin Random House Company
www.penguinrandomhouse.ca

1 2 3 4 5   19 18 17 16 15

For my Grant

THE CENTRE FOR
INTERNATIONAL GOVERNANCE
INNOVATION

Throughout 2014, it was my great good fortune to serve as a senior fellow at the Centre for International Governance Innovation in Waterloo, Ontario. As well as writing for CIGI publications, I devoted the year to this book. To all of the research and senior fellows I worked beside, thank you so much for sharing your insights and your boundless enthusiasm, and for putting up with my rants. A special thanks to Fen Hampson, director of CIGI's Global Security & Politics program, who first suggested I come join the fellows; to David Dewitt, vice-president of programs, who guided me through the year; and to Rohinton Medhora, CIGI's president, who made the year possible.

CIGI's scholars dedicate themselves to understanding how we as a global community govern, regulate, and protect ourselves. If our leaders collectively are able to deter an attack, manage a downturn, or make everyone everywhere a bit better off and a bit more secure, then they have centres such as CIGI to thank for proposing ideas that one day become solutions. I am enormously in their debt, both for the opportunities and the companionship my colleagues offered. You wouldn't be reading this book without them.

Contents

Preface

He is a lion in autumn, weaker than in his prime, but still a force of nature. He faces his fifth, and perhaps final, test as national leader. But in a way, the result won't matter. Whether Stephen Harper wins or loses the general election of October 19, 2015, is moot. He has already reshaped Canada. And Canada will not easily be changed back.

He has made the federal government smaller, less intrusive, less ambitious. He has made Canada a less Atlantic and a more Pacific nation. He has brought peace to a fractious federation. Under his leadership, Canada speaks with a very different voice in the world. He has also given us a very different politics – more intensely partisan, more ideological, more polarizing. This, too, is unlikely to change, now that people are used to it.

And then there is Harper himself. Slow to trust and quick to take offence, brooding and resentful at times, secretive beyond reason, perhaps the most introverted person ever to seek high office in this country, he has nonetheless defeated a plethora of challengers to give Canada its first ever truly conservative government, with profound consequences for the country. He has brought the West for the first time fully into the life of the nation, while making his Conservatives the only conservative party in the developed world broadly supported by immigrants. And he has lasted a decade in office, no mean feat in this democracy or any other.

Though he has few friends, those he does have think the world of what they see as a smart, funny, insightful, loyal, and decent guy. His family likes him, too.

Others see him as autocratic, secretive, and often cruel.

Stephen Harper sees himself as an insurgent, chafing against the political elites of Central Canada and what he believes is their muddled consensus. He rejected them as a teenager, when he first encountered them at the University of Toronto, and has fought them ever since. Though he would never cite John Turner, that fight is the fight of his life.

He has succeeded. More people think like conservatives today than thought that way a decade ago. Even if they don't consider themselves conservative, they believe in lower taxes, less regulation, leaving the provinces alone, letting people get on with their lives. They accept that our federal government is there to protect the border, protect property, protect communities, protect Canada's interests abroad, protect jobs, and otherwise leave well enough alone. While provincial and municipal governments look after schools, hospitals, roads, and other services, Ottawa under Stephen Harper has become a piece of giant software running silently in the background. Though most Canadians never vote Conservative, this Conservative leader has so altered the assumptions of the political debate that his opponents largely accept, though they will never admit it, the version of government he has bequeathed.

Stephen Harper as prime minister has also undermined the prerogatives of Parliament, eroded privacy rights, debased political debate, demoralized the public service, and cheapened the national discourse. He doesn't care. These losses are collateral damage, and not serious damage at that, in his eyes. Others powerfully disagree.

This book is a biography. While situating the life of Canada's twenty-second prime minister in the life of Canada, it seeks first and last to understand the man himself. You will not find in these pages an exhaustive accounting of the events of the three Conservative governments; in fact, the first half of the book is taken up with Harper's life before he became prime minister. We do what we do because we are who we are, and we become who we are early on. I chose to examine certain events closely because I believe they revealed something of Harper the man, rather than just the politician.

Before I began this book, I didn't feel I really knew Stephen Harper, which is the reason I began it. Now I know him better. I hope after reading this you do, too.

John Pearce, my agent, embraced the idea of a biography of Stephen Harper the moment I first raised it, and Douglas Pepper at McClelland & Stewart did the same, serving as editor as well. I owe both of them a great deal, and not for the first time.

John Stackhouse, who was then editor-in-chief of the *Globe and Mail*, granted my request for a year's leave of absence, and David Walmsley, current editor-in-chief, welcomed me back. To both, and to all of my colleagues at the paper I love so much, thank you for granting me the privilege of working with you.

Most of the people I interviewed about Stephen Harper's rise to power (Book One) were willing to speak on the record. Most of those I interviewed about his years in power (Book Two) were not. In either case, each interview subject was invited to review that portion of the manuscript on which his or her contribution was based. Some also read other portions of the manuscript as well. These first readers pointed out many errors, offered invaluable insights, and sometimes raised objections. I listened to those objections carefully, but final authority over the text was mine alone.

To everyone I interviewed, on whatever basis, thank you. You are the book. Simple as that.

Having once served, briefly and badly, as a copy editor and proofreader, I know how vital these contributors are to the final look and credibility of a book. To Tara Tovell, who delivered a meticulous copy edit, and Erin Kern, who ably proofread the manuscript, many thanks. Any mishaps that crept in nonetheless are my sole responsibility.

Finally and foremost, Grant Burke is why I do anything, which is why I have dedicated this book to him, along with my life.

Ottawa
May 2015

BOOK ONE

Rise

ONE

Suburbs

Stephen Joseph Harper was born on April 30, 1959, to Joseph and Margaret Harper of Leaside, Ontario, which made all the difference in the world.

No other Canadian prime minister has been raised in a suburb. Paul Martin was born in the industrial city of Windsor, Ontario, but his father, already an MP, moved the family to Ottawa, in part so that Paul Jr. could learn French in a private school. Jean Chrétien was one of nine children from a working-class family living in the industrial town of Shawinigan, Quebec. Brian Mulroney was born in the shadow of Baie-Comeau's paper mill. Joe Clark grew up in the flood-prone town of High River, Alberta. Pierre Trudeau was raised in a wealthy Montreal home. Prior to Stephen Harper's election, Canadian prime ministers, whether of humble or comfortable birth, had all been raised in towns and cities, and occasionally on farms. None of these places resembled Leaside, the very first planned community in Ontario.[1]

A man named John Lea settled the lands, in 1819, in what is now near-northeastern Toronto. His son, remarkably, built an octagonal house, which he named Leaside. But the real news came in 1912, when the Canadian Northern Railway (CNoR) began buying up the farmers' land and hired the well-known Montreal planner Frederick Todd to design a town. This was unprecedented for Ontario, whose towns were born and grew more or less as nature and market forces intended. Leaside would be different, CNoR's executives predicted: close enough to Toronto for people to commute by train, but with low-priced land that would attract workers and industry.

Perhaps because it was ahead of its time, Leaside was a bust. Toronto was still too far away, and Canadian Northern went under a few years later, ultimately becoming part of the nationalized Canadian National Railway. Frederick Todd's elegant lattice of curvilinear streets – a marked contrast to the traditional grid plan of Toronto and most other Ontario communities – went largely unrealized. By 1929, at the onset of the Great Depression, the population of Leaside was five hundred, give or take.

But as the Depression waned, and Toronto's borders kept moving closer, builders finally started to pay some attention to the town, with its cheap land and lower taxes. After the Second World War, growth accelerated; in 1954, Leaside became a constituent of the new Metropolitan Toronto. Meanwhile, planners pushed Eglinton Avenue east and Bayview Avenue south, finally linking the town with the city.

Leaside was now officially a suburb of Toronto. And it was there that Canada's first suburban prime minister spent his early years. Stephen Harper would, for the rest of his life, think like someone from the suburbs – middle-class, optimistic, conventional. He would look to voters like him for support, and govern on their behalf.

The year in which Stephen Harper was born also sets him apart from every other prime minister. In 1959, the Cold War was at its height. The Soviet Union's *Luna 1* satellite confirmed Russian superiority in space. Fidel Castro had taken power in Cuba. But it wasn't all gloom. The St. Lawrence Seaway opened. Mattel introduced Barbie to the world. *Bonanza* debuted as the first network television program broadcast completely in colour. On the CBC, *Juliette* was almost as popular as *Hockey Night in Canada*, and Wayne and Shuster were already in their third season. And though almost no one knew of it, two American scientists invented the microchip. The United States had already won the space race, and it hadn't even begun.

Stephen Harper was not only Canada's first suburban prime minister; he was the first elected prime minister from the baby boom generation. Jean Chrétien, Paul Martin, and Brian Mulroney were all born in the thirties.

They were all adults when John F. Kennedy was assassinated. Stephen Harper was four.

And he was not just a boomer, he was a particular kind of boomer: one who arrived at the tail end of the boom. The children born of the vets coming home from the war grew up in the 1950s, a supposedly halcyon decade, and fled that stifling paradise in the 1960s. They could afford to rebel: economic growth was strong and jobs were plentiful. The late boomers grew up in a very different world of oil shocks and détente and stagflation and communism on the march. They cut their long hair and looked for work.

Stephen Harper was a kid from the suburbs who came of age in a time of malaise. None of us can escape our upbringing. He never thought to try.

The family had one distinguished ancestor. In March 1774, Christopher Harper left his Yorkshire farm and sailed to Canada with wife, children, a nephew, horses, cattle, and farm tools in search of better land and lower taxes in the New World.[2] The family settled on lands near Fort Cumberland, at the head of the Bay of Fundy, near the neck of land connecting what is now New Brunswick with Nova Scotia. The land was rich and already cleared, thanks to the Acadians who had been expelled by the British two decades before. It was also full of New England settlers who strongly sympathized with their rebellious brethren to the south. When war broke out, the governor of Nova Scotia, Francis Legge, garrisoned Fort Cumberland to quell any nascent rebellion. He also appointed Christopher Harper, whose loyalty to the Crown was absolute, as justice of the peace for the Township of Cumberland. Harper enthusiastically arrested a few suspected traitors, but the British soon found themselves on the defensive; the Americans laid siege to Fort Cumberland in October 1776.

When the invaders paid a visit to Harper in the dead of night, leaving him "much frightened," he and other Loyalists took refuge in the garrison – a wise precaution since the rebels subsequently burnt his home to the ground.

But the invasion failed, and a grateful Britain granted Christopher Harper land in Sackville, in compensation for his burned-out estate. He prospered, becoming the first resident of Westmoreland County to own a chaise. His name appears in local histories of New Brunswick and accounts of the Americans' unsuccessful attempt to make Nova Scotia the fourteenth state.

———————

The story of Stephen Harper's paternal grandfather is a darker tale. Harris Harper, the grandfather Stephen never knew, was principal of Moncton, New Brunswick's Prince Edward School, and leader of the school's cadet core, which won a national championship for marksmanship. Although he was born too late to enlist during the First World War, Harris dedicated himself to military service; he was commissioned as a lieutenant in the reserves during the Second World War and spent his summers drilling recruits in the militia.

On January 21, 1950, Harris Harper left his doctor's office after a routine injection of vitamin B, and was never seen or heard from again. A thousand volunteers scoured the countryside. Police issued cross-country alerts. Someone said they had seen a man matching his description at the Saint John Salvation Army hostel, but it was probably a false lead. Harris Harper was eventually declared dead, and his wife remarried, but it left Faye Richardson, once a lively and happy woman, permanently fearful and protective of her grandchildren.

A teacher who had once worked with him said Harris was prone to depression, had experienced a nervous breakdown some months before, and likely committed suicide.[3] Of course there was gossip about him running away to start a new life. But someone set on such a course doesn't leave an uncashed paycheque on his dresser.[4] To this day, family members dispute the suicide scenario, suggesting he might have been given the wrong injection, become disoriented, and drowned accidentally. Stephen Harper, when he is in Moncton, has been known to ask people if they remember his grandfather, and what they think happened. Whatever happened, things were never the same inside that house again.

A year and a half after Harris Harper disappeared, his son Joseph went down the road.

———————

Joe Harper arrived in Toronto a newly minted chartered accountant in August 1951. He initially planned to return to New Brunswick, but like so many before and after him, he never went back. A young man from a respectable family in those days had three priorities: finding a job, finding a church, and finding a wife. Joe signed on with the accounting firm of George A. Touche & Co., joined Danforth United Church, and met Margaret Johnston at a church social. Three for three. They were soon married and had three boys: Stephen, Grant, and Robert.

Margaret Johnston hadn't intended to go on a date with Joe Harper. She had promised to meet him at a bowling alley after she finished her game, but had already decided to leave early, to avoid him. He arrived even earlier, so there was nothing for it but to attend the concert he had promised to take her to. She was at least hoping for some lively music to get her through this awkward date, but the band played only dirges. It was February 6, 1952. King George VI had died that day.

"Before I met your mother, I really had never been a really happy person," Joseph Harper once confided to Stephen. "After I met her, I have never really been unhappy since."[5] Margaret had moved from a farm in Grey County, south of Georgian Bay, to Toronto a little over two years before the two met, to attend secretarial and business school after finishing grade ten. The war was over, Ontario was growing fast, and a young woman could leave the homestead and know there'd be work for her as a secretary in the city, which Margaret preferred to life on a farm.

Margaret Harper is a quiet but independent woman, with formidable reserves of energy: a decade after her husband passed, she was still riding her bike to the local shopping mall and she shovelled snow through the grim winter of 2014. Once Stephen, Grant, and Rob came along, she devoted herself to making a home for them and her husband, returning to the workforce after they were grown. Though she had moved to the city, her rural ties were still strong. Margaret was one of six children and times were tough during the Depression, but there was always food on the table, and no one was any better off than their neighbour.

The original Johnston homestead dated back to circa 1850, and Margaret had been born there, though her parents moved to a nearby farm — better land; bigger barn — in the early 1950s. Grey County in the 1960s remained firmly rooted in Ontario's settler culture. Not long after the colony was settled in the early nineteenth century, Upper Canada divided into two societies, each hostile to the other. The colony was controlled by a Tory elite known as the Family Compact. Mostly of English or Loyalist descent, these Tories were the closest thing that British North America had to an aristocracy, and the barrier between them and everyone else was not terribly permeable.

Beyond the walls of the Family Compact, the colony and then the province was dominated by farmers, mostly of English or Scottish stock, though in the 1850s and '60s the Irish and Germans arrived. The farmers wanted to sell their grain to the Americans and buy cheap American farm equipment; the Family Compact wanted, and got, high tariffs instead, to protect their own businesses from Yankee competition. The Family Compact worshipped at the Anglican Church; the farmers were more likely to be Methodists or Presbyterians or Baptists. The farmers wanted real representation; the Compact wanted to keep power in the family. In 1837, William Lyon Mackenzie led an abortive rebellion against the Tory aristocracy. When it failed, he fled to the United States, but ultimately returned and served in the new, responsible, pre-Confederation legislature.

While the Tories voted Conservative, the farmers voted Reform, precursor to the Liberal Party, which was led in the years before Confederation by their political hero, George Brown, proprietor of the *Globe*. By the turn of the twentieth century, the farmers were reliably Liberal, because the Liberals were for reciprocity – but mostly because they weren't Tories. Strains of this ancient division lingered in Ontario society until well after the Second World War.

Joseph Harper once said that when he first went up to the farm to meet Margaret's folks, "he was shocked at how anti–British Empire they were."[6] Grey County farmers were proudly Canadian but lacked the anti-American prejudice that infected the Tory elites. That anti-Tory message must have sunk deeply into Stephen as well. For the rest of his life, he would resent and resist the influence of the downtown elites, spiritual descendants of the Family Compact. By the late twentieth century, most of them were voting Liberal or NDP, though some called themselves Red Tories. But it hardly mattered. They were still a closed elite; they were still anti-American; they still condescended to the Grit farmers' heirs. Stephen Harper would become leader of the Conservative Party of Canada. But he would never be a Tory.

Joe Harper exerted a powerful influence on his family, and on the few people he was prepared to call friend. He had strong views, though he typically only shared them with people he was close to. He could be a bit of a raconteur when he felt comfortable with the situation, but he mostly led a very private, self-contained life.

Joe was twelve when Germany invaded Poland, but he served in the army cadets and later became an avid collector of military insignia, eventually publishing two monographs on the subject.[7] At lunch, when all the other workers went out for a sandwich, Joe would take out his badges and work on cataloguing and describing them. Stephen Harper's future obsession with hockey history echoed his father's obsession with military history. His decision to return the word *royal* to the navy and air force and to restore the traditional British pips on officers' uniforms honours his father's love for military tradition.

To those who knew him, there was nothing stereotypical about Joe Harper: His passion for the recordings of Duke Ellington was as thorough as his passion for collecting military insignia. He wore white socks, and only white socks, remembers Gordon Shaw, a co-worker and family friend.[8] He was smart: After four years at Touche he moved on to the accounting department at Imperial Oil, where his analytical skills landed him on a team working with computers, which were just beginning to enter the private sector. He was part of a highly specialized group that, in 1958, installed one of the first commercial mainframes in North America for Imperial Oil in Toronto.

With Joe now an accountant at Imperial Oil, the Harpers decided it was time to buy a house. In 1956, they chose a red-brick, two-storey home with a bay window at 332 Bessborough Drive, in Leaside – population then about eighteen thousand, already a suburb but still with a bit of a small-town feel. Leaside's quiet social solidarity was under increasing strain as the 1950s gave way to the 1960s. The township council considered whether to spend money on fallout shelters for residents. Local merchants complained about big discount stores staying open longer and demanded that council enforce early closing bylaws. A 1962 plebiscite asked residents of East York, the Metro Toronto municipality in which Leaside was now situated, whether they favoured allowing restaurants to sell liquor and sports teams to play on the Sabbath. (Voters said no to booze in restaurants but yes to sports on Sunday.)[9]

The Harper boys were devoted to both of their parents, but it was their father they emulated. Joe Harper powerfully shaped the lives of his sons. Two of Joe's three children, Robert and Grant, are also accountants. The third is an economist by training. (Stephen Harper likes to joke that he wanted to be an accountant, but he didn't have enough personality, so became an economist instead.) Joe Harper was a teetotaller. So is Robert. Grant drinks rarely and Stephen has been known to knock back three or four drinks a year. Joe Harper was a very guarded, introverted man. His sons are introverted, too.

Introverted does not mean shy – introverts can be very effective in public forums. But they are cautious about letting other people into their lives. They look within themselves for strength and energy, rather than drawing energy from contact with others. Joe Harper was very careful about who he allowed to get close to him. Gordon Shaw describes Stephen Harper as "a chip off the old block."[10]

Introversion, like extroversion, exists on a scale. At its extreme, it can be crippling, leaving a person afraid to venture into the world. Stephen Harper is obviously nothing like that. But he is a very solitary man, who does not like crowds or travel or talking to strangers. He keeps his circle of friends small and close, and his family life as private as he can make it. Consider this example: As prime minister, he occasionally ventures out to movie theatres. (He is a huge movie fan, and his compendium of film and television trivia is as impressive as his mastery of hockey statistics.) Invariably, he sits at the back, surrounded by his security detail, making no effort to greet others in the theatre as any typical politician would. Because he is not drawn to other people, he has difficulty trusting them and appears to have difficulty reading them, which could account for some of his hiring decisions in later years. Over time, as he became more accustomed to public life, he became better at managing public gatherings, and even learned to enjoy travel, mostly because of the interesting conversations he had with world leaders at the other end. But there has rarely been a politician elected to high office as temperamentally unsuited to it as Stephen Harper. Circumstances brought him there, not the desire for any spotlight.

Years after he left the Liberal leadership, Michael Ignatieff observed that "people who say politics is acting get it wrong." "You're not playing a role," he wrote. "You're on stage, true enough, but you're playing yourself. People don't have to identify with your life in order to vote for you, but they have to believe that you are who you say you are."[11]

This is true. And it is strangely true that Harper's deep introversion has worked in his favour as a politician. He so clearly did not enjoy the limelight that voters, shaking their heads, grudgingly gave him marks for seeking high office even though its trappings obviously made him very uncomfortable. In any event, Harper's powerfully inward-directed character was rooted in his genes and in the influence of his father.

Joe Harper was an attentive parent who entered into his sons' lives when they were very young. He was keenly interested in whatever they were doing and eager to talk with them about whatever interested them. For example, if Robert was into building model airplanes, Dad would come home with boxes of model airplanes, and they would build them together. With Steve, as everyone called him, it was trainspotting. The two shared a fascination with the coming and going of trains, and would visit the yards together to watch the locomotives and cars shunting back and forth. Other times, he and his dad would hang out at the Leaside train station. "I always remember going there," he recalled, about a year after his father passed away. "It's one of those moments when I could see my Dad standing there just as if it was yesterday, and what I look at now is remembering how young he was. He was younger than I am."[12]

The Harpers were self-sufficient. Though Joe Harper could be gregarious among family and friends, he had no time for the social whirl. "He had lots of acquaintances, but very few close friends," Robert Harper remembers.[13] Margaret was extremely quiet. All three brothers are essentially independent, even sometimes withdrawn, individuals who count on each other and expect little from anyone else. The rest of the world was, and still is, on the outside. And through stories and anecdotes, Joe defined the world outside the family for his sons.

Harper's devotion to his father is deep and lasting. At cabinet meetings or in conversations, he will invoke a story his father once told him; comments or events will remind him of something his father used to say. Joe Harper moulded his son's world view, and continues to influence it to this day. For example, Joe had witnessed the hardship of the Depression, and talked to his sons about his upbringing in New Brunswick and about the suffering of people struggling to find a job. His own family had been forced to tighten their belts, though as a teacher and principal his father was never without work. But Joe preferred private charity to government welfare. As conservatives would put it a generation later, he preferred to give people a hand up, not a hand out. Stephen Harper, as Alliance leader, talked about Atlantic Canada's "culture of defeat," to his everlasting regret.

But nothing Joe Harper transmitted to his son matched the impact of his views on Israel. Harvey Gellman, a pioneer in Canadian computing, worked with Joe Harper on the mainframe computer at Imperial Oil, and became a friend. Born in Poland, Gellman immigrated to Canada with his parents when he was still a child. He lost many relatives in the Holocaust, and his stories left a lasting mark on Joe, who had always hated intolerance, convincing him that the Jews had a right to their own homeland.[14] Joe passed that fervent conviction on to his sons. One of them was able to act on it. Stephen Harper told more than one person how his father had talked to him about the enormous accomplishments of the Jewish people in science and art and business and how they had suffered at the hands of others. His father told Steve he had an obligation to help them whenever he could. As prime minister, Harper fulfilled that obligation.

Joseph Harper died from a chronic heart condition in 2003. In his eulogy, his son Stephen Harper said, "There is no adequate way of saying goodbye to the most important man in your life."[15]

Suspicion of dependency-inducing government programs. Staunch support for Israel. Being there for your children. By deed more than by word, Joe Harper transmitted his values to his children. They would help shape Stephen Harper's world view, and his destiny.

Whenever anyone asks Stephen Harper where he's from, he tells them "I grew up in a small town in Toronto."[16] He spent his first twelve years in Leaside with his brothers, Grant and then Robert. There are two photos of Joe Harper and the three boys taken when the kids were young. In one, they're in casual clothes; in the other, their Sunday best. Joe Harper is clean-shaven, fit, with carefully neutral hair and a serious suburban expression. In both photos, Grant and Rob are smiling. In both photos, Steve isn't. Robert suspects it was because he was self-conscious about the braces on his teeth.

The brothers were, and remain, inseparable. Steve and Grant were roommates after Steve moved to Alberta. Grant and Robert have worked on Harper's campaigns; they share his confidences, they defend him fiercely.

Steve Harper was, you will not be surprised to hear, a very quiet boy, and very studious. "He was the way he is now – quiet and thoughtful," Margaret Harper remembered.[17] He attended Northlea Public School: a classic, two-storey, red-brick building with separate Boys and Girls entrances located two blocks from the Harper home. Teachers remember, to the extent they can, a well-behaved student who – as Harper recalled when he visited the school in 2004 – excelled in math, having inherited the Harper accounting gene.

Though a passionate Leafs fan, he had weak ankles and suffered his first asthma attack when he was three or four, so never joined a team. Robert recalls visiting his brother in the hospital, presumably after an attack, and Grant would listen to his brother, with whom he shared a bedroom, wheezing in the night.[18] The attacks would continue until he was twelve or thirteen, and then go away, returning twenty years later, when he began carrying an inhaler. Harper's asthma was a recurring, defining feature of his childhood. Because he was sidelined from playing sports, he watched and analyzed them instead, plunging into the arcane, obsessive world of sports statistics. His lifelong penchant for collecting and analyzing data began here. At the dinner table, Margaret later recalled, the boys talked about nothing but hockey.

Things were going well for Joe Harper. His skills in accounting, systems analysis, and computers had earned him a promotion within Imperial Oil. One evening in 1971, when Steve was twelve, the Harpers were over visiting one of their close friends, the Grahams, at their house in Etobicoke. (The boys called them Aunt Beryl and Uncle Harry; Harper still visits with Beryl Graham when he's in Toronto and has the time.) Joe mentioned how much he liked their house. Funny, Harry responded, we're thinking of selling it. Really? said Joe, what are you asking? They concluded the deal on the spot, and the Harpers moved across town to 57 Princess Anne Crescent, a spacious bungalow with big windows and a two-car garage in one of the more affluent parts of one of the more affluent suburbs of Metropolitan Toronto in the early 1970s.

Two years later, Steve entered Richview Collegiate Institute, which had a reputation for academic excellence then as now. He chose a punishing syllabus that included five years of French and four of Latin. Even so, from grades nine to thirteen he was at or near the top of every class. He didn't smoke – either tobacco or marijuana – or drink. He concentrated on school, on following sports, and, increasingly, on the subject of politics.

His friend at the time, Paul Watson, who would become a Pulitzer Prize–winning photo journalist, was not so clean-cut. He was a troubled kid who was heavily into drugs, making him an unlikely candidate to be friends with Harper. Steve "always took the conservative side of the debate, and I was the liberal," Watson later wrote. "He was strait-laced and bookish, I was a drug user and big talker."[19] But Richview was a small school, without the cliquish tendency that would otherwise have kept them apart. "We used to talk current events and argue politics for the fun of it," Watson recalled. "I'm not sure what Stephen got out of it, but I liked the mental exercise of trying to score points against brilliance."

Watson remembers a grade ten geography class where the teacher handed out the results of the weekly assignments with the highest mark first. Every week, Steve Harper was first – except for one week. The question was, How many moons has Jupiter? The textbook said eleven, but Harper had just read in *Science* magazine about the discovery of a twelfth moon, so gave the correct answer but was marked down for it. When Harper politely explained that the textbook was out of date, the teacher responded, "Class, what's the best answer? The answer in the text." Harper "took the hit quietly, returned to official perfection the next week, and left no doubt about who was the smartest person in the room," Watson recalled. This is the first recorded instance of Harper butting heads with someone in a position of authority. It would not be the last. In any case, although Harper got the higher marks, their classmates chose Watson as valedictorian for commencement in 1978. The students must have preferred someone with attitude.

The high optimism of the 1960s had given way to the dreary lowered expectations of the 1970s, the decade in which Harper came of age. The hope for a new politics had been replaced by the very worst of the old politics, as Richard Nixon struggled to avoid impeachment and resigned when it was clear that he would fail. The passionate opposition to the Vietnam War turned into quiet embarrassment, as North Vietnam invaded and occupied a defenceless South. Everywhere, America was in decline: its cities burning in race riots, its economy hostage to an oil cartel that wreaked havoc by stratospherically increasing prices. In Canada, stagflation brought low growth, high inflation, and diminished prospects for the young. Every country that had lost the Second World War seemed to be winning the peace, at the expense of unemployed and underemployed tail-end boomers. And after the confident aspirations of Quebec nationalists metastasized into terrorism and the murder of Quebec cabinet minister Pierre Laporte, sovereigntist Quebecers turned to the Parti Quebecois for a political solution. When René Lévesque became premier in 1976, the nation braced for a referendum on independence. Pierre Trudeau – once dashingly insouciant, now mired in constitutional wrangling and failed wage and price controls – remained, nonetheless, the last, best hope for preserving national unity.

Paul Watson was a huge Trudeau fan and founded a Liberal student club at Richview. He convinced his friend Steve to join. Watson grandly aspired to be prime minister. But first he had to win the attention of the local MP and Liberal cabinet minister, Alastair Gillespie. Gillespie had agreed to speak to Etobicoke Centre's Young Liberal Association, a group that Watson had invented, if he could guarantee twenty warm bodies at the meeting. "I roped [Stephen] in because I needed the numbers," says Watson.[20] At the meeting, Harper ended up jousting with one of Trudeau's more influential ministers, challenging the government's policies and generally proving that, once again, "Stephen was probably the smartest person in the room," Watson recalls. And also, no doubt, more conservative than your typical Young Liberal.

Steve also had a bit of advice for his ambitious friend. To advance his standing within the party, Watson volunteered for Gillespie's 1974 re-election campaign, pounding signs in lawns and canvassing from door to door. One day, Harper and Watson noticed Gillespie passing through the riding, the minister surrounded by assistants. "Look around, Paul," Harper told his friend. "Do you see any sign-pounders?"[21] Harper had already realized that the route to power did not necessarily involve climbing through the ranks. Working your way into the inner circles of the powerful was the swifter and surer method.

Steve Harper may have been quiet and studious, but he wasn't so shy that he couldn't run for, and win election to, class representative on student council for a year. And he was aware of girls. Susan Del Giudice took most of her classes with Steve, and one day the tall, geeky kid with a helmet of hair asked her out on a date. "He was the consummate gentleman but painfully shy," the now-retired elementary school principal recalled years later. "He was an incredible writer. He wrote a beautiful letter to me that was very poetic and sensitive."[22] But the date never happened. "Maybe an hour before, he called to tell me that he was unable to go," Del Giudice recalled. "I think his father had something to do with it. He had a very strict upbringing."

Steve was also beginning to show the first signs of a competitive streak, making it onto the school's Reach for the Top team, organized by Paul Watson, which lost to the team that won the national championship. Though asthma kept him from team sports, he became a competent runner once the asthma went into remission.

Despite all that activity – sports, politics, and academic talent so impressive that his grade ten history teacher once led the class in a standing ovation after one of his star pupil's presentations – he also studied piano, passing the Royal Conservatory of Music's grade three theory and grade nine performance exams. While this did not translate into a lifelong passion for the works of Bach or Brahms (Stephen Harper's musical taste gravitated toward pop standards), he could play and sing competently, as a surprised audience at the National Arts Centre was to discover many years later.

In June 1978, Stephen Joseph Harper graduated from Richview Collegiate Institute at the top of his class. His future direction was clear: "He's off to U of T for Commerce or Law," his high school yearbook declared. Business or law seemed natural futures for such an academically gifted young man.

Determined to cram everything into his brain that he possibly could, and like the good Trudeau Liberal that he was, Harper then headed to British Columbia for six weeks of French immersion at the University of Victoria campus, and to visit family out there. Upon his return, he began life as an undergraduate at Trinity College, University of Toronto. And everything fell apart.

If, as essayist and editor B.K. Sandwell claimed, "Toronto has no social classes / only the Masseys and the masses," the Masseys and their friends went to "Trins." Bishop John Strachan founded the college in 1851 in bitter opposition to the Upper Canadian government, which had decided that King's College, which Strachan had also founded, should be secular rather than Anglican. From that day onward, Trinity has fostered a reputation for exclusivity and exclusion. Small, cloistered, its architecture and mores a self-conscious imitation of Oxford or Cambridge, the college educated the sons and daughters of the elite, many of whom had already submitted their children to the academic excellence and social terrors of private boarding schools.

"We are the salt of the earth, so give ear to us," the men and women of college loved to proclaim in their fake Oxbridge accents:

> *No new ideas shall ever come near to us!*
> *Orthodox! Catholic!*
> *Crammed with divinity!*
> *Damn the dissenters,*
> *Hurrah for old Trinity!*

Students wore black academic gowns. At the men's residence, jacket and tie were required for dinner. The food was appalling, but you could leave your coffee cup pretty much anywhere you liked, and someone would silently pick it up and return it to Strachan Hall.

The rituals of the college were bizarre, but proudly held. They included "pouring out," in which second-year students would forcibly eject from the dining hall any man of college who annoyed his neighbours at the table; "deportations," in which second-year students would kidnap first-year students and leave them stranded, sometimes naked, in a park, at Centre Island, or even in another town; and Episkopon, in which the ghost of Bishop Strachan visited the men and women of the college to chastise them for their erring ways, through skits and songs composed by a committee that sought to push the boundaries of sexual – especially homophobic – humour.

Initiation was hell. Days of drinking and hazing culminated in the Cake Fight, in which the students of first year would seek to push through a phalanx of second-year students guarding the gate at Henderson Tower. Though the tower protected the sophomores, the freshmen were drenched in an indescribably foul concoction from the roof above that dedicated students had been preparing all summer. It typically included beer, urine, scraps from the kitchen, yeast, and anything else that could be found and then left to ferment in the heat. Only after surviving this misery were freshmen and -women entitled to don their gowns.

Trinity also offered an excellent education, and the camaraderie of a small college filled with exceptional students. Rather than eating cafeteria-style, the students were served dinner, which brought the entire college together each night (the men at Trinity; the women at their own residence, St. Hilda's), and the discussions and debates this fostered could be the best part of a student's education. But a shy freshman arriving from a suburban, middle-class background, educated at public schools, already suspicious of the Tory descendants of the Family Compact with their snobbish disdain for anyone Not Like Us, could be traumatized by such an environment. Steve Harper lasted two weeks.

Or maybe three. No one can remember exactly; this isn't a part of his life that Harper prefers to talk about. But he was clearly not happy at Trinity. He was put off by the huge, impersonal classes of the University of Toronto. He didn't like the professors who warned the students that the person sitting beside them would be gone by Christmas. He didn't like the pretensions of many of the students. He didn't like any of it.[23]

Robert Harper does not believe that Harper's decision to quit university was sudden; in fact, he believes it was something that had been brewing for more than a year, that Steve didn't know what he wanted to do with his life and wasn't prepared to commit to university until he had answered that question.

But whatever was going through his mind in the months leading up to his decision to quit, the fact remains that in his first encounter with the Upper Canadian elite – the young men and women who would go on to run the businesses, lead the political parties, manage the bureaucracies, and shape the arts and academies of English Central Canada – Stephen Harper decided he wanted none of it, or them. He could have tried to fit in to this new world, which was closed but less impermeable than in the past, but instead he fled from it. His decision to reject that world, and his sense of exclusion from it, would shape his life and his politics. It marked him.

It also produced a deep ambivalence toward academia that would shape the next decade of his life. It would be three years before he returned to university – an eternity for someone that young and that intelligent – and he would drop in and out of school repeatedly during his years as a graduate student. All his life, Stephen Harper has resisted taking orders from other people. Starting with professors.

Or maybe starting with his dad. The news that he was quitting university did not go down well with Joe and Margaret. They couldn't believe their ears. Their eldest son had always worked so hard and done so well. How could he have decided to quit, and so quickly?

Joe had insisted that the boys pay their own university tuition, to instill the notion that a degree was a means to an end, and the end was a good job. In high school, Steve had worked as an office boy in a provincial government office, and as a summer clerk at the local LCBO to help pay for his tuition and books. If he wasn't going to go to university, then he was going to have to earn a living. But doing what? He was nineteen and had only a high school education, but he didn't care. The one thing that both Steve and his father agreed on was that he needed to get a job.

Gordon Shaw was overseeing offices for Imperial Oil in both Edmonton and Calgary. He got a call from Joe Harper, who confessed he had a problem with his son. "We can't get along with him at home," Shaw recalls his friend saying.[24] Was there a job for Steve out there? There was – for an office clerk, in the Edmonton office. Shaw extended the offer. Steve took it immediately. At that point in their relationship, it appears, both Joe and Steve needed to put a couple of time zones between them.

At certain crucial times in his life, Stephen Harper has displayed a tendency to prefer flight over fight. If a situation becomes untenable, he simply abandons the situation, rather than trying to change it to his advantage. Over the years, Harper learned to curb this tendency, but he hadn't yet when he was nineteen. The same week he quit school, he flew west to a new city, a new life, and a new job – though not much of one.

Steve Harper was on his own.

TWO

Lost

He found himself in an entry-level job in a strange city thousands of miles from home with little money for food and rent. For a while he lived at the Edmonton YMCA, before moving to the first of two boarding houses that he stayed at for a year or so – a harsh life for a kid his age from a comfortable suburban world. Eventually, he was able to afford a modest walk-up on Whyte Avenue in Strathcona, which today is home to Edmonton's hipster scene but back then was "a modest street of car dealerships, small shops, the very downscale Army & Navy department store, a western saddlery, a biker bar, a couple of hotels with strippers, and some blue-collar taverns."[1] But for Harper, that first year was an education in how people on the edges of society made out. "Some of the places he lived opened his eyes," Robert Harper believes. Some of his fellow boarders were "people who had terrible lives."[2]

Harper was lost. Alone in a strange city in a dead-end job, a university dropout with no prospects. What did he want? He didn't know. But he was determined not to strike out in any direction until he was certain it was the right one. In the meantime, he would bide his time. This was extraordinary, given who Steve Harper was and where he had come from. There was or is nothing unusual about a student taking a year off before starting college. But Harper wasn't your usual student: he had ranked top of his class throughout high school, and he had grown up in a household with strict standards and high expectations. He hadn't taken a year off before starting college; he had dropped out in first term, which is far more traumatic. And he wasn't backpacking across Europe to see the sights while grieving for an unrequited love. He was stuck in a fluorescent-lit office in Edmonton, working as a clerk. This life would last for three years, from ages nineteen to twenty-two. To drop out for so long at such a young age is a far greater act of rebellion against expectations than smoking up and sitting in. But if Harper was lost, he was prepared to stay lost until he was certain he had found himself on his terms. In the meantime, he'd bring people coffee.

He started out as an office boy, as they were called back then, at Imperial Oil's Edmonton office. His boss was Frank Glenfield, who quickly also became mentor and friend. Glenfield later recalled that Harper was desperately unhappy at first – far from home, alone, and an Easterner with airs, which did not go down well in proud, stiff-necked Alberta. (Edmonton in those days consisted of what one local called "a vast sea of essentially blue-collar working people, and a smaller enclave of government/academic/cultural types.")[3] To make matters worse, he was a huge Trudeau fan – "When Stephen first came to Edmonton, he was a Trudeau Liberal," Glenfield later recalled. "He thought Trudeau was God."[4] In a region where Trudeau was widely detested, Liberals were an endangered species, and there were plenty of men with guns.

But mostly he was just miserable. "He was a very troubled boy when he came," Glenfield believed. "I think what upset him the most was rebelling against what the family wanted him to do. But he wanted to do his own thing. He didn't want to just toe the party line."

Steve was a good worker – happily taking on the most menial of assignments, from delivering mail to handling petty cash. Still, he was lonely and homesick. He was relentlessly self-critical, uncertain over whether he had made the right decision in coming West, yet also determined to find a meaning and purpose to his life. Glenfield started inviting him home for dinner, where Steve would argue with Mary Glenfield about the respective merits of individual members of the Beatles. "He was very self-absorbed," Mary recalled. "I would say he's absorbed by two things. One is himself and the other is: Am I doing the right thing? Am I doing the thing that I should be doing?"[5]

The Glenfields were active in the Edmonton theatre scene, and Steve started accompanying them to auditions and rehearsals, at one point declaring that he thought he had what it took to be an actor, if that's the career he wanted – except he didn't.

He shared his father's aptitude with computer systems, and before long he was given more responsibility with them. After two years in Edmonton, he moved to Calgary, when Imperial Oil shifted its computer operations there. But he never lost his connection with the Glenfields. He'd come up to visit and sleep in a sleeping bag on the living room floor. Many years later, as prime minister, he dropped in on them unannounced, to talk over old times, and when Frank passed away in 2011, Harper delivered a eulogy at the funeral. He once told his wife, "When I'm old, I hope I'm as kind and considerate as Frank."

"Why don't you try being like Frank now?" Laureen retorted. They both laughed.[6]

Three years away from university is an awfully long time for a kid as demonstrably smart as Steve Harper had been at Richview. At one point, he started a course in accounting, but gave it up. He knew how intelligent he was, but he didn't know what to do with it. He refused to take up university unless and until he knew *why* he was going back. No flitting from major to major for him. He just ground it out, and thought, and thought, until finally, in 1981, he was ready.

That September, Steve Harper left his job at Imperial Oil and returned to school, at the University of Calgary. But it was a very different university that he chose, in a very different time, and Harper had become a very different young man. The years in Edmonton and Calgary, and the events that filled those years, had reinforced the conservative streak that Paul Watson had already noticed in high school. And the counterbalancing admiration for Pierre Trudeau had evaporated. In fact he had come to loathe the Liberals, and especially Trudeau. He had become a true Westerner.

Politicians in Ottawa and Toronto had always assumed that the original Northwest Territories – the former lands of the Hudson's Bay Company, which included the Prairies – would hold junior status in Confederation. They would be peopled by the descendants of Ontario settlers, they would serve as a market for the goods being churned out by Ontario factories, and they would be grateful.

But the dire importance of uniting the new country by settling the Prairies before it spun off into its separate regions, the completion of the Canadian Pacific Railway, and the suppressing of the Métis rebellion forced Ottawa to reconsider. Immigrants had to be found, hundreds of thousands of them, and right now. Wilfrid Laurier's minister of the interior, Clifford Sifton, made filling the West with farmers his life's mission. Since it was clear there just weren't enough Canadians at home or Britons willing to emigrate to meet the need, he opened the West to Eastern Europeans – Germans and Ukrainians and others considered too alien ever to successfully integrate into the Western European–based societies of Central Canada, or so many in Central Canada thought. Another crucial source came from south of the border. The American frontier was closed; land was becoming increasingly valuable and scarce, and Alberta in particular gained the reputation for being "the last best West." Between 1898 and 1914, nearly six hundred thousand American farmers or aspiring farmers flooded north into Alberta, contributing to its uniquely populist conservative character.[7]

But the Prairies remained mere oversized colonies, in the eyes of the Central Canadian power elites, which is why when provincehood came, the new provinces were denied control over their natural resources, a power that the founding provinces enjoyed and profited from. The idea that the resources of Central and Atlantic Canada belonged to the people of each province, but the resources of the Western provinces belonged to the entire country, infuriated Westerners long after the situation was remedied by federal legislation in 1930. And in truth, Liberal Ottawa (for Conservative governments were few and fleeting from the end of the First World War until the 1980s) continued to look upon the Prairies' rich resources as a national treasure – something that never applied to Ontario minerals or Quebec hydro.

On February 3, 1947, on Mike Turta's farm, fifteen kilometres west of Leduc, an Imperial Oil drilling team led by Vern "Dry Hole" Hunter (the nickname came from his unbroken string of failed drilling attempts) struck oil, transforming Alberta and Canada. By the 1970s, oil was making Alberta rich and Central Canada jealous. And then came the shocks. Prices rose 400 per cent after a cartel of sheiks embargoed oil production to punish the West for supporting Israel in the 1973 Yom Kippur War. Oil shocks contributed to stagflation, battering the Western economies with low growth, inflation, and high unemployment, though none of this mattered to the blue-eyed sheikhs of Alberta, who profited from the skyrocketing prices. The Trudeau government, determined to protect Ontario industries from the worst of the damage, forced down the price of Alberta oil through export restrictions and other measures through the late 1970s. Western anger over this enforced largesse turned to rage when, in 1980, the newly elected Trudeau government imposed the National Energy Program, promptly wrecking the Alberta economy.

The NEP – three letters that Albertans spit out to this day – had several goals: to preserve Central Canadian industry by pricing Alberta oil below market rate; to raise federal revenues (and correspondingly reduce provincial and industry revenues) through petroleum taxes and other fiscal means; to increase Canadian ownership of the energy sector through the creation of Petro Canada and other measures; and to encourage oil exploration in federally controlled land (so that Ottawa could reap the royalties). The program's components were many and complex, but its impact was immediate and its timing was just awful.

Shortly after the NEP came into effect, the developed world entered a sharp, deep recession. Oil prices sagged, and since the whole point of the NEP was to increase federal revenues, the very raison d'être of the program was now in question. The NEP may have helped cushion the shock of the recession in Ontario, but it unquestionably damaged the Alberta economy, as producers shut down exploration and reduced production since the fruits of their labours were being partially nationalized. And it left Albertans bitterly convinced that Central Canada in general and the Liberal Party in particular didn't give a damn about them. "Let the Eastern Bastards Freeze in the Dark," raged the bumper stickers. But it was a futile threat.

For almost every Albertan, the NEP was personal, and the person to blame was Pierre Trudeau, who seemed perversely determined to alienate and isolate the West. Official bilingualism, part of his general obsession with Quebec; "Why should I sell your wheat?"; flipping the bird to protesters in Salmon Arm, B.C.; and above all, the NEP. The Liberal prime minister appeared neither to understand nor care about Western sensibilities.

Harper had admired Pierre Trudeau's intellectual rigour and his determination to keep Canada together by confronting Quebec separatism. But
Trudeau's apparent contempt for the West, along with the effects of the
hated NEP, brought about a Damascene conversion. In Steve Harper's
young eyes, Trudeau's policies were no longer enlightened; they were
destructive. Who cared about reconciling Quebec, when all around him
people he knew were losing their jobs?

But it was about more than just the NEP. After three years in the West,
this intense, introverted, powerfully intelligent, and passionately questioning young man found that Western conservative values were a natural fit
with his own. Prairie resentment at what Eastern elites had done to the
West matched his own resentment of those elites. And there may have been
something else. In future years, people would wonder why Stephen Harper
was so combative, even vindictive. Whether it is taking on the chief statistician, or the chief electoral officer, or even the chief justice of the Supreme
Court, Harper often presses the attack beyond what even sympathetic
observers consider reasonable or politically wise. Part of the answer may
lie, not in the polarization between Liberals and Conservatives, or even liberals and conservatives, but between established Central Canadian elites
and aggrieved Westerners, reflected in Harper's own youthful experiences.
The senior figures of the public service are part of that elite; the judiciary
belongs as well. And as for the CBC or the political science department at
U of T or the literary crowd – don't get him started. All of this appears to
have crystallized in Steve Harper's young mind in the early eighties with
the NEP. Its residual impact was a terminal loathing of Pierre Trudeau.

Consider this remarkably candid personal essay that Harper penned in
early October 2000, shortly after Trudeau's death. That death and the
state funeral that followed it had transfixed the nation – or at least those
parts of the nation that had been transfixed by Trudeau himself – culmin-
ating in a speech at the funeral by Trudeau's son, Justin, that left observers
either in tears at its eloquence or disgusted by its maudlin theatricality.
Harper, at the time president of the National Citizens Coalition, published
his own reminiscence of Trudeau in the *National Post*. He began by saying
that he had almost met Trudeau in 1977 – probably when he was a Young
Liberal – but that circumstances didn't permit. It was only in the year

before Trudeau's death that he finally encountered the former prime minister, on the streets of Montreal.

"There I came face to face with a living legend, someone who had provoked both the loves and hatreds of my political passion, all in the form of a tired out, little old man," Harper wrote. "It was an experience at once unforgettable, nostalgic and haunting. For Mr. Trudeau had obviously diminished as much as my assessment of him over those 22 years."[8]

He went on to describe Trudeau's contempt for the West, the evils of the NEP – "I came to know many of those who lost their jobs and their homes" – the economic ruin brought on by expanding the welfare state, bloating the bureaucracy, and hog-tying industry with regulations. "From these consequences we have still not fully recovered, and they continue to have an impact on my pay cheque, and my family's opportunities, every single month."

He recanted his once-sincere conviction that only Trudeau could counter Quebec separatism and keep the country together, for the country was atomizing regardless. "Mr. Trudeau won the great political battles of his day only to see the war lost with surprising speed after he left office," Harper concluded. "Yes, he continues to define the myths that guide the Canadian psyche, but myths they are. Only a bastardized version of his unity vision remains and his other policies have been rejected and repealed by even his own Liberal party."

This is where Harper would be at the end of the century. But he was already far along the road when he enrolled at the University of Calgary. The intellectual framework would come later. What mattered was this visceral rejection of Pierre Trudeau, the Liberal Party, and the Central Canadian elites who worshipped the former and sustained the latter. He was outside them. The West, his adopted homeland, was outside them. And yes, it was personal.

———————

Those Eastern elites were also the enemies of an intellectual cabal at U of C. For Stephen Harper was at the university with the strangest political science department in the land.

In 1968, E. Burke Inlow invited a recently graduated Ph.D., Tom Flanagan, to join the political science department of the University of Calgary. The department existed almost entirely on paper, because U of C had only come into existence in 1966. (Harper had rejected one of the oldest academic institutions in the country, and embraced one of the newest.) When Flanagan received the offer, he went looking for a map to find out what and where Calgary was.[9]

Flanagan and Inlow were both Americans. An expert in the Middle East and Iran, Inlow had worked in the Pentagon before being recruited by U of C to help set up its political science department. This would later provide fodder for conspiracy theorists, who believe, as one analyst put it, "he was sent to Calgary by the national security state to do what he could to see that the local academy provided an intellectually safe and friendly environment for US oil interests."[10] Whatever.

But Calgary was and is a conservative town at heart. Reflecting that, many of the political scientists at U of C would prove to have closer intellectual ties to American libertarian thinking than to anything coming out of the Canadian universities to the east, or out of the University of Alberta in Edmonton, for that matter. And with the petroleum industry already a powerful economic force, the university's benefactors would appreciate a school that countered the liberal orthodoxy of the University of Toronto, Queen's, McGill, et al. Besides, the country would surely benefit from having one, just one, department of political science that espoused a more conservative (actually, neo-liberal) point of view.*

---

* Every book on politics struggles to reconcile "liberal" and "conservative." The liberal movement in the 1800s sought personal progress through individual rights, economic progress through free markets and free trade, and political progress through democratic reform. But in the twentieth century, "liberal" evolved to include a greater emphasis on using the powers of the state to fight poverty and protect minority rights. Conservatism became more closely associated with the values that in the previous century had been identified with liberals. And then there are libertarianism, neo-conservatism, and neo-liberalism – which, when you come down to it, might all mean the same thing: minimal government and maximum freedom of individual choice and responsibility. But this is all contained in a footnote rather than in the main body of this text because people know in their gut what the left and right are, what it means to be a liberal or a conservative or a social democrat. To paraphrase from the judge, political ideology is like pornography: hard to define, but everyone knows what they're looking at.

Others saw things differently. First-rate political scientists and economists at the university have been reviled in terms not used by any other academics for any other academics. In a 2004 profile of Tom Flanagan, to cite only one example, Radha Jhappan of Carleton University referred to political science at U of C as "the department of redneckology."[11]

Flanagan joined Inlow at Calgary after obtaining a Ph.D. at Duke University, ultimately reconciling his devout Catholicism with the dictates of democratic political theory by embracing a fierce conservatism, which is why he accepted the like-minded Inlow's offer. Others, of more or less similar bent, joined them, including Barry Cooper, a Canadian who had shared an office with Flanagan at Duke; Rainer Knopff, who made a specialty of criticizing the judicial activism of the Supreme Court; David Bercuson, a Montreal-born historian who focused on Canadian foreign and defence policy – both of which he generally found wanting – and Ted Morton. Morton, another American émigré, was more socially conservative than the others: he campaigned against gay marriage and sought to restrict abortion rights. He also got himself "elected" senator for Alberta (an early demonstration of the principle that senators could and should be elected) though the Chrétien government never gave that election the time of day. Flanagan himself spent much time analyzing Aboriginal claims – which, he concluded, were a distraction from the real problem, which was the reluctance of Aboriginal Canadians to recognize the realities of the advanced, capitalist, liberal-democratic society in which they lived.

They didn't all believe in the same things at the same time. But they shared a general set of common values antithetical to their counterparts in Central Canadian universities. They favoured greater individual freedom and responsibility, smaller government, lower taxes, and provincial autonomy. They were intolerant of the endless federal hand-wringing over Quebec – Quebeckers should make up their mind whether to stay or go, and be done with it – and thought Ottawa was doing the Aboriginal population more harm than good by catering to its leaders' demands rather than promoting personal responsibility and property rights. They were particularly suspicious of the Charter of Rights and Freedoms that Trudeau had managed to insert into the Canadian Constitution. Liberal-minded judges had used and would use the Charter to override Parliament and "read in" rights for minorities of one kind or another, they warned. They also self-consciously fought the stereotype of the academic intellectual. These professors owned guns and fishing rods, travelling to the Arctic each spring to fish for pike and lake trout, and proudly boasted that theirs was the only department of political science in the country that had suspended classes during hunting season.[12]

One day in 1996, Tom Flanagan arrived at the department brandishing a paper and declaring, "Hey guys, guess what? We're a school!"[13] The paper, published by the Johns Hopkins School of Advanced International Studies, was entitled "The Calgary School: The New Motor of Canadian Political Thought," and it declared that the Calgary group had "given birth to a new form of nationalism, that in turn is changing the terms of debate in English Canada."[14] They would change it even more, through their influence on the Reform Party and Stephen Harper.

Harper was smart enough to know that life without a university degree would be no life at all for someone like him. Commerce was out; his ambitions extended far beyond double-entry bookkeeping. But he did like numbers – he was Joe Harper's son, after all. They provided a certainty, a predictability that the woolly-minded theorists in the humanities neither understood nor cared about. Now that he was working in Calgary, the University of Calgary was the sensible choice. So he enrolled as an undergraduate majoring in economics and began reading the *Economist* magazine. Conservative, insouciant, opinionated, comprehensive in its global reach, the *Economist* began shaping his world view as it shaped those of so many young men and women in that tumultuous time.

As any *Economist* reader knew, Margaret Thatcher and Ronald Reagan were imposing a new conservative revolution on their societies. Thatcher had come to power in Great Britain in 1979, and Reagan in the United States in 1981. She was shutting down or selling off money-losing state enterprises, throwing millions of people out of work, but also injecting new life into the moribund British economy. He was facing down striking air traffic controllers, slashing taxes, and launching a new arms race against the Soviet Union, which he referred to as an "evil empire."

Thatcher and Reagan were opposed by progressives who seemed to have no new ideas of their own, other than respecting the status quo, even though years of strikes and deficits and inflation and little or no growth had shown the old ways no longer worked. More effective opposition came, perhaps, from impossibly thin kids with green hair, sporting rings in improbable places, who thrashed to anarchic music and raged against the machine. They were joined, at least in spirit, by grim-faced protesters who demanded an end to the proliferation of nuclear weapons in Europe. Still, nothing could derail the Anglo-American conservative renaissance. And most people preferred disco.

While the Thatcher/Reagan revolution was upending decades-old certainties elsewhere, Pierre Trudeau had other priorities for Canada. As a quid pro quo for rejecting sovereignty in the 1980 referendum, the prime minister had promised Quebec that he would bring home the Constitution and create a new bill of rights, the Charter. Negotiations dragged on for months; premiers made this demand and that; the Supreme Court weighed in; and when the nine premiers of English Canada finally reached a deal with Trudeau, Quebec premier René Lévesque bolted, accusing the others of treachery.

Meanwhile, Canada slogged through the recession, which had become the worst since the Depression. Economic output fell 4.9 per cent over six quarters in 1981 and 1982. (By comparison, the so-called Great Recession of 2008–2009 saw output decline 3.3 per cent over three quarters.) In August 1981, the Bank of Canada rate reached an astonishing 21 per cent, while inflation ran at 12 per cent and unemployment peaked at 13 per cent. People bought the boxy new Chrysler K-Car, not because it was a good car, but because it was all they could afford. But the Japanese were taking over the automobile market, as they had already taken over consumer electronics and household appliances. If they went after aviation and computers, people worried, the North American economy would be finished.

The world was a tumultuous, troubled place in 1981, but it was also exciting, and Steve Harper wanted to get out into it. Although he intended to pursue an advanced degree, Harper didn't want to confine himself to research and teaching at the academy. He wanted to be part of the action, maybe by joining the federal Department of External Affairs and becoming a diplomat. It was all a bit fuzzy, but no fuzzier than you would expect from a slightly-more-mature-than-typical undergraduate.

He was a stellar student, fulfilling the potential he had displayed at Richview but that his very short stint at U of T had managed to short-circuit. A's and A-pluses were standard. He enjoyed living in residence, and was elected floor rep. He had an Ismaili roommate, as he later told the Aga Khan. Though he couldn't play hockey, he coached teams in the intra-mural university league. For the first time in years, life was good. Better than good. He was in love.

Her name was Cynthia Williams. She was a second-year journalism student at Mount Royal University, but she was on the University of Calgary campus because Mount Royal didn't have residences. Harper saw her across a crowded cafeteria, found out who she was, tracked down her phone number, called her, and asked her out. (He may be introverted, but he is also determined.) She knew what he looked like and liked the look – tall, big boned, with a great nimbus of fair hair that almost reached to his shoulders. She accepted. Williams is very much the opposite of Harper: open, energetic, and with an easy, infectious laugh. What did she see in this shy, geeky kid? "He was witty," she recalls, "and we shared an interest in politics."[15]

Williams had learned politics at her father's knee. Cy Williams was a public servant, but at home he had strong views about how his political masters did their jobs, and those views often weren't flattering. Williams was raised in Alberta and Saskatchewan, which meant that, federally, you were either a Progressive Conservative, otherwise known as a Red Tory, or a conservative conservative – Stephen Harper would one day describe himself as a Blue Tory. Williams thought of herself as a conservative of the progressive variety. She practically worshipped Peter Lougheed, who ended thirty-five years of Social Credit government in Alberta when he came to power in 1971, governing as a Progressive Conservative in name and deed until 1985. During those years, he railed against the interventionist perfidy of the Liberals in Ottawa even as he retooled Alberta's society, spending heavily on education, health care, even the arts, and establishing the Heritage Fund to harness oil-industry revenues for future needs.

Harper was attracted to Williams's oppositeness. At parties – and they went to a lot of them – she would talk with everyone while he sat around the table intensely discussing his two great passions: politics and the Oilers. Despite the move to Calgary, Harper's hockey heart remained in Edmonton. He had arrived as the team was transitioning from the WHL to the NHL. Harper was at the Oilers' first playoff game and cheered the team's rise, with Wayne Gretzky leading a band of brothers that included the likes of Mark Messier and Grant Fuhr. Fortunately for their relationship, Williams was an Oilers fan as well, though it was no easy thing to live in Calgary and cheer for Edmonton.

Williams disputes the portrait of Harper as shy, introverted, and withdrawn. "He's not socially awkward," she stresses. "He certainly wasn't back then. He handled himself well. He just wasn't one of those guys who wanted to meet everybody in a room. He wanted to meet someone who had something interesting to say."

One of the things that Williams liked best about Steve Harper was his sense of humour. He was actually a very funny guy, with a razor-sharp ability to parody other people. They enjoyed the same things, especially watching hockey on TV. Williams also had a passion for football – both CFL and NFL – and so Harper ended up watching more of it than he otherwise would have cared to. Neither of them particularly enjoyed cooking, so ordering in a pizza was often the preferred option. Steve had started to get big, thanks to his addiction to pop, fast food, and ordering in.

They never lived together. Each believed that if you were going to co-habit, you should marry. But neither of them was particularly religious; neither of them went to church or talked about their faith, or lack of it. For now, they were both happy to spend a lot of time together, watching sports, watching the news, arguing over sports and the news, talking politics, studying, hanging out with friends. They were a typical college couple.

Despite Harper's interest in things political, he had zero political ambition, and lampooned earnest young students who solemnly declared that they were going to be prime minister one day. But his interest in the foreign service was real, and he soon acted on it. He easily had the necessary marks, and his years of studying French would stand him in good stead, so passing the foreign-service exam was unlikely to pose a problem. Yet there were hundreds of applicants each year from across the country who easily met these qualifications but failed to make the cut. He needed an edge over the competition.

The university offered career counselling for undergraduates, and Harper sought it. You need to pad your resumé, he was told – something that shows your engagement in the community, your leadership potential, your grasp of international issues and politics, and your desire to be in the public service. When Steve told Cynthia, she had just the answer. Williams had always been interested in politics, as a young Progressive Conservative. The two of them should get involved in the local constituency, she told him. This would be the second time Steve Harper had been dragged into joining a political party. But the PCs in Calgary were a much better fit than the Liberals in Etobicoke. Harper never had been a Liberal at heart, and the events of the past few years – overseas as well as at home – had made it seem ludicrous that he had ever joined the party. And his studies in economics – he wasn't yet taking much in the way of political science courses – convinced him that he belonged on the conservative side of the political spectrum. And so Jim Hawkes, Progressive Conservative Member of Parliament for Calgary West, found himself staring one evening at a pair of young faces in the very front row of a room otherwise filled with much older folk.

Hawkes is a genial, courteous, engaging, and, as we will see, very forgiving man. He was also a conscientious MP. Not that he needed to be. Seats didn't come much safer than Calgary West if you were a Progressive Conservative in those days. But Hawkes was not your typical back-bencher. He held a Ph.D. in experimental psychology, and had studied federal job-creation programs in the early 1970s, which brought him to the attention of Joe Clark, who was then working for Robert Stanfield, the party's leader. When Clark succeeded Stanfield as leader in 1976, Hawkes took a leave from his teaching duties at the University of Calgary to help the new leader set up his office. He decided to run himself in the 1979 election, winning his seat and then holding it in the 1980 debacle that upended the short-lived Clark minority government. In that election, Hawkes took two thirds of all votes cast in Calgary West. In 1984, he would get that number up to 75 per cent.

So Hawkes could have coasted. Instead, he worked his riding diligently, which included hosting regular town halls. At this one, the young couple at the front asked a number of questions, though the boy got in more than the girl, and after the event they stayed around to talk some more. Two things became clear to Hawkes from the first: he had two smart, committed young people who wanted to be part of his team. And they both knew a great deal about domestic issues but not the first thing about political organization at the riding level. Before long, both were committed volunteers who also served on the riding executive. And, as it turned out, Hawkes needed them – badly.

As someone whose political career had been promoted by Joe Clark and who had worked in Clark's office when he first became leader, Jim Hawkes was a Clark loyalist to the core. But in the absence of ever actually holding power, the Progressive Conservative Party spent much of its time tearing itself apart. Clark had brought the PCs to government, but only for a few months, and with a very messy ending, when his government lost a budget vote that it should have been able to win in December 1979, and was defeated by a renascent Pierre Trudeau in the ensuing election. Now Brian Mulroney set out to unseat him.

The Quebec lawyer and businessman had come from nowhere to almost win the 1976 leadership convention that chose Clark, and had never really accepted his defeat. He seethed quietly in the background, confessing his frustrations to his closest friends and to friendly reporters, often over too many drinks. But after Clark lost power, Mulroney gave up the booze and launched a campaign to undermine Clark's leadership, portraying him as a loser who, unless he was deposed, would lead the Progressive Conservatives to yet another in their seemingly endless string of defeats. Clark, who was afflicted with chronic poor judgment, called a leadership convention, confident he would win a renewed mandate. Mulroney took it on the fourth ballot.

The winner and his allies set about remaking the party in the new leader's image. That meant replacing Clark loyalists with Mulroney loyalists. And that met turfing Jim Hawkes from his safe-as-houses seat in Calgary West and handing the seat to a Mulroney man. One wintry morning in early 1984, Hawkes's secretary called Cynthia Williams. Hawkes was being challenged for his nomination. Could she help? And would her boyfriend be willing to pitch in as well?

Williams and Harper became card-carrying members of the Progressive Conservative Party and began organizing support. (Remarkably, in light of future events, at this stage in his life Harper was dating a future journalist, hoping for a job in External Affairs, and campaigning for a supporter of Joe Clark.)

The University of Calgary was in Hawkes's riding, and the couple worked hard to sell memberships and deliver those new student members to the nomination meeting. They were so successful that Hawkes easily won renomination. This was a seminal moment for Harper. He enjoyed campaigning at the university residence on behalf of his candidate. He was organized, dedicated, extremely persuasive, and successful. Steve Harper had just had his first taste of partisan political campaigning, and discovered he was very good at it. The introverted, studious student who saw politics as a clash of ideologies actually enjoyed the grubby job of winning votes on the street – or, in this case, the university residence.

Harvie Andre, another Clark loyalist, was also under threat. Harper and Williams went to work to rescue his nomination as well. It was clear to everyone, including Williams, that Harper was exceptionally gifted at organizing and recruiting support. Before long, he was president of the Youth Wing of the riding, with Cynthia as vice-president. A young man by the name of Brian Wik was running for president of the Alberta PC Youth. Harper and Williams went to Edmonton to support his campaign at a PC convention, and by the time it was over, Wik had the job and Williams was vice-president of communications for Alberta PC Youth.

A federal election was imminent. Trudeau, having brought home the Constitution and driven the economy into the ground, announced he would not be running again. The fight to replace him revealed a new and dangerous rift within the Liberal Party. Former finance minister John Turner had quit years ago, impatient with Trudeau's economic policies and with the leader himself. His fellow discontenteds gathered around the Bay Street lawyer, biding their time much as Brian Mulroney had bided his. But there were plenty still loyal to the old leader and the old policies, and most of them rallied instead to Jean Chrétien, who had been finance minister and much else besides in the Trudeau years. Turner won the convention, but not the party, which was now deeply divided between the two camps.

The Progressive Conservatives ran on not much of anything, other than it was time for a change after twenty-one years of near-continuous Liberal rule. Turner proved to be rusty from his years on Bay Street. In the leader's debate, he foolishly declared he "had no option" but to approve a raft of patronage appointments bequeathed to him by the outgoing leader that had riled the public. "You had an option, sir," Mulroney retorted. "You could have said, 'I am not going to do it.'" And the election was over. The PCs won a huge majority government, reducing the Liberals to forty seats.

The West had finally arrived (albeit under the leadership of a Montreal lawyer), or so thought Westerners. From the Ontario–Manitoba border to Vancouver Island, the Liberals had taken a measly two seats. Brian Mulroney had promised to govern like a true conservative. He had fifty-eight MPs from the West, as many as had been elected in Quebec. At the time, the contradiction – the sheer impossibility, really – of a caucus composed in equal measure of Quebeckers and Westerners hadn't sunk in. The Progressive Conservatives owned Ottawa, lock, stock, and pork barrel. The West expected the new administration to deliver.

Jim Hawkes took three out of every four votes cast in Calgary West. Cynthia had been by his side through much of the campaign, accompanying him on stints of door-knocking while also handling campaign communications. Steve spent most of his time at campaign headquarters, organizing an army of volunteers who pounded campaign signs and delivered leaflets. (If he saw no benefit in doing the grunt work himself, he was happy to organize the grunts.)

Despite his enormous victory, Hawkes was unlikely to win a seat in cabinet – his devotion to Joe Clark would count against him, if nothing else. But the veteran MP could count on some interesting work, perhaps even a committee to chair. He needed a new assistant to run his parliamentary office in Ottawa. He asked Steve Harper to join him.

It seemed a natural fit. Steve and Cynthia had been over to the Hawkes house several times, and Joanne and Jim were fond of the young couple. Steve Harper was clearly smart as a whip, dedicated, organized, and loyal. He was older than the typical fourth-year university student, having worked those three years at Imperial Oil, which had given him more practical experience than your average university student possessed. This was a young man worth mentoring, and Hawkes, the former university professor, enjoyed the role of mentor.

The thirty-third Parliament convened on November 5, 1984. Harper wasn't able to be there. He had to finish his courses for his B.A. in economics. But he arrived in Ottawa early in the new year. Before he left, he asked Cynthia Williams to marry him. She happily said yes.

Six years after he'd left Ontario with his tail between his legs, Steve Harper was back, with an important new job and a future burgeoning with promise. Within a year, it would all fall apart, again.

THREE

Epiphany

In 1985, twenty-six-year-old Steve Harper became a legislative assistant, and quickly learned Jim Hawkes's golden rule: either know something or admit you don't.

"With my staff, whoever I hired, when I hired them I would drill them right from the get-go: 'Don't be afraid to not have the answer,'" Hawkes recalls. "'What I can't stand is the wrong answer. If you don't know, I need to know.'" But his new assistant always had the answer, and if he didn't, he knew where to find it. "He was the best I had in all the years," Hawkes maintains. "There were people with Ph.D.s who didn't do as well. He just always had the facts whenever I needed the facts."[1] Immigration rates over the past twenty-five years? Got it. Debt as a percentage of gross domestic product since Edgar Benson was finance minister? Got it. The latest formulation for calculating equalization payments, and the net negative impact on Alberta taxpayers? Funny you should ask.

Harper always had the answers because he worked so hard. He would be at the office when Hawkes arrived in the morning, and there when the MP left at night, which was often after 11 p.m., because the riding was on Mountain Time, two hours behind Eastern Time.

All his life, Harper had relied on mentors, people who could teach him things he needed to know, and in whom this turbulent young man could confide. His father was, obviously, first and most important in this regard.

But sons must make their own way. In Edmonton, Frank Glenfield had fulfilled the role, becoming almost a surrogate father. In Ottawa, Jim Hawkes took over.

The two men would often stay up late, after the work was done, discussing politics and life in general. Hawkes had never had an assistant who talked about himself, his aspirations and frustrations, as candidly as did this new assistant. Six years after he'd abruptly quit the University of Toronto, and even though he now had his B.A. in economics, Harper was still searching, still questioning. What should he do next? Should he go back to school or enter the public service? Or would he be better off in party politics rather than the bureaucracy? He needed to know whether he was taking his life in the right direction. But after a few months in Ottawa, he became convinced of one thing at least: he wanted nothing to do with Ottawa.

The world of legislative assistants is claustrophobic, confined to the febrile contests on Parliament Hill. The hours are brutal and the pay is unimpressive for the skills required. L.A.s are competitive – their own careers track closely those of the MPs they serve. When not trying to convince everyone else of how important they are, they drink together and trade war stories and gossip. Harper referred to them sarcastically as "the future prime ministers" and he had no time for them, any more than he had time for the Bright Young Things at Trinity.[2] Intense, reclusive, he was a poor fit for the incestuous politics and society of the capital.

Ottawa in the early 1980s was only just starting to shake off its reputation as "the town that fun forgot," to quote Allan Fotheringham. White-bred and white bread, its population of federal public servants considered the roast beef at the Chateau Laurier – often referred to as the Third House of Parliament – as haute cuisine. The city had traditionally wasted little money on good architecture, and any attractions, such as the Rideau Canal, had happened along more or less by accident. The wealthiest lived in sprawling piles in the all-but-gated village of Rockcliffe Park, with working-class francophones crammed into Vanier, uncomfortably nearby. Gatineau Park across the Ottawa River was a treasure, but the city of Hull, despite the new and badly designed government buildings, was a place that mainly attracted college students taking advantage of later drinking hours.

Things were changing, though. The Victorian ByWard Market neighbourhood had been saved from the developers and restored. You could find a decent restaurant if you looked hard enough on Elgin Street, which was also taking off. Pierre Trudeau had bequeathed to the city a new national gallery and there was the Museum of Civilization across the river. Both were architectural marvels. High-tech industries linked to defence contracts took root both downtown and in the distant suburb of Kanata. Ottawa was starting to become liveable, although people still joked that the best thing about it was the five o'clock train to Montreal.

Harper was living in a small apartment in Sandy Hill, a turn-of-the-century neighbourhood that mixed established brick houses with student-ghetto apartments. The walk to Hawkes's office in the Confederation Building, just west of Parliament Hill, took about twenty minutes. He ate out of a box, or at fast-food chains, or anyplace else that was cheap.

Hawkes was one of 170 backbenchers in the PC caucus. His experience and ability had earned him the chairmanship of the Commons Standing Committee on Labour, Employment and Immigration, but he wasn't in cabinet, which limited his parliamentary assistant's prospects. Beyond that, Harper realized that getting ahead in Ottawa meant being at the right receptions, saying the right things to the right people, schmoozing and networking, and sucking up, unless back-stabbing was required. All of this was anathema to him. And he arrived, in spring 1985, just as the Mulroney government was suffering its first major capitulation.

Things had begun so well for the Tories. Although the cabinet was an ungainly forty members large, the all-important Priorities and Planning Committee boasted fourteen members from Western Canada and only three from Ontario. And Western priorities were clearly the government's priorities. Energy Minister Pat Carney, from Vancouver, immediately set out to dismantle the National Energy Program. Within a month of the PCs taking office, they had come to an interim agreement with the provinces based on higher prices for oil. By March 1985, Ottawa was out of the energy-price-fixing game completely. The new prime minister met regularly with the premiers, to prove to them that the bad old days of Ottawa using its spending power to dictate policy in areas of provincial jurisdiction were over. The Foreign Investment Review Act, which sought to limit foreign takeovers of

Canadian companies, was replaced with the much more business-friendly Investment Canada.

Most encouraging of all, Mulroney, in a bit of an about-face, signalled his openness to a free trade agreement with the United States. Reciprocity, as it used to be called, was looked upon as a third-rail issue – fatal if touched. It brought down the Laurier government in 1911. Mackenzie King toyed with the notion in the late 1940s, but retreated when push came to shove. Lester Pearson preferred the managed-trade provisions inherent in the Auto Pact. Pierre Trudeau didn't seem to care much about trade or, so it seemed, about the economy in general.

But with inflation, interest rates, and unemployment all absurdly high in the early 1980s, Trudeau launched a royal commission to see what might be done to make workers more productive and the country more competitive. To everyone's surprise, the commission, chaired by former Liberal finance minister Donald Macdonald, recommended negotiating a free trade agreement with the United States – "a leap of faith," the report called it. At the Shamrock Summit in Quebec City in March 1985 – at which Ronald Reagan and Brian Mulroney sang "When Irish Eyes Are Smiling," sending eyeballs rolling across the country – the two sides agreed to launch trade talks.

But other things went less well, at least from Harper's perspective. Finance Minister Michael Wilson warned that the federal deficit was spinning out of control. But when he tried to rein in costs by announcing that federal pensions would no longer increase at the same rate as the cost of living, enraged pensioners took to Parliament Hill. "You lied to us," one protester accused, accosting Mulroney on the front steps of Parliament. "I was made to vote for you and then it's goodbye, Charlie Brown." That quote made sixty-three-year-old Solange Denis instantly famous and sent the Mulroney government into full retreat.* The painful truth was that the Progressive Conservatives didn't have a mandate to eliminate the federal deficit by cutting costs – quite the opposite; Mulroney had proclaimed during the campaign that he

---

* It also explains, according to one observer, why Stephen Harper as prime minister always enters Parliament through a side door.

considered Canada's generous social safety net "a sacred trust." The public wasn't alarmed enough, yet, to face the pain of cutbacks.

Harper was personally involved in a second setback. The Macdonald Commission had also recommended an overhaul of Unemployment Insurance. A program originally intended to provide temporary help for workers who unexpectedly lost their job had morphed into a guaranteed annual income for millions of people in depressed regions of the country – principally Quebec and Atlantic Canada. Returning UI to its original purpose would remove the crutch that was keeping the Maritimes from standing on its own feet. It would revive economies made dependent on federal handouts and encourage workers to move from places where there were no jobs to places where there were.

The Mulroney government responded to the report's recommendation by launching a separate investigation of UI, chaired by former Liberal Quebec cabinet minister Claude Forget, even as the Newfoundland and Labrador government of Brian Peckford established its own commission to study chronic unemployment in Canada's poorest province. Meanwhile, Jim Hawkes's committee on Labour, Employment and Immigration decided to examine both unemployment and immigration. As Hawkes's legislative assistant, Harper found himself immersed in both immigration and employment statistics and their demographic and economic impact. He should have been thrilled. But he could see where the wind was blowing. Hawkes's committee consisted of Members of Parliament from all regions of the country. A Progressive Conservative in Alberta might see UI as a market-distorting, dependency-inducing drag on the economy, but for a Tory MP from Newfoundland and Labrador or Quebec it was all that kept the wolf from their constituents' doors. Besides, people were tied to their communities and unwilling to leave family and friends. Why should they be forced to give all that up for an uncertain future down the road?

Although the Forget Commission echoed the Macdonald Commission in recommending a thorough restructuring of Unemployment Insurance, something that even the Newfoundland and Labrador commission endorsed, Hawkes's parliamentary committee favoured the status quo, which reflected the general mood of the Quebec and Atlantic caucuses. Mulroney embraced the recommendations of his caucus and ignored all the other reports.

By then, Harper had quit his job as Hawkes's assistant. He was homesick. He missed Cynthia. They talked on the phone every night, he got back to Calgary when he could, and she came to Ottawa when she could, but it wasn't the same. He was lonely. One year in the capital had left him with what he thought at the time was a lifelong aversion to politicians. The policy challenges of immigration, employment, and economic productivity intrigued him; maybe there would be a future for him in the public service. Or maybe he could make a mark as an economist at a university. In either case, he needed more than a B.A. He turned his back on Ottawa and returned to Calgary and Cynthia. "He learned to know that he would never be an elected politician," Hawkes recalled. Or so it seemed at the time. "He wanted to influence the world, and going back to get a doctorate would make it possible to really have influence down the road."[3]

Harper had now learned the same harsh lesson twice. From the time of Confederation, Canada had been governed by the politicians, bureaucrats, academics, and journalists in the offices, classrooms, and newsrooms of the cities along or near the St. Lawrence River. The Laurentian elites, they have been called.[4] Their concerns were Central Canada's concerns: reconciling Quebec with the ROC (Rest of Canada – as though three quarters of the population were an afterthought), or at least managing the province's discontents; protecting the manufacturing industries of the heartland with tariffs, even if agriculture and natural resources suffered as a result; warding off the disintegration that always seemed imminent in a fragile, fractured nation by nurturing national institutions such as the CBC, Crown corporations, health care, and cultural values – pride in the new flag, official bilingualism, peacekeeping, looking down on Americans. The other way to keep things together was to transfer wealth vertically – from those who were better off to those who were worse off – and horizontally – from wealthier provinces west of the Ottawa River to the poorer provinces east of it (though Manitoba received equalization and Saskatchewan was usually on the borderline). Above all, they embraced a centrist, consensual, heart-in-the-right-place-but-let's-not-get-carried-away pragmatism that they believed was the only way to manage this fractious federation. They had been at it for more than a century, and on the whole they'd done a pretty good job. But if you were a Canadian watching the 1980s unfold, the whole thing looked increasingly at risk of falling apart, as deficits spiralled, the economy sputtered, social services deteriorated, and the focus on placating Quebec absorbed more and more political oxygen. The body politic in Canada seemed very much in danger of hypoxia.

Stephen Harper could have belonged to this elite. Though partly hereditary, it admitted the upwardly mobile. He had arrived at Trinity College with the right marks, good French (for a Toronto boy), and an obvious interest in public affairs. But these people were not for him. He lacked their conspicuous self-assurance; his suburban middle-class background contrasted with their downtown sophistication. He could have overcome that by distancing himself from his upbringing. But Stephen Harper was proud to be from Etobicoke, and proud to be Joe Harper's son. And whether it was because of the Laurentian elite's increasingly poor performance in managing the economy and politics of the nation, or because of Harper's inherent – though at that point still-evolving – conservatism, or simply because he was an introverted young man who had difficulty fitting in, he had rejected the Laurentian elites, fled Trinity College, and headed West.

Now it had happened to him a second time. He had arrived in Ottawa, part of the vanguard of a new Progressive Conservative government, ready to dismantle as much as possible of the Laurentian inheritance, right the economy and balance the books, and make Western values part of the Ottawa ethos. Instead, the Mulroney government had itself become part of the Laurentian consensus, indistinguishable from its Liberal predecessors. (Though that consensus was starting to unravel over free trade, and would soon do so further over the Meech Lake Accord. More on this later.) The Family Compact ruled in Ottawa as firmly as it ruled in Toronto, only at the national level it formed an (uneasy) partnership with the federalist elites of Quebec. Everyone in Ottawa was a Liberal, especially the Tories. Worst of all, from Harper's perspective, the Mulroney caucus contained within its ranks out-and-out separatists from Quebec. The Progressive Conservative Party was doomed, he believed, by its internal contradictions. A party cannot contain within it both Western conservative populists and Quebec separatists and remain intact.

"Stephen could see fairly early after his arrival in 1985, barely one year into the mandate, that the pull of Quebec nationalism/separatism in the PC

Party meant there was no ability to sustain the coalition," Robert Harper recalls. "On top of the fiscal situation, he saw this as a more critical problem. He believed that you could not grow the Conservative Party by making deals with Quebec nationalists."[5]

Steve Harper had rejected both Toronto and Ottawa. The West was his only real home. So he went home. By autumn 1986, Harper was back in Calgary, back in university, and on his way to being single.

———————————

Steve had hated Ottawa; he told Cynthia it had made him cynical, as though he had contracted some chronic, incurable disease.[6] He was increasingly disenchanted with the Mulroney PCs – with their kowtowing to Central Canadian interests, with their refusal to cut back on entitlement spending, with their cavalier approach to deficits. But Cynthia still believed in the cause. She was active in the Progressive Conservative Youth of Alberta. More than anything else, though, during their year apart they had grown apart. Time zones can be fatal to relationships.

"I was okay with it, because I was changing. I was finding my own voice," says Cynthia. They talked it through, thought about it for awhile, then talked some more. But it was clear to both of them it was over. No one's fault. But still. "I don't want to say one of us broke up with the other," says Williams. "We both knew we had to. But it was still hard. It hit him hard. It hit me hard too." After all, they had been engaged to be married. This was far more than a girlfriend and boyfriend parting ways.

Harper told Hawkes he had to quit the Calgary West Riding Association. He couldn't be on the board with Cynthia. And he wasn't sure he wanted anything more to do with the PCs.

Shortly after the breakup, Harper deepened his friendship with John Weissenberger, whom he had met in 1984 at the Calgary West campaign headquarters. The two began a self-directed crash course in the foundational and modern literature on conservative thought. Only Stephen Harper would get over a breakup by reading Edmund Burke.

Weissenberger's parents had come to Canada in 1952, fleeing from the wreckage of post-war Germany. John was born in 1960, and grew up on

Montreal's south shore, where John's father found work as a teacher in the Protestant board. John came of age watching, with fascination and then alarm, the turbulence of the Quiet Revolution, the high of Expo 67, and the terrible low of the FLQ, who held cabinet minister Pierre Laporte in a house a mile from where the Weissenbergers were living, before taking his life.

John was fascinated by politics and geology. The difference between the two was that there was money in geology. He took his undergraduate degree at the University of Western Ontario, returning to Montreal for his M.Sc., because he missed his hometown and his father wanted him to improve his French. But a geologist interested in oil exploration needed to go west, and Weissenberger did his Ph.D. at the University of Calgary.

More gregarious than Harper, with an easier laugh, Weissenberger was a loyal supporter of the Progressive Conservative Party. In part, this was an inheritance from his father's Continental conservatism, which manifested itself in a fervent belief in John Diefenbaker and everything he stood for. When John came of political age, he supported Claude Wagner during the 1976 Progressive Conservative leadership convention, because he believed the PCs needed a Quebec leader. He campaigned on the campus of UWO during the 1980 federal election, and tried to get involved in the 1983 leadership campaign, only to discover that memberships were hard to come by – the candidates were trying to control who joined the party, in order to ensure that only their own supporters were able to vote for delegates. It left Weissenberger disillusioned with the party, and with politics in general, though he cheered Brian Mulroney on in the 1984 campaign. He even showed up at the Calgary West campaign headquarters to see if he could help. There he met Harper, who was organizing the youth volunteers. They instantly hit it off.

"He was a bright guy, and very knowledgeable about politics," Weissenberger remembers, looking back. "I'd been following politics for a while. So we had common knowledge and common interests."[7] They had more: the one-guy-starts-the-sentence-and-the-other-guy-finishes-it bond of best friends; the easy comfort of being in each other's space; and an evolving, presumptuous, resentment-fuelled conviction that the conservative movement was going to hell in a hand basket, and only they could save it.

After Harper returned from Ottawa in 1986, the two friends were together constantly. One of the things that amazed the young graduate student in economics was that he wasn't actually required to read the foundational texts. No one did any more, one of his professors told him; it was enough to know their general arguments. You can imagine how that went down with Straight-A Steve. He and Weissenberger began wading through the conservative canon, and then talking about what they had read over Chinese food and sodas. (Harper is the kind of Coke drinker who abhors those who, like Weissenberger, prefer Pepsi.) Hume and Mill. Burke on the French Revolution. Adam Smith on the invisible hand of the economy. They read William Buckley's *God and Man at Yale* and watched in delight as he skewered his opponents on PBS's *Firing Line*. They devoured *Alberta Report*, the decade-old magazine published by Ted Byfield that celebrated all things Western and conservative. Though Harper, as an economics student, didn't study much in the way of political science, he and Weissenberger digested the teachings of the Calgary School through articles in Byfield's magazine and by osmosis. Flanagan et al. were part of Calgary's political scene.

They were huge fans of *The Road to Serfdom*, written by the Austrian-born economist Friedrich von Hayek, which was any good conservative's answer to John Maynard Keynes. Hayek argued that fascism and communism were two branches of the same noxious tree: centralized state planning. He warned that the welfare state – which emerged out of the Second World War in the belief that if governments could win the war against fascism then they could win the war against poverty as well – could lead to a similar end, because it robbed the individual of autonomy and responsibility.

But the book that left the biggest impression was *The Patriot Game*, by Peter Brimelow, which got them so excited they ordered ten copies and handed them out to friends. Brimelow was a Brit who lived in Canada for several years in the 1970s, writing for *Maclean's*, the *Financial Post*, and the Sun newspapers, before decamping to the United States. *The Patriot Game* was published in 1986, just as Harper and Weissenberger were launching their self-directed reading program. In the book, Brimelow skewered the conventional wisdoms of Canadian politics and journalism. Canada, he observed, was governed by a small and not-very-permeable class of professional politicians, bureaucrats, academics, and journalists. Though he didn't call them the Laurentian elite, he identified and described them as such. This permanent governing class shared the same progressive (Brimelow would say socialist) assumptions: that resource industries, which dominated the Western economy, were inferior to manufacturing, which dominated the Ontario and Quebec economies and which needed protection from foreign, especially American, competition. Canada, they believed, was best governed through a coalition of Central Canadian – that is, French Quebec and English Ontario – interests. Canadian unity was best fostered by the aggressive intervention of the federal government in areas of nominally provincial jurisdiction, such as health care.

But the model, Brimelow observed, was breaking down. French Canada was evolving remorselessly toward nationhood, even as English Canada fractured into warring regions. (Brimelow saw English Canada as really just a region within English North America, like the American South.) To counter the disintegration, Pierre Trudeau imposed two nation-building exercises: official bilingualism and the National Energy Program. Both were disasters, Brimelow believed. The former failed to appease Quebec, while the latter estranged the West. It made absolutely no sense to encourage people outside Quebec to learn a foreign language that was of no use to them, unless they wanted a career in the federal public service. And the NEP – which Brimelow considered a positively Marxist theft of property – enraged Western Canada, distorted the energy market, and contributed to Canada's relentless economic decline, as Ottawa tried to engineer an industrial strategy better left to market forces.

The net effect of these internal contradictions and the efforts to paper over the cracks "is to create a stagnant pool of professional politicians and bureaucrats, infused with enormous power, and to achieve an illusory stability by suppressing the reality of difficulty and dissent," Brimelow concluded. "Rationales for state power, such as Canadian Nationalism, quickly spring up in such an environment. And manipulation is all too easy."[8] Exactly what Steve Harper had experienced in Ottawa. Exactly.

It was all there: the suspicion that the newly patriated Constitution, with its Charter of Rights and Freedoms, would undermine parliamentary supremacy and empower the judiciary; the conviction that the Progressive

Conservative Party had become an echo of the Liberal Party, which meant that Brian Mulroney would neither want nor be able to undertake major reform. Best of all, for Harper and Weissenberger, Brimelow demonized this centralizing liberal consensus in the person of Pierre Trudeau, and rendered it farcical in the comical figure of Joe Clark.

Clark, wrote Brimelow, once confessed that "when I went into politics I had to choose between learning economics and learning French. And I chose French."[9] And, quoting the book *Contenders*, by Patrick Martin, Allan Gregg, and George Perlin, Brimelow observed that the Alberta-born Clark no longer understood or felt comfortable with the people of his home province. He had become thoroughly centralized.

For Steve Harper and John Weissenberger, as they talked through the book over MSG-infused chicken chow mein in some overlit Chinese food joint in a strip mall, Brimelow's book was an epiphany, putting into words everything they felt and believed but had struggled to fully comprehend: There really was no distinction between the Liberal Party and the Progressive Conservative Party. They were both dominated by Central Canadian liberal assumptions. They both ignored – worse, abused and exploited – the West. They both bought into nation-building, market-distorting federal power grabs that only increased regional alienation, worsened the federal deficit, and dragged down the economy. And if any further proof were needed that Brimelow was right, and that the two big parties were, as former NDP leader David Lewis had described them, "Tweedledum and Tweedledee," then the debacle over the CF-18 maintenance contract delivered that proof in spades.

Brian Mulroney had honestly sought to assuage Western concerns. As we've seen, he dismantled the much-loathed National Energy Program, transformed the Foreign Investment Review Agency into a less-nationalistic Investment Canada, and brought a final end to the century-old National Policy by launching trade talks with the United States.

But for impatient Westerners – and many of them were growing increasingly impatient – it was too little, too slow. The collapse of energy prices had already done in most of the NEP, and Mulroney continued to protect the nationalized oil company, Petro Canada. The Tories' efforts to correct Quebec's rejection of the 1982 Canada Act – the patriated Constitution – ignored

Western demands for a reformed Senate that better represented their interests. And then came the CF-18 affair.

Bristol Aerospace in Winnipeg put in the lowest bid for the twenty-year, hundred-million-dollar maintenance contract to service the new fleet of air force fighter jets. It was also, in the opinion of the Department of National Defence, best qualified for the job. But as early as June 1986, Mulroney was grappling with the possibility of awarding the contract instead to Canadair in Montreal.[10] Quebec politicians and union leaders demanded that any major aerospace contract be awarded to Quebec, which they thought should be Canada's aerospace hub. Quebec MPs outnumbered Manitoba MPs. The cabinet was split; PMO officials grew increasingly impatient as Mulroney desperately sought a compromise between splitting the contract in half and awarding other contracts to Bristol. But there was nothing for it. On the morning of Halloween 1986, the government awarded the CF-18 contract to Canadair.

For many Westerners, this was the final straw. Ted Byfield and writers who contributed to *Alberta Report* went ballistic. It was clear that, no matter who was in charge in Ottawa, in any contest where the interests of Quebec and the interests of the West were in conflict, Quebec would prevail. That's how Stephen Harper saw it, too.

And that's how Preston Manning saw it. All his adult life, Manning had been waiting for the wave. Here it was.

The son of Ernest Manning – preacher, eighth premier of Alberta, and Trudeau-appointed senator – Preston Manning knew the politics of the West better than nearly anyone. Because the West was young, because it was physically and culturally cut off from Central Canada but close to the American West, because its religious traditions tended to be Protestant and evangelical, and because of the many righteously independent farmers who lived there, it was prone to what Manning called a "democratic reform tradition," though most people just called it populism.[11] In the West, and especially in Alberta and Saskatchewan, populist uprisings have been chronic. The Depression spawned both the Cooperative Commonwealth

Federation – which came to power in Saskatchewan in 1944 as the first socialist administration in North America – and the Social Credit Party, which came to power in Alberta in 1935, displacing the United Farmers of Alberta, itself a populist party that fought the federal government for control of natural resources.

Based on the theories of the British engineer C.H. Douglas, social credit sought to eliminate the gap between the value of everything produced and the wealth (or lack of it) that accrued to the workers by direct payments to individuals, which critics instantly dubbed "funny money." Funny or not, the hard-pressed farmers of Dust Bowl Alberta liked the idea and elected the first Social Credit government in the world, led by William "Bible Bill" Aberhart. Aberhart's efforts to bring banks in Alberta under provincial control (banks are federally regulated) and to limit the ability of the press to criticize the government's actions were so wildly out of bounds that the lieutenant governor refused to sign the bills. In any case, they were deemed unconstitutional by the Canadian Supreme Court and the British Judicial Committee of the Privy Council, which was then still Canada's highest court. And just to be sure, the Mackenzie King government annulled the most offensive legislation, invoking the disallowance clause of the Constitution (the last time it was used). It didn't matter. Aberhart's other anti-poverty measures and public works programs made Social Credit immensely popular, and when he died unexpectedly in 1943, the evangelical (and cabinet) minister Ernest Manning took over. Surprisingly, he would govern as a mainstream moderate conservative until 1968. Throughout that time, he continued his radio broadcast, *Back to the Bible Hour*, in which his son Preston often appeared.

In 1986, with Social Credit permanently displaced by the Alberta Progressive Conservatives, Preston Manning worked as a consultant, biding his time. He was convinced that getting involved with any mainstream political party would be a mistake. For one thing, the Progressive Conservatives weren't very conservative, or very attentive to the West. For another, he felt a populist wave building, one that could sweep the West and perhaps the East as well.

The Tories were supposed to eliminate the deficit. They increased it. They were supposed to lower taxes. Taxes went up. They were supposed to dismantle the hated National Energy Program. They dragged their feet. The West wanted a Senate that would represent its concerns in Ottawa. Not a chance. But when Quebec demanded recognition as a "distinct society," Mulroney dropped everything and fashioned the Meech Lake Accord. As he made his rounds as a consultant, Manning could hear the rising voices of discontent. "It was the sound of the wind starting to blow through the prairie grass," as he put it.[12]

And then, like a match to that dry grass, Brian Mulroney yanked the CF-18 maintenance contract away from Winnipeg and gave it to Montreal. "It was one thing to get out-of-control spending, chronic deficits, higher taxes, and anti-Western decisions 'in the national interest' from Liberals," Manning later wrote. "But now, to get the same thing from a Conservative administration that the West had worked hard to elect? It was simply too much to take."[13] In fact Manning had long suspected that Western rebellion would erupt not under a Liberal administration but under a Conservative one, as Westerners realized neither of the big federal parties understood or cared about them.

On October 17, 1986, Manning and a few friends met in a Calgary boardroom. Several of those present were executives in the oil industry. Manning pushed the need for a new political party to represent Western interests. Another group, led by Stan Roberts, the former head of the Canada West Foundation, a local think tank, had reached a similar conclusion. Roberts was a friend of Francis Winspear, an Edmonton philanthropist and businessman, who had offered fifty thousand dollars to set up a meeting of disaffected Westerners looking for alternatives.

Manning's group and Roberts's group decided to pool resources. They drew up papers for the Reform Association of Canada. The association's first task was to organize a Western Assembly on Canada's Political and Economic Future. On the weekend of May 30, 1987, 180 delegates met in a Vancouver hotel, under a sign reading "The West Wants In!" They voted to create a new political party. At the back of the room, a young man had placed a stack of papers – bright yellow, to attract attention – outlining the principles for a new, truly conservative, political movement. That young man was Steve Harper.

At twenty-eight, Harper was getting a bit long in the tooth for starting an M.A., en route to a Ph.D. But then his academic career had been anything but conventional: the false start at the University of Toronto, followed by three years in the workforce, then the second, successful, crack at a B.A. at the University of Calgary, followed by another unhappy year spent working for Jim Hawkes in Ottawa. Now he was back in school, determined to get as much education as he needed for a career in teaching or the public service. That year in Ottawa had convinced Harper that, although he was consumed by policy, he had very little use for politicians. If he were to effect change, it would have to be from within the permanent government: the bureaucracy that developed the plans that politicians implemented. Or so he thought.

His thesis would be on Keynesian economics and what Harper called the "political business cycle."[14] The British economist John Maynard Keynes believed that governments should fight unemployment during economic downturns through some combination of increasing spending and lowering taxes. This approach, of course, creates deficits and increases government debt. When growth resumes, Keynes argued, governments should reduce spending and/or raise taxes to pay down the debt created during the recession. This is called countercyclical spending, and it is the essence of Keynesian economics.

Keynes's critics warned that governments would happily spend during recessions but would lack the will to cut back spending and/or hike taxes during good times. They also predicted that governments would goose the economy by deficit-fuelled spending in the lead-up to an election, in an effort to buy votes. But was this true? Harper's thesis sought to examine Canadian fiscal policy at the federal level from the end of the Korean War to the 1980s, to see if the electoral cycle interfered with fiscal policy to thwart appropriate countercyclical spending.

The results surprised him. While there was evidence that majority governments did cut back on spending immediately after an election, when they wouldn't need to go to the voters for several years, spending didn't necessarily increase before an election, though it seldom went down, either.

"Elections seem to constrain deficit-reducing actions more than they encourage deficit-expanding ones," he concluded. The bigger problem was that, after decades of fiscally conservative behaviour by both Liberal and Progressive Conservative governments, spending went wild in the 1970s, in an effort to decrease unemployment in the wake of the 1973 oil shock. The Trudeau government didn't realize, Harper observed, that the increase in unemployment was not a temporary phenomenon but a structural problem created by the economic damage that OPEC had inflicted on the Western economies. But the Canadian government was hardly unique, he acknowledged; governments throughout the Western world had applied the same failed policies to the same misdiagnosed problem.

Stephen Harper's master's thesis is thorough in its research, sophisticated in its methodology, balanced in its observations, and cautious in its conclusions. It is a fine dissertation that would have made a solid foundation for launching a Ph.D. dissertation on a similar topic. But it took Harper six years to complete the thesis, thanks to political distractions, and by the time he finally finished it was clear he would never be taking a crack at a doctorate. Everything had changed, four years earlier, when Robert Mansell brought Stephen Harper and Preston Manning together.

Mansell taught economics at the University of Calgary. In the 1980s, he had embarked on a series of studies on the economic impact of federal transfers to the different regions. He concluded that the transfers were doubly noxious: they took money from the better-performing parts of the country, especially Alberta, where it should have been productively invested, and handed it to poorer regions, increasing their dependence on Ottawa and preventing them from addressing the structural changes needed to turn their economies around, while fuelling resentment from donor regions.

In the autumn of 1986, Mansell found himself talking to a new graduate student who shared his convictions on the evils of fiscal federalism. Steve Harper hadn't made a huge impression as an undergraduate – though top-flight academically, he was a quiet student who made little effort to get to know his professors – but now that he was embarked on graduate studies, this intense young man appeared comfortable having conversations in the hallway with the likes of Mansell.

"He stood out in so many ways," Mansell said. "He was exceptionally smart, and I don't just mean in a book sense."[15] Harper's data-driven nature, and his year in Ottawa, had combined to make him interested in practical, achievable solutions to the many problems facing the country, from escalating debt to an increasingly sclerotic welfare state to regional tensions to efforts at constitutional reform. "At the graduate level, the discussion tends to focus on theory," observes Mansell, "whereas Stephen was really different in that he'd want to bring into the conversation the consequences – public policy, practical things. He was always asking: 'Would that be practical? Would it really work, given all the complications in our system?' And that was different."

Through the fall and winter terms, Mansell was also interacting a fair bit with Preston Manning. After that October boardroom meeting, and in anticipation of the Vancouver gathering planned for May, Manning was looking for people who could give substance to the as-yet-incoherent movement that might or might not evolve into a new political party. Manning was intrigued with Mansell's arguments on regional development. The new party would need to establish principles and policies on a broad range of subjects: on Aboriginal affairs, agriculture, constitutional reform, fiscal policy, foreign policy, health care, industrial strategy – the A-to-Z of a federal political party's raison d'être. Besides that, Manning was and is intellectually curious, the sort of person who likes to take ideas out for a spin to see how they perform. He would periodically drop by the university for chats with Mansell, who would sometimes invite other professors and graduate students to sit in on the brainstorming sessions. When Manning asked Mansell whether he knew of a student who might be able to do some policy research for him, Mansell's response was, "I've got somebody. He's just around the corner." He invited Harper to one of those sessions in April 1987. Harper brought along Weissenberger, and both met Manning for the first time.

It wasn't just that Harper was a fine and ideologically compatible student. Age and temperament also had much to do with it. "He was twenty-seven at the time, going on forty," Mansell says. "Good values, doesn't have any airs. Not trying to accumulate power or wealth or anything. Just a grounded, well-motivated student, with a passion for politics."

Looking back, Mansell doesn't think Harper was ever cut out to be an academic. Especially in the early years, someone working on a Ph.D. or struggling to achieve tenure "must narrow their focus and then drill down twenty thousand feet." That was never Stephen Harper's way. He was a horizontal thinker, looking for linkages between philosophy, economics, and politics. He was born to synthesize, not theorize.

Something else might also have been at work. Harper was already discovering that he had trouble taking orders from people. This might have contributed to his decision to quit Jim Hawkes's office, and it would certainly become a major issue down the road. Success in graduate studies requires abject submission to professors who can advance your career by offering you a tenure-track position or destroy it by rejecting your thesis. Harper would have been no more comfortable in the cloistered, incestuous world of a university economics department than he had been in the cloistered, incestuous world of Parliament Hill – especially if he was at the bottom of the greasy pole. Mansell knew none of this; he knew only that he had an exceptional student on his hands, one who could help Manning shape the policy of his new party. He was happy to bring the two together.

At one level, Harper and Manning quickly realized that they were meant for each other. Each is essentially diffident, ill at ease in public, and poorly equipped with the skills needed for conventional political success. Manning's high, quavering tenor would rule him out of contention in any casting call for future political stars. Harper's cool, reserved exterior hardly fit with the image of a glad-handing pol. Neither was of a mind to kiss babies in front of the cameras. Both, however, had fine minds, strongly conservative inclinations, and a passion for policy. And as Canadians would soon learn, each had the capacity to convince, based not on charm but on conviction married to powerful reasoning buttressed by a surprisingly strong speaking style.

The Western Assembly in Vancouver in May 1987 had many items on its agenda – devising a plan for a regionally balanced, elected, and effective Senate (Ted Byfield had dubbed it the "Triple-E Senate": equal, elected, and effective); entrenching economic and property rights in the Constitution; creating a Western Canadian common market; changing the approach to Aboriginal poverty; tackling the Meech Lake Accord; and on and on.

But only one decision really mattered. Delegates had to decide whether to (a) work within an existing party (presumably the Progressive Conservatives) to advance Western interests; (b) create a new pressure group to lobby all political parties on Western and conservative issues; (c) create a new political party; or (d) come up with something else.

The banner hanging over the stage said it all. "The West Wants In" was a phrase that first appeared in *Alberta Report*, in which Link Byfield, the son, and Ted Byfield, the father, championed Western and conservative interests. As the columnist Lorne Gunter once perceptively observed, the fact that the phrase contained the word "in" was crucial for the future of the country. Western anger at Central Canada's ignorance and dismissal of its concerns was approaching a flashpoint. Had the Byfields championed the phrase "The West Wants Out," and had Manning embraced it, then at the Western Assembly of 1987 "most of the nearly 100,000 Westerners who eventually joined his Reform Party . . . would have joined a Manning-led separatist movement instead."[16]

Manning offered a different vision, one that tapped into a deep mythical well: "the 'reform tradition' which runs like a broad and undulating stream throughout the length and breadth of Canadian politics."[17] In his speech to the delegates, he invoked the populist waves of reform that had shaped and reshaped the Prairies. But for Preston Manning, populist protest was not only a Prairie phenomenon. It spanned the length and the history of the country. It animated the rebellions of 1837 in Upper and Lower Canada; the crusading reformer Joseph Howe of Nova Scotia; the ecstatic visions of Louis Riel; the Farmers' Movement of the early twentieth century. Elsewhere in English Canada, the spirit of reform had flagged, Manning believed. It was alive in that room, however, on that day.

"And if you are prepared to think of yourselves as Reformers – as people who want change in the conduct of our public affairs and who are prepared to create new structures to secure those changes – then the critics and the commentators who dismiss this assembly as some isolated gathering of Western malcontents will be proved wrong," he urged them. Never mind the quavering, scratchy voice, the gaunt frame, the bobbing Adam's apple, the wonky glasses. Tom Flanagan later observed that there were more than a few people in the room that day who became devoted disciples of Preston Manning, and who never wavered in that devotion from beginning to end. And that speech was the reason.[18]

Robert Mansell was supposed to be one of the delegates, but he had other commitments and sent Harper in his place. Harper arrived in Vancouver with his own agenda, both literal and political. He and Weissenberger had decided to create what they called a Blue Tory network. They would identify and recruit like-minded conservatives inside and outside the Progressive Conservative Party, who would advocate for the principles contained on the sheet of paper that Weissenberger and Harper had drawn up together. Eleven principles made up their "Taxpayer's Reform Agenda." They focused on providing a clearly defined conservative alternative to the "NDP-Liberal-Red Tory philosophy."[19]

But the delegates ignored the kid at the back of the room with his yellow-sheet manifesto. Instead, they voted 75 per cent in favour of creating a new party. Stephen Harper cast one of those yes votes. When he returned to Alberta he told Weissenberger that the new movement was the real thing, and would soon be a party. Both young men decided to go all in. They tore up their PC membership cards – Weissenberger even sent Brian Mulroney a letter explaining why – abandoned their dreams of a Blue Tory network, and became ardent Reformers. For Harper, the years of asking questions were over. He had experienced what he needed to experience, read what he needed to read, and reached his conclusions. From here on in, he would be the one coming up with the answers.

FOUR

Refooorrrm!

Halloween 1987 was a cold, wet, windy Saturday in Winnipeg, where Steve Harper was about to give what would turn out to be the most important speech of his life.

Harper, Weissenberger, and a friend had driven from Calgary in Weissenberger's VW Jetta to attend the founding convention of a new political party, name to be decided. The manifesto that they had printed on yellow paper in hopes it would be noticed had been ignored by the delegates at the Vancouver meeting, but it hadn't been ignored by Preston Manning. He was even more receptive to a memo that Harper had crafted over the summer, advocating the creation of "a genuine conservative party, a Taxpayers party."[1] Manning had been so impressed with the memo that he asked Harper to turn it into a speech, to be delivered at the new party's founding convention. Harper eagerly obliged. In the meantime, he and Weissenberger had established the Calgary West Reform Constituency Association, which, not surprisingly, chose Harper and Weissenberger to attend the founding convention as delegates.

The convention had several priorities: to come up with a name for the new party – the thirty candidates ran the gamut from the Acumen Party to the Western Reform Party – to adopt a set of principles, and to choose a leader. Preston Manning was the favoured candidate, but he was not the only one. Stanley Roberts – who had merged his own plans with Manning's to make the original Vancouver meeting possible – was challenging him. Roberts had spent most of his life as a Liberal, but he had also been president of the Canadian Chamber of Commerce, as well as the first president of the Canada West Foundation. Though Roberts believed the West needed a new political party to represent its interests, he increasingly feared the new party was becoming too much a party of grievance, too conservative, too anti-Quebec. A week before the convention, he announced he would run for the leadership, so as to steer the new party in a more moderate and, to his mind, more electable direction.

For Manning's supporters, this was highly inconvenient. With his Liberal background and centrist views, Roberts in no way represented the populist wave of protest that they wanted the new party to surf. But Roberts was taking his leadership campaign seriously: there was a hospitality suite with free booze, there were posters, there were brightly coloured scarves. There were promises of busloads of Roberts supporters who might show up at any minute. Manning, who had adopted a low-key approach to his campaign, had no hospitality suite, no booze, no scarves.

He did, however, have control of the convention. On Saturday morning, delegates decided that no one not currently in attendance could vote for the leader. So much for the busloads of supporters. Roberts howled, but the truth was he and the new party were a poor fit. He was a centrist, establishment candidate at a convention of contrarians determined to create a populist conservative party. The brightly coloured scarves hurt more than they helped. Roberts walked out, along with a score of supporters whose departure was not mourned. Manning was acclaimed leader.

The delegates chose to call their new creation the Reform Party of Canada, dropping the "Western" reference because the more ambitious among them believed there was potential for a truly national movement. They considered, debated, and adopted a constitution drawn up by Robert Muir, a Calgary lawyer who had helped organize the Vancouver assembly. Its most distinctive provision, Clause 11(c), declared that "the party shall cease to exist on November 1, 2000" unless two thirds of the delegates at a convention voted to keep it alive.[2]

This spontaneous, populist, grassroots movement was the personal creation of Preston Manning. While proclaiming that it governed from the bottom up, the Reform Party somehow managed to be whatever Manning wanted it to be. And while proclaiming that this peaceful, populist uprising transcended ideology, the party mirrored the values and beliefs of Preston Manning, whose values and beliefs were stoutly conservative. Reform would always be like this: avowedly populist, but ultimately under Manning's control; avowedly beyond ideology, but really conservative, and strongly so. The party was the leader.

Before voting Manning in, the assembled delegates listened to Steve Harper speak at Saturday's plenary session on political economics. The speech was long and had a lot of numbers in it, yet when Harper finished he received a standing ovation, and Manning promptly put him in charge of developing policy for the new party. This twenty-something graduate student at the University of Calgary instantly became one of the most senior figures in the Reform movement, all because of that speech, and it's easy to see why.

Harper explained to his sympathetic audience just how badly Westerners were treated, thanks to programs and policies that drained money out of the region to prop up Central Canadian industries and welfare-state policies. The National Policy, the National Energy Program, the bilingualism requirements in the federal public service, the excessive concentration of that service in Ottawa, the excessive concentration of subsidized arts industries in Toronto, the obsession with placating Quebec, the contemptuous dismissal of Western concerns, and especially the entitlement industry generated by the welfare state – out of all of this and more "has grown a highly centralized political culture which is inherently and righteously biased against Western Canada in its values and rhetoric," Harper maintained.[3]

A new party representing truly conservative values and Western interests would act as a brake on such abuses, he argued. It would press for an end to policies that discriminated against the West, for regional development "that encourages development, not dependency," for smaller government and a smaller bureaucracy, for genuine consultation with citizens, for equal treatment of all regions rather than special favours for Quebec.

"In the stale air of politics, what Canada really requires is the sweeping winds of change," Harper claimed. "For the vested interests of the National Policy, the Welfare State, and the Quebec question, this will be a challenge they will resist. In the end, however, these groups will have to cast aside their narrow definitions of Canada in the interests of the country they claim to love, because that country can no longer be built on the economic exploitation and political disenfranchisement of Western Canada."

It brought the audience to their feet.

The speech demonstrated several strengths that would eventually carry Stephen Harper to the prime ministership. Even back then, he was a good writer and a powerful analyst. His logic was remorseless, backed up by facts but appealing to emotions – in this case, a mixture of resentment and the hope for something better. Though sometimes socially awkward, he had a strong speaking style – a cadence that, while hardly conversational, drove the point home to anyone who was willing to listen. Reformers ate it up. *Alberta Report* reprinted portions of the speech along with a picture of Steve Harper and the observation, "The speech was acknowledged by delegates, party officials and media as a highlight of the convention."[4] Manning was equally generous in his 1992 pre-election memoir, saying that Harper's speech offered a solid intellectual foundation for the policies and principles of the party. "People who have been told that the Reform Party consists of well-meaning simpletons mouthing naive solutions to complex problems should study Harper's speech."[5] A star was born. And so was a new political party.

But if *Alberta Report* was enthusiastic about Reform, other media were contemptuous, condescending, and cruel. John Weissenberger recalled a *Winnipeg Free Press* editorial cartoon that, playing on the fact that the convention coincided with Halloween, portrayed Manning with Dracula-like teeth banging a drum over the caption "Join Preston's thump for Jesus," though nothing in the founding documents or resolutions suggested the new party was in the pocket of evangelical Christian zealots.[6] In the *Toronto Star*, Val Sears described the new party as "a group passionately devoted to winning the West by whining about the East," though he had praise for Harper's speech.[7] Weissenberger and Harper were furious. Hundreds of people had met in good faith, worked hard, engaged in civil debate, drafted a constitution, chosen a leader, and launched a new political party, and the press had portrayed them as religious, red-necked yahoos. That bitterness, born in Winnipeg, would grow and deepen in the years to come, as columnists and reporters belittled the Reform Party and the movement behind it. The reflexive, dismissive, ill-informed, and lazy contempt on the part of the mainstream media toward the Reform Party lay at the root of Harper's own contempt for the press in general and the Parliamentary Press Gallery in particular. The feelings would prove to be mutual.

It didn't help that on November 1, the final day of the convention, René Lévesque died. All of Central Canada mourned the passing of a man who had dedicated himself to destroying the country and almost succeeded. Brian Mulroney ordered the flags lowered to half-staff, and described Lévesque as "the greatest democrat this country has ever known."[8] Westerners just shook their heads.

In addition to holding the position of chief policy officer, Harper became the only person apart from Manning authorized to speak on behalf of the party – a remarkable vote of trust in someone still shy of thirty. The two men immediately got to work translating the principles adopted at the convention into policy, which eventually made its way into the first of several Blue Books, as they were called, that would serve as Reform election platforms.

That first Blue Book contained one paragraph that haunted both men as well as the party they created. While not demanding an end to immigration, Reform wanted to end the abuse of Canada's generous refugee policies and to encourage immigrants who were able to contribute to the Canadian economy. So far so good, and consistent with Conservative immigration policy later, in the Harper years. But the Blue Book added that "while immigration should not be based on race or creed," neither "should it be explicitly designed to radically or suddenly alter the ethnic makeup of Canada, as it increasingly seems to be."[9] It is very hard not to conclude from that paragraph that Reform wanted to keep Canada white by limiting immigration from developing countries.

Neither in word nor deed have Preston Manning or Stephen Harper given anyone the slightest grounds for accusing them of holding racist attitudes. And the Conservatives in government have pursued the opposite

approach, by maintaining a large inflow of immigrants from the developing world.

But there were racists in Reform – people who believed that non-white
immigration, which was diluting Canada's European heritage, would lead
the country to ruin. Others, while not explicitly racist, worried about the
difficulties of integrating immigrants from developing countries into a fully
industrialized society. A third group, to which Harper and Weissenberger
belonged, simply objected to Ottawa's starry-eyed obsession with multiculturalism, as though anything of British or continental European origin
was bland, boring, and passé. These combined forces were enough to
convince the party to insert the plank into the platform. But that plank was
toxic, providing critics with a weapon to stigmatize Reform as a party of
bigots. And the simple fact is that no party with such a platform could ever
hope to win a riding in urban Ontario, where immigrants were a fast-
growing segment of the population even back in 1988.

Manning and Harper got along well in those early months simply because
each respected the other's grasp of and approach to policy, and because neither was in the least bit interested in anything else about the other. "Virtually
all of our discussions were at the policy level," Manning recalled later.
"Sandra, my wife, used to remark: 'Do you guys ever talk about anything
other than policy?' The real answer was no. That was the entire basis of our
relationship."[10] Neither would have called the other a friend.

If there was anything that distinguished the two men, besides age, it
was Harper's anger toward the Red Tory movement that dominated the
Progressive Conservative Party, personified by Joe Clark, whom Harper
had singled out in his speech as the embodiment of a Westerner who had
sold out. Manning's approach to politics was always more cerebral and distant than Harper's. The younger man took politics more personally. "I did
get the impression that he was angry and disillusioned with the PCs," said
Manning, but for the most part, "we found ourselves on the same wave-
length and just got at it."

The Reform platform offered a sharp contrast to Brian Mulroney's Progressive Conservative agenda. The PCs had expanded federal bilingualism, passed a new Multiculturalism Act, increased immigration intake to
250,000 people a year, introduced employment equity (another name for

affirmative action, which is another name for job quotas for women and minorities), and run record budget deficits.

That said, the Mulroney government had a trump card when it came to attracting the support of conservatives: on October 4, 1987, after a final, sleepless round of intense bargaining by negotiators, Canada and the United States initialled a sweeping trade accord that would, after more than a century, eliminate at last most of the tariffs that clogged the border. This was bad news for both the Liberal Party and Reform.

Liberal leader John Turner's caucus was split between those who opposed and those who supported free trade, and between those who opposed and those who supported the Meech Lake constitutional accord – an agreement that sought to amend the Constitution so that Quebec could sign it, by acknowledging Quebec as a "distinct society" within Confederation, among other things. Mulroney and the premiers had hammered out the deal at the government conference centre at Meech Lake, in Gatineau Park.

Meech Lake and free trade presented Turner with an almost insurmountable political problem. Both proposals made sense. But to support both was to endorse the governing agenda of the Progressive Conservatives – and, after all, the purpose of the official opposition is to officially oppose. To make matters worse, his fractious caucus was split on both issues, with substantial elements for and against both free trade and Meech Lake. And Turner's control over his caucus and party was shaky at best.

Turner decided to split the difference. The compromises embodied in the Meech Lake Accord seemed reasonable to him. But the free trade agreement was worrisome. The dispute resolution mechanism was weak, and the wording of some clauses appeared to open up the possibility that the United States could force changes to Canadian social programs on the grounds that they represented a subsidy. The Liberal leader decided his party would support the Meech Lake Accord while opposing the trade deal. This, predictably, satisfied no one.

"Dammit, Raymond, you know the deal," Liberal MP Lloyd Axworthy raged at his colleague Raymond Garneau. "I have to support your damned Meech Lake Accord so you better stick with me against free trade!"[11] There could be no better summation of the divisiveness and misery within the Liberal caucus under John Turner. He fought off yet another caucus rebellion and ordered his senators, who still controlled the Upper House, to block passage of the free trade accord until the PCs had agreed to an election. On October 1, 1988, Mulroney visited the governor general, and the date was set for November 21.

At first, things went swimmingly for the PCs. After all, for most Canadians, life was good. The country had emerged from the crippling recession that launched the decade and now enjoyed strong growth, moderate inflation, and a housing boom. The success of the personal computer proved that American enterprise and initiative weren't dead. Japan and Germany weren't so unstoppable any more. Best of all, it was now perfectly clear that the Soviet empire was falling apart, and Canada, in support of the United States and Great Britain, was helping it along quite nicely. Afghanistan had turned into another Vietnam. One geriatric general secretary of the Communist Party followed another into the grave. Brezhnev. Andropov. Chernenko. When Ronald Reagan was asked why he had never held a summit with a Soviet leader, he replied, "They keep dying on me." The much younger Mikhail Gorbachev now sought to reform the Soviet Union from within, and to end the Cold War. But he was racing to avoid internal collapse, and he was losing.

As a staunch ally of Reagan and Thatcher, Mulroney should have reaped the harvest of winning the Cold War. But while his domestic policies differed markedly from those leaders' – Thatcher once sniffily observed that the Progressive Conservative prime minister "put too much stress on the adjective and not enough on the noun"[12] – progressives loathed his government with a fierceness that would not be repeated until Harper led the country. Free trade was controversial, to say the least, and Mulroney's government had endured more than its share of tawdry scandals. During the English-language debate, everything flipped. Mulroney stumbled badly as Turner rounded on him, accusing him of betraying Canada. The Liberals surged into the lead, in one of the most dramatic reversals in public opinion recorded during an election campaign. Turner stormed the country, lambasting free trade in what he called "the fight of my life," and vowing to "tear up" the deal if elected.

But the PCs counter-attacked, using every ounce of their fundraising and organizational power to undermine Turner's credibility, including a truly vicious advertising campaign – "Ten Big Lies," "John Turner Is Lying."[13] Bombing the bridge between Turner and the voters, pollster Allan Gregg called it. Steve Harper couldn't help but notice how well it worked.

There may never be another Canadian election like the election of 1988. The country had split wide open over free trade. Ontario Premier David Peterson campaigned against it; Alberta Premier Peter Lougheed campaigned for it. Most Quebeckers were behind the deal, but in Toronto people like Margaret Atwood and Pierre Berton and Rick Salutin warned free trade would shatter Canada's fragile culture; Mordecai Richler, in response, proclaimed that anything that led to the demise of the "dubious wines of Niagara" was fine by him.[14] As the polls improved for the Liberals, the dollar fell and the stock market swooned, which offered voters a pretty clear signal of how important the deal was for business. The polls swung back. On Election Day, although the Liberals doubled the size of their caucus and the NDP elected forty-three MPs, the largest number in its history to that point, Mulroney secured another majority government, guaranteeing that CUSTA (as the Canada–United States Trade Agreement was inelegantly called) would go through.

It was, by general consent, the most exciting election campaign in a lifetime, which meant it was the worst possible time for the launch of the Reform Party.

Even before the election, 1988 had been a busy year for Steve Harper. He was completing the second year of his master's degree while teaching students part time. And as a designated spokesman for the party, he was travelling across the province, often with John Weissenberger behind the wheel, speaking at small gatherings in church halls and the like. On one occasion, Weissenberger managed to get into a fender-bender, and when the two men finally arrived, very late, at the event, they found a dozen people patiently listening to a tape recording of Harper's Winnipeg speech. But he was learning – slowly, uncertainly – to talk to ordinary voters in support of his ideas. A politician was born.

Manning and Harper also convened a committee, on which both sat along with some constitutional specialists, to draft the wording for an amendment to the Constitution that would entrench a Triple-E Senate. That wording stipulated ten senators would be elected from each province to six-year terms, with powers not dissimilar to the current Senate. On May 28, Reformers chartered a train, the Constitution Express, and rode it to the coast, where the Western premiers were meeting at Parksville, on Vancouver Island. Though the premiers didn't meet with the Reformers, the media picked up on the party's demand for Senate reform, speaking as it did for a large chunk of the West. Why was it that Quebec was having all of its demands met through the Meech Lake Accord, while the West's priority of a reformed Senate was simply ignored? Good question.

Harper and Weissenberger also went to work to create the Reform Party's constituency association for Calgary West, with Harper acclaimed president. He was also acclaimed the candidate for the riding on June 28. Two years before, he had left Ottawa convinced he wanted nothing to do with politicians. Now he was trying to become one. The difference was that he had finally found, in Reform, a political party that mirrored his own beliefs, whose platform he had actually helped to create, as Preston Manning's second-in-command. It was a very, very small pond, but Harper was a very, very big fish in it. He liked it that way.

Calgary West made sense as the riding to run in. He lived there; the University of Calgary was there; he had worked the riding during the 1984 campaign for Jim Hawkes. But that was the thing. He'd be running against Hawkes – his friend, mentor, and former boss. How could he do such a thing?

Throughout his political career, Harper would be accused of abandoning or even betraying colleagues and allies. This was the first of those alleged betrayals. But Harper didn't see it that way. To his family and to his personal friends, he was completely loyal. But politics was politics, a democratic substitute for civil war, and therefore a contest in which all is fair. Besides, he knew he didn't have a chance of winning.

As Hawkes recalls it, "He phoned me and said that 'They want me to run. And I'd like to run against you because you get 60-plus percent of the vote and I won't win but I'll be able to keep my job and I'm trying to do my doctorate and the money is really helpful.'"[15] The affable Hawkes gave his blessing. "I encouraged him to do it, in the sense that I wanted him to get his doctorate and have an impact on the country. I had no thought of anybody beating me, and they didn't."

It was an exceedingly gentlemanly thing to do, though also a fairly safe move. And Steve Harper, as his campaign signs read, was right to assume he didn't have a hope. But something else was also true. Jim Hawkes was not just the Progressive Conservative MP; he was a Red Tory, an ally of Joe Clark, who personified everything craven about the PCs in the eyes of Harper and Manning: selling out the West; obsessing over Quebec; mismanaging the economy. Harper had worked for Hawkes, respected Hawkes, personally liked Hawkes. But ideologically, Hawkes represented what Reformers detested about the big national parties. They were ideologically inseparable.

"This campaign is not about political images or personal relationships," Harper insisted on June 28, as he accepted the nomination for his party. "A vote for Jim Hawkes is a vote for a kind of Red Toryism that appears so similar to the Liberals and NDP on dozens of public policy issues."[16]

Not everyone was so equable. "I was mad at him," recalls Cynthia Williams, who campaigned once again for Jim Hawkes. "I understand now why, that it wasn't a personal thing against Jim. But at the time I was very loyal to Jim. And when I campaign I get passionate about the person I'm promoting, and protective."[17] Not only did Williams do everything she could for Hawkes, she brought her friend Laureen Teskey onto the team as well. In his first election, Stephen Harper's future wife campaigned against him.

By August, the election platform was ready for a Reform Assembly in Calgary to amend or endorse. "The West is not weak," Harper told those gathered. "The West is strong. It is our representatives that are weak."[18] The delegates debated, slightly amended, then endorsed the *Platform and Statement of Principles* – twenty-six pages that laid out a Western-centric and deeply conservative governing agenda for Canada.

Some of the platform's contents would echo down the years, finding a home in the Conservative Party of Canada: calls for a justice system that "places the punishment of crime and the protection of law-abiding citizens and property ahead of all other objectives"; a foreign policy that projects abroad Canadians' commitment to democracy and human rights, rather than "simply adjusting and fitting into the views of foreign governments" in international forums; an end to government funding for lobbying groups, especially those that seek to defend and expand the welfare state; a shift in the immigration system to focus on bringing in immigrants who can contribute to the economy, while cutting back on family reunification; freer trade within Canada and free trade agreements with other nations; daycare funding targeted to parents rather than to daycare institutions; above all, lower taxes and a return to balanced budgets.[19] Those on the right who maintain that the Harper governments to date haven't been sufficiently conservative must also maintain that the heart of the Reform agenda also wasn't sufficiently conservative.

Other parts of that agenda would fall away over the years: the Triple-E Senate, entrenching constitutional property rights; citizen-initiated referenda; citizen-initiated recall of MPs; reducing the number of immigrants who would alter the existing demographic makeup of the country; rejection of official bilingualism across the country; elimination of universality in social programs and a targeting of resources on the most needy; and permission for citizen-initiated plebiscites on abortion or capital punishment. What survived from the original Blue Book and what was rejected tells us much about the evolution of Stephen Harper's thinking over the years, and his growing political pragmatism. He once embraced everything listed in this paragraph. He ultimately jettisoned all of it.

The Blue Book also contained a section promoting sustainable development and respect for the environment. Manning believed, and still believes, that responsible stewardship of the environment is a first responsibility of government. It also reflected his continuing determination that Reform not be seen as primarily a socially and economically conservative party.

Nothing in the platform was of much use, though. Free trade dominated the election campaign; Westerners were fierce supporters of free trade; if you supported free trade your only sensible alternative was to vote Progressive Conservative. The fledgling Reform Party had no money for television or radio ads. Preston Manning confined himself mostly to his riding campaign in Yellowhead, where he was taking on Joe Clark. (The favoured line of Reform supporters at all-candidates debates when confronting Clark: "Why should we vote for you when you won't vote for us?")

Harper ran a solid campaign in Calgary West. He had the experience of the '84 campaign to fall back on, not to mention his passionate conviction for Reform's message. Weissenberger was poll chairman, charged with getting the message to every home in the riding. Both men also lent whatever expertise they had to candidates in other Calgary ridings. The two of them recruited a small army of 250 volunteers, most participating in their first campaign. Those volunteers, who ranged from U of C students to seniors who had voted for John Diefenbaker – one of them had campaigned for Bible Bill himself – were angry about the scandals; they were angry about the deficits; they were angry about the CF-18 contract; they were angry about the government's obsession with Quebec. Harper campaigned relentlessly, knocking on doors from early morning till into the evening. The campaign raised fifty thousand dollars, a better-than-respectable amount for a new party with a candidate not quite thirty years old.

The result was disappointing: not a single Reform MP elected in any of the four Western provinces to which the party had limited itself in its first campaign. Whatever his faults, Brian Mulroney supported free trade with the United States, and that was that. But if you drilled down, there were signs that should have worried any Progressive Conservative political strategist. In Calgary West, Hawkes's vote share dropped from a staggering 75 per cent in 1984 to 58 per cent in 1988. Harper came second, with 17 per cent, ahead of the Liberals and the NDP. Manning did even better, taking 11,136 votes to Clark's 17,847. Manning had secured 29 per cent of the vote, and pulled Clark's plurality from 74 per cent down to 45 per cent. With only 72 candidates in the race, Reform pulled in 2 per cent of the national vote. In Alberta, it polled at 15 per cent. And the party wasn't even a year old when the election was called.

Steve Harper had failed to be elected to Parliament. But he had put up a decent fight. And the Reform Party was anything but dead on arrival. It had a voting base with plenty of room to grow. Harper would grow with it, until the inherent contradictions between his vision for the party and Manning's became more than either of them could bear.

FIVE

Stephen

No one realized how sick John Dahmer was, including John Dahmer, until it was too late. The former high school principal and adult educator had won the nomination for the newly created riding of Beaver River, north of Edmonton. Four weeks after the writ was dropped, Dahmer entered the hospital. He had pancreatic cancer, in an advanced stage. By the time the diagnosis was confirmed, the deadline for candidates to withdraw had passed. Dahmer's name would be on the ballot. Luckily for the Conservatives, Beaver River was rock-ribbed Tory. Although he spent the rest of the campaign in hospital, Dahmer won his riding by seven thousand votes over his Liberal challenger. The Reform candidate, Deborah Grey, a high school teacher, placed fourth and lost her deposit.

Five days after the election, before he could be sworn in as a Member of Parliament, John Dahmer died. Brian Mulroney set the by-election date for March 11, 1989. For Reform, the big question was, Should Preston Manning run, or should the party send Grey back into the fight?

It is exceedingly difficult not to love Deb Grey. A huge-hearted, big-voiced Evangelical Christian who sang in a gospel choir, she also loves to go booting around on a motorcycle, clad neck-to-toe in leather. Though she had no children of her own, she was foster mother to six children, five of them Aboriginal. She tends to sprinkle her conversation with verbal exclamation points – "Dear me!" and "Oh man!" – and her laugh can shake the walls. Her nickname, the Iron Snowbird, came after someone observed that she resembles a cross between Anne Murray and Margaret Thatcher.

Grey was attracted to Reform's populist conservative message. She agreed to run in Beaver River after she found herself sitting on a flight beside Gordon Shaw, who was now a Reform Party organizer. He talked her into it. After taking a leave from her teaching job, Grey campaigned hard in Beaver River. To lose her deposit against a candidate who never even appeared in public was hard to take. And now she had to decide whether to run again, even though she was back to teaching full time. Grey phoned Manning and offered him her full support if he chose to take over the nomination. But after a few days of consultations, the Reform leader decided that parachuting himself into Beaver River would look opportunistic, so he asked Grey to take another run at it. And the thing was, many pundits and politicos thought she had a chance. Voters were angry at the Progressive Conservatives for running a candidate who was clearly too ill to take his seat. The Free Trade Agreement had made it safely through Parliament, though the Liberal-dominated Senate delayed ratification until almost literally the last possible moment. If the West really wanted to register a protest at the Tories' out-of-control spending, voting for Deb Grey was one way to do it.

Grey was utterly surprised when television cameras and reporters from Ottawa showed up at her campaign office on election night, predicting she was going to win. "I could hardly believe my ears," she wrote later. "I had no idea that we could be that close, but I wasn't going to argue with them."[1] Not only did Reform win, but Grey took 50 per cent of the vote. "She smoked 'em," Manning exulted.[2]

Reform didn't know how lucky it was. Not only was Grey a woman, and a very likeable one at that, but her riding contained Alberta's only significant population of francophones, in Lac La Biche–St. Paul and Bonnyville. She utterly contradicted the stereotype that Eastern reporters and politicians had already imposed on Reform as a party of angry and bigoted white men. When David Duke, a card-carrying member of the Ku Klux Klan, was defeated in his bid for governor of Louisiana, Liberal MP Sheila Copps – always an exemplar of understatement – compared him to Preston Manning: "The policies of Preston Manning, which appeal to people's latent fears in a recessionary period, are the same policies that permit a David Duke to come forward in a state like Louisiana."[3] As the visible face of the Reform Party in the House, Grey was the best antidote to such bile. But the Alberta high school teacher was a political neophyte, and as the first Reform MP, she would be the face and voice of the party in the House of Commons. She'd need help.

When Manning first asked him to return to Ottawa as Grey's legislative assistant, Harper said no. He still hadn't finished his master's thesis. And his last stint as a legislative assistant, for Jim Hawkes, had been less than pleasant. But Manning needed someone who could guide Grey through those opening months, while she found her feet and the washrooms, and learned the ways of the Hill. Her learning curve was steep; Grey hadn't even realized that, as a Member of Parliament, she would be expected to spend much of her year in Ottawa. In Alberta, the legislature hardly ever met.* The realization that she would have to move to Ottawa appalled Grey. On top of everything else, she was terrified of flying. "I didn't know that I even needed staff," she recalled, looking back. "I knew nothing about an MP's office."[4]

"This girl needs serious help," Manning told Harper.[5] And Harper no less than Manning understood that the future of Reform would depend in no small measure on how well Deb Grey performed as an MP. So Steve soon found himself back in Ottawa – on a one-year leave of absence from the university – and back in the Confederation Building. Only this time, he knew more than the MP about the party he'd helped to form, the platform he'd helped to write, and the office she held. There were tensions. "Stephen is bright as a whip," Grey said in 2002. "He's a good strategic thinker. But intense: 'You have to do this; you have to learn that.'"[6] William Johnson, an early biographer of Stephen Harper, concluded: "She holds a grudge against him. She is a flamboyant, capable and self-confident woman in her own right, and she did not take easily to being under tutelage."[7]

Not so, Grey retorts. "We got along fine." They were both single, and strangers in a strange capital. They would work late into the night, then go

---

* Between 1988 and 2013, the Alberta legislature sat, on average, fifty-eight days a year.

in search of a meal in nearby Chinatown. "It was very amicable," she maintains, "because I wouldn't put up with not amicable."[8] Besides, Grey points out, if she harboured a grudge against Stephen Harper, she wouldn't have chosen Robert Harper as her next assistant. This may be a case of both sides being right. Grey was intensely loyal to Preston Manning, and as tensions mounted between Manning and Harper, Grey would naturally come to resent Harper's independent-minded ways. But in those days, they were two lonely Reformers without friends in a hostile city. They needed each other.

If nothing else, working for Deb Grey for a year offered Harper a birds-eye view of the second Mulroney administration. There was a lot to see, most of it ugly.

As Harper's M.A. thesis would later demonstrate, governments are more likely to take on tough economic challenges immediately after an election, giving them time to recover from the voters' anger. In his spring 1989 budget, Finance Minister Michael Wilson announced that the government would impose a new tax, the Goods and Services Tax, which would replace the existing Manufacturers Sales Tax. The GST was sound economic policy: it replaced a hidden tax that penalized manufacturers, reducing their competitiveness, with an open, transparent, and efficient tax that would generate much-needed revenue to fight the deficit. But that was the problem. Although Wilson maintained that the GST would be revenue-neutral – that it would take in no more revenue than the tax it replaced – no one believed him and they were right not to. Besides, it would be a headache to administer. The Liberals, the NDP, and the lone Reform MP, Deb Grey, railed against the tax – Reform's position was that the government should cut spending rather than increase revenues to balance the books – and vowed to repeal it if given the chance, leading to the most raucous filibuster in the Senate's history. By the time the GST finally came into effect, in 1991, the Mulroney government was toxic to voters across the land.

The Meech Lake Accord caused an even greater fuss and was the topic of Grey's first speech in the House of Commons – the first address by the Reform Party in the House. The Liberals and NDP continued to support the accord, making Grey a lone voice. But if she was alone inside the

House, she was not alone outside it. Resistance was growing, from premiers who had come to office after the deal was signed; from an angry Pierre Trudeau – "The federation was set to last a thousand years!" he raged. "Alas, only one eventuality hadn't been foreseen: that one day the government of Canada might fall into the hands of a weakling"[9] – from Westerners who wanted Senate reform to be part of any package; and from Canadians who wondered why politicians were obsessing over constitutional reform instead of the economy in general and the deficit in particular. Grey addressed all of these concerns – or rather she and Harper did, with input from Preston Manning.

"The legislative programs of the federal government are too centralized in their orientation, focused on managing Toronto's economic boom and meeting Quebec's constitutional demands, to the neglect of the needs and interests of the more thinly-populated resource-producing areas of the country," Grey declared in a powerful but respectful address.[10] The speech took on the Bank of Canada's campaign, under Governor John Crow, to defeat inflation through high interest rates, which were dragging down the economy, and of course it put the Reform Party on record as opposing the GST.

But the meat of the address concerned the Meech Lake Accord. "Our people are not unsympathetic to constitutional amendments to make Quebec more at home in Confederation," Grey maintained, "but they want concurrent constitutional amendments, namely, meaningful Senate reform, to make the West feel more at home in Confederation. . . . To us, Meech Lake is not an example of democratic Constitution-building, but executive federalism run amok."

Those words made Grey persona non grata in a House that was otherwise unanimously supportive of Meech Lake, whatever some Liberal backbenchers might have grumbled under their breath. But Grey considered her lonely crusade against Meech Lake in the House her finest moment as an MP, and Reform's opposition to Meech put the party on the map, as the only national political voice of opposition to an accord that was facing growing opposition across the nation.

"The Beaver River, I must report, is not a tributary of Meech Lake," Harper wrote and Grey declared, eloquently (even if a river cannot be a tributary of a lake). "Its waters come from different sources and flow in a different direction." The people of Beaver River will want to know, she declared, why this government was so determined to accede to the demands of Quebec while ignoring the demands of the West. "The people of Beaver River are uneasy patriots," Grey and Harper warned, "and look forward to the day when they become truly fair and equitable partners in Confederation." And not only Beaver River was restive.

———————

Reformers gathered for their convention in Edmonton in late October 1989 in high spirits. Not only had they elected their first MP; two weeks before they had also elected a senator. Progressive Conservative premier Don Getty was under intense criticism from Reformers and from Albertans generally over his support for Meech Lake, which the legislature had already ratified. To show he was something other than Brian Mulroney's poodle, Getty agreed under pressure to hold a provincial election to nominate the next senator from Alberta. The Reform candidate, Stan Waters, won the election in a walk, with 42 per cent of the vote. The Tory candidate, Bert Brown, placed a poor third. He was even beaten by a Liberal! Mulroney chose to respect the result, and Waters headed to the Senate.

Manning came to the convention with a speech that had been largely inspired by one element in a memorandum from Steve Harper. In his personal post mortem of the election and the months that followed, Harper had become increasingly convinced that Manning was taking Reform in the wrong direction. With characteristic audacity and unwillingness to defer to authority, he sat down and wrote Manning a twenty-page paper explaining everything that he believed the Reform leader was doing wrong. And Harper was right. Not yet thirty, he understood exactly what it would take to create a natural conservative governing alternative to the Liberals. More than anything he wrote before it, this extraordinary memorandum would guide his thinking and shape his future government. More than any other document or speech, it defined Stephen Harper as a politician.

Harper's concerns were twofold: First, Manning wanted to forge a coalition of Western voters and voters in the hinterlands of Central and Atlantic

Canada. Because the economy of these rural areas was primarily resource-based, Manning was convinced that voters in these regions were natural allies of voters in the four Western provinces. Harper used to joke that "Preston wants to spend all his time in places that end in 'River.'"[11] Second, Manning believed that Liberal, Progressive Conservative, and New Democrat voters in these hinterlands would abandon all three parties in support of a populist movement that took on Central Canada's entrenched elites.

In other words, Manning believed Reform "should emphasize its geographical nature while downplaying its ideological content," Harper summarized, and then swiftly demolished both assumptions.[12] First, the Maritime fisherman, the Quebec dairy farmer, and the Northern Ontario logger depended heavily on government subsidies or tariff protection or Unemployment Insurance or other supports. Why on earth would they get behind a political party that advocated cutbacks to Unemployment Insurance and regional development grants?

Besides, the hinterland-coalition assumption "is based on the failure to recognize the new realities of modern urban populations. . . . Even in a 'resource producing region' like Western Canada, the urban electorate is largely left cold by the rhetoric and issues associated with primary production," Harper wrote. The urban voter "has values and perspectives more in common with other urban centres in Canada than with the immediate hinterland of his own region. Furthermore, our country is today dominated by urban society and will be more so in the future." Harper realized, as Manning did not, that a successful national conservative party would need to attract urban – especially suburban – voters. The cities were the future and must be courted, not alienated.

As for the notion that a grassroots-fuelled, populist party could transcend ideology, Harper considered it ridiculous. Urban voters, especially, cared more about what a party stands for than how it got there, he argued. He predicted that a hinterland-based, grassroots-fed party would win only rural ridings, be constantly starved for cash, suffer from weak organization, face derision from the media, and serve as "an open invitation to fanatics and crackpots." Most important, it would be labelled right-wing whether it claimed to be or not, "because it strongly reflects the conservative values of its rural base." Such a party, Harper was convinced, would never win government.

Before laying out his alternative, Manning's policy director took the Reform leader on a brief, guided tour of the Western world's postwar political history. The unprecedented growth that followed the war had led to the creation of the welfare state, Harper observed, which came under threat when the oil shocks of the 1970s undermined the economic growth needed to finance ever-expanding social programs. As a result, Harper argued, Western societies had bifurcated into two competing political coalitions, both of them primarily urban, professional, and middle-class. One consisted of "social scientists, social researchers, political professionals, educators, bureaucrats, activists and, to a lesser degree, journalists and communicators," Harper wrote. ". . . Unlike the traditional middle class, it draws its income not from market mechanisms, but primarily from the public sector, i.e. from the networking and manipulation of political (or 'social') decision-making structures." He called this coalition "the political class."

Because the political class depends on government revenues for its income, Harper argued, it advocated ever-higher taxation of resources and private-sector incomes, along with deficit financing. This ultimately provoked a reaction from the middle class working in the private sector. "Political realignment in most Western countries today represents a battle over tax dollars between two groups of urban, professional, middle-class voters – the taxpayers of the private sector (the 'Right') and the tax recipients of the Welfare State (the 'Left'). Viable political coalitions become based on these and seek allies among other groups of voters." This crucial paragraph would guide Harper's strategic political thinking for two decades and more.

What, then, would a viable, national conservative party look like? First and foremost, it would be moderate. "An excessive appeal to 'conservative' values can alienate the urban private-sector middle class," he warned. In that respect, he urged Manning to moderate the party's position on immigration. "Our immigration policy risks alienating certain well-integrated middle-class voters of some ethnic backgrounds. It must be seen as strictly a policy of economics and border controls, not cultural adaptation and country of origin." Such an immigration policy, Harper believed, could win over immigrant voters, who were socially and fiscally conservative by nature, yet who traditionally supported the Liberals. He would be proven right.

While the party should appeal to "moderate pro-life voters," it should avoid extreme stands. "The key is to emphasize moderate, conservative social values consistent with the traditional family, the market economy and patriotism," he advised. These three principles would become the bedrock of the Conservative Party of Canada.

A successful conservative party would guide the members, rather than be guided by them. "The Reform Party's policy recruitment of 'membership' (not 'grassroots') should be more targeted at groups and individuals likely to be open to the Party's agenda," he wrote, "as opposed to the agenda being tailored to whoever joins." Under Stephen Harper's leadership, the Conservative Party would devote extraordinary effort and resources at identifying, nurturing, and expanding what would come to be called "the base."

Above all else, a successful governing conservative party would focus on economic issues, especially on "the downsizing of government, particularly central government, in favour of a more decentralized, market-oriented economy." For a decade of government, the Conservatives would own the economy as an issue.

Harper also addressed the most logical and fundamental objection to his hypothesis: Why had Canadian politics not followed that of other Western nations by evolving into coalitions of the Left and Right, competing for power? In part, Harper attributed this failure to polarize to "the inherently bland, non-ideological, apolitical nature of the Canadian population," to the "greater economic options afforded Canada due to its massive resource base and its lack of defence obligations," and to "the especially unrepresentative nature of Canadian political institutions, marked by solidarity, secrecy, centralization and public-sector information systems." But mostly it was the fault of Quebec, which "jealously and carefully guards its interests in the national politics of a country where the majority are essentially foreigners," he observed. This caused Quebeckers to vote as a block, and that block vote invariably captured the national governing party, whether Liberal or Progressive Conservative, leaving both captive to Quebec interests.

"The arrangements designed to include Quebec in a national party, and ultimately the country, have been incompatible with any coherent ideological agenda, especially an Economic Right agenda," Harper theorized. "Therefore a modern Party of the Economic Right must be prepared to effectively ignore the National Unity issue, neglect organizational effort in Quebec, and ultimately risk calling the separatist bluff." Intriguingly, he observed that Joe Clark would have won a majority government in 1979, had the election been fought with the riding distribution in place in 1989. A majority government was possible, he argued, even without support from Quebec. Again, the future would prove him right.

Manning never acted on most of Harper's advice. Although older and more politically experienced, the Reform leader lacked his young advisor's strategic insight. Harper, after all, had been born and raised in an Ontario suburb. He knew the place, knew how the people he grew up around felt, knew how to tailor a conservative message in a way that would appeal to them. He had then lived for a decade in Edmonton and Calgary, absorbing the Western political ethos into his core. He had also spent time in Ottawa. He knew how the senior figures in the major political parties thought, and what their weaknesses were. The accidents of experience, combined with a powerfully analytical mind, had given Stephen Harper the ability to understand how suburban Ontario thought, how Albertans thought, and how the two could be brought together. In his March 1989 memorandum, he offered that insight to Manning. But neither Manning nor Reform were able to embrace such a coalition. It would take another fifteen years before Harper was able to act on his own recommendations, this time as leader of another new party.

But Manning did seize one element of the memorandum with both hands: the Quebec strategy. "The strategy of the Reform Party as regards Quebec must therefore be very careful," Harper had written. "To pursue its agenda, it must insist that the Crisis of National Unity can be resolved only by Quebeckers making an emotional commitment to Canada, not by economic or constitutional appeasement. It must be prepared to negotiate a looser arrangement if this commitment is not forthcoming. Yet the Reform Party must prefer unity." This was exactly the strategy that Manning would pursue.

The October 1989 convention adopted a resolution, which Manning had directed Harper to draft, that held that Confederation "can only be maintained by a clear commitment to Canada as one nation, in which the demands and aspirations of all regions are entitled to equal status in constitutional negotiations and political debate." Further, "should these principles be rejected, Quebec and the rest of Canada should consider whether there exists a better political arrangement which will enrich our friendship, respect our common defence requirement and ensure a free interchange of commerce and people, by mutual consent and for our mutual benefit." The message to Quebec was clear: sign on to Canada or leave. But you'll leave only on terms we all agree to.

In case that message wasn't clear enough, Manning pounded it home at the convention in what came to be known as the "House Divided" speech. He asked the assembly whether three decades of appeasement – official bilingualism nationwide, the 1982 Constitution, the Meech Lake Accord – had placated the concerns of Quebeckers. "No it has not!" he and the crowd answered in unison. "Instead, what the Pearson-Trudeau-Mulroney approach to constitutional development has produced is a house divided against itself. And as a great Reformer once said long ago: 'A house divided against itself cannot stand.'"[13]*

If Quebec was not prepared to accept its place within Canada as a province among provinces, as a region in a nation of regions, as a French fact within a larger English fact, it should go, Manning declared. "We say that living in one Canada united on certain principles, or living with a greater constitutional separation between Quebec and the rest of Canada is preferable to living in a 'house divided.'"

As Harper's memorandum demonstrated, there was space in Canadian politics for a truly conservative party that could offer a governing alternative to the Progressive Conservatives, who had become ideologically indistinguishable from the Liberals. But in the wake of the 1993 election, when Reform laid low the Progressive Conservative Party, ushering in yet

---

* The Reformer was Jesus of Nazareth. Abraham Lincoln famously borrowed the phrase during the debate over abolishing slavery.

another decade of Liberal rule, many Progressive Conservatives angrily chastised Reform and Preston Manning for dividing the conservative movement. "It is when the party, in its broadest form, is united and embraces all strands of conservatism that it has a chance to win," writer and consultant Bob Plamondon wrote in 2006. ". . . the most important lesson Conservatives can learn from losing four consecutive elections is that disunity and division are a guarantee of failure."[14]

Fair enough; it would be Stephen Harper's ultimate task to heal those wounds. But it is also true that there simply was no place for the Reform wing of conservatism within the Progressive Conservative Party under Brian Mulroney or anyone who potentially might replace him. The fact was that, in 1989, three decades of Liberal/PC obsession with accommodating the aspirations of Quebec while ignoring the growing wealth, influence, and resentment of the West; the worsening Canadian economy; and the deteriorating government finances had left millions of Western conservatives angry and alienated. And again, it was personal. Alberta Progressive Conservative MPs were furious at Reformers who questioned their commitment to the West, and who risked fracturing the coalition and returning the Liberals to power, just as Reformers felt only contempt for PCers who had gone east intending to speak for the West in Parliament, only to become "Ottawashed," as Link Byfield put it: defending Ottawa's priorities to the West rather than standing up for the West in Ottawa.

There was also no place in the Progressive Conservative Party for someone like Harper. Twice he had watched the Mulroney government in action while living in Ottawa. Twice he had fled. Stephen Harper in 2003 would bring the fractured conservative movement together. But Steve Harper in 1989 wrote the memorandum and the resolution that drove conservatives apart.

———————

Reform's opposition to the Meech Lake Accord was well judged, politically. Elections in Newfoundland and Labrador and New Brunswick produced governments opposed to the accord; the Liberal Party's position split between leadership candidates Jean Chrétien (opposed) and Paul Martin (in favour). With the accord facing defeat, a commission headed by the youthful MP Jean Charest recommended changes to the deal. This infuriated Lucien Bouchard, the nationalist leader whom Mulroney had first appointed ambassador to France and whom he then enticed into his cabinet. Bouchard crossed the floor and created his own, separatist party, taking a passel of Conservative MPs with him, amply confirming Harper's suspicion that many in the PC Quebec caucus were closet separatists. Well they were out of the closet now. With everything around him falling apart, Mulroney convened a final first ministers' conference in early June, 1990, three weeks before the accord was set to expire if not ratified by all ten provinces. After a week of agonizing talks, it appeared that a new agreement was in place, one that included a vague commitment to future Senate reform. Manning and Harper were as opposed to the new agreement as they were to the old. It didn't matter. Newfoundland and Labrador premier Clyde Wells, who had consented reluctantly and conditionally, backed out, while Elijah Harper, representing aggrieved Aboriginal Canadians who complained they had been left out of the negotiations, held up ratification in the Manitoba legislature. Meech was dead.

Quebec voters were apoplectic. Robert Bourassa warned the rest of Canada that Quebec would choose its own destiny, and that destiny might well include independence. Mulroney launched round after round after round of national consultations, in search of a new consensus, even as Quebec prepared for an October 1992 referendum. Finally, in Charlottetown, on August 28, 1992, the prime minister, premiers, and Aboriginal leaders agreed on a new constitutional arrangement, known as the Charlottetown Accord. This one they decided to put to a national referendum – a vote that created deep divisions within the Reform Party.

Right after Charlottetown was made public, Manning, Harper, Tom Flanagan, George Koch, Laurie Watson, and several others met to consider the party's response. Koch had quit his job as *Alberta Report*'s parliamentary reporter to become a speech writer for Manning. Watson, with whom Koch was and is partnered, was doing communications work for the party. Flanagan and Manning had met at another one of the brown-bag lunches hosted by Robert Mansell at the University of Calgary in late 1990 or early 1991. The professor and the party leader hit it off, and Manning asked

Flanagan to become director of policy, strategy, and communications. As chief policy advisor, Harper now worked for Flanagan, though he was largely absent as he finished off his master's thesis, once and for all.

But Flanagan was not Manning's only, or even principal, advisor. That role was increasingly taken by someone who wasn't even at the meeting: Rick Anderson. Flanagan, Harper, et al. were at first curious about this new arrival, then baffled by him, then resentful of him. By the end, they felt he – and by extension Manning – had betrayed the cause.

Anderson, an Ottawa-based public relations consultant, had worked for both the federal and Ontario Liberal parties. But he had broken with the Liberals and joined Reform. Calm, low-key, quietly competent, deeply plugged-in, Anderson was the kind of professional that Manning believed Reform needed to help it break through east of Manitoba. He had real-world experience in organizing and running a national election campaign, something that everyone else in Reform, including Manning, lacked.

Anderson warned Manning that Central Canada would never endorse a demonstrably right-wing party. This appealed to Manning's conviction that, as a populist party, Reform should focus more on democratic engagement than on ideology. Anderson had told Manning that he was in favour of the Charlottetown Accord, which had the support of all major political parties in the House, all the premiers and Aboriginal leaders, and a healthy majority of the Canadian population, according to the polls. Did that information colour Manning's attitude toward the Charlottetown Accord? There are two different versions of that story.

At the meeting to consider Reform's response to Charlottetown, as Flanagan, Harper, and Koch tell it, the Reform leader appeared to be ready to support Charlottetown. "There were six or eight people in the room, and all of them except Preston remember it as Preston not wanting to oppose Charlottetown," Koch maintains.[15] There were good reasons for Reform to support the accord, such as the fact that it included a modified version of a Triple-E Senate, a core Reform priority.

But Manning insists the others are wrong, that he was opposed to Charlottetown from the start. "I felt it was something that could and should be fought," he later maintained. "It didn't come anywhere close to achieving what Western Canadians would have liked out of it. But I like to consult our people rather than tell them, 'Look, we've decided we're going to fight this and you're going to help us.' I always say, 'Ask first and tell second.'"[16]

Manning maintains that he strongly differed with Harper on the subject of consultation, and that he sees that disagreement as fundamental to Harper's style of governing. "Tom and Stephen were never as inclined to ask the grassroots, as confident that they would come up with the right answer, as I was," he believes. "And that grew more evident as we went down the road."

Consider a political meeting filled with early-stage Reformers. At that meeting, someone might angrily denounce immigrants in racist terms. For Manning, the challenge would be to isolate the speaker, assure him that this wasn't the sentiment of the vast majority of the people in the room, and perhaps even generate a round of applause in support. But Harper, Manning believes, would conclude from that meeting that the party needed to exercise greater control over who it let in.

"I'm not as suspicious of ordinary people as Stephen inclines to be," Manning maintains. "I do believe there is such a thing as common sense." "The common sense of the common people" was a mantra for him. And Manning is much more confident of his ability to control a room. "I also had a fair amount of confidence in my ability to go into these big, wild, grassroots meetings and be able to talk them into taking the position that I thought we should take," he said. "Whereas Stephen and Tom tend to be a lot more reserved." In that sense, at least, Manning was a more natural politician than Harper would ever be. "The wilder elements in our early uncontrolled meetings probably reinforced Stephen's fear that if you left things wide open you'd have all kinds of problems," Manning believes.

While Manning took a long-planned family vacation, Koch sent out a questionnaire to the leaders of every organized Reform constituency – the grassroots. The response was overwhelmingly negative toward Charlottetown. Harper was tasked with looking at the accord's fine print. He went silent for three days, as he parsed the plethora of sections, subsections, clauses, and subclauses. He returned to the group with a revelation: The Charlottetown Accord wasn't an accord at all. It was, rather, a framework for future negotiations. Those who were willing to hold their noses and vote for Charlottetown for the sake of peace would, in fact, not find peace, only endless future rounds of wrangling. For their parts, the riding presidents were powerfully opposed. So was Manning, after he returned.

The upshot is that Manning claims he opposed Charlottetown from the get-go, while his former advisors insist he had to be talked into this stance. A quarter-century later, it hardly matters, except that a river forked in those weeks. Manning began to jettison the advisors who had helped him launch the party, in favour of advisors who could help the party break through. Harper, who was barely in his thirties and had a more-than-promising future ahead of him, could have followed Manning down this new stream. But he took the other fork, leaving the two men too far apart to ever reconcile.

Manning campaigned across the country in opposition to "the Mulroney deal," as he called it (so much for his initial promise to debate Charlottetown on its merits and avoid personal attacks), warning, as Harper had first pointed out, that all people would get for their Yes vote was years of talks and inaction. "If you vote Yes you are following the politicians," he told viewers during a televised debate with NDP leader Audrey McLaughlin. "If you vote No, you are leading them." [17]

The more the public looked at Charlottetown, the less it liked it. On October 26, 1992, referendum night, the accord went down to a resounding defeat, with 54 per cent of the population voting No. Reform had offered an early voice of dissent in a campaign that mobilized the nation against the will of its political leaders. For Preston Manning, it was a triumph.

But not for Steve Harper. In early September, Manning created a steering committee to manage the party's No campaign. Rick Anderson was on it. Flanagan and Harper were not. For Harper, that was it. Though he had given a number of press and television interviews explaining why Reform opposed the deal, he now decided to abandon any national role. It was clear that Manning wanted to take Reform in a different direction.

The day after the referendum result, Manning fired George Koch and Laurie Watson. Flanagan stayed on as an advisor until the summer of 1993, when Manning fired him over his opposition to allowing Rick Anderson to become campaign manager. By then, Harper had already withdrawn from his role of policy advisor, focusing instead on his campaign for Calgary West. He even considered dropping out of the race entirely. Manning saw this as another example of Harper's tendency to abandon the field completely when things don't go his way. "He did have that tendency to go into his own funks every once in a while," Manning observes. "And it usually happened at inopportune times. I attributed it to stress, such as just before an election."[18]

Not only was Harper thinking of dropping out of the race for Calgary West; he threatened to air his grievance in public. A group of Reform insiders met him in summer 1993 and pleaded with him to stay involved and stay loyal. Harper didn't publicly criticize Manning's choice of Anderson for campaign manager, but he withdrew from any national involvement in the election. "This was a blow to our overall campaign effort, and it put more of an overall burden on those who had to fill the gap left by his withdrawal," Manning later complained.[19]

"He thought very seriously about not even running for the party," Tom Flanagan recalls. "He thought about leaving completely. He said he was talked into [staying] by his father and other friends."[20] Joe Harper told his son that he had committed to run in the riding and owed it to his supporters and his own sense of honour to stick it out. However bitter and resentful Harper was feeling, he wasn't prepared to disappoint his father. And there was another reason. He owed it to Laureen.

———————

Steve Harper and Laureen Teskey first met at a Reform Party convention in Saskatoon in April 1991. Harper was so distracted with party business he couldn't even remember the encounter, afterward. The delegates had to make a momentous decision: whether to remain a party of regional protest or to expand nationally. Harper was passionate in his commitment to expansion. He also delivered a major speech at the convention. He rejected special status for Quebec, while also warning the party against taking extreme positions, especially in areas of language and immigration. "Do not allow the party to be shot in the foot on these issues by radical elements, as has happened far too often to new parties," he implored.

The delegates listened. The 1991 Blue Book stripped the obnoxious clauses on immigration from the manifesto, while continuing to insist on

an immigration policy based on economic need rather than family reunification. Most important, delegates overwhelmingly endorsed a proposal,
seconded by Harper, to establish constituency associations and run candidates east of Manitoba in the next election. Though some in the party
wanted to keep Reform a voice of Western protest, most others wanted to
expand. Some of them wore T-shirts with the slogan "The East Wants In."
The vote electrified the convention; they had chosen to create a new
national party. Someone spontaneously broke into singing "O Canada,"
and soon the whole room had taken up the anthem. Those who were there
found it deeply moving.

Laureen Teskey was at the Saskatoon convention because she was at
heart a Blue Conservative rather than a Red Tory. Otherwise, she had a lot
in common with her friend Cynthia Williams. They both worked at a
Calgary firm, GTO printing. Teskey was a graphic artist there. Both women
were opinionated, open-hearted extroverts who loved life and a good laugh.
Teskey was born in Turner Valley, an hour's drive southwest of Calgary.
She described herself as a tomboy growing up, who preferred hockey to
doll houses. As a young woman, she toured the length of Africa, thirteen
countries in all, and acquired a taste for motorcycles. Like Williams,
Teskey studied journalism, but decided it wasn't for her and switched to
photography. That, and her love of computers, drew her into graphic
design. "I couldn't get over being paid for working at something I loved,"
she later recalled.[21] There was a brief marriage to a New Zealander, Neil
Fenton, that ended in 1988, which came as a shock to her. In 1991, she was
interested in Reform, both because it seemed to her a logical alternative
to the centrist, Central Canada ways of the Progressive Conservatives, and
because she thought it would be a great way to meet guys. "If you want to
meet a man, join a political party," was her saying.[22]

Williams was convinced that Laureen Teskey and Steve Harper were
made for each other. Despite the break-up, Harper and Williams had
stayed in touch. They were to meet for lunch, and Williams asked Teskey
to come along. "He asked me later, 'Did you deliberately introduce me to
Laureen?' and I said, 'Yep.' I wanted him to be happy," Williams recalls.[23]

There are other accounts of how the two first got together. Diane Ablonczy
claims she urged Laureen to ask Harper on a date because he was cooped

up in a basement apartment with bronchitis and needed to get out more.[24] Gordon Shaw also says he had something to do with it.[25] A successful match has many fairy godmothers taking credit.

It wasn't exactly love at first sight. Not only did Harper not remember Teskey from the Saskatoon convention, but he was as socially awkward and withdrawn as Teskey was spontaneous and outgoing. However, he did accept her offer to help him with the graphs and charts for his master's thesis, which was finally nearing completion. He dropped by her place often to ask for help, and had a tendency to stay for dinner.

Laureen Teskey was a catch: outgoing, charming, warm, smart, and mighty good-looking. But was Steve Harper a catch? It might not have seemed so at the time. At thirty-two, he was still living in a Spartan apartment that he shared with his brother Grant. He had only two suits, which he rotated for public appearances, and he still hadn't finished his M.A., after six years of trying. For wheels he drove a beat-up K-car. He was anything but svelte.

On the other hand, he was a major influence within a new political party that might be going places. And anybody who knew Steve Harper in those days, from his friends to his professors to Preston Manning himself, knew that he was going places, too. His awkwardness around people was, in its own way, endearing. If he was in a small group, and felt completely comfortable, he could be very funny. Conversation with him was challenging and stimulating. And Steve and Laureen were in love, simple as that.

"I saw it as a good thing, thinking she'll bring him out of his shell," Deb Grey remembered in 2007.[26] Friends who knew them both hoped Teskey would help the glowering, taciturn policy wonk act more like a normal person. "That the rumpled Harper had 'project' written all over him is believed to be part of the appeal for the can-do Teskey," one profile of the prime minister's wife opined.[27]

They were married by a justice of the peace on December 11, 1993, in a small, simple ceremony, with only a few friends present, at the modest house the couple had purchased in northwest Calgary. All in all, it was probably the best thing that ever happened to him. Laureen would offer an emotional anchor that would see Harper through some of his biggest crises. She would turn out to be the only person, after Joe passed away, who could directly and bluntly criticize him. She would become his fiercest defender as well as his toughest critic, at least among those few whom Harper trusted. They would become a political team. Without Laureen, as we'll see, Stephen Harper would never have become prime minister, and would never have survived as prime minister.

Brian Mulroney knew he had no hope of winning a third term. Despite the success of the Free Trade Agreement with the United States, which was expanding into the North American Free Trade Agreement that included Mexico, the failures of Meech Lake and Charlottetown, the hated GST, and the severe recession had made him possibly the least popular prime minister in Canadian history, with one poll putting his personal popularity at 18 per cent. If that weren't enough, two new parties had arisen in protest over the government's perceived failures: the Bloc Québécois and Reform. But perhaps all was not lost; Mulroney had promoted a smart and attractive MP from Vancouver, Kim Campbell, into cabinet. The plan, as he envisioned it, was for Campbell to succeed him, govern for a few months, bring down a budget that finally addressed the problem of the deficit, and then call an election.

The plan worked, at first. Campbell became leader and the party rebounded in the polls, showing the PCs suddenly tied with the Liberals. Convinced that momentum was on her side, Campbell asked the governor general to dissolve Parliament. The election was set for October 25.

Anyone who was around at the time still marvels at the Progressive Conservative campaign in that election: Campbell blithely declaring that unemployment was unlikely to come down significantly until the end of the decade (she was right, but still . . .); vowing to eliminate the deficit without raising taxes but refusing to say how (an election, she declared, was "the worst possible time to have such a dialogue"); and running television ads that appeared to mock Jean Chrétien's facial appearance. ("It's true that I have a physical defect," Chrétien told reporters. "When I was a kid, people were laughing at me. But I accepted that because God gave me other qualities, and I am grateful."[28] The Liberal polling numbers soared.)

One of the biggest problems facing the Progressive Conservatives was that they didn't have a plan, and both the Liberals and Reformers did. The Liberals called theirs the Red Book, a series of specific commitments that Chrétien waved at every stop, telling the voters they could hold him to account if he didn't fulfill each and every promise. Reform's 1993 Blue Book, largely devised by Harper, centred on a "Zero in Three" commitment to balance the federal budget in three years through targeted cuts in spending. To everyone's surprise, the *Globe and Mail*'s editorial board endorsed the Reform approach, saying it was the only credible deficit reduction plan on offer.

Harper's campaign for Calgary West was a family-and-friends affair. John Weissenberger was campaign manager. Laureen designed the signs and brochures. Brother Grant organized the making and distributing of campaign signs, which bore a slight change from the signs of 1988. Then he had been "Steve Harper." Now he was "Stephen Harper." At thirty-three, he was still young for an aspiring MP, and wanted to add gravitas to his campaign. To this day, though, family and older friends still call him Steve (though Laureen has switched to Stephen).

Brother Rob was in charge of door-to-door. Joe Harper watched over the books while Margaret Harper helped out at campaign headquarters. (The Harper clan, at different times and for different reasons, had migrated to Calgary after Steve moved there.) The mood was different from 1988. Money was flowing in, along with volunteers – a thousand of them, or thereabouts. The campaign leadership were hardened veterans now. They had worked the 1988 campaign, the campaign to elect Stan Waters to the Senate, the campaign to defeat Charlottetown. They knew who on the voters list would support them, who might be persuaded, and who was a lost cause. They were able to target supporters and get them to the polls, while wasting no time on hopeless cases. And as the Campbell campaign imploded, they could feel the wave, the broad swing in support away from the Conservatives and toward Reform in Calgary, in Alberta, in the West.

Jim Hawkes could see what was happening on the ground – he had so few volunteers that he had to mail out campaign literature, because there was no one to deliver it door-to-door – but at a certain level, he just couldn't believe it. "We had 60 per cent four weeks before voting, and we had 15 per cent on voting night," he recalled later. "It was just a shock . . . I was totally blind to the fact that we were going to lose."[29] Harper waltzed in with 52 per cent of the vote.

At an all-candidates debate, the Liberal candidate came out in favour of same-sex marriage – an innovative proposal in 1993. Harper responded that political parties shouldn't take stands on issues of conscience, then joked, "I've been on my own a long time, and I have never been asked about my sexual orientation."[30] Hawkes accused his former aide of belonging to a party that was simply Social Credit under a different name. "I think Mr. Hawkes wants to fight the 1935 election all over again," Harper rebutted. Hawkes was frustrated: not only was he carrying the baggage of the Mulroney/Campbell governments, but the National Citizens Coalition, a conservative pressure group, was specifically targeting his riding, because Hawkes had sponsored the legislation that limited third-party advertising during elections. The NCC spent what it could in ads attacking Hawkes in Calgary West. He was taking fire from every side.

Although Hawkes hated losing the 1993 election that put an end to his political career, he bears no ill will toward Stephen Harper, who had visited him in hospital when he fell ill in 1989, who attended his wife's funeral in 2013, and who dropped in on him at Christmas that same year, unannounced. The two sat around the kitchen table and chatted about old times. Looking back, Hawkes figures that, if you're going to lose an election, it might as well be to someone you helped bring along, despite political differences, and who will go on to become prime minister – and a darn fine one, in Jim Hawkes's estimation.

The election of 1993 was one of the most important in Canadian history – second only, perhaps, to the election of 1988. The Progressive Conservative Party, the party of Macdonald and Borden and Diefenbaker and Mulroney, was reduced to two seats – a blow that would prove fatal, although it would take the party a decade to expire. The Reform Party swept British Columbia, Alberta, and Saskatchewan, taking fifty-two seats, including one in Ontario. But the separatist Bloc Québécois would form the official opposition, taking fifty-four seats in Quebec. And yet the Liberals were able to form a majority government, with ninety-eight seats in Ontario. The NDP went from having the best result in its history, in 1988, to the worst, electing only nine MPs and losing party status in the House of Commons.

Stephen Harper was once again returning to Ottawa. But this time it was different. The first two times he had been a legislative assistant, not yet thirty, alone in a city he hated. Now he'd be arriving as a happily married man and a Member of Parliament. And not just any member; despite his difficulties with Manning, Harper was a prominent figure within the Reform Party and could look forward to an important role within the shadow cabinet. All he had to do was watch what he said and remain loyal to the party leader, and he might well lead Reform himself, one day.

But that, as it turned out, proved impossible.

SIX

Temper

Tom Flanagan and Stephen Harper bonded in the months following the failure of Charlottetown and before the 1993 election. Both men were political animals who had been attracted to, and had then distanced themselves from, the Reform Party and Preston Manning. "We would often sit in my office in the late afternoon, talking about Prestonian populism and where the Reform Party was going," Flanagan later wrote. "I was fifteen years older than Stephen, nominally his superior, far better established in terms of professional reputation, but I found him persuasive, indeed almost mesmerizing." Flanagan was fascinated by the thirty-three-year-old's mastery of both long-term strategic planning and short-term tactics to advance his political agenda. "When he got into a political discussion, his china-blue eyes became transfixing," Flanagan observed, "and he could be passionately captivating and mordantly funny by turns. To those who know him well, the real Stephen Harper is very different from the unemotional image that he projects in public."[1]

Flanagan wrote this in 2007, in a book about his years with Harper. Though highly complimentary, the book angered Harper and led to an estrangement between the two men, who haven't spoken to each other since. "I think the problem for Stephen was not what was in the book, but the fact that someone who worked closely with him would write a book about him," Flanagan surmises. Harper once said to him, "Tom, it's always dangerous to share information."[2]

Looking back now, Flanagan continues to admire Harper's strategic sense, and believes he has been an effective, even great, prime minister. But he realizes that the two of them were never close. "His life was always very compartmentalized," he observes. "He had a small circle of personal friends. I was not part of that. I was in a second circle of people who could be useful to him." For example, despite all the time they spent together, Flanagan had no idea that Harper played the piano. The prime minister's appearance at a National Arts Centre gala in 2009, where he played and sang "With a Little Help from My Friends," utterly surprised him.

———————

There are disagreeable aspects to Stephen Harper's personality. He is prone to mood swings. He can fly off the handle. He goes into funks, sometimes for long periods. He is suspicious of others. The public is aware of these traits mostly through what's written and reported in the media. In public, Harper is almost invariably calm, measured, and careful in what he says and how he says it. Yet none of us, watching him, have any difficulty believing that this closed, repressed personality is capable of lashing out from time to time. We all get the vibe. His personality also comes out in the tactics that the Conservative Party uses against its enemies, both perceived and real – which are, in a word, ruthless.

As with most of us, Harper's character flaws are the reverse side of his character strengths: one would not exist without the other. He has been prime minister for a decade not despite these qualities but because of them.

The most cited characteristic of Stephen Harper is his legendary temper. He can descend into rages, sometimes over trivial things, at other times during moments of crisis. A former aide to Harper recalls a time during the 2004 election campaign when things suddenly started to go very badly for the Conservatives, for reasons we'll examine later. Harper was on the campaign bus, in Quebec, leading a conference call with senior campaign staff back at headquarters in Ottawa. "He was very, very angry," the former aide recalls. "It was: 'We are fucking going to do this, and you are fucking going to do that and I want to see this fucking thing done right now.' And then he paused and asked: 'And why does nothing happen around here unless I say 'fuck'?'"[3]

Harper's temper manifests itself in different ways. Some days, he just gets up on the wrong side of the bed. Other times, he flies off the handle when confronted with bad news. That's when the decibel level goes through the roof and the f-bombs start flying. Harper's reaction when he was told in April 2008 that the RCMP had raided Conservative Party headquarters in connection with the in-and-out affair (we'll get to it), carrying out boxes of material past the TV cameras (someone had tipped off the media), was wondrous to behold.

But when Harper is *really* angry at you, he's very calm. He looks you straight in the eye and tells you how you've failed him, and if you are a faithful follower, you simply want to die. The state beyond that is even worse. He simply cuts you out. He doesn't speak to you, doesn't reply to your messages, freezes you out of meetings. At this point, you should be pursuing a new career opportunity.

Another of Harper's less attractive qualities is a perceived lack of loyalty toward others. Flanagan points out that Stephen Harper has betrayed or estranged many in the conservative movement who were at one time senior to him – Joe Clark, Jim Hawkes, Brian Mulroney, Preston Manning. This, Flanagan believes, is the product of Harper's need to dominate whatever environment he is in. "I think he has this very strong instinct to be in charge," he said. "He really wants to be the Alpha figure, and he's achieved that. So part of that is to dispose of anyone who might be considered to be a rival in some sense or another."[4]

But Harper can be equally ruthless to subordinates. We will hear, for example, about Patrick Muttart, a strategic genius who helped bring the Conservatives to power. But a single indiscretion – he leaked a photo that purported to show Michael Ignatieff involved in planning for the 2003 Iraq War, but the person in the photo wasn't Ignatieff – led to him being ejected from the 2011 election campaign and left him persona non grata within the party. When cabinet minister Helena Guergis was accused of being part of an influence-peddling scheme run by her husband, Rahim Jaffer, that included cocaine-fuelled parties replete with prostitutes, Harper dismissed her from cabinet and expelled her from the caucus, even though the more lurid elements of the allegations turned out to be completely baseless. Most famously, he not only accepted the resignation of his trusted chief of staff, Nigel Wright, in the midst of the Senate expenses scandal, but then laid the blame for Wright's decision to personally pay off Senator Mike Duffy's expenses squarely on Wright himself, which many of the former aide's friends considered a shocking act of disloyalty.

And if Harper is not terribly loyal toward others, others are not always terribly loyal toward him. Harper has been through four chiefs of staff since becoming prime minister; his senior press aides leave at the rate of about one a year. And both Flanagan and former trusted assistant Bruce Carson have written kiss-and-tell memoirs about their years with Harper. Carson, who was charged with influence-peddling after he left Harper's employ, confirms that Harper is prone to fits of anger, which he believes lay behind his attack on Supreme Court Chief Justice Beverley McLachlin, after the court nullified his attempt to appoint Judge Marc Nadon to the court.[5]

Flanagan also asserts that "there is a huge streak of paranoia in Stephen. And he attracts people who have a paranoid streak. And if you don't have one to begin with, you develop it, because you're constantly hearing theories."[6] At its root, "looking back, there's a visceral reluctance to trust the motives of other people," Flanagan concludes. "He often overcomes his initial suspicions and will sign on to other people's ideas. But the initial response is always one of suspicion." Flanagan believes Harper is prone to depression. "He can be suspicious, secretive, and vindictive, prone to sudden eruptions of white hot rage over meaningless trivia," he wrote in 2014, "at other times falling into week-long depressions in which he is incapable of making decisions."[7]

These observations came years after Flanagan and Harper were themselves estranged. They also followed an incident that wounded the University of Calgary professor deeply. On February 27, 2013, Flanagan gave a talk in Lethbridge, Alberta, in which he declared, "I certainly have no sympathy for child molesters, but I do have some grave doubts about putting people in jail because of their taste in pictures." Of course, the session was recorded on someone's smartphone, and of course it hit the Internet almost instantly.

Flanagan's statement, however clumsily worded, is consistent with his libertarian views, which he later expanded on in a book, *Persona Non Grata*. But the comments created a firestorm of criticism: The CBC terminated its relationship with Flanagan, who had often appeared on it as a talking head; the University of Calgary rushed to point out he was retiring; Danielle Smith, leader of the Wild Rose Party, condemned his remarks and terminated the party's relationship with its former campaign manager. Preston Manning struck Flanagan from the roster of speakers at a conference hosted by the Manning Centre, his conservative think tank, and warned against "intemperate and ill-considered remarks" that injure not only the speaker but the conservative movement as a whole.[8] (He later apologized and invited Flanagan to speak at a conference the following year.) But one of the things Flanagan found most hurtful was a tweet from Andrew MacDougall, Harper's director of communications at the time: "Tom Flanagan's comments on child pornography are repugnant, ignorant and appalling."[9]

Flanagan's comments on Harper, then, can be taken in two different contexts. As someone who worked closely with Harper from 1992 until 2005, the Calgary university professor is well positioned to assess Harper's strengths and weaknesses. As someone who has been banished from the prime minister's inner circle and repudiated by the Prime Minister's Office, it is only human for Flanagan to bring up what he sees as unpleasant aspects of Harper's personality.

———

Politics and the stock market are the two most ruthless environments outside an actual battlefield. The market creates and destroys wealth; politics creates and destroys power. Power and wealth are both highly prized, and those who acquire large amounts of either are unlikely to be gentle souls. John Turner was disloyal to Pierre Trudeau and conspired to displace him. Brian Mulroney conspired to displace Joe Clark. Jean Chrétien conspired to displace John Turner. Paul Martin conspired to displace Jean Chrétien.

The great majority of prime ministers since Confederation have either been defeated in an election or forced to leave rather than endure defeat. It's a tough game.[*]

Harper, as we have seen, was disloyal to Preston Manning, and would become even more disloyal in the years ahead. Manning believes that Harper was ambitious to replace him as leader of the party. "I never resented the ambitions of the younger guys to be leader some day," he maintains. To remind them of the path to power, he kept a sign on his desk. "He who would be chief among you, let him be the servant of all" (Matthew 20:27).[10]

But others who knew Stephen Harper in the 1990s don't believe he was angling for the Reform leadership. "Everyone regarded Stephen as being second only to Preston within the party, and probably a successor some day, despite his youth," Flanagan recalls.[11] Had he remained in the party and demonstrated loyalty to the leader, he could well have succeeded Manning when the time was right. Instead, Harper left, and after he left, he made no effort to undermine Manning's leadership. He simply quit the party and went elsewhere.

Harper's complicated relationship with Manning stems from one of his core qualities: Stephen Harper is constitutionally incapable of deferring to authority. Gordon Shaw recalls Harper once confessing to him, "I just can't stand to have anyone tell me what to do."[12] This trait stretches back at least to the time he corrected his teacher on the moons of Jupiter. His best friend at high school was another rebel, Paul Watson. Harper rebelled against his parents' assumption that he would go to university and into commerce or law. He felt only contempt for the professors at the University of Toronto who lorded their authority over the undergraduates, warning that half of them would fail. It took him six years to finish his master's thesis, which someone as smart and hard-working as he is should have been able to dispatch in a fraction of that time, whatever his other duties. He only lasted a year working for Jim Hawkes; he only lasted a year working for Deb Grey.

---

[*] Lester B. Pearson, William Lyon Mackenzie King, and Robert Borden more or less departed office of their own volition. John A. Macdonald and John Thompson died in office.

He chafed against the authority of Preston Manning, almost from the get-go.

Such stiff-necked refusal to take orders, such absolute conviction that he is right and others are wrong, such complete unwillingness to suppress that conviction in order to advance his career should have proved professionally fatal. Who among us could have gotten where we are with such an approach? That Harper did survive, and ultimately triumph, speaks both to his talents and his strength of will.

Regarding the absence of loyalty between Harper and his subordinates, George Koch, the former Reform aide to Preston Manning who remains a friend of the prime minister, has an interesting take. Harper, he says, sometimes experiences disloyalty from his aides because he's reluctant to hire anyone he knows and likes. "One reason that he's reluctant to hire friends is that he knows things can go wrong, and frankly, from everything I've heard, when he has to fire someone it's really hard for him and he agonizes over it terribly," Koch said. "And I think that's one reason why he doesn't have this pack of cronies, like conventional politicians, a comet's tail of grazers who follow him wherever he goes. He tends to hire strangers because then it's truly a purely business relationship."[13]

There are advantages to bringing friends into an inner circle: their loyalty is unquestioned; they know the leader intimately; and they can speak more frankly than might someone hired from the outside. But that loyalty has a flip side: it can blind the leader to what's actually happening. A leader unwilling to jettison his close friends and advisors can end up being very badly advised. If Harper wanted his friends with him, John Weissenberger and George Koch and Mark Kihn (we will meet him later) would have been in that inner circle. But apart from a stint by Weissenberger in Diane Finley's office when she was minister of citizenship and immigration, none of them have had anything to do with the Harper governments, other than as friends of the prime minister.

Koch is bemused by Flanagan's assertion that the former strategist and Harper were never really close. "I recall Steve speaking of Tom with respect, admiration, trust, and warmth – as one speaks of a true friend," he says. "Steve later felt betrayed by some of what Tom did, so they are no longer friends. But that doesn't mean that Steve never felt that way." He points out that the Harpers and the Flanagans had Thanksgiving dinner with Koch and Laurie Watson for eight straight years.[14]

John Weissenberger attributes the estrangement between Harper and Flanagan to the latter's decision to break a cardinal rule: never reveal campaign strategies to the opposition. As for the question of the towering temper, Weissenberger believes it's linked to how much sleep Harper is getting and how much stress he's under. "The strengths of introversion are the ability to reflect and focus," Weissenberger observes. "But recharge time is very important."[15] Harper depends greatly on routine. He eats a light breakfast in the morning, has a decent-sized lunch at noon, and dinner in the early evening. (Not to mention the more-than-occasional snack.) When he's at the office, he prefers to work alone, reading memoranda others have prepared. Most important, he needs time to himself each evening, to digest the events of the day and prepare for what lies ahead. When things are hectic, such as in an election campaign, and that routine is disturbed, then he can become irritable or worse. According to those who have worked there, Harper sometimes comes into the office in a great mood, and sometimes in a grouchy mood. When he's in a grouchy mood, stay clear. This is not an unusual state of affairs for a boss.

Harper is more inclined to yell at insiders. Margaret Harper's son seldom raises his voice at strangers or people in no position of power. One sign that you're not on the inside is that he's polite to you. In any case, people who work for Harper quickly learn not to implement orders that he delivers while yelling. Once he calms down, he often decides differently. One former aide noted that when Harper is yelling, it is usually at the situation in general, and rarely at someone who is actually in the room. And even if he does direct his wrath at someone present, former press aide Dimitri Soudas liked to say, "It is an honour and a privilege to be yelled at by the prime minister."

A related trait is Harper's tendency to appropriate the ideas of others without acknowledging the theft. Over and over, you hear the same story: someone lays out a line of argument; Harper derides and dismisses it; weeks later Harper is laying out the same line of argument as if it were his own. In such circumstances, the best thing to say is nothing. Plagiarism from aides is the prerogative of prime ministers.

Concerning Flanagan's contention that Harper is prone to paranoia or depression, Weissenberger simply replies: "Bullshit." Harper does not suffer from depression. Depression is a clinical condition that may be unrelated to external events. When Harper goes into a funk, there's always a good reason. Those funks can be long and deep, combining introspection with sulking with a sudden loss of self-confidence. But he always comes out of them, and over the years he's done an increasingly better job of keeping them under control.

Part of Harper's ruthless political nature, and his alleged paranoia, can be explained by the nature of his opposition. Liberals believe that their chief opponent is the Conservative Party. Conservatives believe that their opponents are the Liberals, the public service, the press gallery, the media in general – especially the CBC – the universities, the cultural industries, the courts, and some elements of big business. Harper, as we have seen, refers to them all as the "political class."

Conservatives believe the entire Laurentian establishment detests them and wants to see them gone. They're right. No prime minister in history and no political party have been loathed as intensely as Stephen Harper and the Conservative Party he created are loathed by the elites of Ontario and Quebec. During a February 2015 run at the National Arts Centre in Ottawa of *Stuff Happens*, by the British playwright David Hare, the audience hissed and booed each night when a photo of Harper flashed on a screen. It's hardly surprising that the party and Harper continue to see themselves as insurgents, even after a decade in power. Insurgents can't fight war according to its accepted rules, because they aren't as powerful as their enemy. So they employ unconventional, often brutal, tactics.

There are plenty of people in this country who think Stephen Harper is evil. They also think he is the worst of an already bad lot. It doesn't matter to Harper. He really doesn't care what they think.

No one had seen anything like the thirty-fifth Parliament, anywhere in the world. The opposition benches were dominated by not one but two new parties, while the Progressive Conservatives and the New Democrats had lost party status in the House. Her Majesty's Loyal Opposition, the Bloc Québécois, was dedicated to the destruction of the country. The most conservative federal party in Canadian history took up most of the rest of the opposition ranks, stridently demanding that the West be heard. The government was the Ontario Party, otherwise known as the Liberals. And they faced a daunting agenda.

In between the election of October 25 and the Throne Speech of January 17, the finance department had announced that the deficit for 1994 would not be $32.5 billion, as forecast in the budget of the previous March, but somewhere close to $46 billion. (The 1993–1994 deficit in fact came in at $42 billion, or $62 billion in today's money, worse than anything the Conservatives ran up to fight the 2009 recession.) The federal debt was approaching 70 per cent of gross domestic product, and the cost of servicing the debt was about equivalent to the deficit itself. At the same time, the separatists in Quebec were on the march, and likely to form the government in the next election, which would almost certainly lead to another referendum on Quebec separation.

Canada was in terrible shape. Misery had been greater in the Depression, of course, and the traumas of the two world wars left hundreds of thousands grieving. But Canada shared those calamities with its neighbours and allies. This was of our own devising.

The critics of the free trade agreement with the United States were right, in the short term. Every city and town with a (Canada) Inc. branch plant watched that plant close, as production consolidated in the United States now that the tariff wall had come down. With inflation once again taking off – it scraped the ceiling of 7 per cent in 1991 – Bank of Canada governor John Crow vowed to bring inflation under control and keep it there, whatever it took, and it took much higher interest rates. All of this arrived with another recession, which was unpleasant in the United States but crushing in Canada, thanks to the branch plant closures, the tough interest rates, and chronic deficits at both the federal and provincial levels that left governments with little freedom to act.

If anyone in the middle of all this had been able to step back and take the long view, they might have noticed that the big picture actually wasn't so bad. The Soviet Empire had fallen. Europe was free at last. The

Americans had shown overwhelming power in crushing the Iraqi invasion of Kuwait. The Japanese economic onslaught had slackened with the bursting of Japan's stock market bubble. There really was only one great power on earth now, and it was a democracy, though smart observers were pointing to the phenomenal growth underway in China, the Tiananmen Square massacre notwithstanding.

The generation that followed the baby boom – Generation X, it was called, named by Canadian writer and artist Douglas Coupland – lacked much of the ingrained racism, sexism, and homophobia that the boomers had inherited and struggled to overcome. The consequences of wide-open immigration were starting to become visible, with Toronto and Vancouver evolving into multiracial melting pots. Personal computers and the operating systems that powered them were getting faster and better. People in the know – though they were very few – were even using their computers to talk to other computers over phone lines using a modem. The world had just embarked, though no one realized it, on a decade of growth and innovation the like of which had never been seen before in so short a space of peacetime. Canada was poised to share in it. All it had to do was keep the country from falling apart while completely restructuring government to encourage growth while eliminating deficits. As it turned out, Jean Chrétien had the experience and the smarts to do exactly that.

Things were different across the aisle. Opposition leader Lucien Bouchard of the Bloc Québécois was an experienced politician, but among the fifty-two Reformers elected to Parliament – some of whom hadn't expected, or even wanted, to be elected – only Grey, Manning, Harper, and Ray Speaker (who had spent thirty years in the Alberta legislature and served in the provincial cabinet) had any political experience. Manning chose to consider this an asset rather than a liability. He was determined that Reform would do things differently. First off, there would be no shadow cabinet. Groups of MPs would focus on different areas of responsibility. There would be no front bench. Manning would sit in the second row. There would be no caucus whip; instead a "caucus coordinator" would consult with MPs, who would have more autonomy than their equivalents in other parties. The party would be frugal. Manning ostentatiously refused the government car and driver that he was entitled to as leader of the third party. Harper announced that all Reform Party members were willing to take a pay cut, to help fight the government deficit. Reformers also rejected the lavish pension that MPs were entitled to. Reform MPs would not be eating in the subsidized parliamentary restaurant or taking advantage of the barber who offered free haircuts. Manning promised that questions from Reform MPs in Question Period would be respectful and substantive. And he committed to consulting the party's membership before taking stands on major issues.

The whole thing was a bust. As the third party, Reform did not get to ask nearly as many questions as the official opposition in Question Period. Manning's thoughtful, respectful tone at first impressed the press gallery reporters who covered Question Period; soon it bored them. One of the purposes of a shadow cabinet is for a particular MP to cover a particular minister, to master the file and to figure out how to get under the minister's skin in Question Period. Reform's committee approach to opposition meant that no one MP was associated with any one issue or minister. Manning's decision to spend two weeks canvassing the party membership before responding to the March 1994 budget meant that his response, when it did come, was virtually ignored. The caucus soon rebelled, and by autumn Reform was acting like a normal party in the House, with shadow critics and pointed questions and Manning sitting in the front row. The honourable members even learned to heckle.

The gestures of restraint were even more unfortunate, and equally short-lived. Harper had declared that the caucus was willing to take a pay cut without first consulting caucus. Some members hotly protested. In the end, most took the pay cut (including Harper and Manning) but many went back to full pay a year later. Some MPs opted out of the pension plan only to opt back in later, to the party's embarrassment. And though Preston Manning didn't have a car and driver, courtesy of the taxpayer, it turned out he was receiving extra funds from the Reform Party – thirty-one thousand dollars a year, it was reported, though in fact there was no fixed sum – in addition to his pay as an MP.

This last issue became a huge problem, and one that deepened the rift between Manning and Harper. It is not uncommon for political parties to supplement their leader's pay. Leading a national political party is an incredibly difficult, time-consuming job, and at the very least, the leader should not be worried about whether he can afford to pay his dry-cleaning bill. The extra money would allow Manning to dress properly, and would pay for Sandra Manning to accompany her husband on travel across the country and internationally. But at a time when Reform was campaigning to cut back on the pay, pensions, and perks of parliamentarians, the secret fund looked terrible. It certainly looked terrible to Harper. He was Reform's representative on the Board of Internal Economy, which was investigating the issue of MP pay and pensions. Harper got on that board when caucus voted to put him there, rejecting Manning's candidate. The Reform leader was facing a rebellion within caucus, and Harper appeared to be at the pointy end of that rebellion.

News of the secret payments to Manning broke in the *Globe and Mail* in late March 1994. To this day, no one knows who the source was. Some people wondered whether Harper himself leaked the information to the press, or was instrumental in having the material leaked. Tom Flanagan only knows that Harper was aware of the private fund and anxious for it to be made public. "I know he told me about it and encouraged me to get it out into the media," Flanagan later recalled.[16] At the time, Flanagan was working on a less than complimentary book about Preston Manning. Harper provided him with so much inside information – dirt, really – that Flanagan jokes Harper should have demanded recognition as co-author. The leader and his former aide were no longer merely estranged. They had become enemies.

A few days after the original story appeared, Harper was quoted in the *Calgary Sun* saying, "The whole idea of non-accountable expenses is not acceptable" and "The compensations are not consistent with what the party is asking of Parliament."[17] So now the rebellion was in the open, gloves off.

Manning lets criticism roll off his back. But others don't. The next day, the party's executive council fired off a letter reprimanding Harper for his comments. "We are appalled," the letter stated. "We accept that Mr. Harper disagrees with and questions our decisions, however, we are disappointed that he did not make use of the Constitutional mechanisms established by members at the last Assembly to deal with such issues.

Mr. Harper did not even place a phone call to the appropriate Committee members to get the facts or to register his concerns prior to expressing himself in the media."[18]

With the rebellion in full swing, caucus sided with Harper. A few weeks later, they elected him to the Reform MPs' ethics committee, again choosing him over Manning's nominated candidate. The fact was that, in the eyes of at least some Reform MPs, Harper was looking like a better, more capable leader than Manning. Nonetheless, Harper's decision to complain to the media about the conduct of his own party's leader was deeply disloyal and in bad form, no matter how you look at it. Had an MP tried anything like it when Harper became leader of the Alliance and then the Conservatives, that MP would have been ejected from caucus within hours.

———————————

Unfortunately for Manning, he had no choice but to keep Harper. At thirty-four, the young MP was one of the most attractive faces of a party that many, especially many in the press gallery, considered a party of yahoos. He was one of only four Reform MPs who could speak French, he handled questions from reporters well – Tim Harper (no relation) of the *Toronto Star* declared that Harper was known as "the 'respectable' Reformer" – and he was capably handling the most difficult issue facing the party, the unity issue.[19]

As Intergovernmental Affairs critic, Harper was the most senior voice in managing the party's stand on the file, apart from Manning himself. At first, the party tried a low-key approach. Lucien Bouchard and Jean Chrétien tore at each other in the House, day after day after day, on the Quebec question. Not looking to be the third man in a fight, Reformers preferred to talk about the government's desperate finances, the still-high unemployment numbers and other issues that mattered to most Canadians, inside and especially outside Quebec. But on September 12, 1994, the Parti Québécois defeated the Liberals in Quebec, and Jacques Parizeau became premier, portending another referendum on separation. Reform was going to have to confront the Quebec question, whether it wanted to or not.

In those early weeks, all national parties struggled to find their footing. Jean Chrétien at first seemed to suggest that the Constitution contained no provision for a province to secede, and he was sworn to uphold the Constitution. Harper took a slightly different approach: the Constitution could be amended to permit the secession of a province, he believed, but only if all provinces agreed to that secession. "I would maintain that it is the duty of the federal government which purports that national unity is its highest priority to recognize that it does have an obligation to uphold the Constitution," he told the House of Commons on October 19. "I would also note that politically there would be considerable advantage for it to make clear to the people of Quebec that when they are being told that separation can be achieved unilaterally that this is legally untrue. In fact, it would also be politically untrue, politically unfeasible to pursue in that manner."[20]

Reform more or less held to that line for a year. But as the actual referendum approached, Manning and Harper changed course. They'd heard from angry constituents in their ridings: Quebec should decide once and for all whether it was in or out, which was in line with what the West had always thought. When Parliament returned in September 1995, Manning and Harper both declared that a Yes vote of 50 per cent plus one would constitute the end of Quebec within Canada. But Reform was determined not to be completely sidelined by the October 30 referendum. Two weeks before the vote, the party released its "New Confederation" proposals, co-written by Harper and a young conservative writer (and future MP), Scott Reid. Consistent with the bedrock Reform principle that there could be no special treatment for Quebec, it argued for the broad devolution of power from Ottawa to the provinces in the areas of culture and language, along with regional unilingualism. No one paid any attention, as Bouchard replaced Parizeau in leading the Yes campaign, and support for a Yes vote surged in the polls. A shaken Chrétien went on television to beg Quebeckers not to leave. Tens of thousands from outside Quebec rushed to Montreal for a unity rally just before the vote. On referendum night, the result was terrifyingly close: 50.58 per cent No; 49.42 per cent Yes. How long would it be till the third referendum, and what were the chances that the forces of unity would prevail?

Stephen Harper decided he wasn't willing to gamble with that question. On October 30, 1996, he introduced Bill C-341, the Quebec Contingency Act. His private member's bill had three main provisions: First, any future referendum on separation must have a clear question, with the federal government deciding whether the wording was sufficiently clear. Second, in the event of a Yes vote on a clear question, the federal government could enter into negotiations on secession, but only in cooperation with the provinces, and with the result put to a national referendum in which a majority of citizens outside Quebec had to approve secession. Third, any unilateral declaration of independence by Quebec would have no meaning under federal law.

"These proposals avoid the mistakes of the past, ensure a respect for our legal order and ensure that all Canadians, including Quebecers, have a role in shaping their future," Harper told the House.[21] Of course, as a private member's bill, the Quebec Contingency Act had no hope of passage without the support of the government; it died on the order paper, as so many. But Harper's bill was remarkably prescient, foreshadowing the Clarity Act with which the Chrétien government would confront the dangers of another referendum. Chrétien agreed with Harper: Ottawa could enter into sovereignty negotiations with Quebec, but only after securing a yes on a clear question and in consultation with the provinces.

But by the time Bill C-341 died, its fate was moot. For even as he introduced the legislation, Stephen Harper was preparing to leave Ottawa yet again.

It's easy to discern in retrospect, but Stephen Harper just wasn't very good at being a subordinate. Those who have worked closely with him say that he tends to form early, emphatic opinions. Sometimes he takes strong stands in order to challenge others; convince him he's wrong and he'll happily climb down off his high horse. At other times, he simply makes up his mind and that's that. Such firm-mindedness is a mixed blessing. Vacillation can be a fatal flaw in a leader, wasting time and sapping morale. (Paul Martin's reputation as "Mr. Dithers" would prove fatal to his premiership.)

But bull-headedness can blind you to reality, especially if reality suddenly changes. Harper's stubbornness has led to more than one policy or political disaster. On balance, though, his ability to correctly analyze a situation and act firmly to address it has been more a strength than a weakness. It has brought him three election victories and a decade of power.

But anyone who's always convinced he's right and isn't afraid to say so can be a pain in the neck, especially if that person sits in caucus. "Stephen had difficulty accepting that there might be a few other people (not many, perhaps, but a few) who were as smart as he was with respect to policy and strategy," Manning wrote a few years later, more in anger than in sorrow.[22] But Manning was fortunate, in a way. Brian Mulroney and Paul Martin conspired to undermine Joe Clark and Jean Chrétien respectively. Stephen Harper, when things didn't go his way, simply walked away.

On January 14, 1997, Harper surprised the members of the Parliamentary Press Gallery by announcing that he was resigning his seat in Parliament to spend more time with his family – Ben had been born the previous April, and Rachel would come along a couple of years later – and to take a job at the National Citizens Coalition. For the assembled reporters, Harper's decision made little sense. Though they were aware of the tensions between Harper and Manning, the young Calgary MP was the most articulate, sensible voice in the party, apart from Manning himself; the talking head that every network wanted for a political panel; the one you went to when you needed a quote. He was Manning's natural successor and the Reform MP most obviously capable of one day becoming prime minister. One reporter bluntly asked Harper if he was waiting for Preston Manning to leave. But Harper said he had no desire to ever lead the Reform Party, and later events would prove that he meant it.

In March 1995, Harper wrote an essay for the *Globe and Mail* entitled "Where Does the Reform Party Go from Here?" In essence, he was taking his 1989 memo to Manning public. In the essay, Harper warned that all four opposition parties were in danger of becoming "sectarian" – protest parties representing certain regions or ideologies, unable to establish a national mandate.

In Reform's case, "the impression is that the party wants either to form a majority government right away or to pack up and go back to the farm," he wrote.[23] But a populist party of no fixed ideology that hoped to form the government by surfing the grievance-du-jour would wait a very long time, and the party was set to expire, according to its own constitution, in 2000.

Reform needed "to accept itself as the principal force of the democratic right in Canadian politics, like the Conservatives in Great Britain, the Republicans in the United States or the Christian Democrats in Germany," Harper urged. That meant "fighting all elections, federal and provincial, from the broad right of centre, not just planning to fight one election around the protests of the day.

"Sectarianism is a possible outcome of a strategy of simple populist protest," he concluded. "But with the right decisions, Reform can emerge as the critical element in the development of a broadly based national alternative to the Liberal government." Once again, Harper laid out how a conservative party could win power in Canada. Once again, Manning ignored him.

Instead, Reformers appeared willing to double down on the social-conservative agenda. At a party gathering in 1994, the membership passed a motion opposing same-sex marriage. That December, Preston Manning released a caucus statement opposing the inclusion of homosexuals in the Human Rights Act. Harper was offside with his party on both positions. "I think it's perfectly legitimate to have moral objections as well as moral approval of homosexuality," he said, "but I don't think political parties should do that."[24] Those who, to this day, continue to harbour suspicions that Harper has some hidden social agenda that he would impose on the country given his druthers should note that from the earliest days of Reform and through his years as an MP, Harper opposed and warned against allowing the party to become hostage to social conservatism.

Harper might also have left because he thought Reform was going to be trounced in the upcoming election. "I think one of the reasons he left in '97 was that he thought we were going to lose, and he didn't want to go down with the ship," Manning later opined.[25] In early 1997, the Liberals were riding very, very high. They had discovered the secret formula to electoral success in the 1990s: talk like a liberal; govern like a conservative. It worked for Bill Clinton in the United States and Tony Blair in Great Britain, and it worked splendidly for Jean Chrétien in Canada.

The Liberals had finally and successfully confronted the budget deficit. They had little choice. By the time they took power in 1993, the combined federal–provincial deficit had reached 8 per cent of the nation's GDP, twice the OECD average. In 1994, Finance officials watched in fear as a Canadian bond issue sat unsubscribed until almost literally the last minute. The *Wall Street Journal* had dubbed Canada "an honorary member of the Third World."[26] This was utterly unsustainable. Mexico and Sweden had already gone through financial crises; Canada might be next. Roy Romanow, Saskatchewan's NDP premier, got the ball rolling in 1991 with severe cuts to government spending as the path to balancing the province's books. Ralph Klein followed suit in Alberta when he became premier in 1993. Mike Harris surged to power in Ontario in 1995 with his Common Sense Revolution of spending cuts, tax cuts, and a balanced budget.

The Tories at Queen's Park were a special case. Neither Reformers – obviously, they weren't from the West and, more important, they had no interest in social conservatism – nor Red Tories, such as had dominated the provincial party for decades, Mike Harris's team in many ways foreshadowed the Conservative Party that Stephen Harper would forge in the next decade. If he had stayed at the University of Toronto, he might have met some of them, such as Tony Clement, who was one of a cabal that had captured the university's tiny Conservative Club and transformed it into a neocon hotbed. He might also have met Clement's friend, a brilliant young student named Nigel Wright. Clement and Tom Long, who'd gone to Western, joined forces with other young, like-minded worshippers of Thatcher and Reagan to help Mike Harris, an affable MPP from North Bay, capture the destitute Progressive Conservative Party from the Red Tories, just as Clement had done at U of T. They would play an essential role, down the road, in uniting the conservative movement, and in Harper's government.

The same year that Mike Harris came to power in Ontario, Paul Martin vowed to eliminate the federal deficit "come hell or high water." The cuts to federal and provincial spending programs were brutal: thousands of public servants lost their jobs, hospitals closed, pot holes didn't get filled, classrooms bulged with students. But it worked. Canada put the brakes on a debt-to-GDP ratio worse than any in the OECD except for Italy's by achieving a net federal–provincial balanced budget by 1997. Strong economic growth, low inflation, and declining bank rates helped, along with targeted tax increases. At the federal level, it was a huge boon that there was no effective opposition: the NDP wasn't even a recognized party in the House of Commons, and the Bloc Québécois had no relevance outside Quebec. The real pressure for reform came from Reform, and it was forever urging Martin to move faster. With his political flank covered, the Liberal finance minister was able to eliminate the deficit in two years, which meant the party would go into the next election with the books balanced and tax cuts on the horizon. Naturally, Reform slumped in the polls.

If Harper did think that Reform was in for a licking, then he was surprised. So was Jean Chrétien, by how poorly the Liberals did in the election of 1997. Liberal cuts to Unemployment Insurance hurt the party in Atlantic Canada, to the benefit of the PCs. The Bloc lost a few seats in Quebec, and Reform increased its seat count to sixty, making it the official opposition. Things might have gone even worse for the Grits, had vote-splitting on the right not allowed the Liberals to once again take practically every seat in Ontario. And with the Progressive Conservative Party winning twenty seats in Quebec and Atlantic Canada under Jean Charest, it was virtually tied with Reform in the popular vote. The division on the right was now entrenched: neither party was going to disappear; neither party could win government.

It was time for some serious thought on how to unite the conservative movement. But Stephen Harper would be largely absent from that debate. To everyone's surprise, he had taken himself out of the political game. At least for the moment.

SEVEN

Exile

For the next three years, Stephen Harper would give up the role of politician and become instead an ideologue. He would reposition himself as a conservative purist, railing against the failures of a quasi-socialist nation in thrall to corrupt, Central Canadian elites. He would also give up the role of politician in exile and immerse himself more fully in the role of father and husband living in his adopted hometown of Calgary. On a personal level, these were some of the happiest years of his life. But with each passing year, he would become progressively more impatient with national politics, as conservatives sought but failed to displace the Liberal hegemony. Freed from party discipline, and with no one to answer to but his conscience and his board of directors, the new president of the National Citizens Coalition would pen some of his most provocative lines, including passages that would come back to haunt him.

Yet at the same time, his political thinking matured, became more nuanced. At his very best, he glimpsed the promised land of a governing conservative coalition and how it might be achieved. He became a conservative Jekyll and Hyde: dispassionately analyzing the steps needed to forge a governing party of the centre-right, while raging against the perfidy of the Laurentian centre. And then, quite abruptly, he would face a choice: to continue in the exile of commentary, or to return to the arena, this time in a bid to lead the movement he had almost given up on.

In May 1996, while he was still an MP, Harper attended the Winds of Change conference in Calgary, hosted by pundits David Frum and Ezra Levant. About a hundred prominent conservatives met behind closed doors for two days to hash through the differences between the Reform and Progressive Conservative parties, in hopes of finding common ground. It would turn out to be the first of many failures in the effort to unite the right. Although the politicians, journalists, and policy wonks at the conference agreed among themselves that a good first step would be to run only one right-of-centre candidate in the upcoming by-election in Brant, a southern Ontario riding, Jean Charest made it clear that the PCs had no intention of cooperating with such a plan. Charest spoke for most Progressive Conservatives, who blamed Reformers for shattering the conservative coalition in the first place. It also wouldn't be out of place to say they viewed Reformers as a bunch of rednecks – and probably racist rednecks at that. Reformers, for their part, looked upon the PCs as ideologically bankrupt. The two sides were far, far apart, and it seemed it would be a long time, if ever, before they would be able to work together as one.

Strangely, one of the leading figures in the original schism now wanted to heal it. Stephen Harper gave a speech at the conference that turned out to be the only memorable thing that came out of it. The speech offered the latest stage of evolution in Harper's political thinking. In some ways it contradicted his arguments to Manning of 1989; in some ways it deepened them.

Harper maintained that conservatives had only come to power – Bennett in 1930, Diefenbaker in 1958, Mulroney in 1984 – when the party of the day was able to craft a three-legged coalition: traditional Tories in Ontario and Atlantic Canada, Western populists, and nationalist Quebeckers. Mulroney, he argued, had overreached by incorporating out-and-out separatists into the coalition, which then shattered into its component parts: Central and Atlantic traditional Tories (Progressive Conservatives), Western populists (Reform), and Quebec nationalists (Bloc Québécois). The solution was to reunite the movement by offering a genuinely conservative party (the Reform part) that nonetheless accepted the wisdom of incremental change (the Tory tradition) and that respected Quebec's aspiration to be the master of its own destiny (Quebec nationalists) while also respecting the rights of other provinces and regions. Tom Flanagan was so impressed that he phoned Laureen Harper and exclaimed, "Stephen sounded like a prime minister today!"[1] As the U of C professor later observed in his book *Harper's Team*, Harper would employ exactly the reasoning of his Winds of Change speech to become prime minister, first by taking over the leadership of the Western populists (Reform), then by co-opting the Ontario and Atlantic Tories (merging the Alliance with the PCs), and finally by roping in nationalist Quebeckers (the 2006 election).

The speech attempted to reconcile an internal contradiction within the conservative movement and within Harper himself. The Reform MP viscerally distrusted the power elites of the Laurentian establishment in Central Canada. But he also recognized that millions of voters were comfortable living within the political space created by that establishment. In 1989, he had warned Manning that a conservative party must be moderate and pragmatic, or it would alienate urban, Central Canadian voters. In the next decade, he would take this further. As he would declare in a speech in 1998, "Governing requires a conservative temperament. This temperament includes a respect for tradition, a penchant for incremental change and a strong sense of honourable compromise. These qualities are not developed overnight and cannot be adequately embodied in a single individual. They are embedded in institutions. The Progressive Conservative Party is such an institution."[2]

Stephen Harper is a true conservative, and would lead Canada's first truly conservative government. But he is a Jekyll conservative and a Hyde conservative. The Hyde conservative is reflexively suspicious of institutional power and the elites that hold it. His Hyde conservatism embraces minimalist government, minimal regulation, unfettered free trade, but a strong security state. Stephen Harper as Hyde is emotionally and ideologically raw. Hyde has propelled him throughout his life, has given his politics meaning. Without Hyde, Stephen Harper would never have had the strength of will to become prime minister.

But already in the late 1980s, and increasingly in the 1990s, the Jekyll conservative had begun to emerge. William F. Buckley–style derision of the post-war social welfare state, Peter Brimelow–style indignation at the hypocrisy of the Central Canadian consensus, and Calgary School–style contempt for centrist Liberal platitudes only got you so far. Toryism – with its emphasis on caution, tradition, and a *noblesse oblige* responsibility for the better off toward the less fortunate – exerted a powerful influence within the Progressive Conservative Party. Marrying the ideological rigour of Reform to the pragmatism of the PCs was the real coalition, one Harper would ultimately pursue and perfect. Yet that merger contained within it almost intolerable tensions. Harper would embody those tensions as he sought to personally recreate the conservative movement in his own image. He could never, ever be a proper Tory. But to govern, he had to be a Tory, at least in part. And he wanted to govern.

The Winds of Change speech contained one other interesting element. In his 1989 memo, Harper had dismissed the Quebec nationalist element of the conservative coalition as unattainable and ideologically irreconcilable with a Reform Party that preached equal provincial rights. Besides, the more nationalist the Quebecker, the further on the left he or she was likely to be found. There simply was no room for such a constituency inside a conservative coalition. Yet by 1996, Harper was convinced that Quebec voters could and should be pursued. By 2006, he would be successfully pursuing them. But by 2011, he would have abandoned the hunt. There was another leg to the stool, as it turned out, that didn't require Quebec votes. But we're getting ahead of ourselves.

———————

Think tanks and pressure groups have three purposes: to advance their agenda; to raise money; and to win market share away from other think tanks and pressure groups. In Stephen Harper, the NCC found an engaged, effective president.

The National Citizens Coalition was founded in 1967 by Colin Brown, who had made his money in insurance and who stoutly opposed public health care – or "socialized medicine" as he and his allies preferred to call it. On the spectrum of conservative pressure groups, the NCC was as far to the right as you could get and remain respectable. Harper joined it in the early 1980s, after Brown set the NCC against the National Energy Program. Its motto, "more freedom through less government," fit Harper's ideological inclinations nicely. It has also campaigned against allowing in Vietnamese boat people in 1979–1980 (a stand it later regretted) and against limits to third-party advertising during election campaigns (the NCC, remember, campaigned against Jim Hawkes in 1993), and against the long-form census when that issue emerged in 2010. Former *Sun* journalist David Somerville took the helm in 1986. Somerville was a colourful character who led with his gut, sometimes creating "cash-flow" problems, to use the euphemism. But he made one inspired decision, which would have a major influence on Stephen Harper and on the future of political campaigning. In 1982, when he was vice president of the NCC, he hired Arthur Finkelstein.

Finkelstein was Brooklyn born and bred, a political brawler who had already developed communications, polling, and election strategy for Ronald Reagan and Jesse Helms. Somerville brought him in to professionalize the NCC's operations in the wake of the coalition's ill-managed opposition to the Clark government's efforts to settle Vietnamese boat people. Finkelstein was (and is) "tough as nails," remembers Gerry Nicholls, who arrived at the NCC in 1985 to do communications work. "He used to scare the crap out of me."[3]

For fourteen years, Finkelstein travelled up from New York to the NCC's offices in Toronto once a month to offer strategic advice. "He taught us everything about how to communicate," remembers Nicholls. "How to raise money, how to direct-mail fundraise, how to do thirty-second ads in a way that got your message out there. He taught us the importance of using emotion in getting your message across, how to generate buzz, just all the nuts and bolts of how to run a professional, effective communications campaign."

More than anything else, Finkelstein drove home the power of the attack ad. The two most powerful political emotions are fear and hate, he told Nicholls and Somerville and the half dozen others who made up the NCC's permanent staff. Stoke those emotions in your viewers, listeners, or readers, and you'll have the basis for an effective campaign. "He was vicious, and he taught us how to be vicious too," Nicholls recalls. The favourite image used by the NCC under Finkelstein's tutelage was the pig, usually lined up at a trough or wallowing in muck, to represent politicians in their natural habitat. Cartoon pigs. Photographs of pigs. Videos of pigs. Finkelstein wanted to dump a truckload of live pigs onto Parliament Hill, but they talked him out of it.

With money raised from Finkelstein's direct mail campaign, the NCC was able, in 1996, to launch Tales from the Tax Trough, a series of books that highlighted government spending on useless studies (one such study compared hockey coaches and symphony conductors) and effete causes (such as a canoe museum).[4] The organization helped fund court challenges to Quebec language laws, the right of unions to donate to the NDP using members' fees, and the like. The NCC became very good at stoking popular outrage at abuses by big government and big labour – even big business, through their opposition to corporate welfare.*

Harper arrived determined to change all of this. He wanted the NCC to focus more on policy, on articulating and advocating reforms to the public service, on fiscal policy, on the regulatory state and similar measures. "He wanted the NCC to be less of a street gang and more of an organization that got involved in sophisticated ideas," said Nicholls, who became vice-president under Harper. "He didn't want to use pigs and stuff like that." There was a huge culture clash between the NCC as it was and as Harper wanted it to become. Nicholls argued with his new boss, telling him over and over, "If you're going to get a message across, if you're going to have something that resonates with the public, then you have to use emotion. And you have to use a short, simple, concise argument, one that appeals to their heart or one that gets them outraged. And that's what the NCC was good at. This was not Fraser Institute kind of stuff. This was pigs."

There were also – surprise! – tensions between Somerville and Harper. Harper had reason to be grateful to Somerville, who had long been impressed with the Reform MP and political analyst, and who had hand-picked him as his successor. But once again, Harper had difficulty following someone

---

* Progressive critics have often accused the NCC, which does not reveal its donors list, of being funded by powerful and shadowy corporate interests. *Au contraire*, says Nicholls. There are some donors who cut large cheques, but they are mostly businessmen who own medium-sized enterprises. The bulk of the donations are small and come from individual citizens. In that respect, the NCC's funding resembles that of the Reform/Alliance/Conservative party.

else's lead, even during a transition. Although the NCC had always been based in Toronto, Somerville lived in Calgary, and Harper was determined to keep it that way. For the months during which Harper was vice-president under Somerville, the two shared a tiny office, which didn't help. Harper wanted to be in charge. Somerville wanted to stay in charge, at least until Harper was ready to take over. Somerville assigned Harper menial tasks, like clipping out and filing newspaper stories. Harper seethed, but in this instance bided his time. And with each passing month, the incoming president took firmer control, as Somerville increasingly deferred to the new boss. From then until now, Harper would never be subordinate to anyone.

Harper also came to absorb and master the dark arts of political marketing. Although Finkelstein ended his relationship with the NCC a year before Harper arrived, the old master's attitude and strategies infused the organization, and were literally embodied in his disciple, Nicholls. Harper's biggest contribution was to impose greater fiscal discipline and planning rigour on the NCC. Whether taking on the Canadian Wheat Board monopoly, the ban on third-party political advertising campaigns, or Elections Canada rules that forbade broadcasting election results in time zones where polls were still open, Harper planned his campaigns meticulously, considered every possible contingency, and ensured that the money was in place. Only then would he launch.

Stephen Harper is not only the first suburban prime minister and the first boomer prime minister. He is also the first Canadian prime minister with extensive first-hand knowledge of political marketing and communications. "Throughout my time with him he would personally reference [NCC] campaigns that he ran," Harper's political marketing guru, Patrick Muttart, would later say. "He ran an organization that was in the business of erecting billboards, running direct-mail campaigns. So I don't think we've ever had a prime minister who had direct personal experience being a marketer."[5]

Nicholls also watched Harper take on the job of manager for the first time in his life. He was impressive in his ability to define responsibilities and to get staff to execute. But he was no cheerleader. "If you didn't do your job you knew about it, and you knew about it in no uncertain terms," Nicholls recalled. "I remember somebody once went up to him and said 'it's not my fault.' And his response was 'I didn't say it was your fault, I said it was your responsibility.' He was that kind of guy. No nonsense, no excuses. Do your job or else. And being called on the carpet by Stephen was not a pleasant experience, not because he'd freak out, but because he was so coldly analytical."[6] When Harper unleashed the full measure of his displeasure on an employee, it could be devastating. "Sometimes he would manage by fear. But he was very analytical about it. If he thought the best way to get people to do something was to scare them, he would scare them."

Nicholls is not the first to point out that his relationship with Harper deteriorated after his old boss moved on. When Harper became prime minister, Nicholls argued that the NCC should hold their former president to the same standard they held his predecessors. Tensions between Nicholls and the board eventually led to his departure. But although he offers a pretty unvarnished opinion of Stephen Harper as an employer, Nicholls remains essentially admiring of what Harper accomplished at the NCC and on the national stage.

Mark Kihn offers a somewhat different perspective. Kihn has a background in both journalism – before joining the NCC, he had owned several agriculture-based magazines – and fundraising. He is a talker. He had once been a paid announcer for the Calgary Stampede cattle show. After chatting with Harper at an event in November 1998, he received a phone call from the new leader of the NCC offering him a job as fundraiser, and to handle advertising. Six months later, Kihn was on the job working with Harper in the Calgary office. They became, and remain, good friends.

One thing that Kihn discovered, as others would in the leader's office and the PMO, is that Harper takes a very long time to make up his mind. Yes, he is quick with an opinion. But if a major decision needs to be made, Harper likes to mull it over on his own, look at it from every angle, then go away and think about it by himself before announcing what he and the organization are going to do. (We saw an example of that when he disappeared to ponder the Charlottetown Accord.) Kihn remembers a day when Laureen Harper called him up and asked, "Mark, what's going on?" Her husband was even more silent than usual. Not only was he not talking, he was even not eating – and that was serious. Kihn told her of a major dilemma that the NCC was wrestling with. Ah, Laureen Harper replied, that explains everything.[7] (This could also tie in to Tom Flanagan's suggestion that Harper sometimes lapses into depression. George Koch believes that people observing Harper sometimes confuse depression with brooding: "He has a tendency to isolate himself, monk-like, while he wrestles with problems.")[8]

Kihn agrees that when Harper was his boss he could be a bit of a taskmaster. "He was a demanding boss, I'll not deny that," he agrees. The NCC was a small shop with a large mandate, and Harper expected people to work as hard and as well as he did. Kihn remembers a particularly frantic day when he was tasked with buying commercial time on every single radio station in Alberta. Somehow, he pulled it off, a feat he considered Herculean. "But with Stephen it was, 'Huh. Okay. Next.'" But he points out that if Harper set a high bar for others, he set it for himself as well, and people worked hard to meet his standards. "Maybe, on occasion, he came apart a little bit by raising his voice, but that's normal for a high-performing boss."

Harper also became very good at getting his mug on television and his byline in newspapers. He was a regular on CBC and CTV news shows – deriding the House of Commons pledge to eliminate child poverty in the year 2000 as "the high water mark of political stupidity in this country," and condemning penalties on foreign-owned publications selling into Canada as "old fashioned protectionism."[9] Don Newman, who hosted a politics program on CBC's cable news channel back then, recalls a panellist who lobbied to get on the air, came well prepared, and got the better of his left-wing counterparts more than once.[10]

He gave speeches and wrote articles. One, with Tom Flanagan, fleshed out two foundational political notions: First, Canada was not really a functioning, multi-party democracy. "Although we like to think of ourselves as living in a mature democracy, we live, instead, in something little better than a benign dictatorship, not under a strict one-party rule, but under a one-party-plus system beset by the factionalism, regionalism and cronyism that accompany any such system," they wrote in the now-defunct *Next City* magazine.[11] To counter the Liberal hegemony, they called for the reunion of "the three sisters" of conservatism (named after the peaks along the highway to Banff). Flanagan came up with the metaphor after listening to

Harper's speech at the Winds of Change conference – the sisters, of course, being traditional Tories, Western populists, and Quebec nationalists:

> Reformers will have to realize that there is something genuinely con-servative in the Tory penchant for compromise and incrementalism. Tories will have to admit that compromise, to be honourable, must be guided by underlying principles, and that Reformers are not extremists for openly advocating smaller government, free markets, traditional val-ues and equality before the law. And both will have to recognize that Quebec nationalism, while not in itself a conservative movement, appeals to the kinds of voters who in other provinces support conserva-tive parties. The Bloc Québécois is strongest in rural Quebec, among voters who would not be out of place in Red Deer, except that they speak French rather than English.[12]

The appeal to Quebec nationalists seems strained, though appealing to Quebeckers by offering greater internal autonomy – something that would also be on offer to other provinces – was part of both Reform's and Harper's mantra. Rather improbably, the article also argued for electoral reform that might introduce proportional representation in the House of Commons, an idea Harper swiftly abandoned once it became clear that the Conservatives might actually win power the old fashioned way.

Harper also tackled the bugbear of bilingualism. Canadians, he argued in a 2001 op-ed piece, were no more bilingual today than when Pierre Trudeau first foisted the ideal of everyone speaking both French and English on the nation. Only 17 per cent of Canadians speak both French and English, he observed, and most of them either live in Quebec or near the Quebec–Ontario or Quebec–New Brunswick border. The federal pub-lic service draws heavily from their ranks.

"The Liberals, of course, believe emphasizing Canada's 'Frenchness' will encourage more loyalty to Canada among Québécois," he opined in the *Calgary Sun*. "But as Quebec becomes more French and the rest of Canada becomes more English, it really means the Québécois identify more with Quebec than with Canada. So there you have it. As a religion, bilingualism is the god that failed. It has led to no fairness, produced no unity, and cost

Canadian taxpayers untold millions. I guess that's what happens when you mix church and state."[13]

This reference to bilingualism as "the god that failed" is a line that Harper's opponents would use against him for years to come, along with his criticism of the "culture of defeat" in Atlantic Canada. In the same vein, there is the infamous speech Harper gave right after the 1997 election, to the Council for National Policy, a conservative American organization that was meeting in Montreal. "Canada is a Northern European welfare state in the worst sense of the term, and very proud of it," he told them.

Canadians make no connection between the fact that they are a Northern European welfare state and the fact that we have very low economic growth, a standard of living substantially lower than yours, a massive brain drain of young professionals to your country, and double the unemployment rate of the United States.

In terms of the unemployed, of which we have over a million-and-a-half, don't feel particularly bad for many of these people. They don't feel bad about it themselves, as long as they're receiving generous social assistance and unemployment insurance.[14]

The speech is also telling for Harper's characterization of Canadian federal politics. The governor general, he told his American friends, is appointed by the prime minister. The Senate is appointed by the prime minister. The Supreme Court is appointed by the prime minister. The House of Commons, in a majority government, is in thrall to the caucus of the majority party, and that caucus is in thrall to the prime minister. Rather than having a system of checks and balances, Canadian politics can be described as "unpaid checks and political imbalances," Harper concluded.

The address shows Harper at his funniest. He describes the NDP as "proof that the Devil lives and interferes in the affairs of men." On the question of school prayer, he predicted, "as long as there are exams, there will always be prayer in school." And he repeated a good joke. A constitutional lawyer dies, goes to heaven, and meets God. "God," the lawyer asks, "will this problem between Quebec and the rest of Canada ever be resolved?" God thinks about it and replies, "Yes, but not in my lifetime."

"Don't be offended," Harper added. "The joke can't be taken seriously theologically. It is, after all, about a lawyer who goes to heaven."

––––––––––––

During his years at the NCC, for the first time in his life Stephen Harper was returning home at night to his wife and children and living in his own house. Domesticity suited him, at least in the short term. Harper at home is at his most suburban: TV, games with the kids, managing a typical two-income household. Laureen, who had kept the name Teskey, had her own very successful graphic design and desktop publishing firm, and the two of them shared domestic chores, including cooking. (Harper is rather proud of his homemade pizza.) After dinner was done and the dishes put away, there might be TV. Stephen Harper was a passionate *Seinfeld* fan, and can quote entire episodes, or so it seems. He also, inexplicably, was and is a dedicated viewer of *Coronation Street*. He is emphatically *Star Trek* over *Star Wars*, and loved to watch old episodes of *The Twilight Zone*. While averse to participating in any form of sport, including golf, he enjoyed going to a driving range and whacking at a bucket of balls. It's a pastime he and Ben shared, when Ben got older. He's also fond of mini-golf. (The image of Stephen Harper hunched over a putter, preparing to attempt to put the ball through the blades of the windmill is, well, arresting.)

Privately, these were happy years. For the first and, as it turned out, last time, the family was together and living in Calgary, Harper's adopted and only true home. Though he worked hard at the NCC, there was time to be with the family and to read, one of Harper's favourite pastimes. He is a voracious consumer of books on history, biography, and politics. (Fiction, not so much.) When Ben was old enough, Harper started taking him to hockey games. (When they moved to Ottawa, Harper always found time to watch his son play – on the same team, it turned out, as NDP MP Paul Dewar's son. The two men sat in different parts of the stands. Harper was no doubt disappointed when an older Ben Harper switched from hockey to volleyball, on the grounds that there aren't a lot of girls around a hockey rink at six in the morning.)

Ben and Rachel Harper are, by all accounts, remarkably well adjusted considering they were raised in Canada's most public private home. Ben is more like his mother and Rachel like her father. Kihn taught both of them to drive. With Ben, from the start, it was "How fast can we go?" In contrast, Rachel would consider, and worry, about the possibilities of collision presented by the oncoming car, and how calamity might best be averted. Though Rachel was a baby during Harper's NCC years (Laureen dubbed her "Mini-me"), she and her dad later bonded watching *Coronation Street* and *Murdoch Mysteries*. Rachel followed her brother in pursuing volleyball as a sport, and she is also likely to beat you at table hockey and ping pong. The family still enjoys playing board games. Dad takes as much pleasure in winning as the children do in beating him.

Besides work and home, there was politics. It was still in Stephen Harper's blood. And by 2000, his blood was boiling.

The times following the 1997 election were frustrating for everyone who wasn't a Liberal. The Progressive Conservatives had made a comeback, but not much of one. Reform was the official opposition but couldn't break through in Ontario. The Liberals had purloined key elements of Reform's economic agenda; they were about to do the same on the national unity file, by ceding broad new powers not just to Quebec but to all provinces, while introducing the Clarity Act, which would make it harder for Quebec to leave Canada without the consent of Ottawa and the other provinces. Conservatives could take comfort in the fact that Canada had shifted to the right in the 1990s. Balanced budgets, free trade – the Mulroney government negotiated the North American Free Trade Agreement, which expanded CUSTA to include Mexico, but the Liberals ratified it, albeit grudgingly – and even lower taxes were the new orthodoxy. But in terms of political power, they had nothing to show for it.

And once again the political landscape was shifting. Jean Charest was about to go up the road.

Under Charest, the Progressive Conservatives had picked up twenty seats, mostly in Atlantic Canada and Quebec, and were now officially the fourth party in the House of Commons. But Charest was personally disappointed. He had dreamed of official opposition status, as a bridge to government in the next election. He knew that vote-splitting had kept both Reform and Progressive Conservatives out of Ontario, while for the PCs, the West was now wilderness. With the PCs holding only twenty seats, his prospects of becoming prime minister anytime soon were somewhere south of remote. And Charest was needed elsewhere, as pundits, professors, and personal friends kept reminding him. Quebec would soon be going to the polls, and for the sake of the nation, Charest needed to take over the Liberal leadership. Business leaders were particularly insistent; the threat of separation was a drag on the economy and an unwelcome variable for investment. It was a big move, and one that his own caucus stoutly opposed, but on March 27, 1998, Jean Charest announced he would resign as leader of the Progressive Conservative Party of Canada and seek the leadership of the Liberal Party of Quebec.

Within the PCs, there was considerable interest in trying to draft Stephen Harper for leader. On its face, the logic was compelling: Harper was an intelligent and relatively moderate Reformer who would represent a natural bridge to the reunification of the divided right. MPs Jim Jones and John Herron and Senator Gerry St. Germain approached Harper about running. And he gave it some serious thought. But Harper ultimately decided he wasn't prepared to betray his Reform roots, and truth be told, there was so much hostility toward his candidacy within the PC Party that he probably wouldn't have won if he had run.[15] The flirtation was significant, though. Harper might have been through with the Reform Party when he resigned in 1997, but he wasn't through with the idea of politics. Clearly, he didn't intend to stay at the NCC forever.

In November 1998, the Progressive Conservatives chose Joe Clark to lead them once again. Clark was convinced that, with his national profile, he could lead the PCs to power within two elections, giving him a second term as prime minister. For that reason, and because he was temperamentally inclined to loathe Reform and everything it stood for, Clark proscribed any talk or action to unite the right.

That proscription probably doomed the United Alternative movement – as Preston Manning dubbed his own effort to unite the right – from the start, but Manning kept pushing anyway. Remember the auto-destruct clause in its constitution that would terminate the Reform Party if it had not achieved power by 2000? Well Reform would certainly not become government before then. And Manning, who had pushed hard for a breakthrough in Ontario, only to see the party lose its sole seat in the province, now accepted that vote-splitting was preventing either Reform (which he still insisted was not inherently conservative) or the Progressive Conservatives from breaking through.

In a series of studies, consultations, votes, and assemblies, Reform ultimately agreed to disband and relaunch as the Canadian Conservative Reform Alliance, or CCRA, at its founding convention in February 2000. When the new name was unveiled, it only took minutes before delegates – and delighted reporters – realized that if you added "party" to the name the acronym would be pronounced "CRAP." The next day, the party's name was changed to Canadian Reform Conservative Alliance. It didn't matter. Among supporters and neutral observers, the name that stuck was Canadian Alliance, or Alliance. Its detractors always called it CRAP.

Despite the embarrassing rollout of the party name, the Alliance boasted two potential strengths lacking in its Reform predecessor. First, it had the support of provincial conservative activists in Ontario. This was no small thing. Mike Harris's Common Sense Revolution agenda had led to strikes by teachers and public servants, Days of Action when labour unions banded together to shut entire cities down, and protests and demonstrations over the forced amalgamation of the municipalities in Metropolitan Toronto into a single city. But Harris, advised by the same young Turks who had crafted the Common Sense Revolution, and who were now either in cabinet (Tony Clement) or the premier's office (Guy Giorno, another charter member of what critics called "The Little Shits"), had won a second solid majority government in 1999. If the New Blue Machine could be successfully yoked to Reform's Western base, then a breakthrough in Ontario, producing a minority Alliance government after the next election, was a real possibility.

The Alliance's second strength was that, in an effort to broaden its base, the party had dropped its covertly hostile approach to Quebec. Manning even began speaking of the desirability of recognizing Quebec's unique status within Confederation, while still insisting that all provinces needed to be treated equally. That would never be enough for an Alliance break-through in Quebec, but it might be enough to assuage the fears of Tory voters in Ontario.

But Harper was dead set against the United Alternative. Since it had no support from the federal Progressive Conservatives, he viewed it as simply a rebranding exercise for Preston Manning's private, personal party. The NCC commissioned a poll that showed 48 per cent of Reformers favoured the United Alternative, while 47 per cent opposed it. "These results con-firm that the Reform/UA has become a house divided against itself,"[16] Harper declared, in a conscious echo of Manning's famous speech.

But Harper wasn't exactly absent from partisan politics. He kept in touch with his former colleagues in caucus by phone, and if an MP was in town, Harper would take him or her out to lunch. He had no defined pol-itical ambition, but Kihn, who was with him throughout his NCC tenure, has no doubt Stephen Harper was continuing to think about his future, and what part politics might play in it.

Manning and Harper both assumed that Manning would lead the new party. But others had different ideas. After all, Manning had led Reform for twelve years, through three federal elections, without coming close even to forming a minority government. A new party needed a new leader. Tom Long, political advisor to Mike Harris, challenged Manning, and so did Stockwell Day, treasurer in Ralph Klein's Alberta government. (Keith Martin, a fiscally conservative but socially liberal Reform MP, also ran, but was not a factor.) Day was younger than Manning, ruggedly good-looking, more charismatic, could claim his own sliver of credit for Alberta's eco-nomic miracle, and, unlike Manning, could speak French. More important, the former Pentecostal preacher could rally Christian conservatives who complained that Manning, preacher's son though he was, hadn't advocated against abortion or homosexuality. "If this party decides that it's going to make abortion one of the top two or three issues we're going to run on in the next election, we're going to lose,"[17] Long warned, when Day promised he would permit citizen-initiated referenda on limiting abortion rights, on preventing the extensions of homosexual rights, on bringing back capital punishment, and on other aspects of the social-conservative gospel. But it didn't matter. Day's record in government appealed to fiscal conservatives, even those of the urban variety, who merely rolled their eyes at his social-conservative messages, assuming they'd be dropped or downplayed once Day became leader. After two rounds of voting by party members, Day took the Canadian Alliance away from Preston Manning. The Reform story was truly over.

Stockwell Day, it was said, could deliver an entire budget speech in the Alberta legislature from memory, which says much about Day's memory and about the complexity of Alberta budgets. (The province at that time had no deficit, virtually no debt, and a flat income tax.) Ontario-born; Quebec-, New Brunswick-, and Ontario-raised (his father worked for the Zellers department store chain); bilingual; socially conservative; of deep and sincere faith, he had worked as a deckhand, auctioneer, lumberjack, salesman (perhaps his true calling), youth minister, and Pentecostal school administrator, before running successfully for the Alberta Conservatives in 1986. He is a born-again Christian who accepts the literal and infallible truth of the Bible. (Liberal campaign worker Warren Kinsella mocked Day's faith during the 2000 election by saying on television, "I just want to remind Mr. Day that *The Flintstones* was not a documentary." Why evangelical and fundamentalist Christians are subjected to derision that would never be tolerated if directed at other faiths, or even other Christian denominations, remains an enduring mystery for this writer.) As a cabinet minister in Ralph Klein's government, he tried to have provincial funding for abortion services cut off, and advocated using the Constitution's notwithstanding clause to reverse a court-ordered ban on discrimination against homosexuals. Klein slapped him down both times, but Day quickly became a charismatic and popular advocate for Canada's Christian conservative movement. (His suggestion that serial killer Clifford Olson ought to be released into the general prison population so "moral prisoners will deal with it in a way which we don't have the nerve to do"[18] helped rather than hurt his cause within that constituency.)

Day brought to the reincarnated Reform Party pizzazz, new ideas (including extending a flat income tax to the national level), and a moral fervour that Preston Manning had either lacked or suppressed. But he had absolutely no experience leading a political party, much less a brand-new one that was recovering from the inevitable factionalism of a leadership race, and in which both Ontario Tories who had supported Long and Reformers who had supported Manning were nursing bitter grudges. Immediately upon winning the leadership on July 8, 2000, Day sought a seat in Parliament. Amazingly, Joe Clark still hadn't entered Parliament, almost two years after winning the Progressive Conservative leadership. Day's decision to run forced Clark to run as well, and after MPs in both parties stepped aside in deference to their leaders, both leaders won by-elections on September 11 and were in Parliament for the autumn session a week later. A week after that, Day made a suicidal mistake. Rising in the Commons to confront Jean Chrétien, he accused the prime minister of being offside with Finance Minister Paul Martin, and with his own caucus, on taxation.

"Will the Prime Minister, who disagrees with his finance minister on the high marginal rates of taxes and who now disagrees with his MPs, do one of two things?" Day asked. "Will he either resign because he has no support over there or call an election based on his record of being the highest taxing leader in the G7 countries?"

"I will never be afraid to go in front of the Canadian people with my record and the record of the Liberal government," Chrétien retorted.

Day shot back: "In the court of public opinion I find the Prime Minister in contempt of the people for not answering these questions. I have no further questions for this uncooperative witness."[19] He must have thought that was terribly clever.

Day was inordinately proud of his ability to think on his feet, to speak without notes, to improvise, to act outside the box. The press were still recovering from a conference he had held after the by-election, in which he arrived and left by jet-ski, wearing a wetsuit. Now he was daring the prime minister to call an early election. Chrétien, who would probably have called one in any case to exploit the Alliance's unsteady first steps, was happy to oblige. The poll was set for November 27, and the Liberals won it in a walk.

Had Stockwell Day waited a few months, learned on the job, consolidated his control over the former Reform caucus, developed a coherent

platform, adapted the old party's election machinery to the new party's
needs, courted the Ontario provincial conservatives, made a few mistakes
and learned from them, the new Alliance might have made serious strides.
It was better funded than the Progressive Conservatives, and had a stronger
base and greater potential in exploiting the popularity of the Harris government in Ontario. (The tragedy in Walkerton in May 2000, when seven
people died and many others became ill from drinking water infected with
E. coli bacteria, had already damaged the government's popularity, but its
electoral machine remained intact and could have been an invaluable
resource.) Instead, Day welcomed a snap election in which he bumbled
from gaffe to gaffe. It was probably all over on day two, when the Alliance
leader summoned journalists to Niagara Falls to illustrate the brain drain
of Canadian talent to the United States due to high taxation.

"Just as Lake Erie drains from north to south, there is an ongoing drain
in terms of our young people, in terms of our country," Mr. Day asserted.

But, um, the Niagara River flows south to north, from Lake Erie to Lake
Ontario, someone pointed out.

"We will check the record," he said. "If someone has wrongly informed
me about the flow of this particular water, then I will be having a pretty
interesting discussion."[20]

Oh dear.

In the end – and after a leaders' debate in which Day held up a sign on
which he had scrawled "No two-tier" health care, to general amazement –
the Liberals won another majority government, with 172 seats, up 17 from
1997. The Alliance gained on its Reform predecessor, with an increase of
6 seats, to 66. The Bloc, Conservatives, and NDP were all down. Joe Clark
had taken his once-proud party from 20 seats down to 12, a humiliation.
But it was Alliance supporters who were most chagrined. All the agonies
and struggle over four years: the Winds of Change conference, the United
Alternative movement, the creation of the Canadian Alliance, the two
rounds of the leadership campaign that tossed Manning overboard, the
election – for what? Six seats, and no breakthrough in Ontario. The old
Reform Party with Manning at its head would probably have done at least
as well.

Everyone was angry. Stephen Harper was angrier than most.

In a way, Harper had little reason to be upset. He had opposed the United Alternative project from the start, had written against it, had even avoided the founding meetings, sending John Weissenberger to scout the situation instead, lest anyone think he was still in the game. He had supported Tom Long, though only nominally, during the Alliance leadership campaign, and had focused most of his energies in 2000 on *Harper v. Canada*. This was a court challenge that the National Citizens Coalition had brought against the Liberals' latest amendments to the Canada Election Act, which once again prohibited third-party advertising during federal election campaigns. (In 2004, the Supreme Court would uphold the spending limits.) So why was he so fussed by the result? Partly, it was the way in which it had come about. During the campaign, Chrétien had joked that he really didn't like the West very much and preferred to campaign in the East. "I like to do politics with people from the East," he confessed. "Joe Clark and Stockwell Day are from Alberta. They are a different type."[21] It was a terrible thing to say about Joe Clark.

The Liberals generally ran a foul campaign. Future critics of Conservative hardball tactics forget that in 2000, the Liberal leader warned that the Alliance appealed to "the dark side that exists in human beings."[22] In case that was too subtle, Immigration Minister Elinor Caplan warned that the Alliance was supported by "Holocaust deniers, prominent bigots and racists,"[23] while Markham Liberal candidate John McCallum claimed that "at best, the Canadian Alliance tolerates the presence of new Canadians."[24] In French, Chrétien warned that "The proposition of Stockwell Day is to destroy Canada."[25] This wasn't a campaign of right versus wrong; this was a campaign of good versus evil. Harper would never forget the Liberal tactics. And he learned a lesson: the best way to protect yourself against a low blow is to land your own first. "Exactly," Arthur Finkelstein would have said.

But the larger message of the 2000 election, as far as Harper was concerned, was that the West was officially out. Nicholls, NCC vice-president at the time, says that in the wake of the election he wanted to write an op-ed piece blaming Stockwell Day for the debacle. No you won't, Harper told him – it would contradict the op-ed he was writing. The message of the election, Harper advised Nicholls, was clear. "It was Ontario saying no, not to the Canadian Alliance, not to Stockwell Day, but to Alberta."[26]

Harper's op-ed was a howl, screamed from rock bottom.

"The latest dribblings from the mouth of Canada's Prime Minister . . ." is how his December 8 essay in the *National Post* began.[27] The article – a screed, really – is Harper in despair, absolutely convinced that everything he had sought to achieve – a principled, moderate, national conservative party based in the West but with appeal in the East, able to form government and to govern well – had turned out to be an illusion.

"A shrewd and sinister Liberal attack plan" to "pull up every prejudice about the West and every myth about Alberta that could be dredged" turned out to have "enormous market in the country," he raged. The result "stripped away any veneer of openness to reforming Canada." While Alberta "has opted for the best of Canada's heritage . . . an open, dynamic and prosperous society in spite of a continuously hostile federal government," the rest of Canada "appears content to become a second-tier socialistic country" led by a "second-world strongman appropriately suited for the task."

The time had come, Harper concluded, for Albertans to "begin building another home – a stronger and much more autonomous Alberta." The government in Edmonton should follow the example of the government in Quebec City and make Albertans *maîtres chez nous.*" The article did not advocate outright separation from Canada, only a greater degree of provincial autonomy. Harper warned, however, that "separation will become a real issue the day the federal government decides to make it one."

The *National Post* essay, more than the infamous Firewall Letter that followed a few weeks later, properly reflects Harper's mood at the time. But the Firewall Letter,* or the Alberta Agenda as it was properly called, got far more attention, in part because it was addressed to Premier Ralph Klein, and in part because Harper's signature wasn't the only one on the document. Flanagan also signed, and Ted Morton and Rainer Knopff, also of

---

* The term was greeted with horror by progressives, including Progressive Conservatives in Alberta, because people believed the letter advocated a scorched-earth policy, such as a firewall created to contain a forest fire. But the term, according to its authors, referred to a computer's firewall.

the Calgary School, along with Andrew Crooks, chairman of the Canadian Taxpayers Federation, and Ken Boessenkool, an economist who was policy advisor to Stockwell Day when he was Alberta finance minister. Flanagan held the pen, and others contributed suggestions, but the idea of the letter was Harper's.

Banking, but by no means dousing, the anger that raged in Harper's essay, the open letter to the premier repeated Harper's earlier claim that the Liberal election campaign represented a direct assault on the province. One prominent feature of that campaign had been ads and speeches attacking the private delivery of some medical procedures in Alberta. Those services had been in place for years, and Ottawa had never been concerned about them before, but now they were presented as proof that conservatives were going to push for "two-tier" health care: a private service for the affluent; a public service starved of funds for everyone else.

For the authors of the Firewall Letter, these and other Liberal mendacities from "a misguided and increasingly hostile government in Ottawa" demanded a defensive reaction: greater autonomy for Alberta.[28] Specifically, the letter recommended that Alberta create its own pension plan; collect its own income tax; establish its own provincial police force; assume full provincial control over health care, even if that meant contravening the Canada Health Act; hold a provincial referendum on Senate reform; and (somehow) end the flow of wealth out of Alberta to the rest of Canada.

"It is imperative to take the initiative, to build firewalls around Alberta, to limit the extent to which an aggressive and hostile federal government can encroach upon legitimate provincial jurisdiction," the authors concluded. Many of the proposed measures were, in fact, quite modest. Quebec has its own pension plan and collects its own income tax. Ontario and Quebec have their own police forces. Other proposals had been debated for years. But tied together with fierce rhetoric, in the wake of the 2000 election, the letter created a sensation.

For Stephen Harper, this was the end of a very long road. Twice he had gone to Ottawa as a legislative aide, hoping to effect change. He had returned a third time as a prominent Member of Parliament in the Reform insurgency. But he had left after it became clear to him the insurgency had failed. He had watched that failure made manifest in the disastrous Canadian Alliance campaign. The right remained divided. The Liberals would govern forever. Paul Martin would replace Jean Chrétien and eventually some other Liberal would replace Paul Martin. If ever a party did unseat the Liberals, its conservatism would exist in name only. The Western conservative impulse had been banished from Central Canadian consideration. Every conservative principle Stephen Harper had thought through and then fought for had been rejected. Alberta was on its own, and so was he.

Although the Firewall Letter's primary motivation – and its ultimate impact on Stephen Harper – was to alert the nation to Alberta's anger, it was also fraught with implications in his home province. Some saw the letter to Klein as a way for Harper to create political space for himself at the provincial level, much as Jean Charest had moved from federal to provincial politics. "There were those who felt the Alberta premiership was virtually Harper's for the taking – either by elbowing aside Klein or by creating a new party and sweeping away the PCs," George Koch believes.[29] Klein's government was already growing soft. Spending was going back up, some of his hardcore ministers – like Day – had departed, and Klein kept refusing to tackle the heavy lifting in intractable policy areas. He would threaten to authorize much more private medicine and flout the Canada Health Act, for example, but then do nothing. Might Harper jump into provincial politics? Some thought it likely, though Ted Morton, a charter member of the Calgary School who later served as finance minister in the Ed Stelmach government, believes that Harper never seriously entertained provincial leadership aspirations.

But if he lacked ambitions provincially, Ottawa seemed farther away than ever: a Liberal bastion, with the opposition leadership firmly in Stockwell Day's hands. On the day the Firewall Letter was published, Stephen Harper would have laughed in scorn at the suggestion that five years later, almost to the day, he would be elected prime minister.

EIGHT

Faith

Early in his tenure at the National Citizens Coalition, Stephen Harper was talking with Gerry Nicholls about social conservatives. Pandering to social conservatives was a political dead end, Harper maintained, because the movement was out of touch with the mainstream of Canadian culture. Nicholls, who calls himself "a libertarian atheist," started going on about "those crazy religious guys." Harper looked at him sternly.

"Gerry, make no mistake," he declared. "I am a Christian."[1]

Harper's pilgrimage, as one author calls it,[2] from teenage agnostic to adult evangelical Christian mirrors his political conversion from uncertain liberalism to devout conservatism. He would temper the tenets of this acquired faith while never abandoning its core principles. A careful, measured, some would say fence-sitting approach to the so-con element of the conservative coalition would serve Harper well, as he returned to the political arena in the biggest gamble of his political life: wresting the leadership of the Canadian Alliance from Stockwell Day.

———

When Steve Harper was growing up in Leaside and Etobicoke, the Harpers attended the United Church along with everyone else, or so it seemed. The United Church, a union principally of the Methodist and Presbyterian churches (though some Presbyterians and Methodists refused to go along), was by far the largest Protestant denomination in Canada. Up until the 1960s, many English Canadians considered it more respectable to be Protestant than Catholic. This was less true in Toronto, where Irish, Italian, and Eastern European immigrants wove the Catholic Church into the religious fabric of the city. But for good WASPs, Catholicism was still a bit suspect, a legacy of the religious wars that had wracked the British Isles from the Reformation until the Battle of the Boyne. Even in 1960, John F. Kennedy's Catholicism was an issue he had to address and overcome before he could become president of the United States. Catholics, some people thought, took their marching orders from Rome; the Pope meant more to them than the prime minister or president; Catholics were vaguely untrustworthy. Such sentiments could still be found in the shires of Central Ontario when Stephen Harper visited Grey County as a boy.

Which is not to say the Harper family was in any way anti-Catholic. It is simply to say that Stephen Harper was raised in a conventional sub-urban Toronto household of the 1960s, which meant the family worshipped at the local United Church. At one point, the United Church even shared its hymnal with the Anglican Church, further cementing its respectability as a pillar of the establishment, with the added benefit that United Church congregations got to sing all the best hymns.

But Harper's move to Alberta threw his faith into disarray, as well as his politics. In high school, he had described himself as a "skeptical agnostic." In Alberta he became a believing, practising Christian. And he left the United Church – or, to steal from Ronald Reagan, the United Church left him.*

Roiled by the social turmoil of the 1960s and '70s, and alarmed by declining membership, the United Church began transforming itself into the New Democratic Party at prayer, as some dubbed it. To the dismay of many of its congregants, the church opposed the war in Vietnam and offered aid to American draft dodgers (1968). It declared abortion to be

---

* When asked why he abandoned the Democratic Party and became a Republican, Reagan said he didn't leave the Democratic Party; the Democratic Party left him.

"a personal matter between a woman and her doctor" (1980). It boycotted South African investments (1986). It accepted gays and lesbians into the church (1984), approved the ordination of gay ministers (1988), and urged Parliament to legalize same-sex marriage (2003). The evolution of the church away from what used to be considered orthodox Christianity reached its zenith – or nadir, depending on which side you were on – in 1997, when moderator Bill Phipps questioned the divinity of Christ. Long before then, theologians and ministers within the United Church were speculating on whether the Resurrection was literal or metaphorical.

Harper arrived in Alberta in 1978 as an agnostic – dismissive of the anti-scientific and anti-intellectual nostrums of the Christian Church, but willing to believe that there might (or might not) be an intelligence behind the order of things. It was not, however, something he devoted much thought or energy to. During his years with Cynthia Williams, the two neither attended church nor talked much about religion. When they became engaged, Williams recalls, Harper told her "He didn't want to get married in a church."[3] "I think he just felt that that confined him. We were both outside-the-box people," is how she accounts for it. "He was never really religious."

But after the break-up, as Harper and John Weissenberger launched into their own self-directed reading program, that reading included the works of the Christian apologists C.S. Lewis and Malcolm Muggeridge. And they became increasingly critical of the trend toward liberalism within the mainstream Protestant churches. "We both felt the church was moving in a certain direction, and had its reasons for doing so, but we weren't going to move with it," Weissenberger recalls.[4] He stayed within the Lutheran Church, but sought out a more conservative congregation. Harper left the United Church and spent a bit of time in the Presbyterian Church, before embracing an evangelical congregation.

Harper was not attracted to Pentecostals, who believe Christians can be infused with the Holy Spirit, causing them to speak in tongues and giving certain among them the power to heal sickness through faith. He is not a fundamentalist, demanding a literal acceptance of every word in the Bible as divinely ordained. But he did convert to the belief that we are all sinners (Romans 3:23), that the wages of sin is death (Romans 6:23), and that salvation lies in accepting Jesus Christ as your personal saviour (John 3:16).

The mainstream Protestant churches, while not rejecting this Christian core, prefer to emphasize instead that there are many paths to embracing the divine, including non-Christian ones.

There is another reason Harper prefers evangelical churches, such as Bow Valley Alliance Church, the first evangelical church he worshipped at in Calgary. These churches tend to be large (Bow Valley had a congregation of about 1,500 people back then), and it is possible to attend them anonymously, which suited Harper's non-demonstrative approach to faith. "I can't say he was a super-frequent church goer," says Weissenberger. "But the thing about those churches is that they're very big and open and you can come and no one is going to scrutinize." Nonetheless, "his faith is more profound than mine," Weissenberger maintains. "He talks about it much more comfortably than I do – not that we really talk about it very much. But he has a profound faith, and it's part of his world view. And he's not shy to talk about it."

Actually, he is shy to talk about it. Very rarely has Harper ever discussed his Christian faith in public. One exception was a 1995 interview with the now-defunct *Ottawa Times*. "I'm not a person who was born with a particular set of values and has held them my whole life," he told the interviewer. "I like to think that the values I hold today are in the process of a life of education."[5] He went on to explain that "twenty years ago, when I was a teenager, I would have been an agnostic, central Canadian liberal. And my life experiences have led me to come to other conclusions about life and political values . . . both intellectually and spiritually."

He did not claim to have worked out as rigorous an approach to his Christian faith as he had to his conservative political beliefs. "I wouldn't say I have a well-developed theology," he explained. "But my personal religious views, which I tend not to make much an issue of publicly, would probably be categorized as conservative Christian views." As for which denomination he embraced, "I am an adherent in the Alliance Church, but I am not a member at the moment."

In a 2005 book on Harper's religious faith, the writer Lloyd Mackey credits the influence of Preston Manning in helping shape Harper's beliefs. Manning says that isn't the case. The two never really discussed religion, he maintains.[6] But Manning's influence on Harper might have been more profound than the older man realizes. Tom Flanagan recalls Harper telling him that Manning's example of living a Christian life without trying to impose that life on others deeply affected the young man.

In any case, Harper's faith is personal and private, even within his own family. Although Laureen Harper was raised in the United Church, she became a non-believer, disillusioned by the role that religious conflict played in the break-up of her parents' marriage after twenty-nine years. The Harpers avoid going to church together, and never expected Ben and Rachel to attend.

Mackey's book, *The Pilgrimage of Stephen Harper*, seeks to demonstrate that Harper's Christian faith has guided his values and shaped his politics in a positive way. Marci McDonald, in *The Armageddon Factor*, makes the same claim, but asserts that the religious influence is entirely negative. For McDonald and those who share her view, Harper and his social-conservative supporters are plotting a takeover of Canadian politics and society that will transform Canada into something approaching a theocracy. Harper's tendency to say "God bless Canada" at the end of his speeches is, in the eyes of these critics, a coded signal to true believers that Harper is one of them and is waiting for the Rapture. Actually, he says "God bless Canada" in imitation of Ronald Reagan and other Republican presidents, just as he wears a Canada flag lapel pin in imitation of the American flag that U.S. presidents wear. But for these conspiracy theorists, it's all part of a grand scheme, just as Harper's support for Israel is linked to the belief of some evangelicals that an independent Israel is a necessary precondition for the return of Christ, and that Canada, too, must be returned to the path of righteousness as we approach the End of Days.

The theo-con conspiracy "is, in fact, being promoted in Ottawa by an aggressive and organizationally savvy band of conservative Christians with increasing ties to the Conservative government," McDonald warns. ". . . slowly, covertly, the political process is being co-opted by an extremist version of Christianity – one ultimately shaped by what I call 'the Armageddon factor.'"[7]

Both Mackey and McDonald are wrong. As we've already seen, through his years in Reform and during his time at the National Citizens Coalition, Harper warned against letting the conservative movement be co-opted by social conservatives. And as we will see, he ran against the social-conservative wing of the Alliance when he took on Stockwell Day for the leadership. As prime minister, he took no meaningful action against same-sex marriage – his sigh of relief was almost audible in 2006 when members of his own cabinet and caucus joined with the opposition to vote against reopening the question – and he prohibited any debate on abortion rights. Mackey is correct in asserting that Harper's religious beliefs have informed his values, but that means nothing. Everyone's religious beliefs, or the lack of them, inform their values. They make us part of who we are. But that does not translate into an agenda. Paul Martin, a Catholic, was the prime minister who gave Canada same-sex marriage. Under Brian Mulroney, also a Catholic, abortion became legal in Canada. Under Stephen Harper, an evangelical Protestant, both measures were upheld.

As for McDonald's assertion of a dark evangelical conspiracy to hijack the politics of the nation, if anyone wrote about Jews the way she writes about Christians, they would deserve all the trouble they'd be in.

Stockwell Day's misjudgment in urging Jean Chrétien to call an election in the autumn of 2000 turned out to be a symptom of a chronic condition. In the weeks and months that followed, Day's staggering propensity to make the worst possible decision, no matter what the situation, brought the Canadian Alliance to the brink of extinction – a remarkable feat of self-destruction for a single politician.

In retrospect, it's amazing that the Liberals didn't use the Goddard lawsuit against Day during the 2000 election. (They must have felt they had the situation well in hand and didn't need to.) In April 1999, when he was Alberta's treasurer, Day had written a letter to the *Red Deer Advocate* complaining about the actions of Lorne Goddard, a local lawyer and school board trustee. Goddard was representing a man charged with possession of child pornography. Goddard "is reported to have said that he actually believes the pedophile had the right to possess child porn," Day complained. The letter went on to say that "Goddard was elected to protect children. Also, by extension, Goddard must also believe it is fine for a teacher to possess child porn. Perhaps even pictures of one of his own students, as long as he got the photos or video from someone else."[8]

The letter showed appalling misjudgment. Day either did not understand or simply rejected the fundamental right of the accused to a fair trial and the fundamental duty of a lawyer to defend his client. Goddard sued Day for six hundred thousand dollars. Rather than apologize and settle, Day dug in. Because he was a provincial cabinet minister at the time, Alberta taxpayers were responsible for his legal fees. When costs reached eight hundred thousand dollars, the Klein government ordered Day to settle or pay for his own defence. Day ultimately settled, apologized, and contributed sixty thousand dollars of his own money to the settlement, by mortgaging his house. But by then it was March 2001, and the Goddard lawsuit had seriously damaged his credibility.

There was more, so much more: It came out that the OLO (Office of the Leader of the Opposition) agreed to have the party pay Alliance MP Jim Hart fifty thousand dollars to step aside so that Day could run in his riding. A police investigation ultimately concluded that the money was not a bribe, but still. . . .

There was the gumshoe who was hired to spy on the Liberals, or maybe on dissident Alliance MPs. Or maybe he wasn't hired. Maybe Day had never met him. Maybe he had. The story kept changing by the day, which made for a lot of bad days.

As staff members began quitting or were fired, Day brought in conservative pundit Ezra Levant to handle communications, which is rather like hiring an arsonist to put out a fire. He encouraged Day's demand for complete loyalty from caucus — "If I kill my grandmother with an axe, I want you to say 'She had it coming,'" he told MPs[9] — without doing anything to earn that loyalty. Instead, one controversy followed another.

It all culminated in an awful, awful caucus meeting on May 2, 2001. MPs had demanded that Day present a strategic plan for reversing the Alliance's disastrous slide in the polls. (At the beginning of the 2000 election, the Alliance had reached 33 per cent in one poll. By May 2001, support was down to 13 per cent.) Instead, Day and party strategists presented the MPs with some woolly strategy for winning an election three years down the road, and then demanded unanimous support for the plan. There was a near riot, which didn't deter Day from leaving the room and then declaring to reporters that caucus had endorsed the plan (and him) unanimously.

First, Art Hanger, the blunt former police detective who was now MP for Calgary Northeast, demanded Day step down. Hanger was turfed from caucus, along with Vancouver Island MP Gary Lunn, who supported him. And then, on May 15, eight grim Alliance MPs, led by former House leader Chuck Strahl, publicly announced that they had lost confidence in their leader. "We realize that by speaking out there are implications, including the fact that we will be suspended from caucus," Strahl acknowledged. "But we are convinced that over the past few months the current leadership has exercised consistently bad judgment, dishonest communications, and lack of fidelity to our Party's policies."[10] Others joined the "Rebel Alliance," as reporters dubbed it. The Democratic Representative Caucus, as the dissidents preferred to be called, began meeting with Joe Clark's Progressive Conservative caucus. Their ranks now included Deb Grey, who had quit as deputy leader and then left the Alliance caucus in disgust. Joe Clark's dream of absorbing the Reform rebellion back into the Progressive Conservative Party under his leadership now appeared to be on the brink of fulfillment.

Even Alliance MPs who weren't prepared to bolt from the party were in open rebellion against Day. Facing a vote of non-confidence by his own caucus, Day announced on July 17 that he would step down as leader ninety days before a leadership vote, the date of which would be set by the National Council. Leadership contests require time for candidates to organize, meaning this intolerable situation would go on well into 2002. Many within and outside caucus were convinced that the Alliance, now broke and deeply unpopular, would collapse before then, with the PCs picking up the pieces. There was only one way to hold the shattered party together. On August 13, Stephen Harper issued a press release, saying that he would soon be stepping down as head of the National Citizens Coalition. Everyone knew exactly what that meant. Harper was going to run for leader.

He had never entertained the thought of leading the Reform Party. The membership was loyal to Manning and he was not. Too many Reform supporters would never forgive him for abandoning the leader. He flirted with the idea of trying to capture the Progressive Conservative leadership, but it would have been too much of a betrayal of past principles and allegiances. He never contemplated running for the Alliance, a party that he thought was a mistake in the first place, and offered only nominal support for Tom Long's campaign. But when Stockwell Day took the leadership away from Manning, the calculus changed. Manning was no longer the dominant force within the party, though part of Day's many troubles stemmed from Manning loyalists who pounced on the new leader once he became vulnerable. (Day's much bigger problem was his unwillingness or inability to bring his and Manning's supporters together.)

When Day's shaky leadership led to further splits, Harper began to despair, but he also began to calculate. According to George Koch, he opposed the Democratic Representative Caucus, which he believed was an insurgency by Manning loyalists against Day's leadership, the very last thing the already schismatic right needed. His greatest fear was that the Alliance, which by late spring 2001 was polling in single digits, would collapse, allowing Joe Clark's Progressive Conservatives to absorb the remnant. Everything would be lost, including a genuinely conservative alternative to the Liberal hegemony. By late spring 2001, Harper was beginning to consider the possibility that he might run for the Alliance leadership himself.

As it turned out, his decision to quit Parliament in 1997 had been remarkably prescient. Moving to the NCC removed him from the inevitable internecine strife as the United Alternative movement morphed into the Canadian Alliance, while allowing him to retain a national profile as a thinking, moderate, maybe even electable conservative. Once Day began to implode, it was obvious to anyone, even the press, that Harper was the logical choice to replace him.

The situation brought two powerful elements in Stephen Harper's character into conflict. He was ambitious. Even after stepping down as an MP, he had sought through the NCC to influence the conservative movement. Also, he was young and most of his career, whatever that career may be, still lay ahead. A return to politics had always been in the cards.

But he was ill-suited to being a leader, and he knew it. He was uncomfortable with crowds, uncomfortable with strangers. He lacked the ability to inspire of a born leader. Instead, he led by example and through discipline. Discipline was something the Alliance badly needed at that point. But could Harper lead?

He didn't like being part of a team. He could never work under another's leadership. He only lasted a year working for Jim Hawkes, and another working for Deb Grey. He resisted Preston Manning's direction, and ultimately left the caucus when it was clear Manning wasn't prepared to remake Reform in Harper's desired image. He chafed while waiting for David Somerville to leave the NCC. He was and is a loner.

But by leading, he could at least be lonely at the top. He could reshape the Alliance into the socially moderate, fiscally conservative party based in the West but with appeal to both rural and suburban Ontario. He could realize the vision of his 1989 memo to Manning. And he would be giving, rather than taking, orders.

"Don't do it!" warned the *Globe and Mail*'s Jeffrey Simpson. "You're too ideological to succeed in Canadian politics."[11] In its own way, opprobrium from the dean of the press gallery pundits was the best endorsement Harper could hope for.

Even so, Harper approached the decision gradually, even reluctantly. In April 2001, he met with Day at Ted Morton's house and offered to help him in any way he could. Two months later, with things going from bad to worse, Harper and Tom Flanagan had dinner with Ezra Levant, whom Day had finally fired as communications director; Sean McKinsley, who had been Day's deputy campaign manager in the leadership race; Ken Boessenkool, who had signed the Firewall Letter and who had been a Day advisor; and Gerry Chipeur, a Calgary lawyer who hosted the dinner at his house and who had hired Levant after he left the Alliance. The consensus around the table was that Day's leadership had been fatally weakened. Everyone at that table urged Harper to run for leader to replace Day. Harper was non-committal.

In July, Boessenkool arranged for Day and Harper to meet at the Calgary Stampede. Are you planning to step down? Harper asked Day. Day denied he was. Harper said he wasn't sure he believed him. The next day, at

Robert Harper's daughter's birthday party, Stephen lamented to his brother that the Alliance was falling apart and into the hands of Joe Clark.

"You know what you can do about it," Robert replied.

"What can I do?" Harper asked.

"You know what you can do," his brother repeated.[12]

Harper was reaching out to Alliance MPs to gauge support. About ten were already on board. All those lunches whenever a Reform/Alliance MP passed through Calgary had borne fruit. Members of the Calgary School were writing newspaper op-eds urging him to run. Harper himself was giving speeches, warning that in all this fratricidal manoeuvring, one crucial thing had been lost: a common commitment to an ideas-driven conservative party that could offer a meaningful alternative to a Liberal Party increasingly mired in accusations of corruption and enmeshed in a civil war of its own. Paul Martin was openly attempting to force Jean Chrétien out of the leadership, even as the *Globe and Mail* had begun publishing stories about a program consisting of government contracts to sponsor events in Quebec, in which the money seemed to have just disappeared. There might not be anything to it. But then again, there might.

Day's announcement on July 17 that he would step down ninety days before a leadership vote had been followed by the party executive setting March 2, 2002, as the date for that vote. It was time to decide. On August 10, a core group of Harper supporters met with the NCC president at the 400 Club, a private Calgary business club (now defunct). The group included Robert Harper, John Weissenberger, Tom Flanagan, Ken Boessenkool, Mark Kihn, George Koch, and Eric Hughes (a friend from Harper's university days). By then, Harper had told his brother that he was in fact going to run. Now it was all about planning. At Boessenkool's urging, he sent out the press release three days later saying he was leaving the NCC. "My own view is that, had he not done that, the Alliance might have simply ceased to exist," Boessenkool later recalled.[13]

On August 18, the group met again at Flanagan's house for a dinner of chicken and potato salad. They talked logistics: building a campaign team, raising money, winning caucus support, installing phone lines, that sort of thing. The team agreed to work as a Draft Harper committee, with a more professional organization taking over the actual campaign once it launched.

In the meantime, Flanagan would be in charge, backed up by John Weissenberger. "I was excited as a kid at Christmas," Flanagan later recalled, "and I didn't sleep at all that night – the first of many sleepless nights over the next five years."[14]

But this was going to be no cakewalk. Day still had a base of support within the Alliance membership. The Christian right was in his corner, and would be buttonholing potential supporters in parking lots across the nation after church services, exhorting the faithful to join the Alliance and support Stock, one of their own. Harper had been out of politics for more than four years. He had no machine, and less money. Truth be told, the whole thing was in danger of crashing before it was even launched.

———————

No one outside the tiny bubble of Canadian federal politics noticed or cared about any of this, of course. It had been such a year. The very foundations of American democracy had been shaken by the 2000 presidential election, the results of which were so close that the Supreme Court eventually had to rule on whether a recount of votes in Florida should go ahead. The judges appeared to vote along strictly ideological lines, bringing George W. Bush to power and the court into disrepute. Beyond politics, the U.S. economy was shuddering. The end of every decade appears to be accompanied by economic pain. This time it was the bursting of the dot-com bubble. The 1990s had witnessed the miraculous arrival of the Internet, which allowed everyone to connect to everything, and Google, which helped guide them to where they were going. Everyone had a scheme; everyone was going to make a billion. But everyone's thinking was premature, as declining confidence sent the American economy into recession, taking the Canadian telecommunications giant Nortel with it. And then the planes struck the towers and the Pentagon, and suddenly everyone was vulnerable, everyone was frightened, everyone was angry, and no one was quite sure who the enemy was. In all of this, who cared about a race to see who would lead a Canadian political party that never had a ghost of a chance of coming to power? The Alliance leadership campaign was a third-tier story in a world suddenly gripped by a crisis of confidence. Only for those few, very few, people actually engaged in the fight did it mean anything at all. But for them, especially for Stephen Harper, it meant everything.

The plan was, first of all, to run a Draft Harper campaign that would keep the candidate's name in the news before the race formally kicked off. The team drew up a brochure that emphasized Harper as a true Reformer; one of his campaign themes would be that the Alliance, in its efforts to appeal to Progressive Conservatives, had lost its conservative soul. Flanagan and Weissenberger called MPs for support and, most important, hired experienced organizers, led by Brian Mulawka, who had managed campaigns for Reform MPs in the past. Money started arriving in dribs and drabs, bolstered by a twenty-thousand-dollar cheque from Scott Reid, now an Alliance MP and a true believer in Stephen Harper. Individuals on the team also wrote cheques for the campaign. The team got its hands on the membership lists of four ridings, and conducted a quick-and-dirty poll. It showed that Manning was still the most popular figure in the movement, Harper was number two, and attitudes toward Day were strongly negative – almost as negative as they were toward PC leader Joe Clark. So that would be the plan: Harper would be the true heir of Preston Manning – oh, the irony! – the leader who would save the conservative movement from the clutches of the Red Tory turncoat from High River. Everything was in place for a big rollout in December, followed by a national campaign. And then they ran out of money.

A September 12 launch date was scrubbed due to the horrific events of the day before. And then September turned to October turned to November, and still there was no campaign headquarters and no coherent campaign plan. Rather than duck, Harper personally called or met with all of the paid campaign staff to tell them they were fired. Then he went into a classic Stephen Harper funk.

Flanagan and Weissenberger and Kihn and the other core supporters met on their own. Did they want Harper to win the Alliance leadership? Yes. Were they prepared to run the campaign on their own, unpaid? Yes. Flanagan had zero experience as a campaign manager, but he was only teaching part-time that year, so would have the most hours free. Weissenberger had run Harper's '93 campaign in Calgary West, and had the most experience. Kihn was a formidable fundraiser for the NCC, and would now devote those skills to fundraising for Harper. George Koch would come up with the campaign brochure, aided by Flanagan, and generally help out; his wife, Laurie Watson, would work on production through her communications firm. Ken Boessenkool would work on speeches. Devin Iversen, a staffer in the office of MP Rob Anders, another staunch Harper supporter, offered to draw up a membership database and create a phone campaign.

Flanagan went to Harper's house. "Look, you've got a group of people in Calgary that are absolutely committed to seeing you win," he declared. "We know you're going to win, and we're going to stick with you through this whole thing."[15] Harper wasn't convinced. Once again, he was thinking of walking away. A day later he still hadn't made up his mind. People were losing patience. But now Laureen stepped in.

If the Harpers are a political team, and they are, part of Laureen's contribution is to buck her husband up when he's down. At critical moments in his career, she has shown greater faith in Harper's ability to overcome obstacles than he has himself. This was one of those moments. Her approach was to tell him to put up or shut up. "If you don't think you should do it, you should quit now," she told him.[16] Harper pounded the table with his fist. He was in.

Over and over again – at the University of Toronto, when he worked for Jim Hawkes, in his confrontations with Preston Manning – Harper had responded to crises by walking away. This time, challenged by Laureen, he decided to keep going. He would never walk away again.

The new campaign budget was set for $250,000. Staffing would be mostly voluntary – just the core team, backed by the staffers of supportive MPs. Weissenberger and Koch found some cheap office space in a Calgary strip mall for campaign headquarters. Volunteers scraped together the $25,000 entry fee and the 300 signatures needed to enter the campaign. As it turned out, Harper's campaign had greater fundraising potential than he himself suspected. All he needed was a focused team dedicated to identifying, and then raking in, donations. Kihn and Koch leaned on Calgary business executives for support. Some big cheques came in from semi-retired types who no longer had to kowtow in hopes of government contracts. A direct mail campaign in the form of a letter from Harper himself was also productive. Eschewing the big rollout, Harper flew to Ottawa on December 2 and held a press conference to announce he was running. The campaign slogan: "Getting It Right."

The campaign now had $100,000 in the bank, and access to 300,000 names of current and former Alliance and Reform Party members. More than anything else, Harper's campaign consisted of mining this database for support and donations. It would turn out to be all he needed.

Each paid-up Alliance member could cast a mail-in ballot, with the results of the vote announced March 22. If no one got 50 per cent on the first round, the top two contenders would square off in a second round. Because there was no riding-by-riding component, Weissenberger chose to create only regional organizations to sell new memberships and recruit support from existing members. He controlled the tour (well, Harper did, really, but Weissenberger managed the details) while Flanagan ran the business side. The campaign sent out a direct mail appeal in December to 70,000 existing Alliance members. The take: $400,000. Money was off the table as a problem. By the end of the campaign, the team had raised $1.1 million from 9,800 donors, with the average donation $116. Team Harper finished with money in the bank, one of the lessons learned that would be applied to future campaigns: Keep the team small and on the same page. Rely as much as possible on volunteers. Avoid consultants and elaborate regional organizations. Stay small and nimble.

But even as money receded as a problem, a new one emerged. In late January, Flanagan met with Harper's caucus supporters. More than two dozen had signed on, compared to eleven for Day. But the MPs had a warning: The Day campaign was on a drive to sell new memberships in churches, nursing homes, and social-conservative groups. Harper's team had focused on winning over existing members; what if Day flooded the party with new ones? The membership cut-off was only five weeks away.

Devin Iversen came up with an inspired invention: a stripped-down version of a predictive dialler. This machine allows a computer to directly call phone numbers in a database, connecting whoever answers to a volunteer who asks a few questions (Who do you support for leader of the Canadian Alliance?) and/or trolls for a donation. The team now expanded the operation into a proper telemarketing campaign. Weissenberger lived with a phone in his ear, begging MPs to mobilize their supporters to sell memberships. Things were tense. When the campaign learned that Campaign Life, the anti-abortion group, was selling memberships on behalf of Day, it filed an objection with the party's chief electoral officer, who ordered the practice stopped. Flanagan also went to the media, complaining that the Day team was trying to hijack the party by flooding it with social conservatives.

Harper's last-minute campaign generated 16,000 new members, but Day's campaign had signed up 29,000 and claimed it was in the lead. "Leadership Race Too Close to Call," the *Calgary Herald* declared.[17]

The contest was about more than just the leadership. The Alliance was on the brink of collapse. It no longer knew what it stood for. A large chunk of the former caucus was now sitting with the Tories. Two minor leadership candidates, MPs Diane Ablonczy and Grant Hill, were advocating a merger. Harper was running against any merger, because "Joe Clark and the Tories don't agree with a single thing that this party stands for." Day, meanwhile, wanted to define the Alliance as a coalition of populist social conservatives. "Have you had enough of being continuously scolded by the elites for not thinking properly or voting correctly?" he asked supporters.[18]

The party gathered in convention – perhaps, some thought glumly, for the last time – in Calgary on March 20, 2002. The results of the first ballot were a shock for Day's campaign and for many reporters. Stephen Harper: 48,561 (55 per cent); Stockwell Day: 33,074 (37.5 per cent). Neither Ablonczy nor Hill made it to 4 per cent.

Stephen Joseph Harper, having won easily on the first ballot, was leader of the Canadian Reform Conservative Alliance and leader of Her Majesty's Loyal Opposition. The man who could never follow another leader now had to convince a broken party and a skeptical country to follow him. But first, he had to go back on his word.

NINE

Frustration

In the late 1940s, Grattan O'Leary of the *Ottawa Journal* launched a campaign to provide a residence for the leader of the Opposition. If nothing else, it would offer solace to the endless string of Conservative leaders who would never become prime minister. They settled on Stornoway, a gracious, light-filled mansion (eight bedrooms and five bathrooms) in the exclusive enclave of Rockcliffe Park. Though smaller than 24 Sussex Drive, in some ways it's more comfortable and pleasant to live in than the prime minister's official residence. That hasn't tempted any of its residents to avoid the move to New Edinburgh.

Soon after becoming Alliance leader, Harper took possession, with Laureen and Ben and Rachel joining him in August. The Harpers' tenure at Stornoway came in the wake of a decade of controversy over the residence. Bloc leader Lucien Bouchard had refused to occupy the house, preferring to live across the river in Gatineau, Quebec. Preston Manning had jokingly proposed turning 541 Acacia Avenue into a bingo hall to save the taxpayers money, but when he became leader of the Opposition in 1997, after much agonizing, he moved in. He had learned that the Opposition leader's budget for social events, along with a car and driver/security person, was attached to the residence rather than the leader's office. Still, many of the Reform old guard considered it a betrayal. But Harper had never made an issue of Stornoway, and Stockwell Day had preceded him there in any case, so once again having the Opposition leader in the residence became simply a matter of course.

Harper's most urgent priorities were to get himself elected to Parliament and to end the infighting within the Alliance caucus. The two turned out to be related. Preston Manning stepped down from Calgary Southwest in early 2002, making it clear that this would be an ideal by-election for a joint Alliance–PC candidate. Ezra Levant, a mischief-maker if ever there was one, had already taken control of the riding association and proceeded to make himself the Alliance nominee. In response, the PCs put forward Calgary lawyer Jim Prentice, a quality candidate who would be a big get for the PCs if he won the riding. The Liberals were rumoured to have a high-powered candidate of their own ready to launch, who would go straight into cabinet if the by-election went their way. Suddenly, Calgary Southwest had gone from being rock-solid Alliance to a three-way toss-up. Even though the Alliance leadership race was still underway, Levant (being Levant) had already launched a harsh pre-writ campaign against "Kyoto Joe" Clark, including billboards announcing himself as "Loyal to Calgary."

Harper wanted Levant to step aside and allow him to run. After Harper won the leadership, the two talked by phone, but Levant refused to back down. It was up to the grassroots supporters in the riding to decide whom they wanted as their nominee, Levant told reporters on March 27, and the grass-roots had nominated him. Chrétien, delighted by this latest bit of Alliance infighting, had set the by-election date for May 13. Was Harper's leadership going to begin with a turf battle over which riding he would run in?

But the Alliance caucus, party executive, and membership had had it up to here with infighting. Levant was deluged with complaints from Alliance supporters and columns slagging him for putting his own interests ahead of the party. Shaken, he stepped aside the very next day. Prentice withdrew from the race in deference to the new Alliance leader. The Liberals, now that there was no prospect of a split right-wing vote, returned to the time-honoured tradition of running no candidate in a by-election to send the leader of the Opposition to Parliament. The NDP ran Bill Phipps, the divinity-doubting former moderator of the United Church. With much of his leadership team now running the by-election campaign, Harper cruised to victory.

The Calgary Southwest riding association was rotten with dead wood. It was also deeply in debt, thanks to Levant's lavish pre-campaign spending. The executive council of the party (the national governing body) was similarly faction-ridden, with many of its Day-supporting members skeptical about the new leader who had suddenly been thrust upon them. Most pressing of all, a dozen former Reform/Alliance MPs were still sitting alongside the Progressive Conservatives, who were pressing them to take out party memberships. Some of the best-known and most respected former Alliance MPs were in the Democratic Representative Caucus, including Deb Grey, Chuck Strahl, Jay Hill, and Monte Solberg. Harper had criticized the DRC, before and during the leadership campaign, for splitting from the party. Now he needed to get these Manning loyalists back in the fold.

But things were breaking his way. On Wednesday, April 3, 2002, the Rebel Alliance met in caucus. It was clear that many of them were reluctant to join the Progressive Conservatives. People like Deb Grey simply had no history with that party. That weekend, Harper reached Grey on her cell-phone. Would she come back? "Stephen, you know I have always been a Reformer and always will be," she assured him. "That's where my heart is."[1]

The following Monday, Harper met with most of the DRC. The window to join the Alliance was open, he told them, but it will close. No one has to apologize for anything, on either side. Simply pay the ten-dollar membership fee to rejoin the party, apply for re-admission to caucus with a letter of support from your constituency executive, and you'll be welcomed back. Former Alliance MP Inky Mark decided to stay with the Progressive Conservatives. Jim Pankiw, who had been accused of making racist comments, was refused admission to the Alliance and Progressive Conservative parties, and sat out the rest of the term as an independent before going down to defeat in the 2004 election. Everyone else decided to return. On April 10 they said their goodbyes to their former PC seatmates, and on April 17 joined the Alliance MPs in caucus. There were a couple of short speeches, and then everyone carried on as if nothing untoward had happened. One of the most bizarre episodes in Canadian parliamentary factionalism was at an end. But it had not been for naught. For several months, Reform/Alliance/DRC MPs had sat with Progressive Conservative MPs. Each side discovered that the other side was much easier to get along with, personally and ideologically, than they had suspected. It was a beginning, of sorts.

_____

Stephen Harper was back in Ottawa, though this fourth time in much nicer digs. But for Laureen, it was a hard transition. When Harper had quit the NCC to run for the Alliance, the income from her design and publishing business had been all that kept the family afloat. Luckily, that business had been so successful that Harper enjoyed referring to himself as a "kept man."[2] But to follow her husband to Ottawa, Laureen had to give the business up and become simply the wife of the Opposition leader – a housewife, in other words. Times had changed since Joe Clark was derided as a wimp because his wife, Maureen McTeer, had not taken his name. But even in 2002, staying in Calgary to run a business while her husband served as Opposition leader would have raised eyebrows and excited rumour. Besides, the kids needed Mom and Dad in the same town.

It was hard going, at first. Ottawa was and is a quintessentially Laurentian city. Red Tories could fit in well enough, but a Calgary ex-Reformer who was raised on a farm, rode motorcycles (Laureen has had a lifelong passion for them and currently owns a Yamaha), and had a technical certificate rather than a university degree simply wasn't going to be accepted by the sort of people who decided who was and wasn't One of Us. She was lonely.

But it is not in Laureen Teskey's nature to mope. She became heavily involved in her children's local public school and joined a basketball team. The avid hiker had all of Gatineau Park – thirty-five thousand hectares of woodland mere minutes from Parliament Hill – to play in. And Ottawa had evolved beyond the comfortable, closed living rooms of the substantial houses in the Glebe or mansions of Rockcliffe Park that housed the Laurentian set. The booming tech sector had brought new energy, new restaurants, and new night life. (Not that Stephen Harper was ever going to go dancing with his wife in the ByWard Market. He was more likely to be sighted, as he sometimes was, in the lineup at the local Harvey's.) And of course, Laureen immersed herself in the political career of her husband. Over the course of the next two years, she stopped calling herself Laureen Teskey and became Laureen Harper.

There was no honeymoon for the reunited Alliance, which was still in seriously bad shape. Despite the leadership race, party membership had fallen to 124,000, less than half of what it had been in 2000, during the previous leadership race. A raft of pundits, from one end of the Dominion to the other, wrote columns dismissing Stephen Harper as too extreme and the Alliance as too West-centric to ever win government in an essentially liberal country where Central Canada elects the government. Richard Gwyn of the *Toronto Star*, Edward Greenspon and Hugh Winsor of the *Globe and Mail*, and Barbara Yaffe of the *Vancouver Sun* all wrote essentially the same column. "His thinking on most matters starts from an economically conservative base in a country that is neither conservative nor comfortable with ideology," is how Greenspon put it.[3] There were many squibs of that ilk. Harper's victory had given the Alliance a small bounce in the polls, but only to 15 per cent, essentially tying it with the Progressive Conservatives. And the party owed its riding associations $2.3 million.

At a policy conference in Edmonton on April 4, while the talks with the DRC dissidents were still underway, Harper vowed to put the party back on its feet financially and make it competitive in the next election. His solid fundraising performance revealed that donors were willing to take out their chequebooks now that Day was no longer in charge. As for becoming electorally competitive, delegates started by avoiding anything that smacked of social or economic extremism. Resolutions to abolish the Charter of Rights and Freedoms, to prohibit stem cell research, to allow private payment of publicly funded health care services were all defeated. And the Alliance no longer supported Day's flat income tax.

The day before the convention, Joe Clark phoned Stephen Harper, and the two agreed to meet the following Tuesday. On its face, this made no sense. "Joe Clark has refused every offer of cooperation for over three years," Harper had declared in his leadership campaign pamphlet. "He is intent on creating a second liberal party. Until there is a new leader of the PCs we are the sole conservative alternative for Canadians in the next election. It's time to focus our efforts on this party."[4] Harper and the party had rejected the campaigns of Diane Ablonczy and Grant Hill, who favoured union. Now, mere weeks after winning the leadership, he was willing to meet and talk with Joe Clark? They weren't going to be discussing the weather.

There was even less apparent reason for Clark to talk to Harper. "The Alliance party is fundamentally offensive," Clark had declared after the 2000 election. "It's an alliance of people who don't like other people, the very opposite of the inclusion that characterizes our party. In those parts of the country that are a base for us, any kind of association with the Reform/Alliance would give those seats to the Liberals."[5] Yet he was the one who had phoned Harper, not the other way around.

The reason for the conversation was twofold. For one thing, each leader wanted to secure the support of the Alliance defectors in the DRC. They could only do that by showing that they had negotiated in good faith to end the split. For another, both parties needed money, as corporate donations had dried up almost completely. The donor base of the conservative movement wanted union. Neither leader could afford to be seen as intransigent.

On the Tuesday after the convention, one day after Harper had talked to the MPs in the Rebel Alliance, the two leaders met in Clark's office for ninety minutes. The talks collapsed before they had barely begun. Clark wanted to pursue a process: the two parties, negotiating as equals, would launch a joint examination of how to avoid vote-splitting in the next election. Harper had a much bolder proposal: the two parties would immediately sit together as one in the House of Commons, while plans were launched for a formal union – followed, no doubt, by a leadership contest. Clark would have none of it. The Alliance had more than sixty MPs (the exact number depending on who returned from the DRC); the PCs had twelve. Their caucus would be swallowed up, with hardly any of the major critics' portfolios going to Clark's team. Clark must also have known that, in any leadership contest, Harper would have some support among the Progressive Conservative membership and total support among the Alliance membership. Clark could not possibly beat him.

Nor could he win this argument. The day after the Harper–Clark meeting, the Rebel Alliance went home. Talk of merger would have to wait until someone other than Clark led the Progressive Conservatives, Harper told reporters. And there things stood, as spring gave way to the hot summer of 2002.

———————————

Not long after the merger talks collapsed, Harper made one of the worst mistakes of his leadership. In late May, he told a reporter for the New Brunswick *Telegraph Journal*, "I think in Atlantic Canada, because of what happened in the decades following Confederation . . . there is a culture of defeat that we have to overcome."[6]

It was his father talking as much as him. Joe Harper had strong views on the Maritimes from which he'd come. The independent fishermen who had tended their own gardens and relied on their own resources had become addicted to Unemployment Insurance and lost their sense of initiative, he once complained to a reporter.[7] Steve Harper had inherited Joe's conviction that the Liberals in Ottawa had crippled the Maritimes with addlepated and graft-ridden regional development programs and ever-more-generous welfare (that, in truth, was what Unemployment Insurance in the region had become) for the locals when those programs failed.

Now, in 2002, Stephen Harper was promising that if he became prime minister he would act "dramatically and very rapidly" to end regional supports, replacing them with tax cuts and infrastructure investment. "Traditional regional development programs are not very successful," he maintained. "They grossly distort the market and they not only fail to develop a lot of profitable enterprises, but over a long period of time they have detrimental effects on potential opportunities." And lest there be any misunderstanding, he concluded, "Atlantic Canada's culture of defeat will be hard to overcome as long as Atlantic Canada is actually physically trailing the rest of the country. When that starts to change, the culture will start to change too."[8]

Harper later said that the remarks had been taken out of context. In what possible context should they have been taken? His remarks were triply damaging. They gave the Liberals fodder both when Harper said them and later, in the 2004 election. They angered Atlantic Canadians, further dimming the party's already dusky prospects of ever electing anyone in the region. And they bolstered the arguments within the Progressive Conservative caucus and membership that union with these Prairie radicals was out of the question.

As for whether he was right, well, there is a strong case to be made that equalization payments, generous Employment Insurance benefits (the Liberals euphemistically changed the program's name from Unemployment Insurance in 1996), and regional development programs have failed to revive the Maritime economy, and may even have harmed it by distorting market forces and, yes, creating a culture of dependence. But Atlantic Canadians reject that analysis, blaming factors such as geography, the St. Lawrence Seaway, and Central Canadian neo-colonialism for their chronically underperforming economies. In any case, what Stephen Harper said was something no politician can say in Canada. In the 2006 campaign he made a point of apologizing while he was in the Maritimes. And once he became prime minister, Harper retained the regional development grants and equalization payments. Only in the area of Employment Insurance did he make reforms, and those reforms were not sufficient to alter labour markets in the region.

Other than that great gaffe, Harper was settling in as leader rather well. He had imported a number of people from the leadership campaign into his office. Tom Flanagan was chief of staff, though he was delayed in getting to Ottawa because of teaching commitments. Flanagan had originally planned to sign on as director of operations, with Stockwell Day's chief of staff, Jim MacEachern, staying on. But that didn't work out, and by mid-summer Flanagan was in charge. John Weissenberger decided to stay in Calgary. He enjoyed his life as a geologist for a petroleum firm, and had no desire to uproot the family. Besides, Harper wasn't pushing him to come – as we've noticed, he was reluctant to put friends in positions of responsibility inside his office. Carolyn Stewart Olsen took over as press secretary. Harper had gone through two press secretaries during the leadership race, before hiring Stewart Olsen. She was quiet, trustworthy, loyal, and instinctively hostile to reporters. Perfect. Though Harper had had a relatively good relationship with the press as an MP and as head of the National Citizens Coalition, he was deeply suspicious of the national press gallery, which he saw as self-important, ill-informed, cozy with the bureaucracy, ideologically sympathetic to the Liberals (some of them perhaps even closet NDP sympathizers), and reflexively hostile to anything conservative or Western. The job of his press secretary was to manage the trickle of information that the Alliance would deliver to the press, and otherwise to keep them as far away from the leader as possible. Stewart Olsen did her job so well that she stayed on as press secretary until Harper appointed her to the Senate in 2009.

Ray Novak became his executive assistant. As a graduate student in politics at the University of Calgary, Novak had done some work for Harper at the NCC. From the day of his hiring until now, he has been Stephen Harper's most devoted aide: low-key, extremely competent, utterly devoted to the leader. You've seen him often, but haven't noticed him. In the photograph with Harper greeting the foreign leader, addressing caucus, talking (infrequently) to reporters, Novak is the young, thin, good-looking guy in the background, going unnoticed. When Harper moved into Stornoway, so did Novak, into a loft over the garage. He often ate meals with the family, and practically became one of them. With each passing year, Novak would take on more and more responsibilities – organizing touring and scheduling overseas trips, and handling ever-more important files. At the height of the Senate expenses scandal in 2013, when chief of staff Nigel Wright was forced to resign, Novak took his place. He was thirty-six.

Devin Iversen, he of the famous improvised predictive dialler, worked in operations. Jim Armour, who had handled communications for the Reform Party, became Stephen Harper's first director of communications, responsible for crafting and delivering the strategies for getting the Alliance message out to the public, while at the same time doing everything possible to discredit the other parties' messages. Phil Murphy, who had deep links to the Reform Party and was already in the OLO, became deputy chief of staff, handling much of the day-to-day operations while Flanagan focused on party organization and preparing for the election expected in 2004. That autumn, Ken Boessenkool, the economist and co-signer of the Firewall Letter, arrived as senior policy advisor.

Flanagan could afford to be virtually a part-time chief of staff because in many ways Harper was his own chief of staff. He liked to meet directly with the communications team, say, rather than having them go through

Flanagan or Murphy. This hub-and-spoke method worked best for a leader who wanted to know and direct everything and everyone in his office. Of course, it had its downside (and has had the same downside to this day). Harper is a taskmaster; he has no hesitation in telling you exactly what he wants from you, and no hesitation in telling you if he believes you haven't measured up to expectations. There have, from that day to this, been very few people who feel comfortable contradicting, warning, or offering contrary analysis to the leader, as a result of which Harper sometimes leads his team straight off a cliff. A communications team that was doing its job, for example, would have known that Harper planned to condemn Atlantic Canada's "culture of defeat" and would have talked him out of it. But they didn't, and so they couldn't.

"He demands a lot from other people, but he also demands a lot from himself," observes Mark Kihn. "And sometimes, frankly, he demands maybe too much, or doesn't allow for human foibles, whether his own or others', to come into play."[9] But as Kihn also points out, there was much to be said for what critics derided as Harper's control-freakish handling of his office. He knew, for one thing, exactly what was going on in it. People who had a concern or suggestion could raise it with him directly. For many years, chief of staff Jean Pelletier had acted as gatekeeper to Jean Chrétien, protecting the Liberal leader from those seeking his time and attention. Chrétien never really understood how deeply Martin had turned the party against him until it was too late. The Board, as the circle of advisors surrounding Paul Martin was known, jealously protected access to Chrétien's successor; groupthink – everyone seeing things the same way, as they walk together toward disaster – would prove fatal to that administration. Harper was much more connected personally with what was going on around him in his office, the caucus, the party. But most important, Stephen Harper was and is a clever (though by no means infallible) tactician and a far-sighted strategist. Under his leadership, his office effectively executed his personal directives, and a decade of power suggests those directives were more often right than wrong.

On May 21, 2002 – a cool, wet day in Ottawa – Stephen Harper once again swore an oath of loyalty to the Queen and once again became a Member of Parliament, this time for the constituency of Calgary Southwest.

At the ceremony, surrounded by a small knot of family and friends, he signed the register and then suggested Ben sign as well. Then he shrugged. "We'll worry about the dynasty later," he joked, to general laughter.

The first exchange between Harper and Chrétien was great fun. The gaunt, laconic prime minister whose suits never quite seemed to fit, and who famously was known to be fluent in neither official language, welcomed the eighth leader of the Opposition to sit across the aisle from him. "Perhaps in terms of security a seat belt should be put on his seat because it is called the ejection seat," Chrétien joked, and ended with this heartfelt wish: "I want the new Leader of the Opposition to have many, many years to learn how to do the job on the job."[10] It was a typically incoherent Chrétienism, and typically endearing.

But Harper gave as good as he got. "I was four years old when the Prime Minister first took his seat in the House of Commons," he told the packed House. "What is not known is that of course I was an avid reader of *Hansard* at the time. I recall reading some of the early speeches of the Prime Minister and turning to my mother, who is here today, and saying: 'Mom, someone has to do something to stop that guy.'"

"I am his eighth Leader of the Opposition," he went on. "However, I am in a privileged position in that besides myself and my party, the Deputy Prime Minister, the Minister of Canadian Heritage, the Minister of Industry and of course the Minister of Finance are all wishing that I will be his last opposition leader."

He also thanked Stockwell Day for his service as the previous Alliance leader, and John Reynolds for his work as interim leader. Reynolds is old school in the best sense: a big, affable back-slapper of a man who, as interim leader of the Alliance after Day stepped down, helped heal some of the trauma within caucus by taking up residence in Stornoway and inviting MPs over for a chat and a drink, or two, or ten.

"Mr. Speaker, you do have to tell him that he has to return the contents of the wine cellar," Harper urged. "I insist on this."

"I think that is an internal party matter," the Speaker, Peter Milliken, demurred.

In a year, more or less by accident, Stephen Harper had gone from being the head of a small conservative pressure group to leader of the Opposition and the most likely candidate to defeat the Liberal government. Except, history and conventional wisdom held that he and his party were too far to the right ever to win government. The real question, according to conventional wisdom, was whether and how Paul Martin would be able to force Jean Chrétien to step aside as prime minister. After the 2004 election, in which the Liberals looked set to win two hundred or more seats, either the Alliance or the Progressive Conservatives might be so weakened that one might agree to merge with the other, conventional wisdom speculated. Until then, conventional wisdom dictated, the Liberals could count on clear sailing. But once again, for the umpteenth time, conventional wisdom would make an ass of itself.

———

It took months for the smoke to stop rising from the rubble of the World Trade Center. America was angry and afraid. Within weeks of the attack, the Taliban had been swept from power in Afghanistan, but that was hardly satisfying, and besides, Osama bin Laden got away. George W. Bush became the voice of an enraged nation, as he brought in sweeping anti-terrorism legislation and demanded that everyone on the planet declare whether they were with the United States or against it. But who really could be against it? Russia was prostrate, thanks to incompetent and corrupt leadership; China was rising but not risen; and Japan had entered its second decade of decline. The American hegemon was raging against mosquitoes.

To its north, Canadians revelled in prosperity and worried about the border. The Americans were letting fears for their security trump economic self-interest, as they tightened the rules on who and what could cross the 49th parallel. There was no appetite in Canada for toppling dictators just for the sheer pleasure of it. In any case, we were on top of the world. Shame about Nortel, but otherwise the economy weathered the bursting of the dot-com bubble nicely. Budgets were balanced and taxes were coming down as far as the eye could see. No one knew that this prosperity was autumnal, as banks in the United States and overseas went searching for exotic instruments to widen their profit margins and fatten the bonuses of overdressed jocks who ruled the financial services sector and the world. Too bad Paul Martin wouldn't let the dull old Canadian banks slip their regulatory leashes so they could play with the big boys on Wall Street. But there wasn't any wolf on Wall Street or Bay Street who could match the finance minister when it came to ambition.

Just as Jean Chrétien never got over losing the 1984 Liberal leadership contest to John Turner, Paul Martin never got over losing the 1990 leadership contest to Jean Chrétien. During the first Liberal government, the two men worked cooperatively to fight the deficit and Quebec separatism. But by the second term, Martin was already starting to pressure Chrétien to step aside in his favour. After the 2000 election, that pressure became relentless. Martin had the support of most Liberal MPs, especially those who hadn't been favoured with cabinet posts. His people increasingly dominated the national executive; most of the riding associations were controlled by Martinites. The Martin machine even controlled who was able to receive an application to join the Liberal Party. Faced with an open mutiny by his finance minister, Chrétien dismissed Martin from cabinet in June 2002. Actually, Martin said he was fired; Chrétien insisted he resigned. The joke around Ottawa was "Paul Martin got quit." But that only cleared the decks for a more open confrontation. Chrétien faced a leadership review in February 2003 that he was unlikely to win. Half the caucus was in open rebellion. Finally, at a caucus retreat in Chicoutimi, Quebec, on August 20, 2002, Chrétien announced he would step down as Liberal leader – in February 2004. Paul Martin would have to cool his heels for another eighteen months.

But everyone knew what would come after those eighteen months: a campaign toward an election victory as impressive and implacable as the *Juggernaut* (the title of *Toronto Star* reporter Susan Delacourt's book on the Liberal civil war)[11] that Martin had assembled to unseat Chrétien. Martin understood Quebeckers' aspirations better than Chrétien, and would score major gains against the Bloc Québécois. Paul Martin empathized with Western discontents – why and how, he couldn't say, but no matter – and he would eat into Alliance support in the West. Martin, it seemed certain, would win a two-hundred-seat majority government in 2004, leaving both separatists and conservatives in disarray.

Funny thing, though: since August 2000, *Globe and Mail* reporters Daniel Leblanc and Campbell Clark had been writing about government sponsorships for sporting and cultural events in Quebec. No one seemed able to explain where the money had gone. The *Globe* stories prompted the new public works minister, Don Boudria, to call in Auditor General Sheila Fraser to have a look at three of the contracts. In May 2002, just as Stephen Harper assumed the leadership of the Alliance, Fraser reported an "appalling" lack of control over spending on the sponsorship program, saying the government officials involved "broke just about every rule in the book." She sent her report to the RCMP and announced that her department would now conduct a full audit of the entire sponsorship program. The report would be ready in late 2003. That would be around the time Paul Martin took over as prime minister.

The same week that Chrétien told his caucus that he would be stepping down in a year and a half, Progressive Conservatives met in Edmonton to prepare for yet another leadership race. Joe Clark had had enough. "The good news is that I am widely trusted and popular," he offered in an August 6 statement announcing his resignation. "The bad news is that we cannot translate those qualities into votes for the party."[12] The plain fact was that, under his leadership, the PCs had lost about a third of the public support they had enjoyed when Jean Charest was leader, and in the 2000 election had lost a third of the MPs who had been elected under Jean Charest. Clark had failed to win over the dissident Alliance MPs when Stockwell Day was imploding, and had rejected any meaningful effort to cooperate with the Alliance when Stephen Harper took over. Fundraising efforts had failed, the caucus – such as it was – was restive, and no one could give you a straight answer as to what the Progressive Conservatives stood for.

There was a pattern here: Clark was prime minister for only nine months because, in 1979, he refused to condescend to secure the support of the tiny Social Credit caucus for his first budget, losing the vote and the election that followed as a result. In 1983, after two thirds of the delegates at a Progressive Conservative convention voted in support of his leadership, he decided that it wasn't enough, and called for a leadership convention, confident he could defeat Brian Mulroney. Wrong. In his second bout as leader he had taken a Progressive Conservative Party that was in a modest, tentative recovery and sunk it to the brink of extinction. And still he would not cooperate with the Alliance, just as he had refused to cooperate with Reform or with the Mike Harris Progressive Conservatives in Ontario. It had often been said of Clark that, just like Palestinian leader Yasser Arafat, he never missed an opportunity to miss an opportunity. Now, with the majority of his own caucus threatening to campaign against him at the August convention, he decided he'd had enough. "The Conservative Party," Tory stalwart Hugh Segal observed, "was just about done."[13]

When Clark stepped down, a door opened. Harper had always said that the Alliance and the PCs would never be able to get together while the former prime minister was at the Tory helm. Now, with him gone, Harper immediately proposed a joint leadership convention – in effect, the union of the two parties. Nobody took him seriously, so all Harper could do was perform his duties in the House, work to build the Alliance, and wait for the result of the leadership vote on June 1, 2003.

Nova Scotia MP Peter MacKay was the favourite from the start. He was young; had an interesting background as a Crown attorney; regularly topped the annual *Hill Times* survey of sexiest male MPs;[14] had been raised in a political household as the son of a prominent federal Tory, Elmer MacKay; and presented a smooth, affable, intelligent face to the world, though his bare-bones French was a concern. His main opponent was Jim Prentice, a savvy Calgary-based lawyer and party loyalist who had stepped aside rather than run against Harper in Calgary Southwest, and advocated cooperating, though not merging, with the Alliance. Scott Brison, a young Nova Scotia MP and Clark loyalist, was also in the game. But the wild-card was David Orchard. Once described by Joe Clark as a "tourist" in the Progressive Conservative Party, the Saskatchewan farmer ran for the leadership in 1998 and 2003 on a platform opposing both free trade with the United States and cooperation with Reform/Alliance. The party had become so weak that Orchard commanded about a quarter of the delegates when the leadership convention got underway in Toronto. MacKay was in the frustrating position of having the most support of any candidate at the brokered convention but not enough for a clear win. When Scott Brison finished last on the second ballot and was forced to drop out, he took his supporters over to Prentice, making Orchard the kingmaker. Since Orchard was vehemently opposed to cooperation with the Alliance, the Orchard delegates should have gone over to MacKay. But rather than take a chance, MacKay acceded to a hastily negotiated agreement that was literally scrawled out on a piece of paper. He promised:

1. No merger talks or joint candidates w Alliance, maintain 301.*
2. Review of FTA/NAFTA – blue ribbon commission – with DO [David Orchard] choice of chair. Rest of members to be jointly agreed on.
3. Clean up head office including a change of national director with consultation, and some of DO's people working at head office.
4. Commitment to make environmental protection front and centre, incl sustainable agriculture, forestry, including reducing pollution through rail.[15]

It was a remarkable document, combining elements of policy minutiae (reducing pollution through rail?), sweeping principles (no merger talks), and naked power politicking ("some of DO's people working at head office"). MacKay got the word *talks* taken out of the first clause, convinced Orchard that they needed to jointly agree on the trade commission's chair, and then signed the paper. Orchard duly delivered his block of Orchardistas at the next ballot. MacKay won the leadership, and sealed the fate of the Progressive Conservative Party.

On May 12, 2003, in the midst of the race for the Progressive Conservative leadership, a by-election was held in the Southwestern Ontario riding of Perth–Middlesex. The outcome of that by-election had as much influence on the fate of the Alliance and PC parties as anything that occurred on the floor of the Tory convention. "The road to merger began in Perth–Middlesex," Tom Flanagan believes.[16]

Perth–Middlesex is a riding of farmers and actors. The largely rural

---

* That is, the party would field a full slate of candidates in all 301 ridings in the next election.

Southwestern Ontario constituency is home to Stratford, site of the Shakespearean festival. Until the schism, it had been reliably Progressive Conservative. But the Liberals took it in the 1993 sweep of Ontario, and held it in 1997 and 2000. The MP, John Richardson, was not well, and stepped down in 2002. After a six-month delay, Jean Chrétien called the vote for May 12. He may have been hoping that a leaderless Progressive Conservative Party would increase Liberal chances of holding the riding.

The Canadian Alliance was weak in Perth–Middlesex: the party had placed third in 2000; the constituency association was a closed fiefdom; and the Alliance nominee, business owner Marian Meinen, lived outside the riding in London. Nonetheless, Harper wanted a good result, to show that the Alliance had breakthrough potential in rural Ontario. When it became clear that local forces wouldn't be enough, he sent Doug Finley into the riding to shore up the campaign. Finley was a gruff, plainspoken Scot who liked a drink, and a cigarette to go with it; he worked his first political campaign in 1966, when he helped send the first Scottish National Party MP to Westminster. After immigrating to Canada, he worked for the Liberals, then the Progressive Conservatives, and finally the Canadian Alliance, as his youthful Marxism migrated farther and farther to the right. He had been turned down for the job of director of political organization in the Alliance, which was a mistake, because it was clear that Finley knew what he was doing. He took charge of the sad-sack campaign team and began organizing the few available volunteers, while Flanagan poured in help from outside. Mark Kihn put together a simple radio ad campaign; Devin Iversen fired up the predictive dialler; staffers were encouraged to take a week or two off and head down to the riding; and Harper himself visited five times during the campaign, even holding a caucus meeting there. None of it did even the slightest bit of good. PC candidate Gary Schellenberger, a local business owner and a councillor in the regional government who had run for the seat twice before, squeaked in with 33.8 per cent of the vote to the Liberals' 30.5 per cent. The Alliance finished a poor third, with 17.5 per cent.

Harper was bitterly disappointed by the Perth–Middlesex result. He was trying to reposition the Alliance as a sensibly conservative party with no hidden social agenda that rural Ontario voters could comfortably support. And yet he had lost, not just to the Liberals but to the PCs – at a time when the party didn't even have a leader. If that's the best the Alliance could do under Harper, with the party pouring everything it had into the contest, what were the chances of a breakthrough in the general election?

In late June, four weeks after Peter MacKay won the leadership of the Progressive Conservative Party, he walked up to Stephen Harper in the lobby of the House of Commons. Parliament was about to rise for the summer. After it returned in September, Jean Chrétien would step down as Liberal leader in favour of Paul Martin, who would almost certainly call an election in 2004. The polls had the Liberals at over 50 per cent.

"You and I have to talk," MacKay said.[17] Then let's talk, Harper replied. It had started.

TEN

Union

Why merge now? The timing seemed wrong. Both Stephen Harper and Peter MacKay had only recently won the leadership of their respective parties. An election was only a year away, maybe less. There was a good argument for Harper to try his luck with an election, hoping that the result would leave the Progressive Conservatives so weakened that the remnant would have no choice but to let itself be absorbed by the larger party. For his part, MacKay had seen that the PCs still had strength in rural Ontario, courtesy of Perth–Middlesex. Polls showed that most voters who inclined Liberal had the Progressive Conservatives as their second choice. If the Tories could make significant gains in Ontario in the 2004 vote, then at the very least they would be able to negotiate a merger from a position of strength.

But in reality, both parties desperately needed to unite. The Paul Martin juggernaut was coming, threatening to erode the Alliance base in the West and potentially obliterate the Progressive Conservative base in Atlantic Canada. The polls in June 2003 had both parties in the mid- to low teens, and both Harper and MacKay faced the prospect of leading a party that would be weaker after the election, threatening their leadership. For MacKay, the situation was particularly grim. Any serious seat loss would deprive the PCs of party standing in the House of Commons, putting them right back to where they were after the 1993 election, this time with

virtually no hope of a comeback. Senior figures in the Conservative move-
ment – Brian Mulroney; former cabinet ministers Don Mazankowski and
Barbara McDougall; current and former premiers such as Ralph Klein,
Bernard Lord, Mike Harris, and Bill Davis; and senators such as David
Tkachuk and Gerry St. Germain – were all publicly or privately urging
talks. St. Germain had crossed the floor from the PCs to the Alliance in
2000, in despair over Clark's leadership and the Tories' dismal prospects.
Belinda Stronach, scion of Frank and CEO of auto parts maker Magna
International, was working the phones and the backrooms, offering to help
facilitate a merger. Hugh Segal, now at the Institute for Research in Public
Policy, was also pushing for talks. The party rank and file had made it clear
they were sick of campaigning against fellow conservatives. Conservative
fundraiser Irving Gerstein had worked miracles with the party's finances,
selling the headquarters in Ottawa and restructuring the debt. But the deal
with David Orchard and the threat that the Tories might reverse themselves on free trade had effectively ended any hope of funding from the
business community. The "party was bereft," Segal observed after the
fact, "with too little traction or relevance in the business capitals to mount
a campaign."[1]

Most important of all, Preston Manning and Joe Clark were both gone
from the scene. Each was so hated by partisans on the other side – Manning
had shattered the conservative coalition; Clark was a Liberal in all but
name – that reunion was impossible while either held sway over either
party. But now Stephen Harper was leading the Alliance. He was moderate
(for a former Reformer), bilingual, pragmatic, and eager to deal. MacKay
was young, a strong voice for Atlantic Canada, and fresh off his leadership
win. Yes, there was that deal with the devil David Orchard. But MacKay
had gotten the word *talks* stripped out of the no-merger clause. So there
would be nothing wrong with talking. And as for a merger itself, well, the
party membership would have the final say.

Even before their brief conversation in the House of Commons opposition lobby, each leader had been sending the other signals. On June 16, at
a party fundraiser, Harper launched his "common cause" initiative, arguing that the Alliance and PCs should field joint candidates in the next
campaign. Three days later, at a speech to party loyalists, MacKay replied,

"I'm open and I'm interested" in talks aimed at fielding joint candidates, at least in some ridings.[2] After that brief exchange in the opposition lobby, Harper and MacKay met in Belinda Stronach's office at Magna International in Toronto on June 26. They agreed to exploratory talks, with Labour Day as the deadline for moving ahead or calling the whole thing off.

Each party appointed three emissaries to conduct the talks. For the Alliance, Harper selected Ray Speaker, the former Alberta cabinet minister and Reform MP; Gerry St. Germain, who had ties to both camps; and Scott Reid, his loyal Ontario MP who would liaise with caucus. MacKay asked Bill Davis, Don Mazankowski, and Newfoundland and Labrador MP Loyola Hearn, who was PC House leader, to represent the Tories. All six agreed to take on the assignment, but Davis and "Maz," as Mazankowski was affectionately known, had busy schedules, and it was August 21 before all six representatives met in person, at a hotel near the Toronto airport. At that meeting, Mazankowski dropped a bombshell: The Progressive Conservatives were willing to negotiate a full merger of the two parties. The talks should not be about cooperation. The talks should be about union.

When the Alliance team reported the proposal to Harper, it seemed like a dream come true. Any merger would really be a takeover of the small, weak Progressive Conservative Party by the much larger Canadian Alliance. But time was running out. Martin would be prime minister in four months. As well, Chrétien, responding to the sponsorship scandal, had brought in new legislation severely restricting corporate donations to political parties. Instead, parties would mostly be publicly funded based on the results of the popular vote in the last election. With 40.8 per cent of the vote in 2000, the Liberals would have more money to campaign with than the Alliance (25.5 per cent) and the Progressive Conservatives (12.2 per cent) combined. But if the parties merged, they would at least be able to put up a credible fight. Harper's instruction to the negotiating team was explicit: Give up anything, if you must, but get a deal. Well, almost anything. The new party must be called the Conservative Party. And the new leader must be directly elected by the party membership. Everything else was on the table.

The two men could not have been more different: MacKay steeped in the PC tradition (his father Elmer had been a cabinet minister in Brian

Mulroney's government); Harper a son of Reform. MacKay a proud Maritimer; Harper an adopted Westerner who talked about Atlantic Canada's "culture of defeat." MacKay a rugby-playing jock; Harper a piano-playing geek. Any time Peter MacKay slapped Stephen Harper on the back, Harper must have cringed.

But despite all this, the Alliance leader was wooing the PC leader. Harper knew MacKay would need the most generous terms possible in order to sell the union to his membership, and was willing to do everything within his power to help him. As to who would lead the new party, he was willing to take his chances. With one member, one vote, the Alliance base would overwhelm the Tory ranks, and the Alliance base, Harper calculated, would vote for him.

Talks accelerated, with the surprised Tory negotiators winning round after round. The Alliance team jettisoned the party's resistance to official bilingualism. Instead, "English and French have equality of status in all institutions of the Parliament and Government of Canada," the terms of union declared.[3] The new party would inherit the Conservative Party's name, minus the "Progressive." The party would be one that "reaches out to all Canadians, not just like-minded conservatives," and would strike "a balance between fiscal accountability, progressive social policy, and individual rights and responsibilities." Joe Clark could have written that one. Specifically, the party would embrace universal public health care. No two-tier, once and for all. There were no provisions for citizens' initiatives or referenda. And the Triple-E Senate, the holy grail of the Reform Party, disappeared. Quebec, which had caused so much constitutional and political grief for so many decades, with Tories promoting and Reform opposing special status for the province, wasn't even mentioned.

The merger would be an alliance of "equal partners," even though the Alliance had three score MPs and the PCs a dozen, even though the Alliance had 110,000 members and the PCs only 40,000 (many of them Orchardistas who would bolt for the NDP or the Greens or the Martians if the parties merged). The provincial wings of the Progressive Conservative Party would become the provincial wings of the Conservative Party. Each party would elect the same number of members to the new governing council. The new party would assume the Progressive Conservative Party's debt. (The Alliance was debt-free; Harper had already fulfilled his pledge to put the party in the black.)

But there were roadblocks. Every time the PCs got close to the altar, they hesitated. Their emissaries cancelled one of the planned meetings. Harper sent MacKay his own set of proposals, directly. MacKay rejected them. The two leaders and their House leaders met for dinner on September 14 and agreed to talks that would begin on September 22 and would conclude either with a final agreement or the end of merger discussions completely. But the CBC got word of the talks and ran a story about merger negotiations on September 18.[4] The Tory caucus was in an uproar. MacKay assured them that nothing would be agreed to unless they agreed to it. The talks on September 22 and 23 ended with what the Alliance side thought was an agreement in principle. But on a September 26 conference call, the Tory side balked. They still hadn't offered their own detailed counter-proposal. Harper called off the talks and went public with his frustration, releasing the Alliance proposal he had sent to MacKay. "What we need them to do, if they are serious, is to tell us where they stand," he told reporters. "Otherwise we are at a dead end."[5]

The problem was the leadership selection process. MacKay rightly feared that the one member, one vote system would hand the leadership over to Harper, or someone else from the Alliance side. The union of equals would be a sham. Instead, the Tories proposed a system in which each member of the new party would cast a vote within his or her own riding. Each riding would be awarded a hundred points. If one candidate received 60 per cent of the vote in that riding, he or she would score sixty points in that riding. This meant that a riding in, say, northern Quebec, where only ten votes were cast, would have the same weight as a Calgary riding where thousands of votes were cast. On the one hand, the system would be less democratic; on the other, candidates would be forced to run a truly national campaign. And a candidate from the Progressive Conservative side of the party – Peter MacKay, for instance – would at least have a chance.

Harper wouldn't budge. One member, one vote was sacrosanct within the Reform/Alliance movement, and he certainly had to think twice about abandoning that principle with his leadership on the line. Would he compromise his chances of winning the leadership in order to unite the parties?

On October 8, Harper learned that MacKay was boarding a flight to Toronto after Question Period. He rushed to the airport and boarded the same flight. At the Toronto airport, he urged MacKay to meet with him that evening. That night, at Belinda Stronach's house, Harper offered a compromise. MacKay shook his head. On October 10, Harper counterproposed again. He'd accept the leadership selection formula if the PCs would accept an Alliance formula for adopting policies at the next convention. MacKay turned him down. The two sides kept talking over the Thanksgiving weekend. By now, Harper was convinced the merger would happen. On October 14, a Tuesday, Harper and MacKay talked by phone, with others listening in. Characteristically for both men, Harper was in his constituency office in a strip mall in Calgary; MacKay was in his home in New Glasgow, Nova Scotia, nursing a knee injured in a rugby game. During the conference call, which lasted an hour, it became increasingly clear to everyone that they had a deal. In essence, Harper had caved on everything. Leadership selection, convention votes – the Tories could have it all their way. MacKay was left with absolutely nothing to object to. If Paris was worth a mass, Harper had decided, acquiring the Progressive Conservatives was worth any concession he had to make. The two leaders initialled and released the agreement the next day.

"It's like Christmas," Harper told reporters at the press conference. "I have a reputation of not getting excited too often, but I actually had difficulty sleeping last night."[6]

It was already after Thanksgiving, so there was little time to work with. Both sides had agreed to hold a ratification vote among the members by December 12, and the forces of reaction against the merger were powerful. David Orchard sued, naturally. MacKay had unquestionably broken their contract by agreeing to merge the PCs with the Alliance, violating his written promise. "The Conservative Party of Canada, if formed, would be an illegitimate creation conceived in deception and born in betrayal," Orchard protested the day after the deal was announced.[7] But the legal action went nowhere; courts are traditionally very reluctant to interfere in the internal workings of political parties, and judicial nullification of the merger of two political parties would have been interference of the highest order.

Not surprisingly, Joe Clark wanted nothing to do with the new party. After the merger was completed, Harper and MacKay asked Clark to be interim leader. It would have been a distinguished end to his political career, but Clark not only turned them down, he proceeded to campaign against the merger. "The long-term result would be to make Canadian politics less competitive, by closing down the only national party whose base is broad enough to provide a genuine alternative to Liberal governments," he predicted. He was wrong, for the umpteenth time.[8] When the deal was finally consummated, he left the united caucus to sit as an independent. "This is not my party," Clark said after the merger. "This is something entirely new. . . . I will not be part of this new party."[9] It was the biggest floor-crossing in Canadian history – a former prime minister abandoning his own party – and it got things off to a rocky start.

Other Tories defected as well: André Bachand of Quebec; John Herron of New Brunswick; and, most famously, Scott Brison of Nova Scotia. Bachand retired at the end of the term; Herron ran for the Liberals and lost; Brison ran for the Liberals and won, ultimately becoming a cabinet minister. Brison had no intention of serving under the leadership of a right-wing Albertan, as he saw Harper. Veteran Tory senators Lowell Murray and Norm Atkins also refused to join the new caucus. Manitoba MP Rick Borotsik stayed in caucus but opposed Harper for leader, didn't stand for re-election, and endorsed the Liberals. On the Alliance side, Esquimalt–Juan de Fuca MP Keith Martin joined the Liberals.

The question was whether these defections, coupled with the votes of the Orchard block of PC members, would be enough to prevent ratification of the merger. Harper was confident he had overwhelming support among the Alliance membership, but would the Tory base, what was left of it, prove too Red? But just as the courts shut down any hope of preventing a merger legally, so too a sudden rush to buy Progressive Conservative memberships before the November 15 cutoff swamped the Red Tory ranks. The word on the street, though it was never proven, was that Alliance members were buying PC memberships in order to guarantee ratification. On December 5, 95.9 per cent of Alliance members voted for the merger; the next day,

90 per cent of Progressive Conservatives said yes. There are tin-pot dictators who would envy such results.

Harper now found himself in the same vulnerable position that Preston Manning was in after the Reform Party morphed into the Canadian Alliance. Although he had been Alliance leader for less than two years, he was the face associated with the old party, and with Reform before that. The PC side of the party would be desperate to find a different leader, someone who could transcend the schisms of the past. Someone like Mike Harris, perhaps? Or what about Bernard Lord, the young, bilingual, Quebec-born, New Brunswick–raised dynamic premier of New Brunswick, who had wowed the Edmonton PC convention back in 2002? And then there was Peter MacKay. He was an equal partner in the merger; his campaign team from the spring leadership race could easily be revived; he would certainly be a more appealing face for voters in Atlantic Canada, and possibly in Ontario as well.

Unfortunately for the Ontario PCs, blame for deaths due to tainted water in Walkerton, Ontario, had been laid squarely at the feet of the Harris government, which had loosened health and safety regulations. Harris had stepped down, and his replacement, former finance minister Ernie Eves, had led the party to ignominious defeat at the hands of Dalton McGuinty's Liberals in early October 2003. Besides, Harris didn't know a word of French. After a few days of febrile speculation, he let it be known he wasn't interested. And Bernard Lord had a near-death experience in the province's June 9 election: his majority was so thin that if he resigned to run federally, the government would likely fall. He was only thirty-eight. He'd have another chance, or so it seemed.

Time, or the lack of it, was also on Harper's side. Six days after the PCs voted for union, Paul Martin became prime minister. He could call an election any day. (In light of future events, immediately seeking a fresh mandate might have been a smart move.) The Conservative Party of Canada would hold its leadership vote on March 20, counting on common decency (of which Paul Martin has his fair share) to keep the Liberals from calling an election.

But the best news for Harper was that, after all the agonizing over the leadership selection process, his most dangerous potential opponent decided not to run. MacKay was exhausted from the leadership campaign, the unhappy months of grappling with a party on the brink of extinction, and the emotional turmoil of the merger negotiations. He knew he would have a hard time winning over Alliance supporters in the West. And he had the millstone of the Orchard agreement around his neck. While Red Tories denounced him for betraying that agreement, Blue Tories damned him for signing it in the first place. He decided to bow out. MacKay also would have suffered from something Jim Prentice quickly learned when he tested the waters: nobody in corporate Canada wanted to donate to the campaign of a candidate from the PC side of the party.

That left only two other contestants – both of them highly improbable candidates for either Stornoway or 24 Sussex Drive. Tony Clement had been one of Mike Harris's most loyal and effective cabinet ministers. But he had lost to Ernie Eves in the 2002 leadership contest, the Tories had lost the 2003 election, and he had lost his seat in that election. He had no money, no machine, and a resumé whose last page looked just awful. Running for the leadership of the Conservative Party of Canada would help him transition from provincial to federal politics, but winning that leadership was never in the cards. I met him for breakfast in an Ottawa hotel halfway through the campaign. He had already conceded defeat.

Part of his problem was Belinda Stronach. Yes, the beautiful, wealthy auto parts heiress had decided to run, and she was in it to win it. Stronach was taking a large measure of the credit for bringing the two parties together. (In truth, she deserved a fair measure of credit for getting the two sides to start talking, but after that it was all Harper and MacKay and the emissaries.) She had all the campaign resources money could buy. On the spot, she assembled a team led by veteran political strategist John Laschinger, who had run Peter MacKay's leadership campaign. With money no object, Lasch (as he is known) put together a formidable operation taken largely from Mike Harris's former machine – people who might otherwise have worked for Tony Clement. Anyone who knew that machine knew that names like Deb Hutton, Guy Giorno, and Janet Ecker (who had been in cabinet) were to be reckoned with. Across the country, Stronach had Rod Love, the man behind Ralph Klein's campaigns (and Stockwell Day's, for what it was worth), and Rick Anderson, Ian Todd, and Morten

Paulsen from the Reform/Manning camp. Political operatives this good had to be taken seriously. Most important, the Stronach team bought up every living, breathing Tory organizer in Quebec. Giving in to MacKay on the equality of ridings principle might indeed prove fatal to Harper's chances if Stronach could control most or all of the seventy-five ridings in that province.

Most of all, she lacked baggage, which Harper had already accumulated. There was his historic opposition to any special status for Quebec. Though Harper had mostly avoided social-conservative issues as an MP, he had campaigned against the Chrétien government's plans to legalize same-sex marriage, going so far as to send a letter to twenty-six thousand ministers and other religious leaders, asking them to circulate a petition aimed at stopping the legislation. Though Alliance supporters strongly opposed same-sex marriage, PC supporters were much more inclined to favour it. By running in defence of low taxes and balanced budgets, while protecting the rights of women and sexual minorities, Stronach had the potential to bridge the gap. Based in Toronto, she could expand the reach of the party into urban Ontario. And with all that money, she just might be able to swamp her competitors in membership sales. She was so unknown in political circles that she became a wildcard. As the race got underway, Harper was genuinely worried that Stronach could take the leadership away from him.

He needn't have been. Belinda Stronach proved, hearteningly, that the best political operatives money can buy can't protect a manifestly unqualified candidate from public embarrassment. At her opening speech and press conference to announce her candidacy, her delivery was beyond wooden. She gripped the lectern as though it were a life preserver, interjecting "you know" into every other sentence. She admitted to knowing nothing about military affairs, and as far as the economy was concerned, she believed government should "grow the pie." It didn't help that the reporters in the room were hostile. This neophyte had been endorsed by Bill Davis, Mike Harris, and Ralph Klein. Everyone who was anyone was behind her campaign, either to prevent the Alliance from taking over the PCs, or because they had been bought. Did that entitle her to a shot at becoming prime minister of Canada? As it turned out, all it entitled her to was a speech, a press conference, and a spate of scathing reviews. "Pathetic," declared veteran CTV commentator Craig Oliver, who urged the thirty-seven-year-old political neophyte to "back out of this thing before it becomes a terrible embarrassment."[10]

Harper's strategy was simply to win the same support he had won last time, with largely the same team. But he also liked to quote a line of Tom Flanagan's: "In the first race, we could win by building on strength; in this race we have to address our weaknesses."[11] That meant breaking out of his (and the Alliance's) Western stronghold and building a machine in Ontario, Quebec, and Atlantic Canada. He recruited Michael Fortier, a Montreal investment banker, as campaign co-chair, while expanding the voter ID and GOTV (get out the vote) operations. Provincial co-chairs were added as the campaign progressed. Harper's greatest asset was Doug Finley, who had impressed with his efforts in Perth–Middlesex, despite the disappointing results. Finley was a huge fan of integrating information obtained from membership and donor's lists, combining that data with information obtained from door-to-door canvassing, and pouring it all into databases that made it possible to concentrate on identifying and recruiting potential supporters and donors. Harper made him director of operations for the campaign. The team's other great asset was the Alliance party. Flanagan had been putting together a national campaign operation, including regional campaign machines, to prepare for the 2004 federal election. That entire operation took a leave of absence and went to work for Harper. With that much firepower, how could you lose?

And in fact, Harper couldn't lose. He was overwhelmingly the logical choice for leader among the three candidates. Clement's team was so incensed at getting knee-capped by Stronach that it virtually became a surrogate team for Harper. Stronach learned (as Laschinger had warned her) that it's no easy thing to recruit members to a political party, and it's even harder to get them to mail in a ballot. The challenge is triply difficult if your strategy is Quebec-based and the candidate speaks no French and has no other meaningful basis of appeal. And as the campaign unfolded, Stronach's weaknesses only became more manifest. She was weak on policy, weak on communications, weak on – well, you name it.

Harper had also crafted a sly, clever strategy to limit Stronach's appeal by painting her as a child of privilege who was out of touch with the values of ordinary Canadians. And he did it without ever mentioning her name. "I warn you that I am no Paul Martin," Harper declared at his splashy campaign kick-off on January 12, 2004.

I have not been packaged by an empire of pollsters and media managers. I have not been groomed by the experts and the influential. I was not born into a family with a seat at the cabinet table. I grew up playing on the streets of Toronto, not playing in the corridors of power. When I left home for Alberta, I had to get a job. I wasn't on loan to the corporate elite. I'll never be able to give my kids a billion-dollar company, but Laureen and I are saving for their education. And I have actually cooked them Kraft Dinner – I like to add wieners. When my family goes on vacation, it isn't in a corporate executive jet. I pay for a ticket and we stand in line to get a seat with everyone else.[12]

This was as close to a public persona as Stephen Harper would be able to muster: the ordinary guy, the family man who gets his coffee at Tim Hortons (or would, if he drank coffee) and his hamburgers at Harvey's. A hockey dad. He would cultivate that persona with limited success. Stephen Harper in a sweater looked no more natural and at ease with himself and the world than Stephen Harper in a suit. But if the ploy failed to convince voters that he was your next-door neighbour who sat in coach with everyone else, shoving his carry-on under the seat, it at least reminded voters that he came from where they came from, that his values were fundamentally their values, and that his opponents' emphatically were not. He said it about Paul Martin, though everyone knew he was talking about Belinda Stronach. It worked for him then, and it would work for him later against Martin, Stéphane Dion, and, especially, Michael Ignatieff. The strategy only began to fail when he painted the same portrait of Justin Trudeau. By then, voters had stopped caring.

If Harper needed any more help, and he didn't, nomination races were underway for the new party in the lead-up to the expected election. Most of the candidates were pro-Harper, and any members they signed up to vote for their nomination became de facto Harper supporters as well, though it doesn't appear that many of them voted. In fact, when the results were released on March 20, at a rather tepid celebration in Toronto, only 47 per cent of eligible voters had cast ballots. The results appeared ideal: under the hundred-points-per-riding system, Harper secured 56.2 per cent of the points; Stronach earned 34.5 per cent; Clement garnered 9.4 per cent. The victory was seen as a solid win for Harper, but also as a respectable performance by Stronach, showing that the Progressive Conservative side of the party had voting clout and would have to be taken seriously. But in fact, the result only convinced Harper of the distortions that the equality of ridings principle had introduced into the race. He had actually taken 69 per cent of votes cast, while Stronach had taken only 26 per cent. In a closer race, a candidate could easily lose on points while winning the popular vote. But efforts to correct this anomaly would bring Harper only grief.

The vote mattered in another context not really grasped at the time. Despite doing badly, Tony Clement didn't walk away from the new Conservative Party. Neither did other Mike Harris Conservatives. Clement blamed Stronach, not Harper, for his poor showing. Everyone looked upon the new Conservative Party as a merger of the Canadian Alliance and the Progressive Conservatives. In fact, it was a tripartite union of those two and the "Mike Harris Party." The results of the leadership race convinced those Ontario PCs that the party was for real, Stephen Harper was for real, and it was time to sign on. Harper would benefit enormously from this down the road.

On the day of the vote, Harper kept to his hotel room, sending Flanagan over to the convention to collect the vote totals. As was typical for Harper, there were no celebrations afterward. The next morning, the entire team was on its way to Ottawa to prepare for a national campaign that could be underway any day.

In the space of less than two years, Stephen Harper had waged a campaign to become leader of the Canadian Alliance, fought and won the by-election in Calgary Southwest, convinced Peter MacKay to merge his party with the Alliance, and won the leadership of the new Conservative Party of Canada. He deserved a vacation, but of course he didn't take one. The past was prelude: the real race was about to begin. Harper was about to take his first shot at becoming prime minister. Amazingly, he appeared to have a credible chance. Because against every expectation, including his own, the Liberal juggernaut had gone into the ditch.

On November 14, 2003, at Toronto's Air Canada Centre, Paul Martin greeted about eight thousand adoring delegates, virtually every single one of whom was there because they supported him as leader. The highlight of what was purportedly a leadership convention, but was really a love-in, was Bono's speech. U2's front man confessed, "I'm a little shy – you know, I'm not used to speaking to crowds of less than 25,000," but he managed anyway. "It's not just that everybody likes Canada," he told the adoring throng. "Everybody respects Canada because something is going on here. You've avoided a stigma that's attached to the West . . . that other parts of the world regard with such suspicion."[13]

For his part, Martin promised delegates a Canada transformed. "I believe that we are at a moment of great opportunity, and that we have the national will and the sense of purpose to seize it," he told the crowd and the nation watching on TV. "This country belongs to us, and we belong to it."[14] What did that mean? Who cared? Paul Martin was going to heal his party's wounds and the nation's divisions by sweeping every region of the country in an election landslide. He predicted it himself, during a golf game with Brian Mulroney, industrialist Paul Desmarais, and George Bush Sr.[15] No one – not Martin, not the others in the foursome, not Martin's band of senior advisors, not the opposition, not the press gallery – no one expected any other result in November 2003.

Of course, there was the irritant of Sheila Fraser's upcoming report on the sponsorship program. The original release date of November 2003 had been delayed because Jean Chrétien prorogued Parliament to give the new administration a clean slate. The new release date was February 12, 2004. Martin had two months as prime minister to prepare.

As the February date approached and the press was increasingly filled with stories about what the audit might reveal, Martin and his advisors debated the best approach. Try to minimize the impact by simply handing everything over to the RCMP and then saying the government can't comment on an ongoing investigation? Or meet the challenge head on? The advantage of the latter approach was that it would allow Martin to isolate himself from events that happened on Jean Chrétien's watch. Martin had been campaigning against Chrétien for years. Blaming him for everything that was wrong with the party and the country was in his DNA and that of his advisors. The message track would be: This is all about a few Chrétien Liberals and their cronies doing Lord knows what in Quebec, and we're going to find out what they were up to and fix it.

What Team Martin couldn't quite grasp was that they were facing an avalanche of bad news. The report was overwhelmingly damaging to the Liberals. A hundred million dollars had gone missing. It was supposed to have been spent sponsoring events in Quebec. It hadn't. Where had the money gone? That wasn't a job for an auditor. The same day that the report was released, Martin announced a public inquiry headed by Quebec judge John Gomery into the sponsorship program. The prime minister vowed to find out who had robbed the public purse, to get the money back, and to throw the book at the offenders.

The problem with this approach was simple but damning: Martin had been finance minister throughout the debacle. How could he not have known what was going on? He tried to answer this question the next day. "Some can't understand how as a Quebec minister I could not have known about the conduct of this program," he said at a press conference, reading a prepared text. "Well, the fact is that very few Quebec ministers did. Furthermore, it is no secret that I did not have an easy relationship with those around the former prime minister. It stemmed primarily from the fact that we held different views on Quebec," as a result of which, "my advice was not routinely sought on issues related to Quebec."[16] Lame.

How lame? On January 1, 2004, the Liberals stood at 51 per cent in the polls. By mid-February they had dropped to 36 per cent. The Liberals have never gotten that lost support back. Not even to today.

The only party ready for an election in April 2004 was the NDP, under its new leader, Jack Layton, the moustachioed former Toronto councillor who combined eye-twinkling charm with a fierce determination to revive the New Democrats as a credible national party, and who tended to be underestimated as a silk-stocking socialist dilettante. Notwithstanding Sheila Fraser's report, the Liberals should have been ready: Paul Martin had been chasing the job of prime minister for half a decade; he had been Liberal leader since November 2003 and prime minister since December. But the campaign was supposed to have centred on obtaining a national mandate to govern as a truly national party by winning new seats in Quebec and Western Canada. It had not been geared toward sheer survival, and as the fallout from the findings on the sponsorship program accumulated, survival was the new, frightening goal for Martin and the Board. As for Stephen Harper and his team, they were exhausted: Over the past two and a half years, they had waged a campaign for the leadership of the Canadian Alliance, for the Calgary Southwest by-election, and then for the leadership of the new Conservative Party. Now they faced a formidable Liberal machine and a party with all the advantages of incumbency. Their own party, which was days old, had no settled policies, little infrastructure, and a campaign team that desperately needed a vacation. Instead, they upped the pace.

Ian Brodie completed his M.A. and Ph.D. in political science at the University of Calgary in the early 1990s and so got to know Stephen Harper, Tom Flanagan, and the Calgary School. He was teaching at the University of Western Ontario when the Perth–Middlesex by-election was called, and he commuted from London to help with the campaign. The thin, intense but cheerful and dedicated conservative enjoyed the grunt work of a constituency campaign, and soon was considered part of the Harper team. By March 2003, he was executive director of the Alliance and one of Harper's most trusted aides. He ran the 2004 leadership campaign tour, improvising as he went along. After the victory, Harper dispatched Finley and Brodie – they had become a team – to organize the new Conservative Party headquarters, a nondescript floor of a nondescript office building a few blocks from Parliament Hill. The new party, because it was a new party, had no field or fundraising operations in place. No one there even knew how to charter a bus or plane. Ken Boessenkool had been working on a policy platform during the leadership campaign and was now in charge of policy, strategy, and communications, which included beating the platform into the heads of former Alliance and PC MPs seeking re-election, as well as those of the newbies who had won nominations in ridings not formerly held by Conservatives. And who were these newbies? Were there any anti-Semites, homophobes, former criminals, or just basically unsavoury characters among them? Finley, who was in charge of field operations, set out to find out. Tom Flanagan, as campaign manager, worked with Harper and others on the advertising strategy.

Harper demanded that Martin delay an election until fall because, well, just because. He couldn't readily admit that his own party was in no position to campaign. He knew that if he were Paul Martin, he would take advantage of the Conservatives' disorganization just as Jean Chrétien had taken advantage of the new Alliance's lack of preparedness in 2000. To his surprise – and Harper afterward told anyone who would listen that he thought it was the single biggest mistake Paul Martin ever made – Martin did delay, at least for a few weeks. He couldn't wait any longer than that. A six-month delay might reverse the shaky polls, but Chrétien-era cabinet ministers and MPs had signalled they wouldn't be running again. If they were asked to stay on another six months, some would just quit, forcing dangerous by-elections. Besides, the Liberals didn't have much in the way of a governing agenda. They had been preparing for an election campaign, not a Throne Speech. And yet, the longer Martin waited, the better the chances that the turmoil surrounding the sponsorship affair would subside. Gripped by an indecisiveness that would prove characteristic, Martin delayed the spring election until almost the last possible minute, then had Parliament dissolved on May 23, with an election set for June 28. That window gave the Conservatives the time they needed to prepare. Well, almost.

The Liberals used the weeks between Harper becoming leader of the Conservative Party and the dropping of the writ to attack the new leader over the many things he'd said during his days as a Reformer and his time at the National Citizens Coalition. But the most effective attacks centred on Harper's position on Iraq. When Jean Chrétien had announced that Canada did not, could not, and would not support the American-led coalition that was planning to topple Saddam Hussein, Harper had delivered one of his most powerful speeches of protest in the House of Commons.

On March 20, 2003, as coalition forces prepared to invade Iraq, Harper rose to berate the Chrétien government's decision not to support the invasion. The operation lacked United Nations sanction, Chrétien had said, the case that Iraq was seeking to manufacture chemical weapons had not been sufficiently made, and the Canadian population (certainly in Quebec and in much of Ontario) did not support invasion. Harper, in rebuttal, was at his most eloquent. "This government, in taking the position it has taken, has betrayed Canada's history and its values," he told the House of Commons.

> Reading only the polls and indulging in juvenile and insecure anti-Americanism, the government has, for the first time in our history, left us outside our British and American allies in their time of need. However, it has done worse. It has left us standing for nothing, no realistic alternative, no point of principle and no vision of the future. It has left us standing with no one. Our government is not part of the multilateral coalition in support of this action and it has not been part of any coalition opposing it; just alone, playing irrelevant and contradictory games on both sides of the fence.

"This is not an act of independence," he concluded. "In fact, as we find ourselves isolated from our allies, we find ourselves under the government more dependent on them than ever before, economically, culturally and, of course, militarily."[17]

But Harper had wandered into quicksand. Unlike the Liberal prime minister, he lacked decades of experience on the world stage, taking the measure of other leaders and their agendas. Harper's agenda came from the *Economist*, and the *Economist* was behind the invasion. Harper and the *Economist* (and the *New York Times* and this writer) were wrong. By 2004, Iraq was clearly turning into a quagmire, and Chrétien's refusal to allow Canada to be dragged into it seemed inspired. The Liberals accused Harper of being a warmonger who would have embroiled Canada in an unwinnable conflict. Not so, Harper replied; the Alliance only wanted Canada to offer moral support, and besides, the Liberals had left the armed forces so run down that no other support would have been possible. But that's not what Harper was saying in 2003, and when Tonda MacCharles of the *Toronto Star* reminded him, he became visibly angry, offering Canadians their first glimpse of the soon-to-be-notorious Harper temper. The Liberals had scored a hit.

There were bigger problems. Election laws allowed the party to spend $17.5 million on the campaign, and chief fundraiser Irving Gerstein had cleared the campaign to spend the full amount. But the Alliance had never run a national campaign, and the Progressive Conservatives had become so weak that they had also focused on areas of strength and potential growth. The party had only weeks to come up with a national tour, a national advertising campaign, and support for candidates in formerly no-go regions, especially Quebec. Talent was also an issue. Flanagan, for example, was by nature and profession a university professor, not a campaign strategist. Brodie likewise. There was talent to be found in the Stronach and Clement camps, but no time to identify and integrate potential assets. Even Harper, despite his political and marketing skills, was unfamiliar with running as a party leader in a general election. But the biggest problem was not the campaign mechanics or money or readiness. The biggest problem was that no one expected the Conservatives to win, including the Conservatives. If you don't expect to win, you don't plan for it.

Remarkably, none of that mattered, at first. Because Team Harper had been through so many campaigns, and because everyone knew and trusted everyone, the infrastructure came together quickly, including setting up and staffing a war room, identifying winnable ridings and flowing support to those riding campaigns from head office, and establishing an advertising campaign, with ads in the bank ready for the launch. The campaign platform, "Demand Better," was leaked before it was ready to be released, but the press was favourable. The centrepiece was a 25 per cent tax cut for middle-income Canadians, along with a two-thousand-dollar tax deduction for each child. There was also money for infrastructure and for research and development, to be paid for by limits to the growth in government spending and an end to corporate subsidies (an essential plank in many conservative campaign platforms, though not in any conservative governing agenda). There were commitments to toughen criminal penalties and eliminate the long-gun registry, and a promised one-billion-dollar increase in defence spending, with more to come.

In the end, Team Harper was "almost miraculously well prepared" for the election, Flanagan later judged, "considering how little time was available."[18] There was money, a budget, a television advertising campaign (at least for the opening of the campaign), a fully scheduled tour with the logistics worked out, a properly staffed war room – even a platform. And there was CIMS (the Constituent Information Management System) – the Conservative Party of Canada's inheritance from the grassroots nature of the Reform Party. Because Reform could never rely on big corporate donations, it had to raise money through a large number of small donations by party supporters. That, along with the populist nature of Reform, got the Reform, Alliance, and Conservative parties thinking hard about their base – talking to it, listening to it, and counting on it for political and financial support. It also encouraged the creation of a database that allowed the party to track first its own supporters, and then the larger voting public. CIMS was still in its infancy in the 2004 campaign. But it would grow in size and sophistication with every election and every fundraising quarter.

In the beginning, things went well. The negative ad "Carousel" showed janitors throwing bags of money into the dumpster while calliope music played. Other ads emphasized Harper as a caring, competent, trustworthy leader ready to govern. The tour proceeded smoothly, with Harper condemning Liberal waste and mismanagement, while also rolling out major chunks of the forty-four-page platform. Meanwhile, the Liberal campaign – "Choose Your Canada" – was relentlessly negative, as Martin warned of Harper's "hidden agenda," of extreme social conservatism and U.S.-style private health care. The net effect actually increased support for the Conservatives, who went from about three points behind the Liberals at the start of the campaign to being tied or slightly ahead by week three. The best asset, at least at first, was Harper himself.

Elections are occasions when the great body of the Canadian electorate who do not follow politics from day to day acquaint themselves with any new arrivals to the scene. So there was a new conservative party led by a new guy who wanted to become prime minister. He was tall, really heavy, with a helmet of greying medium-brown hair. Fleshy, almost pouty lips. Intense blue eyes. A strong jaw that saved him from having a double chin. A stooped slouch for a walk.

Harper's singsong way of speechifying got better over time – at his best he could actually speak quite powerfully. But he could never convince anyone that his public voice was his real voice, because it clearly wasn't.

Jack Layton, Michael Ignatieff, Justin Trudeau, and their ilk were born with the gift or honed the skill of speaking naturally. Harper never did. It contributed to the public perception – an accurate one – that he didn't enjoy public speaking, or public anything for that matter. But he was clearly smart, and strangely comfortable in his own skin. The public discomfort actually worked in his favour, making him seem less like a born politician, less of a narcissist who craved applause. More like an accountant, really. And after two decades of Brian Mulroney, Jean Chrétien, and now Paul Martin, and in the wake of the sponsorship scandal, an accountant might be just what the country needed.

The closed nature of Canadian politics, in which only the party faithful choose the leader, makes it possible for a Stephen Harper to emerge and lead. He would never have survived the caucuses and primaries through which Americans choose their leaders. Whether countries are better led by technocrats or by charismatics is beyond the scope of our tale. But to anyone who has watched both of them, it's no surprise that, of all the G8 leaders, the one Harper personally got on with best is Germany's dour but exceedingly competent Angela Merkel.

In the leaders' debates, Stephen Harper delivered a calm, measured performance that reinforced his stature as a potential prime minister. The polls showed the Conservatives steadily climbing, opening a real gap between themselves and the lagging Liberals. A majority Conservative government, which had seemed inconceivable at the start of the campaign, now appeared possible. On June 10, halfway through the campaign, the *Globe and Mail*'s Jane Taber got a huge scoop. Liberal campaign chair David Herle, in a conference call with fellow Liberal campaigners across the country, had declared, "We are in a spiral right now that we have to arrest."[19] (Unknown to Herle, someone had given Taber the access code to the conference call, allowing her to listen in.)

The Liberals set out to arrest that slide with the most negative television ads ever aired on Canadian television. Those who believe that the Conservatives sank to new lows with their ads attacking Stéphane Dion and Michael Ignatieff should refresh their memories via YouTube. While the Conservatives were undoubtedly effective in branding the future Liberal leaders with saturation pre-writ advertising, in terms of the actual content of the ads, the Tories have never come close to the public slandering Harper received in, for example, the Liberal "Truth" ad.

It opened with tanks rolling across a desert and an aircraft carrier plowing through seas as a woman narrator solemnly intoned, "Stephen Harper would have sent our troops to Iraq." [Debatable, though he did support the invasion.] "He would spend billions on tanks and aircraft carriers." [*Aircraft carriers?*] With a pistol pointed straight at the viewer, the narrator warns that the Conservatives would weaken Canada's gun laws [the Conservatives did promise to scrap the long-gun firearms registry] and scrap the Kyoto accord. [They did, years later.] Then: "He'd sacrifice Canadian-style health care for U.S.-style tax cuts." [No. The Conservatives had committed to protecting health care funding and the public health care system.] As a woman rocked back and forth on the floor in a hospital corridor, the ad claimed, "He won't protect a woman's right to choose." [Utterly false. Harper had vowed that a Conservative government would take no action on abortion rights or services.] "And he's prepared to work with the Bloc Québécois." [Huh? As it would turn out, all parties worked with the Bloc at one time or another in the minority government that resulted.] "Stephen Harper says that when he's through with Canada, you won't recognize it. You know what? He's right."[20]

"When I'm through with Canada, you won't recognize it." Everyone knows Stephen Harper said that. Every second anti-Harper post on the comment threads quotes it to this day. The Liberal attack ad asserted it. But it's false. The closest Harper ever came to saying anything like the contents of that quote was his victory speech at the 2004 Conservative convention. In that speech, he declared: "We can create a country built on solid Conservative values, not on expensive Liberal promises – a country the Liberals wouldn't even recognize."[21] He has, and perhaps they don't, but that statement is light years from the one in the "Truth" ad. Yet it has become the political equivalent of the urban myth.

"U.S. style attack ads came to Canada with a vengeance in the June election,"[22] Jonathan Rose at Queen's University wrote after the dust had settled. He went on to describe the Liberal ads as "savage" and warned that Canadians "have every reason to fear that attack ads of such ferocious intensity, in which all pretence of decency is abandoned, may become a permanent and negative part of our political culture."

But the ads did their job, causing swing voters to think twice about swinging Conservative. On top of that, the Conservatives were running out of gas. Lacking time and resources – and not convinced they could win anyway – Flanagan and company had only put together a script for the first half of the campaign, planning to improvise once they had a sense of how things were going. But that meant they had nothing in place to build on the Conservatives' momentum. They lacked the experience and flexibility that veteran campaigners would have brought to an opposition-party campaign under relentless bombardment from the governing party. Worst of all, they lacked a script: Harper had already announced and re-announced every sentence in the platform. If the Tories didn't have anything to offer about themselves, reporters happily accepted the material sent along from their opponents. The Liberals pounced on a spate of Tory "bozo eruptions" (first coined in the Bill Clinton years) from candidates who seemed to confirm that the Harper Conservatives were a bunch of right-wing wing nuts with a hidden agenda that they would spring on an unsuspecting public if they were ever trusted with power.

There was rural Ontario MP Cheryl Gallant comparing abortion to the terrorist beheading of a hostage. There was B.C. MP Randy White telling a documentary filmmaker that the Conservative Party could use the not-withstanding clause of the constitution to roll back court-mandated rights for homosexuals. "To hell with the courts!" is how he colourfully put it.[23]

Worst of all, there was Stephen Harper himself. John Weissenberger has noted that, as an essentially introverted person, Harper needs time to himself. He prefers a predictable routine around eating and sleeping, with a minimum of disruptive travelling. He is not now, nor has he ever been, comfortable with travel. The election campaign involved nothing but travel, little sleep, constant interaction with other people, and little time alone. As the weeks went by, the strain started to show. Harper was becoming increasingly ill-tempered, especially when it became clear that there really was no script in place for the last phase of the campaign.

Bend turned to break on June 17, eleven days before polling day. Back in 1999, the British Columbia Supreme Court had decreed that "artistic merit" could be a defence in some instances where someone was in possession of child pornography. Ever since, the Alliance had been trying to get that loophole closed, while Liberal governments were content to let it alone. On June 17, media reported that a pedophile had told the court that child pornography had led him to kidnap, rape, and murder a little girl, Holly Jones. The Tory war room decided to use the new hook to contrast the Conservative and Liberal stands on child pornography. Unfortunately, the headline of the news release, which was itself poorly worded, was "Paul Martin Supports Child Pornography?" It was as vile, at least, as anything the Liberals had thrown at the Conservatives. Harper should have disowned it. Paul Martin wasted no time telling reporters that Harper had reached a new low. "This is personal," he told reporters, quietly. "I am a father and I am a husband. And he has crossed the line and should apologize."[24]

Indeed he should have, and moved on. Instead, during a quick conference call with his communications team, Harper leaped on the advice of his young advisors to double down. (Tom Flanagan, who wasn't on the call, later joked that if the advisors had been married as long as he had, they'd have known that the best way to handle any situation is to just apologize.)[25] The press release was recalled and reissued with a less offensive headline. But Harper refused to apologize. Instead, trapped by the side of the campaign bus in Drummondville, Quebec, surrounded by reporters barraging him with hostile questions, he lashed back. When Robert Benzie of the *Toronto Star* asked him if it was in "bad taste" to link Paul Martin to child pornography, even as a sensational trial was underway, Harper shot back, "What's in bad taste is the Liberal Party's record on child pornography. And I will not make excuses for it, and I will attack them on it, and if they want to fight the rest of the election on it, good luck to them."[26]

That night, before the story had made the national news, the Tories' internal polling showed them at 41 per cent support, more than enough for a majority government. A day later, it was 31 per cent.[27] More than anything else, that press release, and Harper's bitter defence of it, cost him the election. He was devastated, withdrawing into himself, refusing even to talk to senior staff. No one could even get him to discuss strategy for the last week of the campaign. He was at the lowest point that those closest to him had ever seen.[28]

As the momentum shifted, the veteran Liberal organizers improvised, something the Conservatives seemed unable to do. On the final day before the vote, Martin campaigned frantically, dipping his toe in the Atlantic in the morning and in the Pacific in the evening, with several stops across the country in between. Harper should have been doing the same thing. But he was inside himself now, avoiding reporters and campaigning with little energy, and he ended the campaign in Alberta, in what was supposed to have been a triumphal return home, rather than in Ontario, where votes were up for grabs.

Still, it was a surprise: With 36.7 per cent of the vote, Paul Martin had won a minority government, with 135 seats. A juggernaut it was not, but it was at least an unqualified win. The Tories had dropped back farther than they had expected, to 99 seats and 29.9 per cent of the vote, only four points better than Stockwell Day's performance in 2000. With 15.7 per cent of the vote and 19 seats, Jack Layton had pulled the NDP out of its decade of decline.

Harper was crushed by the result. He had allowed himself to imagine that he might form a government, at one point even speculating publicly that he could win a majority. (That in itself was a mistake.) He had a transition team at work planning the move into the Langevin Block and 24 Sussex Drive. And in the end, he hadn't even cracked 30 per cent.

"I'm always willing to serve, so I'm going to take a little bit of time with my family," he told reporters on the campaign plane the next day, when someone asked whether he would stay on as leader. "And obviously I'm already talking to people across the country."[29] That was enough to launch a spate of stories speculating on whether Stephen Harper was going to quit.

Either way, he had some serious thinking to do.

ELEVEN

Winning

No one on Stephen Harper's team thought for a moment that he might quit after losing the election. His public ruminations about considering his options, Tom Flanagan believes, were simply a ploy "to test sentiment in the party. If there was to be any attempt to overthrow him, he wanted to flush it out early."[1] But the members and the caucus were happy with his leadership, as they should have been. The Conservatives had lost because they had initially not expected to win. Their goal had been to establish a beach head in Ontario and hold the tottering Liberal juggernaut to a minority government. Not only was Paul Martin's government reduced to a minority, it was weak and unstable, requiring the consent of two opposition parties to survive any vote of confidence. And the Conservatives had picked up twenty-four seats in Ontario, compared to two for the Alliance in 2000 (when the PCs had been shut out).

Still, Harper kept a low profile in the summer of 2004, and part of the reason was that he was licking his wounds. Apart from his hopeless-cause quest for a seat in Parliament in 1988, he had never been beaten in a campaign. It hurt. He went to ground for a few weeks, at least publicly, though he was actually busy crossing the country, often with Laureen, attending endless barbecues and listening to the concerns of the base. Meanwhile, his campaign team generated a blizzard of post-mortem memoranda, while pollster Dimitri Pantazopoulos conducted surveys to determine whether the election campaign had damaged the Conservative brand or the Stephen Harper brand. Short answer: no.

The team drew three broad conclusions. First, the advertising campaign had been woefully inadequate. The next time, there would have to be more of it, it would have to be better, and it would have to be more flexible, with ads that could be written, shot, and released mid-campaign, guerrilla-style, to counter Liberal attacks. The previous advertising firm was let go, and Flanagan recruited Perry Miele, who had done advertising for the Harris Conservatives. Copying the Liberal approach, Miele recruited a team from different firms who would come together to fight the election, and then return to their former jobs.

Second, they needed a platform that had the approval of party members and that would lay to rest the hidden-agenda charge that had damaged them so badly in the last campaign. Rather than work it out exclusively in the OLO, Harper and his advisors charged caucus committees with devising policies on key issues such as taxation, industrial strategy, the environment, and defence. But, as is always the case, the leadership and composition of the committees were tailored to produce outcomes that the leader wanted in the first place. The committee that looked at the Tory commitment to scrap corporate subsidies, for example, soon discovered that eliminating those subsidies would, among other things, sink the aviation industry, especially Bombardier, which was competing with firms in other countries where subsidies were rampant. Since the aviation industry was centred in Quebec, getting rid of the subsidies would also doom any Tory hopes for gains in that province. The committee recommended that the platform be changed and subsidies retained.

Which leads us to the third lesson that the Conservatives drew from the election: they had to get serious about Quebec. This was Harper's own personal priority, one he took so seriously that Flanagan and other advisors complained that the leader was obsessing over Quebec when he should have been focusing more attention on Ontario. But Harper was convinced that he could never win government without attaching the third leg to the stool that had supported Conservative governments in the past: Quebec nationalists, added to Prairie populist conservatives and Ontario and Atlantic Canadian Red Tories.

Harper put himself in charge of the Quebec file. He placed Josée Verner on the OLO payroll. A former political staffer in the Bourassa government, Verner had done well in her campaign to win a seat in Quebec City, coming second to the Bloc. Harper also put Verner in caucus, to give the party a francophone voice, and he hired several staffers from Quebec, charged with creating a separate organizational, advertising, and communications strategy for the province. He also insisted that the party's first policy convention be held in Montreal. Quebec would never again be an afterthought in campaign strategy.

It didn't work, at least at the beginning. Changes as fundamental as making the Conservatives sellable in Quebec take time. The Quebec wing of the Conservative Party would remain small, disorganized, and afflicted with infighting. Harper soon realized he needed a different Quebec lieutenant.

Paul Martin and Jack Layton had the same problem: with only nineteen MPs, the NDP didn't have enough votes in the House of Commons to sustain the government. For previous Liberal minority governments, the key to success was to govern with the support of the New Democrats. Much of the Canadian social safety net had been woven by Liberal prime ministers acting more or less in concert with the NDP leader: Lester Pearson and Tommy Douglas; Pierre Trudeau and David Lewis. But Martin's minority government would need the support of either the Conservatives or the Bloc Québécois to survive any confidence vote.

Layton tried anyway, offering to cooperate with the Liberals in crafting a Throne Speech and a governing agenda that both parties could embrace. But at a meeting at 24 Sussex Drive on August 23, Martin turned him down. "You're two votes short, Jack," he pointed out.[2] So the NDP switched tactics: not long after that failed meeting with Martin, Layton met in Montreal with Harper and Bloc Québécois leader Gilles Duceppe. The three leaders agreed to impose conditions on the upcoming Throne Speech – such as lowering taxes on lower-income Canadians – without which they would bring down the government.

They also agreed to send Adrienne Clarkson a letter, under their joint signature. Dated September 7, 2004, it pointed out to the governor general that "you could be asked by the Prime Minister to dissolve the 38th Parliament at any time."[3] If the GG did receive such a request, they wrote, "this should give you cause, as constitutional practice has determined, to consult the opposition leaders and consider all of your options before exercising your constitutional authority." In other words: If Paul Martin asks you to dissolve Parliament and call an election, please don't do anything until you've talked to us.

Apart from being impertinent – if circumstances warranted, Clarkson might come to the opposition leaders; but it was not for them to come to her, which is why she ignored the missive – it was a mistake, one that would haunt Harper four years later, as he fought off attempts by the other parties to defeat his government and form a Liberal-led coalition. In any event, Martin rejigged his Throne Speech at the last minute to secure Conservative and Bloc support. The only lasting legacy was one of mistrust by each party leader for all the others.

Before that launch of the thirty-eighth Parliament, Paul Martin offered by example an object lesson in how not to manage federal–provincial relations. During the 2004 election campaign, Martin had vowed that, if elected, he would convene a first ministers' meeting that would "fix medicare for a generation." There would be more federal money for health care, he promised, but there would also be clear national goals to improve performance and to measure that improvement. He and the premiers would meet "not just for lunch or dinner or even a weekend, but for as long as it takes to put in place a health care system that is properly funded and clearly sustainable."[4]

For Harper, co-author of the Firewall Letter, the very idea was offensive. In order to balance the budget, the federal government had cut health care funding to the provinces. The cuts led to overcrowded emergency wards, unbearable wait times for essential services, and a chronic shortage of doctors, from general practitioners to specialists. Whether the cuts were necessary or excessive is something that's still being debated, but what could not be debated was that, by 2004, the budget had been balanced for the better part of a decade, and the provinces needed and wanted the money back. But like Jean Chrétien before him, Paul Martin was determined to attach strings to any increase in funding: in particular, some kind of accountability mechanism that would require the provinces to meet goals set by Ottawa in exchange for the returned funds. Health care was a provincial jurisdiction. As far as Harper and the Conservatives were concerned, Ottawa should simply restore the transfers to their proper level and let the provinces get on with it.

The Liberal government had trapped itself. The goal was to wrangle with the premiers until they agreed to Ottawa's terms. Instead, Paul Martin found himself in a room filled with premiers united in purpose. He had agreed to meet "for as long as it takes." Very well. Let's see how long it would take him to cave in to their demands. Those demands were simple: vastly more funding than Martin had originally promised, with absolutely no strings attached. The premiers behaved like a bunch of schoolyard bullies. At one point, they simply refused, en masse, to show up for a meeting, leaving the cameras to pan across the vacant chairs. In the end, Martin had no choice but to give in. Had he won a majority government, he could have adjourned the conference and rebooted the negotiating process. But he was weeks away from convening a minority Parliament; he had to have a deal. In the end, Ottawa promised a forty-one-billion-dollar infusion in health care funding over ten years. The provinces promised to report on how well they were doing in reducing wait times. But it was up to them to decide when and how they would report, and Premier Jean Charest refused to go along in any case, so Ottawa made a separate side deal with Quebec. Some critics, including William Johnson, Stephen Harper's first biographer, complained that the side deal with Quebec opened the door to "asymmetrical federalism," in which each province negotiated separate agreements with Ottawa. He had forgotten that this had always been Stephen Harper's – and Preston Manning's – position: no special status for Quebec, unless that same status is available to every other province.

In any case, Harper drew a far more important lesson about first ministers' conferences: they are a bad idea. They are an especially bad idea if the topic is in an area of provincial jurisdiction. All that results is provincial extortion papered over with mumbles about national standards. "This will never happen when I'm prime minister," Harper told his aides. And it didn't.

In February 2005, the Gomery Commission moved to Montreal, to hear from some of the key players in the province's advertising industry. The commission had already heard that advertising firms in Quebec that were friendly with the Liberal government had taken the government's money in order to promote Canada at cultural events, but that no work was done. Where had the money gone? And who was in charge?

Chuck Guité was the public servant responsible for the program. But he said he was only taking orders, although who he was taking them from was not at all clear. Gomery ordered Jean Chrétien to the stand. Relations were already poisoned between the judge and the former prime minister, after a January interview in which Gomery derided golf balls with Chrétien's name on them, paid for by the program, as "small-town cheap." When Chrétien testified in February, his contempt for the commission, everyone on it, and the prime minister who had created it, was as palpable as his swatting away of questions was masterful. He was proud of his government's efforts to promote national unity in the wake of the 1995 referendum. If mistakes were made or crimes committed, those responsible should be punished. He wasn't to blame. And he ended his testimony by producing from his briefcase a series of autographed golf balls that he had been given by U.S. presidents and other famous figures. If his golf balls were small-town cheap, he parried, then so were Bill Clinton's. Compared to the old lion's performance, Paul Martin's testimony seemed quite believable when he insisted he knew nothing about the sponsorship program because Chrétien never told him anything or asked his advice. The prime minister suddenly seemed very small.

All this, and a federal budget, too. Initially, Harper was willing to vote for the budget, since it ramped up spending on the military and, even better, introduced a phased-in series of cuts to corporate income taxes. But that goodwill evaporated on April Fool's Day, when the Gomery Commission lifted a publication ban on testimony from Jean Brault, the former head of the Montreal ad agency Groupaction. Brault testified – *confessed* would be a better word – that he was part of an intricately organized and thoroughly corrupt money laundering scheme. In exchange for lucrative sponsorship contracts, he would funnel much of the money from those contracts to the Quebec wing of the Liberal Party, while keeping some of the proceeds for himself. So that was it: The sponsorship program was about channelling federal funds to the Liberal Party in Quebec through friendly advertising agencies, with everyone taking a piece of the action along the way. It was appalling, and once again public support for the Liberals plummeted – this time, to well below 30 per cent.

Stephen Harper ordered Tom Flanagan and Doug Finley to accelerate candidate nominations. He was going to change his mind about the budget and force a spring election.

The Tories had just come off a highly successful policy convention in Montreal. The convention had two purposes. The first was to show that the party was serious about appealing to voters in Quebec. To that end, Ian Brodie, Doug Finley, et al. had pushed the skeletal riding associations in that province to send a robust delegation of Quebeckers to the convention. Harper had already given a speech mooting the possibility of devolving some federal authority over culture and communications to Quebec. He unhelpfully held up Belgium, one of the most dysfunctional federations on the planet, as a model. (The French-speaking Walloons and the Flemish are so at odds with each other in that country that it's a major challenge just to put a government together and keep it running.) Pundits and political opponents leapt on the inapt comparison, but Harper's larger point was that a flexible federal system of government shouldn't be afraid to experiment. He was offering Quebeckers an alternative to the Liberal obsession with preserving unity by constraining provincial autonomy. The better way, Harper argued, was for Ottawa to stick to its areas of jurisdiction – fiscal and monetary policy, defence, criminal justice, and the like – and let the provinces be provinces: autonomous in their spheres of jurisdiction, such as health, education, social welfare, and overseeing the municipalities.

The second purpose of the convention was to slay the dragon known as the hidden agenda. At any policy convention, regardless of the party, the goal is the same: to let the delegates openly debate contentious issues, and then engineer a result that suits the party leader. At this, the Conservative management team proved brilliant. Take abortion, for instance, the most contentious issue on the agenda. Many delegates favoured legislation to protect the life of the fetus. But the popular will in Canada favoured preserving a woman's right to choose. And the PC side of the party was as pro-choice as some old Reformers were pro-life. The Liberals used the abortion issue as proof that if Stephen Harper ever became prime minister, he would ram anti-abortion legislation through Parliament. What to do?

Before the convention, caucus unanimously declared that MPs would vote their conscience on any issue related to abortion, regardless of the convention outcome. In his speech to the delegates on Friday night, Harper declared that he would never, ever as prime minister legislate on abortion. In the workshop that first debated the motion, emotions ran high. But when the issue came to a vote at the plenary session, the anti-abortion forces were handily defeated. Case closed.

Same-sex marriage was another potentially schismatic issue. Jean Chrétien had put forward legislation to legalize marriages between two people of the same sex, and then promptly referred the matter to the Supreme Court for review. Meanwhile, provincial courts of appeal were ordering provincial governments to permit same-sex marriage, on the grounds that prohibiting them violated the Charter rights of gays and lesbians to equal treatment before the law. When the Supreme Court affirmed that the legislation was constitutional, Paul Martin reintroduced the bill, and then called for a free vote.

Harper found himself pulled in two directions on same-sex marriage. On the one hand, the social-conservative wing of the party strongly opposed allowing gays and lesbians to marry. And many immigrant Canadians were also skeptical. In China, the Philippines, and India, the three biggest source-countries of immigrants, homosexuality was still socially and legally stigmatized. The Conservatives had launched ads in ethnic media declaring that the party opposed same-sex marriage, hoping to increase support among new Canadians, who traditionally voted Liberal. But opposing same-sex marriage too strenuously would lend credibility to the Liberal portrait of the Conservatives as a bunch of crypto-Republican evangelical rednecks. And it would swing the focus in the next election away from Liberal incompetence and corruption and toward social values and the Charter. What to do?

At that time, Stephen Harper's views on homosexuality matched those held by the roughly half of Canadians who opposed same-sex marriage, according to most polls. He had no particular problem with homosexuality and didn't believe that gays and lesbians should be discriminated against. But neither did he believe they deserved special, specific protection by law or in the Constitution. "Regarding sexual orientation – or more accurately, what we are really talking about, sexual behaviour – the argument has been made by proponents of this position that this is analogous to race and ethnicity," Harper told the House back in September 2003, during an early debate on same-sex marriage legislation. "This position was not included in the Charter of Rights when it was passed by Parliament in 1982," the Alliance leader went on. "It was not included, not because of some kind of accident or oversight. It was not included deliberately and explicitly."[5] In other words, if it was good enough for Trudeau and the other Fathers of Confederation 2.0 not to extend full equality to gays and lesbians, then it should be good enough for us. Apart from Harper's startling deference to Trudeau, what mattered in his speech was the use of the word *behaviour*. Homosexuality was a lifestyle choice, he was saying, and thus not worthy of constitutional protection and certainly not something to be sanctified by letting gay and lesbian couples marry.

Harper's own upbringing, his friends and family, his associates in Calgary, his Reform colleagues, his time at the National Citizens Coalition had all left him isolated. He hadn't met many people who were comfortably gay and conservative, and Harper didn't tend to associate with people who weren't conservative. His views would evolve, just as society's evolved. In his case, that evolution would be influenced by the large number of gays and lesbians who worked for him – during the second administration, people joked that the Prime Minister's Office was in thrall to a gay mafia – and by increased contact in general with people, some of them conservatives, who had become more open about their sexuality. The passage of same-sex marriage legislation in 2005 encouraged that openness; the debate around it encouraged it even more. Today, the Harper government has made championing the rights of sexual minorities part of its foreign policy. The Harper government even supports an underground railroad to spirit Iranian gays and lesbians to Canada, where they are promptly granted refugee status. At the 2005 convention, delegates resolved that any vote on same-sex marriage would be a free vote, with each MP welcome to vote his or her conscience. Case closed.

Official bilingualism (full support, ending what was once a key Reform grievance); recognition of a "fiscal imbalance" between the federal power and the Government of Quebec (the Liberals denied there was such an imbalance); support for supply management (which protected dairy and poultry farmers); elimination of any support for direct democracy, such as citizen recalls of MPs. Case closed, closed, closed, closed.

It all went swimmingly. Harper used a teleprompter for the first time during his big convention speech, markedly improving his delivery, and 84 per cent of delegates endorsed his leadership. The whole thing went off without a hitch, with one very large exception that would come back to haunt the Conservative leader a few weeks later.

Hasting–Frontenac–Lennox and Addington MP Scott Reid was a Harper loyalist of the first order. He worked with Harper on crafting Reform's stand during the 1995 referendum. He contributed heavily to his Alliance leadership campaign. He was Ontario organizer for his Conservative Party leadership campaign. He was one of the emissaries during the merger negotiations. Yes, he had blotted his copybook by ruminating about the wisdom of official bilingualism during the 2004 campaign, but he was still an important figure on the Reform/Alliance side of the party, if only because he had managed to win a seat in Ontario.

So everyone knew that Stephen Harper was backing Reid when he proposed at the policy convention that rules be modified for the next leadership campaign so that very weak ridings didn't have the same voting weight as very strong ones. It was a modified version of the proposition that Harper had fought for and lost during the merger negotiations. When the motion was passed at a workshop session Friday morning, Peter MacKay went straight to the microphones. "This party is in real jeopardy, in my view," MacKay warned.[6] The Conservative Party was founded on the principle of equality of ridings, he told reporters. Without that principle, "there wouldn't have been a merger." Belinda Stronach was also talking to delegates and reporters. She and MacKay had become romantically involved, and their joint opposition threatened to undermine the convention. It dominated news coverage in the Saturday papers, overshadowing Harper's speech.

He was beyond furious, kicking a chair – twice. But there was nothing for it. The weighted-riding proposal was deep-sixed at the plenary meeting, and everything else went down well enough that the press forgot about the spat and concentrated on the party's success at laying the hidden-agenda argument to rest, at least to the extent it ever could be. Back in Ottawa on

Monday, MacKay and Stronach were summoned to the leader's office. Harper employed the management-by-fear approach that Gerry Nicholls had witnessed at the NCC. Besides, he was still really mad. The message was delivered "in salty language and high volume."[7] They had undermined the party leader, and had almost ruined the convention. They had aired an internal disagreement in front of the press (for Harper, a particularly egregious sin). If they had wanted the resolution axed, then they should have worked within the rules and talked to him or his assistants. And he delivered an ultimatum: Are you in or are you out?

MacKay, abashed, apologized and said he was in. But Stronach left in a huff. The daughter of Frank Stronach was not used to being spoken to in that tone of voice. From that moment, both she and Harper knew that a clock was ticking. Harper was convinced that Stronach would soon leave caucus. As a wealthy Toronto businesswoman, he told his aides, she was used to having her own way, and certainly didn't need an MP's salary. Harper was used to having his own way, too. In the past, whenever he didn't get it, he left, and he assumed she would do the same. The problem was, he needed her vote, at least for a few more weeks, to bring down the Martin government.

The revelations of fraud, corruption, and bribery flowing out of the Gomery Commission had crippled the Liberal administration, leaving Paul Martin in mortal danger of defeat in the House and on the hustings. Brault was talking about secret meetings in restaurants in which bags, literally bags, of cash were passed across the table. The Conservatives and the Bloc Québécois were as resolved as ever to force an election. Ian Brodie, as head of the Conservative Party, was trying to whip things into shape, though that shape wasn't encouraging. The platform was complicated, the messaging not well thought out, the scripting half finished. And most of the candidates hadn't been nominated. Harper gave him five weeks to get everything in place.

Desperate, Martin went on television April 21 to plead for a delay. Why not let Judge Gomery complete his work? Why force an election now, when the commission was still underway? He promised he would call an election within thirty days of Judge Gomery's report, which meant sometime in early 2006. "Let Judge Gomery do his work," he pleaded. "Let the facts come out. And then the people of Canada will have their say."[8] It would have sounded more convincing if the Liberals hadn't been trailing the Conservatives in the polls, and if it hadn't already been clear what Gomery's report would conclude.

Martin got partway to salvation by renegotiating the budget, which had yet to be passed in the House, with Jack Layton. The corporate tax cuts were out, replaced with $4.6 billion in new spending on NDP core issues, including housing, post-secondary education, and the environment. With Layton and his party on board, Martin still had to find two votes. The Liberals probed to see if any Conservative MPs might be tempted to cross the floor. The crucial vote was set for May 19.

Bruce Carson had joined Harper's office in August 2004, as director of policy and research. The leader knew some, but not all, of his aide's checkered past, which included disbarment plus a jail term for fraud. But Harper wanted someone on his team to the left of him, from the PC side of the party. Carson had roots there, and he was a loyal and competent aide. He was also a friend of Peter MacKay. On May 17, Ray Novak pulled Carson out of a meeting. Harper needed him immediately: "Stronach is going over to the Liberals," Novak explained as they hurried to Harper's office. "We have to go upstairs and see Peter. He is a mess."[9]

The night before, Stronach had confessed to her boyfriend that she had secretly and successfully negotiated with the Liberals to cross the floor. Things like that can strain a relationship. When Paul Martin entered the National Press Theatre with the new, and single, minister of human resources and skills development, as well as minister for democratic reform, in tow, reporters actually gasped. "The significance of her decision is not that it necessarily alters the outcome of Thursday's vote," Martin insisted, with a straight face, as the press theatre erupted in derisive laughter.

There was still one vote to be found. Everything hinged on Chuck Cadman. The former Reform and Alliance MP had lost the nomination in his Surrey North riding to a challenger, and so had run, and won, as an independent. But by then he already had cancer, and in May 2004 was near death. As a former Reformer, Cadman should have supported the Conservatives. But he also had to consider his pension situation, which would be improved if he remained a sitting MP. And after all, did he want to be remembered as the man who brought down a government?

Carson and other representatives pleaded with Cadman. Later, there were allegations that Tom Flanagan and Doug Finley had offered to provide Cadman a life insurance policy to substitute for the pension that would be lost if Parliament were dissolved, which could be construed as a bribe. There were also claims that Harper might have known of the offer, something he stoutly denied. The Conservatives sued the Liberals over the allegations, but the lawsuit was eventually dropped, no charges were ever laid, and the matter faded from sight. Passions were running high in the third week of May 2005. On May 19, Cadman rose with silent dignity in support of the government. Following parliamentary tradition, Speaker Peter Milliken broke the tie by voting for the government as well. Parliament continued.

In the final days, Harper actually didn't want the government to fall. The party had taken a hit in the polls in the wake of the Stronach defection; he'd be entering the election on a down note. Once again, he and his aides agonized over what they had done wrong. Once again, they had been on the cusp of victory, only to let it slip away.

It had been clear from the get-go that Belinda Stronach would be a challenge. She was a powerful, wilful person with great political ambition but little political experience. Harper could, and should, have kept her close, given her positions of responsibility, sought her counsel, made her feel welcome. She could have been a conduit to the voters in the 905 belt surrounding Toronto, whose support the Conservatives sought so desperately. Instead, he yelled at her, and she yelled back. On May 2, as the caucus debated whether to push for the government's defeat, Stronach told a reporter she thought it was wrong to force a second election in less than a year. Harper was livid. Once again, she had gone to the press rather than having her say behind caucus doors. He summoned her to Stornoway. "You'll never have a future in this party, you're too ambitious," he thundered. "If we lose the confidence vote I will hold you personally responsible."[10] But in fact he was responsible, at least in part, for her defection. He simply couldn't manage his temper and her ambitions. Harper was as intolerant of any challenges to his authority as leader as he had been unwilling to submit to authority when he was younger.

In retrospect, most Conservatives were convinced that losing the vote on May 19 was the best thing that could have happened. "It was a blessing in disguise," Tom Flanagan concluded. With the NDP and Stronach both siding with the Liberals, "the strategic configuration shifted against us," he believed. "We would have been sailing against the current, propelled by an overly detailed platform without dramatic selling points and steered by a scripting team scrambling to get a few days ahead. It would have been hard to win under those circumstances."[11] The Tories still weren't fully prepared for an election. And it was becoming increasingly clear that some personnel changes were in order. The extra six months bought the Conservatives the time they needed to hone a winning campaign.

But at the time, losing the vote hurt like hell.

"I do not believe the party leader is truly sensitive to the needs of each part of the country and how big and complicated Canada is," Stronach said at her press conference with Martin. To which Harper replied: "I've never noticed complexity to be Belinda's strong point."[12] Ouch.

Once again Stephen Harper had "gone dark," as his staff called it: breaking off contact with colleagues and withdrawing into himself. Once again he emerged rejuvenated and determined, launching himself on a summer tour of the barbecue circuit that culminated in an embarrassing photo of him dressed like a cowboy, replete with ill-fitting vest, at the Calgary Stampede. But he was also making changes. Harper and Flanagan agreed that the Calgary prof should step aside as campaign manager in favour of Doug Finley, who had demonstrated greater ability at managing the tactical side of the election operation. But Flanagan also offered Harper some strong advice. The leader's obsession with approving every press release, every detail of election planning, every everything, was creating chaos in the party and in the OLO – which, by the way, was in need of a thorough housecleaning. Harper took that advice. To the extent that this micro-manager was able, he relaxed his grip a bit and let the campaign team be the campaign team.

Ian Brodie moved over from the party office to become chief of staff while Finley focused on organizing the party itself. Together, they convinced Harper to bring Patrick Muttart on board, in charge of strategic planning. As a teenager, Muttart had worked on the Hill for Preston Manning. Then he moved to Navigator, Jaime Watt's powerful communications firm, where he learned the dark arts of polling, advertising, and media management. He was a natural, able to literally envision the potential universe of the Conservatives' voting base and those outside the base who might nonetheless be persuaded to vote for the party. He sharpened the campaign message and stripped the platform down to a few essential bullets. He also drew up a set of archetypal voters who might cast a Conservative ballot, and then fashioned particular messages focused on each archetype. They included Dougie, a young tradesman from a small town, and Eunice, a widow in her seventies, and Steve and Heather, a couple with three children in the suburbs. (Zoe, a bistro-loving single woman living in a condo in a city like Toronto, they ignored completely, because she would never, ever vote Conservative.) It was Muttart who focused the campaign's attention on winning over what he called "aspirational" suburban voters, who were doing okay, trying to do better, and hoping things would be better still for their kids. Many of them, especially in the suburban and exurban rings around Toronto and Vancouver, were immigrants. They tended to be more economically and socially conservative than many native-borns. They too were a potential pool of new Conservative voters. Muttart's mastery of the suburban zeitgeist would prove crucial in the coming years.

There was another, equally important acquisition. Gatineau councillor Lawrence Cannon was as deeply embedded in the Quebec Liberal aristocracy as you could get: Both his grandfathers had been federal Liberal cabinet ministers. Other ancestors had served in the Quebec National Assembly. Cannon himself had served as an aide to Robert Bourassa, and then later as a cabinet minister. But he was furious with the federal Liberal Party over the sponsorship scandal, which was driving support toward the Parti Québécois and increasing the likelihood of another referendum on separation. Paul Terrien, a speechwriter for Harper, was a friend of Cannon's, and knew of his unhappiness. Would he consider switching sides? Cannon replied, "If I ever do that, my grandfathers are going to turn over in their graves. So would my mother and everyone else."[13]

But the March policy convention in Montreal convinced him that the Conservative Party had shed its so-con image (Cannon is a liberal on social policy) and by April, with Cannon ancestors spinning wildly in their resting places, he was the candidate for Pontiac, a large, rural riding north of

Gatineau, across the river from Ottawa. He was soon much more. Cannon was appalled by the disorganization in Quebec: the backbiting, the lack of discipline, the ties to Mario Dumont's ADQ (Action démocratique du Québec), which Cannon regarded as an unreliable ally. He wrote a memo recommending major changes. Doug Finley embraced them and him. Cannon was brought into the OLO as deputy chief of staff and made deputy director of the party, with a mandate to reorganize the Quebec operation. Cannon recruited former Mulroney supporters, and convinced Harper to begin mentioning Mulroney in Quebec-related speeches. Those speeches, successors to the Belgium brouhaha, increasingly spoke of Quebec as a partner in Confederation, with a distinct language and culture, deserving of respect and special status. And so yet another core Reform principle, equal treatment for all provinces, was quietly laid to rest.

But these shifts were accompanied by dozens of firings, which produced negative newspaper headlines. Harper's tour of the barbecue circuit was ignored by the press, except for the embarrassing cowboy photo. The Stronach affair and the opposition's botched effort to bring down the government had boosted the Liberals in the polls. Instead of being ten points back of the Conservatives, they were now ten points ahead and more. Some former Conservative candidates in Quebec called on Harper to depart. Carol Jamieson, a Toronto organizer and Joe Clark supporter who had opposed the merger, wrote an email to fellow Tories declaring, "He should resign and get the hell out of my party. He's a disaster."[14] She and the Quebec malcontents had all supported Belinda Stronach in her leadership campaign.

In fact, the Tories were much better positioned than many believed. Harper's barbecue-circuit tours of 2004 and 2005 improved his retail politicking skills, taking them from just awful to barely adequate. He would never be good at it, but at least he started to get less cringingly bad at it. Muttart and Brodie and Finley were knocking the OLO, the campaign organization, and the campaign messaging into shape. And in September, they finalized the most important element of the campaign strategy: the promise to cut the GST.

The Conservatives, and the Alliance and Reform before them, had promised cuts to income taxes. But Ralph Goodale had already lowered income taxes, and so had premiers in several provinces. And the thing was, taxpayers didn't notice. That was partly because federal income tax cuts were offset by tax hikes in other areas – increases in Canada Pension Plan premiums, in user fees, in property taxes – and partly because the average paycheque goes up and down throughout the year, as CPP and Employment Insurance levies are applied or removed, along with union dues, company pension plan deductions, and the like. Most important, almost a third of all Canadian workers don't make enough money to pay income tax. Conservatives examining the issue in caucus, the leader's office, and the party couldn't find a tax cut that was meaningful and visible and comprehensive – with one exception. At least as early as June, Harper had been mulling the possibility of cutting the GST.

As it happened, Ian Brodie and Doug Finley were coming to the same conclusion on their own. Who didn't hate the GST? Canadians were reminded of it every time they pulled out their wallets. The Liberals had promised to scrap it, and then reneged. The tax was too vital a source of revenues to be abolished. But why not knock a point or two off it? Cutting the GST would be a highly visible and popular move. It would stimulate consumer spending – though the robust Canadian economy of 2005 hardly needed more stimulating – and it would benefit lower- and middle-income earners, because the GST is regressive; the poor must pay the same rate of tax as the rich when they buy a pair of shoes. Most of all, it would signal to Canadians that a Conservative government was determined to give back to the taxpayer money that the government shouldn't be collecting in the first place, given the size of the federal surpluses. As someone with an M.A. in economics, Harper knew that economists would howl. The GST is a highly efficient tax – well nigh impossible to avoid and virtually immune to loopholes. But Harper wasn't after the economist vote. Cutting the GST by two percentage points, at a cost to the treasury of five billion dollars, would become the centrepiece of the Tory platform.

Paul Martin wanted to focus on yet another first ministers' meeting, this time on Aboriginal issues. That would be followed by a budget that would serve as a springboard for the winter 2006 election that he had promised. But Stephen Harper had a different timetable. Never mind the polls that had the Liberals ten to fifteen points ahead; he was determined to bring down the government. Harper was ready, the team was ready, and it was time. The arrival of the first volume of John Gomery's report on November 1 offered a proximate cause: The report exonerated Paul Martin of any personal responsibility, which was damning in its own way, since it meant he had no idea what was going on in the Chrétien government, even though he was finance minister. More damning was the "culture of entitlement" within the Liberal Party that the report concluded led to the scandal. The dip in the polls for the Liberals was only fleeting, but Harper didn't care. He was going to defeat the Liberals over sponsorship now, not at the time of the Liberals' choosing.

This time he had Jack Layton on board. Layton and Harper actually got along reasonably well, for political and ideological rivals. Though they were polar opposites in terms of personality, Smiling Jack and Grim Steve were both skilled political operators who were positioning their parties against the Liberal behemoth. Layton concluded he had spent too much of the 2004 campaign attacking the Conservatives, which had only driven voters into Liberal arms. This campaign, he would attack the Liberals from the left even as the Conservatives attacked them from the right. Polarization served both leaders' interests.

The two met privately in mid-November and agreed on a strategy: Layton would demand new and stricter health care regulations to prevent privatization of health care. Martin would refuse. Layton would put forward a motion for Parliament to be dissolved on the first week of January (to avoid campaigning at Christmas). If the Liberals refused that as well, Harper would move non-confidence, and the NDP would join the Bloc Québécois in supporting the motion.

It worked out exactly as they predicted. With a substantial lead in the polls, and sponsorship finally behind them (or so they hoped), Martin's team was ready for an election. All sides agreed to delay the vote of non-confidence until after the Kelowna first ministers' meeting, which reached an accord to spend five billion dollars annually on Aboriginal housing, health care, and education. The next day, the government was defeated. The Kelowna Accord would disappear, setting a record for the briefest shelf life of any federal–provincial agreement.

From the time the writ was dropped until people had finished opening their Christmas presents, not much happened. The Liberals focused on Stephen Harper. Stephen Harper was George Bush. Stephen Harper would ban abortion. Stephen Harper would privatize health care. Stephen Harper would trash the Charter of Rights and Freedoms. Paul Martin's biggest promise was to ban handguns, which made no sense since handguns are already banned, other than for gun collectors and target shooters who hold special permits. Gun violence wasn't a problem in cities because people were breaking into homes and stealing vintage Lugers. The guns were coming in illegally across the border. But that didn't matter. What mattered was making the pre-Christmas campaign a referendum on Scary Stephen Harper.

The Conservatives did exactly the opposite. Rather than attack Martin and Liberal corruption, Harper spent every day promoting new Conservative policies, with particular emphasis on cutting the GST. Liberal strategists were amazed and delighted that the Tories were firing all their guns before Christmas, in the phony-war part of the bifurcated campaign. But Harper's team wanted to use the time to counter the Scary Stephen Harper message by showing a calm, reasonable, convincing Conservative leader who had a bunch – not a large bunch, but still a bunch – of strong new ideas to save the taxpayers money and clean up the mess in Ottawa. Stephen Harper would cut the GST. Stephen Harper would tighten oversight of federal spending. Stephen Harper would crack down on lobbyists. The Liberals wanted to create a national subsidized daycare program; the Conservatives promised to give the money directly to parents. When Liberal strategist Scott Reid said that people would just spend the money on "beer and popcorn," he rendered daycare toxic as an issue for the Liberals.

Harper countered the Liberals' hidden-agenda charge by vowing never to legislate on abortion. As for the same-sex marriage bill, which had finally passed Parliament the previous June, he would hold a free vote on whether to revisit the issue. If Parliament voted no (which everyone knew it would, because almost nobody wanted to reopen the debate) then that case would be closed as well.

One big change for Stephen Harper in this campaign involved travel. In the 2004 campaign, the team and accompanying reporters rose early and bused or flew to the day's event, leaving Harper exhausted by the end of the day. In the new routine, the campaign would travel to the location of the next day's event at the end of the campaign day. That meant arriving late in the evening (or even early in the morning), but Harper didn't mind because this allowed him to sleep in a bit before the post-breakfast announcement-du-jour. Then, after taking questions from reporters, he would rest until the afternoon event, which might be a roundtable with working families, or a tour of a factory floor or the like, followed by a campaign rally in the evening, and then on to the next locale, before bed.

Muttart was behind simplifying the message, focusing on strong visuals – like slapping a "5% GST" label on everything in a store – and portraying the Liberals as elitist. The Liberals wanted to cut income taxes – nice, if you've got a great big income, not so nice if you're the rest of us. The rest of us want to see the GST go away. The Conservatives would toughen penalties for crime and crack down on rules that coddled offenders. Critics protested that crime was not a serious problem, that crime rates were coming down, and that punishing offenders too severely only increased the chances that they'd reoffend. Didn't matter. The people who know all those things have alarm systems to protect their houses. Everyone else is worried about the rash of break-ins in the neighbourhood.

To some observers, none of it seemed to be working. Pre-writ, the Liberals had flooded the country with forty-two billion dollars in unbudgeted spending commitments. Amazingly, Ottawa could afford it. Growth was strong; both unemployment and interest rates were low; alone among G8 countries, Canada was recording a budget surplus (and had been since 1997). The polls had the Liberals in a comfortable lead of about ten points at the beginning of the campaign, and nothing changed during Yuletide.

Except that the Tories had managed to define the campaign. They were proposing; the Liberals were responding. And something was even happening in Quebec. Martin had draped himself in the flag, challenging Bloc leader Gilles Duceppe to debate him anytime, anywhere. (Happy to, Duceppe replied, which caused Martin to withdraw the invitation.) Harper, in contrast, paid tribute to the aspirations of Quebeckers to protect their language and culture. He was calmer than Martin, more reasonable. His French had demonstrably improved. In a December 19 speech in Quebec City, he talked of Canada as a nation founded in Quebec, by the French. He talked of an "open federalism," one that respected provincial jurisdictions and that was sensitive to the responsibilities of the

Quebec government to protect the province's language and culture. He would invite Quebec to join Canada's table at UNESCO; he would end the so-called fiscal imbalance in transfers that allegedly punished Quebec. "This outrageous spending power gave rise to domineering and paternalist federalism, which is a serious threat to the future of our federation," he lamented. ". . . the functioning and the very spirit of the Canadian federation are at stake." He pledged "to build a stronger Quebec within a better Canada."[15] The Quebec press paid the speech serious and favourable attention. It was the first good press the Conservatives had received in the province in years.

Pre-Christmas, either the Conservatives had taken control of the election agenda, which they would exploit in the final weeks of the campaign, or they had shot their bolt and were still behind, depending on how you looked at it. In the Tory war room, there was quiet confidence that the party had control of the election. Maybe the war room was deluded. We'll never know, because in what was supposed to be the lull of Christmas week, the Liberals lost the election.

Fifteen-year-old Torontonian Jane Creba was leaving a Pizza Pizza on Yonge Street just north of the Eaton Centre, with her sister. It was Boxing Day, and the downtown was packed with shoppers. Suddenly, horrifyingly, a gun battle erupted between two street gangs, right there, practically at Yonge and Dundas. Creba was killed. Six others were wounded. The nation was shocked by such a brazen, wanton crime. It had been a bad year for shooting deaths in Toronto – fifty-two in total. Overall, Toronto's crime rate matched that of other Canadian cities, and was drastically below the American homicide rate. But that didn't matter. Street gangs battling it out in the shadow of the Eaton Centre on Boxing Day. What was the country coming to?

When Ben Harper was born, the Harpers had moved from their small white stucco house in suburban Calgary to a larger white stucco house in suburban Calgary. That Christmas, as with every Christmas before and since, they were back home celebrating the season with family and friends. But within hours of the shooting, Harper told reporters, "This is the first government in our history that seems unable to enforce our gun laws, and I think obviously this is just the consequence of 12 years of lax criminal justice law enforcement."[16] The next day, he went to the site of the shootings, to unveil (really to reannounce) his program against violent criminals: less parole, more jail time, tougher sentences, more police.

Martin mourned the loss of life and reminded everyone of his promise to ban handguns. But he added, in reference to the shootings, "I think, more than anything else, they demonstrate what are in fact the consequences of exclusion."[17] So it was society's fault that these young men had decided to turn Yonge Street into a killing field.

What Harper said was bunk. There isn't an expert on gang violence on the planet who will attribute the roots of that violence to lax gun laws. But what Martin said was also bunk. Society has been struggling to deal with what used to be called juvenile delinquency for decades, and as far back as 1957 *West Side Story* had lampooned the futility of the attempt. "Hey, I'm depraved on account I'm deprived!"[18] What mattered for electoral purposes was that Harper had sounded tough, and Martin weak, on an issue that was suddenly top-of-mind for every voter: gang-related violence.

Things got infinitely worse two days later. In November, Finance Minister Ralph Goodale had announced there would be no tax changes to income trusts. Businesses were converting themselves from corporations to income trusts to take advantage of the favourable tax status, and Goodale had warned he might close the loophole, before changing his mind. There was some odd market activity in advance of the announcement, and NDP MP Judy Wasylycia-Leis had sent a letter to the RCMP asking them to investigate the possibility of insider trading. Such letters are standard opposition party tactics. The letters are routinely ignored, but sometimes you get lucky with the media: "Opposition Demands Police Investigation of . . . ," reads the headline.

Remarkably, on December 23, the RCMP faxed a reply to Wasylycia-Leis's office, saying it had indeed launched a criminal investigation. When she didn't acknowledge she had received it – the office was closed for the campaign – they helpfully phoned the Winnipeg constituency office four days later to alert her staff. On December 28, Wasylycia-Leis held a press conference in Toronto, revealing that the finance minister was under police investigation. Suddenly, the sponsorship scandal and Liberal corruption were back front and centre.

There are those who believe to this day that RCMP commissioner Giuliano Zaccardelli let it be known the RCMP was investigating Goodale in a deliberate bid to undermine Paul Martin's campaign, for reasons that can only be guessed. According to this theory, the Conservatives didn't win the election on their own, and the Harper government was therefore illegitimate. But this ignores the fundamentals of the campaign. The Conservatives had dominated the agenda since the beginning; the legacy of the sponsorship scandal was going to haunt the Liberals one way or another; Martin had mishandled the Jane Creba shooting. Still, it is incontestably true that the RCMP announcement whacked the Liberal campaign upside the head. They never recovered.

The Tory momentum was reinforced on January 2, when Harper re-released his platform, this time as five short, sharp, clear priorities, a Patrick Muttart repackaging of the once far-more-elaborate suite of policies: an accountability act to clean up corruption in Ottawa; a reduction of the GST from 7 per cent to 5; a tougher approach to crime; money for child care that parents could spend as they wished; and a reduction in health care wait times.

Harper would pound those five themes every day until January 26, starting with that January 2 campaign relaunch. In contrast, Paul Martin began his post-holiday campaigning with a stop in a bagel shop. Then the campaign plane broke down. In the days that followed, things went from bad to worse to worst. As the Liberals finally unveiled their campaign platform, much of it seemed stale, because the Tories had already announced something similar. That's the advantage of getting your message out first. Besides, a mole inside the Liberal campaign leaked the platform to the Tories, who strategically released it bit by bit, constantly undermining the Liberal announcement. A series of Liberal attack ads sent in advance to the media on CD ROMS and posted, very briefly, online accidentally included one ad that the party had never intended to use, because it was so over the top: "Stephen Harper actually announced he wants to increase military presence in our cities. Canadian cities. Soldiers with guns. In our cities. In Canada. We did not make this up."[19] Actually, they did make it up. The Conservatives had talked about the possibility of stationing troops near major urban centres to respond to natural disasters. But the ad was not about where troops should be optimally deployed. It was about the Conservatives imposing martial law, which is why the war room axed it. Which is why, when reporters saw it, they had a field day.

Martin tried a game-changer of an announcement during the English language debate: a Liberal government would introduce a constitutional amendment to eliminate the notwithstanding clause that allows governments to protect legislation from a Charter challenge. (Quebec governments, for example, use it to protect laws limiting the use of English on signs.) But Martin changed no game; the ploy looked like what it was: desperate. To borrow from Kim Campbell, an election is no place to discuss constitutional reform.

One thing saved the Liberals from a complete rout. The Tories had scripted announcements for every day of a five-week campaign. But Martin had decided on an unusually long eight-week campaign. Brodie and Finley and company managed to stretch things out, but ten days before the vote, Harper ran out of script for the second election in a row. And as is his wont, once he was forced to improvise, he messed up.

The smell of majority government was in the air. Harper was campaigning hard in Quebec, where *La Presse* had endorsed the Conservatives, an almost unheard-of gesture for a francophone newspaper toward a party leader from outside Quebec. All the Tories needed to do now was calm the fears of anyone who still worried about the hidden-agenda bogeyman.

What Harper wanted to tell Canadians when he talked to reporters on January 17 was that institutional checks would limit the power of any government seeking to impose reforms outside the national consensus. What he said was, "The reality is that we will have, for some time to come, a Liberal Senate, a Liberal civil service . . . and courts that have been appointed by the Liberals. So these are obviously checks on the power of a Conservative government."[20]

To many ears, Harper was saying that, indeed, he did have a secret agenda, but don't worry, folks, the Senate, the public service, and, if all else fails, the courts would rein him in. That's hardly reassuring for someone who fears the Conservatives are going to take away a woman's right to choose or a gay couple's right to marry. The Liberals flooded the airwaves with a series of attack ads, from which the troops-in-the-street spot had been culled. The Bloc Québécois, now more worried about the Conservatives than the Liberals, trained their guns on Stephen Harper, scary right-winger. Harper, with nothing left to say, limited himself to friendly campaign rallies and avoided reporters almost completely.

In the end, Patrick Muttart's strategic genius, the mostly effective Tory war room, the advertising campaign, and the drive to target and get out the vote were enough on election day. Just. With 36 per cent of the vote, and 124 seats, the Conservatives had a weak minority government, the first Conservative election victory in almost twenty years. Paul Martin had driven Liberal support down to 30 per cent, the worst showing ever for a Liberal Party other than John Turner's 1984 debacle. But the vote was efficient – that is, the vote splits in close races often favoured the Liberals, who held on to 103 seats. Jack Layton had a good election, growing his caucus by 10 seats to 29, on 17.5 per cent of the vote. But once again the NDP didn't have enough seats to prop up the government. The Bloc dominated Quebec, with 51 of 74 seats.

But if anyone looked at the numbers carefully, there were reasons for Tory optimism and Liberal concern. The Tory result in Ontario had grown from 24 to 40 seats, including a few suburban ridings outside Toronto and in Ottawa. The Conservatives had taken 10 seats in Quebec, mostly in the Quebec City area where Lawrence Cannon's political ties ran deep. The Liberals, for all intents and purposes, now controlled only English Montreal, Toronto, Vancouver, and Atlantic Canada. Was that a strong base from which to rebound? Or a final, eroding bastion?

Two currents flowed through the hotel suite, as Harper watched the returns with Laureen, the children, staff, and a few friends. One was grim: This would be a very weak government, a far cry from the majority that the campaign team had thought was in reach. Stephen Harper, perpetual tactician, was already calculating the odds that the government might last mere months, and those odds looked good. But on the other hand – they had won! For once, he chose to revel in the good news rather than chew over the bad. Harper had a great big grin on his face as he and Laureen discussed the results in the hotel corridor. Preston Manning was there. Despite everything that had gone on in the past, this Conservative government would be heir to its Reform ancestor, and Manning deserved to share in the glory of that night. There was some impatience at how long it took Martin to call to concede defeat. The Tories didn't realize he was also making the decision to step down from the leadership that night.

Harper's victory speech was unusually personal. "To Ben and Rachel, your dad's heart aches when he does not get to spend as much time with you as he would like, and I love you very much," he told them, the ecstatic crowd at the Telus Centre in Calgary, and the nation. "To Laureen, a day never goes by when I am not in awe of how you have managed the surprises of this marriage. Your love and support keeps me going."[21]

His tribute to Paul Martin was gracious, and the heart of his message was that he would do all that was in his power to govern for all Canadians, regardless of political persuasion. But there was one line that stood out, as he directly addressed voters in the various regions of the country. "To the people of the West, let me say one thing and let me be clear," he told them. "The West is now in. Canada will work for all of us."

"It was electrifying," George Koch remembers.[22] Twenty-seven years before, a discouraged college dropout, fleeing failure, had arrived in a West increasingly estranged from the Laurentian centre. He and his adopted homeland had chafed together at their exclusion, lashed back against it in a new political movement, watched that movement fail to break through, struggled to save a Western conservative voice, struggled to merge that voice in a national conservative chorus, struggled to sing of victory across the land. Now there he was, up on the stage with his family, victorious. From mailroom clerk to prime minister. And he had only just begun.

BOOK TWO

Power

TWELVE

24

They had, they thought, very little time. When the celebrations ended and the campaign team woke after too little sleep, a grey dawn and a fragile future greeted them. Yes, they had won, but with only 124 out of 308 seats. The regional breakdowns were even more alarming. The Liberals had taken more seats than the Conservatives in Ontario, in Quebec, and throughout Atlantic Canada. The old Reform base of the Prairies and British Columbia had delivered the votes needed for the Tories to squeak through. But unless the Conservatives could sink deeper roots in Central and Eastern Canada, this minority government could prove ephemeral.

Jack Layton had once again grown the New Democrats, who now had twenty-nine seats. The Bloc Québécois had a solid contingent of fifty-one. That meant that the Liberals could defeat the Conservatives with the help of any other party. And Stephen Harper was convinced that they would, just as soon as they had a new leader. They could all be back in an election campaign that autumn. The Conservatives needed to get the key elements of their election platform through Parliament as quickly as possible. That way, if they were forced back into a campaign they'd at least have something to run on.

They were wrong, as it turned out, though in a good way. Harper was the first to notice the counter-scenario, as he perused a copy of the *Calgary*

Herald that morning on the flight back to Ottawa. Pierre Pettigrew in Montreal. Tony Valeri in Hamilton. Reg Alcock in Winnipeg. Anne McLellan in Edmonton. All major losses suffered by the Liberal front bench. Other heavy hitters – former deputy prime ministers John Manley and Sheila Copps, to name only two – had been pushed out by Paul Martin. For the first time in its history, the party did not have a field of A-quality talent ready to challenge for the leadership. The Liberals, Harper told his advisors on the plane, were in a lot of trouble. Even he did not realize, however, that the once natural governing party was already well into a decade of decline that would, for starters, turn this fragile minority Conservative government into one of the longest-lasting in Canadian history.

———————————

Stephen Harper was still asleep in Calgary when Derek Burney got to work in Ottawa on the morning of January 24. Big, blunt, gruff, strong-willed, immensely experienced, and, at his best, deeply wise, Burney had served as Brian Mulroney's indispensible chief of staff during the Canada–U.S. free trade talks, before being sent to his reward as ambassador to the United States. When Kim Campbell succeeded Mulroney, the outgoing prime minister's strong advice to her was, "Get yourself a Derek Burney to run your PMO."[1] During the 2004 election campaign, when it appeared the Conservatives might win, Harper had asked Burney to work on a transition plan. Though it turned out not to be needed, Harper learned a lot about the inner workings of government just by reading Burney's plan. So it was no surprise that in 2006 Harper tapped Burney once again to lead the transition team. This time, the plan would actually be used.

The orderly transition of power is the glory of democracy. The public service prides itself on being able to serve whichever party and leader the people choose. Well before Election Day, the various departments had put together briefing packages on how the Conservative platform might be implemented. Alex Himelfarb, Clerk of the Privy Council, had talked to Ian Brodie, Harper's chief of staff, and to Burney, to let them know that the mandarinate was ready to implement a smooth transition. By 10 a.m.

Eastern Time, January 24, Burney and Bruce Carson were ensconced in offices on the fourth floor of Langevin Block, across the street from Parliament Hill. Langevin houses the Prime Minister's Office (the political staff who serve the PM) and the Privy Council Office (the clerk and senior staff who run the bureaucracy and advise the PM). Today, Langevin Block, even more than Centre Block (home to the Senate and House of Commons), is the real nerve centre of the federal government. Prime ministers typically work either out of an office in Langevin or in the more ornate office in Centre Block. Jean Chrétien governed from his Centre Block office; Harper prefers to work out of Langevin Block (though he will transfer his flag to Centre Block if the House is sitting or he is meeting with cabinet or caucus). The choices complement Chrétien's more distant and Harper's more hands-on approach to day-to-day government.

Harper wanted a swift transition. He gave Burney's team until February 6 to get everything ready. "Everything" really meant two things: choosing a cabinet and a cabinet structure. As a former chief of staff to Brian Mulroney, Burney rather liked the cabinet structure Mulroney had used. He recommended it to Harper, who agreed.[2] In essence, two cabinet committees would run the government. Priorities and Planning, which Harper would chair, would do what its name suggested: set out the agenda for the government. Operations, which would be chaired by Jim Prentice, would handle strategic communications, while also attempting to douse any political fires that might erupt from one day to the next.

One thing that bemused Burney was Harper's decision not to have a deputy prime minister. Some have assumed that Harper didn't want to name someone who could be seen as a potential successor, in case caucus became restless. It has also been speculated that Harper didn't want a deputy because he wanted to be completely in charge. But another rationale figured more strongly in 2006. Harper didn't pick a deputy prime minister because he couldn't decide which track he should pursue toward majority government.

In the 1989 memo to Manning, Harper argued that a well-defined but moderate conservative party could find strong support among suburban voters in major cities in Ontario. But the Conservatives had been largely shut out of the 905 belt of ridings surrounding Toronto (named after its area code). If the party wanted to grow its support in the 905, then the obvious choice for deputy prime minister was incoming finance minister Jim Flaherty, who had won in the eastern 905 riding of Whitby–Oshawa.

But in the 1996 speech at the Winds of Change conference, Harper had reverted to the traditional notion of how Conservatives cobbled together a coalition: by harnessing nationalist Quebeckers to Western populist conservatives and Ontario Red Tories. The Conservatives had made impressive gains in Quebec, electing ten MPs. Should Harper pursue Quebec? If so, then Lawrence Cannon, his Quebec lieutenant and the incoming minister of transport, would be an obvious choice. Harper didn't know which track to take and didn't want to signal his choice until he was ready to make it. As for naming Prentice his number two, that was a nonstarter because both men hailed from Calgary, and the government was already top-heavy with Albertans.

There has to be someone the bureaucracy can turn to when you're away, Burney explained. Make it Prentice, Harper replied. With that call, and by putting Prentice in charge of Ops, Harper was making the Calgary MP effectively the number two in cabinet. But he also gave Prentice Indian and Northern Affairs – traditionally a graveyard of political ambition – to keep his ambitious lieutenant in line. (Prentice had, after all, run for the Progressive Conservative leadership in 2003.)

As for cabinet itself, that was going to be tough. No one in caucus had any experience in a federal cabinet apart from Rob Nicholson, who had served in Kim Campbell's blink-of-an-eye administration. The good news was that Harper had inherited the core of the Mike Harris cabinet. With the Liberals now ensconced at Queen's Park, Jim Flaherty, John Baird, and Tony Clement had decided it was time to head up Highway 401 to Ottawa. Clement had won the narrowest of victories in Parry Sound–Muskoka, in Ontario's cottage country, finally breaking a string of defeats; Flaherty had translated his Oshawa-area provincial seat into a federal seat with the support of essentially the same voters; and Baird had swapped a suburban Ottawa provincial riding for a nearby federal riding.

Responsible for almost 40 per cent of Canada's population and GDP, the Government of Ontario is big and complicated. Graduating to the federal level wasn't a major challenge for any of the Harris troika. So Harper put the three veterans in charge of implementing the five key promises of the election platform. In Finance, Flaherty, a plain-spoken Irishman who had also served as Mike Harris's finance minister, was tasked with producing a budget that would implement the first tranche of the GST cut and with designing a child care benefit for parents. John Baird, a fierce Tory partisan who occasionally grapples with anger-management issues, but who is also whip-smart, had learned how to bend the bureaucracy to his will at Queen's Park. He was sent to the Treasury Board, charged with implementing the Accountability Act, the Conservative response to the sponsorship scandal that aimed to make the federal government both more open and more responsible in how it spent taxpayers' money. Clement, who had been highly effective as Ontario's health minister during the SARS outbreak, was sent to Health to implement the patient wait-times guarantee. That guarantee would come to nothing, since Harper didn't believe in dictating health care policy to the provinces, but at least the government had to be seen to be trying.

These three Harrisites, along with a couple of other key players, would become the core of the Harper cabinet, and would cement one of Harper's greatest political accomplishments: bringing and keeping Ontario provincial Conservatives into the Conservative tent. Mike Harris Conservatives were well to the right of the province's Red Tories, but they obviously weren't Westerners and had no interest in social conservatism. Throughout the 1990s, the Conservatives at Queen's Park had kept their distance from both Reform and the PCs. But in Stephen Harper, they found a leader whose views closely mirrored their own, who seemed able to reconcile the differing strands of the conservative movement, and who appeared to have the makings of a genuine national leader. By 2006, the Mike Harris Conservatives were as fully committed to Stephen Harper as they had been to Harris. Their contribution to his success as prime minister would be enormous.

As the de facto leader of the Progressive Conservative wing of the new party, Peter MacKay was handed Foreign Affairs, which was once as prestigious a post as Finance, though it had become a bit of a revolving door during the Chrétien and Martin years. Vic Toews, a voluble former Crown attorney and minister of justice in Manitoba, was handed the Justice portfolio, charged with implementing the Tories' tough-on-crime agenda. It was good that Toews was from Manitoba: getting a proper geographical mix is important for any cabinet. With so many MPs from Alberta, much of the talent in the Conservative caucus simply couldn't be used. The biggest problems were Toronto, Montreal, and Vancouver. The Tories hadn't elected a single MP in any of Canada's three largest cities. Toronto could be taken care of by MPs like Jim Flaherty, whose riding was close to the city. Harper's solution to the Montreal problem was to place Michael Fortier, the Montreal lawyer and businessman who had co-chaired the Conservative Quebec campaign, in both the Senate and in cabinet, as minister of public works. In the complex, unwritten constitutional conventions of Westminster, such a practice is permitted – Joe Clark and Pierre Trudeau both appointed senators to cabinet – but frowned upon. Ministers should be able to face and answer critics in the House of Commons, and Fortier's appointment was criticized by the opposition and by some pundits.

But that was small potatoes compared to the storm that surrounded David Emerson. Emerson has a perfect resumé, starting with a Ph.D. from Queen's. He twice served as a deputy minister in the British Columbia government – in Finance and as deputy premier – and had also been CEO of the Western Bank of Canada and of Canfor, the forest products company. There were also several other stints, such as leading the Vancouver International Airport Authority. Paul Martin enticed this king of all trades into federal politics, parachuting him into the riding of Vancouver Kingsway, and then appointing him as industry minister. Now Emerson was simply an opposition MP. That hadn't been part of the plan.

The day after the election, Emerson bumped into the garrulous John Reynolds at the Vancouver airport. The two men got to talking. Emerson was naturally unhappy. He wasn't a politician, and had no desire to be one. He had agreed to go into the Martin government as industry minister because there were things that he believed needed to be done that only the federal industry minister could do. Now he was stuck in the opposition backbenches, which was not the sort of place someone like David Emerson wanted to be.

Reynolds, whose back-slapping amiability had helped keep the Alliance together when he was interim leader, had just the solution to Emerson's problem. He passed the nub of the conversation to the Conservative transition team, with a strong recommendation that Emerson be wooed. Within days, the outgoing Liberal cabinet minister was in Ottawa, in talks with the incoming prime minister. Why not come on board as international trade minister? Harper urged. Emerson was trying to negotiate an end to the softwood lumber dispute with the United States, a critical irritant between the two countries. Claiming that Canadian lumber exports were subsidized, the Americans had slapped on a tariff that was crippling the B.C. lumber industry. If Emerson stayed with the Liberals, someone else would solve the softwood problem. But if he crossed the floor, he'd never even miss a day of work. Emerson happily agreed. Technically, Harper never asked Emerson to cross the floor and join the Conservative caucus. He could have sat as an independent had he wanted to. But Emerson was happy to switch parties. For him, such things were small beer.

It was a huge win for Harper, who now had an MP and cabinet minister from Vancouver – and no ordinary cabinet minister at that. But the voters of Vancouver–Kingsway were not happy; they had sent a Liberal to Parliament, and now they were being represented by a Conservative. Social activists, who aren't hard to find in Vancouver, were livid, and vowed to defeat Emerson in the next election. They didn't get the chance; Emerson decided one term as a Tory was enough. But it was one heck of a shock when he showed up at Rideau Hall for the swearing-in on February 6.

That day was a mix of giddy exhilaration and steely determination. The new ministry looked like a bunch of kids at graduation, beaming with pride as they recited their oaths and shook the governor general's hand. Later, as Harper prepared to chair his first cabinet meeting, Bruce Carson turned to the new prime minister and affirmed, "Stephen, we really did it."

"Yes, Bruce, we really did."

"Now you have to go and chair your first cabinet meeting."

"Yes I do. Where do I do that?"

"Follow me."

When they reached the cabinet room, Carson had to point out the chair – "the vacant chair with the high back" – where Harper was expected to sit.[3]

The message that Harper delivered to cabinet was clear and emphatic. Each minister had received a mandate letter, spelling out his or her duties and responsibilities. Those letters, which had been drawn up during the transition, conformed to the election platform. Getting that platform implemented, and swiftly, was the top priority of each and every one of them. He expected them to behave honestly, to act within the rules, and never to abuse the authority and responsibility of their office. If they did abuse that office, they would be gone. Protecting the integrity of the government – protecting the prime minister, as leader of the government – was the highest priority. From day one, the Conservative government was really the Harper government.

There was another message that Harper delivered that day and reinforced in the days after. Message discipline was everything. Ministers were not to speak with reporters unless and until they had cleared it with the Centre, the Prime Minister's Office. Permission would not often be forthcoming. For major events, Harper himself would give the final yea or nay. The same applied to senior public servants. The Conservatives aimed to control the message, and to deliver that message directly to constituents through advertising or, when necessary, through carefully managed interaction with the press. Thus was born the reputation of the Harper government as a small band of secretive, anti-democratic control freaks led by a control freak-in-chief.

Harper's cabinet structure evolved little over the years. Ops (the Operations Committee) met on Monday; P and P (Priorities and Planning) on Tuesday. Caucus met Wednesday and cabinet met twice a month, though it functioned largely as a talking shop and a rubber stamp. Harper made little secret of his impatience with some meetings of the full cabinet. As for the two key committees, P and P gradually ceded primacy to Ops, where PMO staffers worked closely with key cabinet ministers on the vital issues of the day. When it came to priorities and planning, the prime minister handled those files himself.

The National Capital Commission, which looks after federal properties in Ottawa, wanted the Harpers to delay their move into 24 Sussex Drive. The Martins had complained of the cold and draft, and the thirty-four-room mansion lacks central air conditioning. No serious work has been done on the building since the Mulroneys lived there. A 2008 auditor general's report estimated the house needed ten million dollars in upgrades, which would take up to fifteen months to complete. But Harper insisted on moving in immediately. With a shaky minority government, he needed the legitimacy of living in the prime minister's residence. The symbolism of staying in Stornoway would be terrible, reinforcing the impression that the Conservatives were interlopers who had come to power by some freakish accident and would soon be returned to opposition, their natural home. As for the cold and the draft, they would wear sweaters, Harper assured his landlord.[4]

One key to understanding Stephen Harper is to realize that he never stops. Recreation for him is switching from analyzing finance department statistics to analyzing hockey statistics. He doesn't channel surf: he plunges into *Coronation Street* – a show he is obsessed with – or memorizes *Seinfeld* episodes. He spends little time in quiet reflection, and none just lying on the beach. Luckily, when you're prime minister, finding a way to fill your day is never an issue.

A typical day in the life of Canada's twenty-second prime minister, and his family, has changed little between 2006 and now. Harper is usually out of bed between six and seven. He and Laureen start out with a review of the relevant media. Harper concentrates on watching the Radio Canada TV news or the TVA network, in order to improve his French. (In the early years of his prime ministership, he was also using a French tutor for one or two hours once a week. Eventually, he was able to speak fluently, though with a heavy English accent.) The joke is that Harper watches Rad-Can in the morning to work on his French and get his heart pumping. Though he looks at the front pages of the major papers, paying particular attention to the *Ottawa Citizen* because it's the local rag, Laureen is the one who deep-dives into the press, often tipping him to stories or columns to which he needs to pay attention. Laureen Harper is as outgoing an extrovert as her husband is a closed introvert. But don't let that cheerful exterior fool you.

Prime ministers' wives play differing roles, depending on how engaged they are politically and on their relationships with their husbands. Maryon Pearson never really liked being wife of a prime minister at all; Margaret

Trudeau wasn't interested in her husband's work, nor he in sharing it with her; Mila Mulroney focused on key charities that she could contribute to. But Aline Chrétien was her husband's closest confidant, and everything they did they did together, in politics as well as in life. In that sense, Laureen Harper is much more similar to Aline Chrétien than to her predecessors.

Remember, Laureen Harper met her future husband at a Reform convention. Although she had campaigned for the PCs in 2008, that was because of her strong support for free trade. By conviction, she was always much more of a Reformer. As a married couple, the two cooked together (under her tutelage, Harper turned into a pretty decent cook) and talked politics together. At critical moments – such as when Harper was thinking about abandoning the run for the Alliance leadership – it has been her voice he has listened to, and hers alone. While Laureen may not weigh in on the conditions under which she believes state-owned enterprises should be allowed to acquire strategic Canadian assets, her political antennae are acute. On the truly big issues, he has rarely, if ever, acted contrary to her wishes. It's not that Laureen has a veto; like most married couples, they are more likely to work things through until they find themselves both on common ground.

Laureen has also been known to chide the prime minister for being such a cold fish, especially in public. But if anyone appeals to her to get her husband to be more forthcoming (or to lose a little weight), she is likely to shrug and reply, "That's Stephen." She is also utterly unforgiving of anyone who betrays or undermines the Conservative cause in general or her husband in particular. Her temper can be the equal of Harper's. If Harper walks into work waving a piece of paper, chances are it's something that's bothering "Mrs.," as the PMO staff call her, and he'd better not be sent home without an answer. As one person close to the situation observed: "God help you if you got on the wrong side of Laureen Harper."

When Ben and Rachel were younger, after the couple organized breakfast, they generally saw them off to school. This led to one of Harper's deepest embarrassments. After the 2006 election, but before his swearing-in, the prime minister designate walked the kids to school, something he did whenever he could as Opposition leader and tried to continue as prime minister. Ben was nine, by then, and Rachel six. On that day, they faced a barrage of photographers and cameras, who were invited to watch the new prime minister being a normal dad. Though Harper knew the press would be there, the situation threw him. Impulsively, he reached out to Ben and shook his hand, something he would never have done otherwise. That was enough for bloggers and commentators to conclude that Stephen Harper was an emotionally sterile father (and human being) who couldn't even muster sufficient intimacy to hug his son.

Harper was deeply hurt. It was partly his fault, of course, for mismanaging the photo-op so badly. But in truth, he has worked hard to be there for his children, despite the demands of his job. Harper is much different around children than around adults. For instance, he's a sucker for a baby; although he doesn't kiss them in public, he loves to hang out with them in private. One day, when he was leader of the Opposition, Ian Brodie brought his newborn daughter, Chloe, into the office. Although Question Period was fast approaching, Harper got lost in the world of this new child. As he stood there, patting her back to get her to burp, alarmed staff pointed out that Question Period was minutes away, and there was a very high risk that an infant was about to vomit on his suit. Harper didn't care. So to be described as disconnected from his children was painful. It was something Harper has never forgotten or forgiven. And it did nothing to improve his already suspicious approach to the fourth estate.

Each day, the prime minister's motorcade makes the five-minute drive from the official residence to the Langevin Block at around 8 a.m. The RCMP varies the route, sometimes crossing over to Quebec and back, to keep things unpredictable. Although the motorcade avoids lights and sirens, transponders switch traffic signals to green as the entourage approaches intersections. Over the years, as Canada's commitment in Afghanistan and other parts of the region have deepened, along with Harper's commitment to Israel, the motorcade has become longer and security tighter.

Typically, the first meeting of the day is with senior staff, to discuss Question Period. Even if the House isn't sitting, the meeting pretends it is. Focusing on Question Period is a good way of confronting the issues du jour, and how the government is handling them. Harper is typically asked if he has anything he wants to bring up first. Sometimes he does. Sometimes he raises something brought to his attention by Laureen, but often he simply lets staff tell him what they think he needs to know.

Then it is on to what is often the most important meeting of the day, known as the "clerk's meeting."* Alex Himelfarb, who served as clerk of the Privy Council under both Chrétien and Martin, stepped aside after a few months, and Kevin Lynch took his place. The former deputy minister of finance combines a fine mind and a determined character with a low-bridge approach to discussions and possible disagreements with the prime minister. The meeting may involve routine or not-so-routine prime ministerial appointments, issues raised by the bureaucracy, or a general debate over a priority policy issue. The clerk's meeting often runs until noon, when Harper breaks for lunch – usually a sandwich and bowl of soup brought to the office from 24, which he eats directly out of the Tupperware. He prefers to eat lunch alone at his desk, poring over government documents, which might be announcements referred to as MEPs (message event proposals). In its early days, Canada's New Government, as it branded itself on every press release and website, was determined to control the flow of information to the public. A minister who wanted to make an announcement would have to have his or her staff prepare an MEP describing what event was planned and what the message would be. Harper often personally reviewed and approved – or vetoed – MEPs from ministers. Though Patrick Muttart was in charge of overall management of the government's brand, Harper also carefully supervised how his administration presented its face to the world. It was, and continues to be, the same with every aspect of policy and planning. Nothing of importance is decided until the PM signs off on it.

Harper often drives bureaucrats to distraction with his passion for

* This was the case in the first government. As we will see, the frequency of this meeting changed after 2008.

reading complex background documents. While many prime ministers, from Winston Churchill to Jean Chrétien, preferred to peruse one- or two-page summaries and recommendations of issues requiring a prime ministerial decision, Harper prefers to read the background documents as well. Over the years, he has developed certain passions. One very esoteric preoccupation is with border disputes. Harper can tell you the complete history of every border dispute involving Canada and another nation, how it was resolved, and what disputes (there are several minor ones, as well as the larger Arctic claims) remain. He also made himself an expert on equalization issues, which dominated the first administration in the effort to eliminate the so-called fiscal imbalance.

After lunch comes Question Period prep, if the House is sitting. This is an innovation introduced by the Conservatives, carried over from the party's time in opposition. In those days, MPs would practise how they planned to grill the minister across the aisle. Harper almost always attended, along with Question Period coordinator Jason Kenney. Kenney didn't like the job of choosing who got to ask questions, because it made him unpopular. When he complained to Harper, the prime minister replied, "Why do you think I chose you, Jason? You don't have any friends anyway." The practice has continued since the Conservatives formed the government, with cabinet ministers and parliamentary secretaries taking turns grilling each other. Harper is almost always present, and since the sessions usually wrap up around 1:45 p.m., half an hour before Question Period actually begins, this is a good time for a cabinet minister who needs to bend the boss's ear to have an informal chat.

Harper typically attends Question Period two or three days a week, absenting himself on Mondays and Fridays. He answers questions put to him by the leaders of the other three parties, leaving ministers or parliamentary secretaries to respond to questions from opposition critics. He has adopted a patient, low-key approach to responding to questions – facing the Speaker directly, rather than the questioner – occasionally raising the temperature if he wants to take a jab at one of his opponents. He keeps the famous Harper temper firmly in check.

After Question Period, Harper typically works alone in his office, unless he is in meetings. Those meetings might be with the finance minister, if the budget is coming up, or a premier, or a visiting head of government. But generally he prefers to work alone. Stephen Harper may be the most solitary prime minister we have ever had. (Mackenzie King at least had the ghost of his mother for company.) Although he will ask relevant staff to offer their opinions on an important issue, he hates sitting around with others, blue-skying or talking through an issue. His thought process is linear, and it requires solitude to function.

Around 6:30, he returns to 24 Sussex Drive for a substantial but simple meal. The Harpers are very meat-and-potatoes; the fine wines in the cellar get dustier by the year. After dinner, it might be a visit to a hockey rink to watch Ben play, or a school gym to watch Rachel dance. They might settle in to watch TV, or Harper might closet himself in the study off the master bedroom to read and work on files. Calls to staff in the evening are rare, and calls after 9 p.m. rarer still. As noted above, Harper might attend the movies, alone or with family members, arriving unannounced and sitting at the back (though he also likes to sneak in to matinees, when there are fewer people). In that jam-packed brain of his, he has an enormous store of movie trivia.

Before bed, for many years he often worked for a bit on his book, a history of the early years of the Toronto Maple Leafs. After the book was published in 2013, he took up Spanish. Why? Something to do. (Remember, he took five years of Latin in high school, along with French.) This is also when he works on his journal.

Harper has been keeping a diary of sorts since he became prime minister. It grew more or less haphazardly out of the detailed schedule of his day that is printed out for him each morning by staff. After a particular meeting, or at the end of the day, on a flight, or when he otherwise feels like it, Harper jots notes beside the itinerary of his impression of this meeting, that leader, this briefing, that phone call. The more interesting or important the event, the longer and more detailed the annotations. Not only do they serve to remind him of who has committed to what, they also allow him to talk to himself about what is going on in his life and in the government.

Harper likes a good seven or eight hours' sleep, and is typically in bed between eleven and midnight, often before Laureen, who is more likely than he is to be out at a social event – often accompanied by John Baird, who quickly became her friend.

This was the life of the Harpers in 2006, and it remained their life for as long as he was prime minister.

The new government's first initiative was to introduce the Accountability Act. In essence, this piece of legislation responded to and implemented the recommendations of the Gomery Commission. The act's most important feature was to reduce the maximum individual contribution to a political party from five thousand dollars to one thousand dollars, while also going one step further than the Chrétien government by prohibiting corporate donations of any kind. As a result, the new rules forced political parties to target a broad range of individual donors for support. The reforms almost destroyed the Liberal Party, which had traditionally relied on corporate contributions, and which lacked even a centralized database of donors. But it was a huge boon for the Conservatives, which is why Harper pushed the measure through. The Reform Party was never loved by corporate Canada, which largely looked upon the movement as a bunch of disruptive interlopers. This left Reform no choice but to depend on individuals willing to donate relatively small sums to sustain the cause. As it perfected the art of fundraising, Reform and then the Canadian Alliance became extremely good at identifying and cultivating potential donors, who also became the electoral base of the party. So while Chrétien eliminated the ability of corporations with deep pockets to influence the government agenda, Harper ended the ability of a wealthy individual to cut a five-thousand-dollar cheque. This also gave the Conservatives an enormous, though temporary, fundraising advantage. The other parties, in order to survive, had no choice but to identify and cultivate their base as well. Over time, they got better at it. But from the time Paul Martin stepped down until the day Justin Trudeau became leader, the Conservatives routinely raised as much money as the Liberals and NDP combined. It was a classic case of doing well by doing good.

The act also prohibited anyone who worked in government from lobbying for a five-year period after they left government. Conservatives themselves would later complain that this made it very hard to acquire ministerial staff – people who work directly for a minister, rather than belonging to the public service. But if someone decides to work for a minister in the hope that they can later translate the experience into work as a lobbyist, that person shouldn't be working in government in the first place. The Accountability Act ensured that Ottawa would never have its own K Street, the thoroughfare in Washington where powerful lobbying firms practically dictate the legislative agenda of Congress.

Other measures added a new auditing function to line departments, and protected whistleblowers who brought public attention to abuses inside government. The whistleblower protection proved to be weak, and the auditing functions further gummed up works that were already jammed. But the most disappointing aspect of the act was the sidetracking of the Public Appointments Commission, which was to oversee the appointment of officials to government agencies, boards, and commissions, eliminating patronage in such appointments. The commission ran up against opposition parties keen to show that they had this government on a short leash. When Harper nominated Gwyn Morgan, a respected businessman and prominent Conservative, to head the commission, the other parties used their majority on a parliamentary committee to reject the candidate. Harper, angry at the rebuke and embarrassed by the public humiliation Morgan had endured, scrapped the commission. It was a serious mistake. First, Harper was letting his temper get the better of him, which is poor leadership. Second, because he failed to persevere, public appointments under the Conservatives became every bit as patronage-ridden as they were under the Liberals. So much for openness and accountability. It was a tremendous opportunity lost.

Overall, however, the Accountability Act was more a plus than a minus, reducing outside financial influence on government decision making, severing the link between governing and lobbying, and reducing the possibility for abuses inside line departments. It also resulted in the creation of the parliamentary budget officer position, one that Harper would come to wish he had never thought up.

The other major priority in spring 2006 was Finance Minister Jim Flaherty's first budget, which set in motion a suite of tax reductions that continue to this day. Fulfilling the promise of the election platform, the budget reduced the GST by one percentage point, with the promise of a further reduction to come. The government also began lowering the corporate tax rate, which would eventually decline from 21 per cent to 15 per cent. These and other measures substantially reduced the tax burden for both individuals and business. Combined with declines in provincial corporate taxes, Canada would emerge within six years as the only member of the G7 that ranked among the top ten countries in the world in corporate tax competitiveness, according to a Forbes survey,[5] with rates considerably lower than the United States or Japan, though still higher than that notorious tax haven, Sweden.

There was another piece of good economic news that spring. In mid-March, Ian Brodie convened a gathering of senior PMO staff. Kevin Lynch and Industry Minister David Emerson were also there. Then Harper walked in to announce that the government had a deal on softwood lumber. The dispute had been dragging on since the late 1990s. It was the chief irritant in Canada–U.S. relations. It had damaged the lumber industry across the country, hitting British Columbia especially hard. David Emerson, as both Liberal industry minister and Conservative international trade minister, had been working hard to resolve the problem. But a deal was only reached after President George W. Bush called Harper to say that he thought the time was right to get an agreement through Congress. In essence, the Americans would lift the tariff, while keeping $1.5 billion of the $5.5 billion in penalties that the United States had levied on Canadian softwood lumber imports. It was a lot of money to leave on the table, but a deal was a deal, and Harper jumped at the opportunity. The agreement was announced publicly in April, and the PM declared the vote on the legislation to ratify the agreement would be a vote of confidence. The Liberals and NDP kvetched, but the Bloc agreed to support the bill. The softwood lumber dispute was finally over. Finally.

———————

Being prime minister also involves travel, one of Stephen Harper's least favourite activities. He avoided it before he became prime minister, confining himself mostly to trips to the United States. Travel disrupts his schedule, and he's never at his best when his schedule has been disrupted. He is incurious about museums and monuments and vistas. Since he doesn't easily engage with people in the first place, the thought of seeking out and connecting with new and strange situations and people leaves him cold. He'd rather look down at a book than up at the Eiffel Tower. His response to travel hasn't changed that much as prime minister. He suffers from jet lag; is unimpressed with the food on CF-01, the modified Airbus 310 that prime ministers use for overseas travel (it is used to transport troops when the PM doesn't need it); and is bored by most foreign conferences with their endless talk and little action. In the first government, Harper tried to avoid travel when the House was in session, because the government could be defeated at any time. He rather resembled the African strongman at risk of being replaced by a coup while overseas at a Commonwealth conference.

His first international jaunt was also one of his most embarrassing. Harper attended the Three Amigos summit in March 2006 at Cancun, with George W. Bush and Mexican president Vicente Fox. During a walk among Mayan ruins, Bush and Fox wore carefully casual white shirts and cotton trousers. Harper tried to match the look but ruined it with a multi-pocketed vest. "He looks like he's going hunting," offered one fashion consultant.[6] (At the *Globe*, a wag circulated a photo of the three men, with the cutline, "Presidents George W. Bush and Vicente Fox tour Mayan ruins accompanied by an unidentified fly fisherman.") Shortly thereafter, Harper hired Michelle Muntean, a former makeup artist at CBC, to manage his look. At first she was placed on the PMO's staff, but her salary was transferred over to the Conservative Party when eyebrows were raised. Under Muntean's guidance, the hair was kept in place, the vests disappeared, and Harper's wardrobe ceased to interest anyone at all, which is how he likes it.*

---

* Muntean does have one eccentricity: she's a mystic, and quite an enthusiastic one, as the prime minister's staffers discover if they sit beside her on a long overseas flight aboard the CF-01. There is no evidence, sadly, that Harper has ever sought her guidance.

Joe Harper and his three sons. Steve, on the right, isn't smiling. It may be
the braces. DIMITRI SOUDAS

The track team at Richview Collegiate. Steve is back row, centre. Also, Steve Harper as
a lanky long-distance runner. DIMITRI SOUDAS

The not-so-faithful servant: Preston Manning and Steve Harper, circa 1990.
MARK KIHN

Pile on: Reporters grill a trapped Stephen Harper over his accusation that the Liberals are soft on child pornography. That scrum probably cost the Conservatives the election and deepened Harper's contempt for the Parliamentary Press Gallery. THE CANADIAN PRESS//FRANK GUNN

On top of the world: Stephen, Laureen, Ben, and Rachel, election night 2006.
THE CANADIAN PRESS//AARON WHITFIELD

Touring Mayan ruins in an unfortunate vest. Harper with Mexican President Vicente
Fox and U.S. President George W. Bush at the March 2006 Three Amigos summit.
After that, he got a fashion consultant. THE CANADIAN PRESS//TOM HANSON

Tense talk: Harper with Barack Obama at the APEC summit in Hawaii, November 2011, soon after the U.S. President vetoed the first proposal for the Keystone XL pipeline.
REX FEATURES

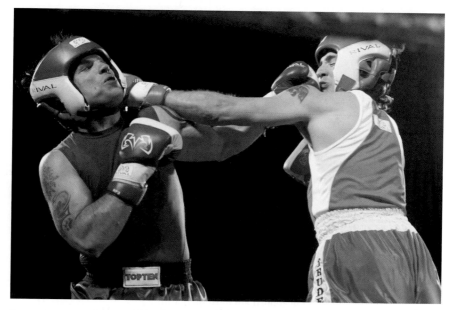

Justin Trudeau wins the Liberal Party leadership by defeating Conservative Senator Patrick Brazeau in a boxing match. THE CANADIAN PRESS//JAKE WRIGHT

In happier times: Harper and Chief of Staff Nigel Wright. PRIME MINISTER'S OFFICE

Tom Mulcair reveals that his true calling might have been a Crown prosecutor as he grills Stephen Harper over the Senate expenses scandal in 2013. THE CANADIAN PRESS// SEAN KILPATRICK

Not the best of friends. By 2013, when this picture was taken at the G20 summit in
St. Petersburg, Harper was one of Russian President Vladimir Putin's fiercest critics.
THE CANADIAN PRESS//ADRIAN WYLD

Nine years and counting: Stephen Harper in the House
of Commons, January 28, 2015. THE CANADIAN PRESS//
SEAN KILPATRICK

One other incident in the early life of the government revealed much about the PM's thought processes, and about his relationship with his new finance minister, Jim Flaherty. Income trusts had been bedevilling federal governments for years. In essence, companies that converted themselves into income trusts were able to flow earnings into the trusts and then back out to investors, avoiding corporate income tax. This might limit a company's ability to invest resources in, say, research and development, but it made the company highly attractive to investors. In the low-interest environment of the early 2000s, more and more Canadian companies began converting themselves into trusts, in order to avoid taxes and increase shareholder value. Liberal finance minister Ralph Goodale initially tried to rein in the trusts, but then backed off under pressure from Bay Street and pension funds. (The surge in the stock market before that announcement led to the RCMP investigation that helped defeat the Liberals.)

The Conservatives had vowed that they would never tax income trusts. But after coming to power, they found the facts on the ground belied their low-tax ideology. Companies were converting themselves into income trusts left and right. Alarmed officials in the finance department warned that the government was going to lose five hundred million dollars over four years in foregone corporate tax revenue, and that the situation was getting worse. Harper and Flaherty talked back and forth about it for weeks. Each was hoping to be convinced by the other. The arguments coming from officials in Finance were compelling. Not only were the tax implications severe, but companies would be starving themselves of capital needed for investment. Mark Carney, then a senior official at the department, put together the new regulations that would tax the trusts. But the Conservatives had promised in the election campaign not to tax them, and Harper hated to break that promise.

Then came word that both Telus and Bell Canada, which in Stephen Harper's eyes were prime examples of companies that should be focusing on new investments, instead announced that they too were converting into income trusts. Both Harper and Flaherty were now convinced. After close of trading on Halloween 2006, Flaherty announced new measures to tax income trusts. Thousands of investors howled, but even much of the corporate sector supported the move. Dodgy tax dodges don't help anyone over time. And Harper had shown that, given compelling evidence, even he could change his mind.

———————

In some ways, minority government brought out the best in Stephen Harper. Two of his government's most unexpected moves were influenced by opposition leaders. One of them was the residential schools apology.

Harper had no intention of fulfilling the commitments Paul Martin had made to First Nations, non-status Indians (as they are known under the Indian Act), Métis, and Inuit in the Kelowna Accord. Martin had made those commitments without booking the dollars in the 2005 budget. No doubt they would have been part of the 2006 budget, but Harper had other plans for the five billion dollars that implementing the accord would cost over five years. His position was clear: "If I had $5 billion to give away, I would give it to the farmers."[7] But there was five billion dollars on the books specifically to settle the residential schools class action lawsuit. The schools predated Confederation – the Gradual Civilization Act, the name of which tells us all we need to know, was passed by the Province of Canada in 1857 – and continued into the 1970s; the last school closed in 1996. The government funded the schools, about 60 per cent of which were run by the Catholic Church, though Protestant churches were also heavily involved. The overt purpose of the schools was to "kill the Indian in the child," as the saying went. The children were isolated from their parents and reserves, forcibly discouraged from speaking their native languages, and sometimes physically and sexually abused. For years after the schools finally closed, the federal government and Aboriginal leaders had been negotiating compensation for those who had suffered this mass program of attempted cultural genocide. The Martin government had come very close to a settlement. What should the Harper government do? Harper called in former Supreme Court justice Frank Iacobucci to review the file. He concluded that, while there was a legal case for arguing that Ottawa was not compelled to offer compensation, evidence of abuse was so strong, and the government had been negotiating for so long, that the Aboriginal peoples would have a strong case in any lawsuit.

Jack Layton was also convinced that the federal government needed to apologize and compensate, a point he made repeatedly whenever he and Harper met. It isn't uncommon for a prime minister to meet with opposition leaders, especially in a minority Parliament. Sometimes such a meeting involves negotiations over a bill; sometimes the prime minister wants to apprise leaders of a sensitive issue involving national security. As we've seen, Harper and Layton actually got along reasonably well. Each was a savvy political operator who respected the other's tactical skills. And each realized that the Liberal Party was their common enemy, though Harper repeatedly puzzled over Layton's attacks on the Conservatives, especially at election time, when the Liberals were the NDP's real competition.

Harper decided to write the apology himself. He rejected advice from the justice department to be careful in his wording, lest the apology increase the government's legal liability. The speech went through many drafts – whether writing a speech himself or rewriting someone else's effort, Harper can be obsessive in reworking drafts of speeches.

Initially, he resisted the idea of allowing Aboriginal leaders onto the floor of the House of Commons, which he believed was a space where only elected Members of Parliament should be permitted. But when Layton tipped him that the Liberals planned to introduce a motion inviting Aboriginal leaders onto the floor, Harper nipped that in the bud by asking Phil Fontaine, National Chief of the Assembly of First Nations, and other Aboriginal leaders to join him in the Commons.

On June 11, 2008, Harper rose in a hushed and solemn House to apologize to Canada's Aboriginal peoples on behalf of the government and people of Canada:

To the approximately 80,000 living former students and all family members and communities, the Government of Canada now recognizes that it was wrong to forcibly remove children from their homes, and we apologize for having done this.

We now recognize that it was wrong to separate children from rich and vibrant cultures and traditions, that it created a void in many lives and communities, and we apologize for having done this.

We now recognize that in separating children from their families, we undermined the ability of many to adequately parent their own children and sowed the seeds for generations to follow, and we apologize for having done this.

We now recognize that far too often these institutions gave rise to abuse or neglect and were inadequately controlled, and we apologize for failing to protect you.[8]

It was a powerful and moving moment in the life of Canada's Parliament, and well received by Aboriginal leaders and somewhat surprised commentators in the media, who had never witnessed such a display of empathy and understanding from the prime minister. The Harper government's actions in attempting to improve the lives of Aboriginal Canadians often angered their leaders. Internal disagreements undermined a landmark effort at education reform. Chiefs furiously resisted federal efforts to force them to disclose their salaries. The Idle No More movement gained national attention as a protest against federal neglect of Aboriginal people on reserves. And Aboriginal resistance to the Northern Gateway pipeline would undermine efforts to build that pipeline. But on this day, at least, and on this issue, at least, there was healing.

Opposition antics were behind what might have been the most surprising move by the Conservative government in the thirty-ninth Parliament. On Wednesday, November 22, 2006, shortly after 9 a.m., Intergovernmental Affairs Minister Michael Chong bumped into his deputy minister, Louis Lévesque, outside Centre Block. What are you doing here? Chong asked. Lévesque had been summoned to the Prime Minister's Office to consult on a resolution recognizing Quebeckers as a nation.

Chong was stunned. This was the first he'd heard of the resolution. To be sure, the idea had been in the air for months. The Quebec National Assembly had unanimously passed such a motion earlier that year. Michael Ignatieff, the leading candidate in the Liberal leadership campaign, advocated recognizing Quebec as a nation within Canada. The evening before, the Bloc Québécois had tabled a motion of its own in the House of Commons. And Harper had mentioned to Chong and others that the question was going to have to be dealt with. But neither Harper nor any of his advisors had told Chong that Harper planned to pre-empt the Bloc motion with a motion of his own. The minister might never have heard about it until that morning's weekly caucus meeting, had he not come across his deputy minister. And the fact that the Centre had summoned Chong's deputy minister, without first consulting and briefing Chong, spoke volumes both about Harper's trust in the minister, and about how he expected Chong to react.

Later that morning, at caucus, Harper rolled out his plan. That afternoon, the government would propose "That this House recognize that the Québécois form a nation within a united Canada." Chong was one of the first to the microphones to object. The resolution was a mistake, he warned. It would provide the sovereigntists with ammunition in a future referendum. But Harper was adamant. Every Conservative was expected to support the motion, or risk expulsion from caucus.

In the coming days, Chong spoke with as many people close to Harper as he could, including Jim Flaherty, the political minister for Ontario. His staff reached out to staff inside the Prime Minister's Office. Surely there was a way to reword the motion that could accommodate Chong's concerns. But the Centre ignored the flares being sent by the intergovernmental affairs minister. Finally, on Monday, just before Question Period, Chong met privately with Harper. The prime minister couldn't understand the minister's complaint. The motion had no legal weight; it wasn't part of the Constitution; it was purely a symbolic gesture. The Progressive Conservative side of the party, to which Chong had belonged, had favoured Joe Clark's notion that Canada was "a community of communities." There was no good reason, Harper argued, for Chong not to be on board.

But in fact, the PCs had always been divided on that subject, and Chong had never accepted the community-of-communities interpretation of the federation. And as for Harper's argument that the Conservative motion would short-circuit the Bloc's efforts to present a similar motion with more separatist-friendly wording, Chong believed the better alternative would be for the prime minister to rally the other federalist parties to defeat the motion, as Chrétien had done in similar circumstances when he was prime minister.

Chong had a point. Steve Harper, Reform policy chief, would never have supported such a motion. He would have seen it as pandering to Quebec, and as further proof of the need for a Reform alternative to the governing Conservatives. Stephen Harper, Reform MP, wouldn't have supported it, either, as Intergovernmental Affairs critic. He would have demanded stronger limits on the ability of Quebec to secede, and such a motion could have the very opposite effect. Stephen Harper, president of the NCC, would have campaigned against this partial concession to the notion that Quebeckers formed a distinct society within Canada. So why had Stephen Harper, prime minister, personally put forward the motion?

Partly, the move was based on political calculation. One path to a majority government, Harper calculated, involved a bigger breakthrough in Quebec than the ten seats they had won in the last election. This offer of recognition might help. He had already accorded Quebec a seat at Canada's table at UNESCO. The 2007 budget was going to address the alleged fiscal imbalance. Recognizing Quebeckers as a nation within Canada might make the Conservatives more attractive than the Liberals to non-sovereigntist Quebec voters. And Harper had learned on the job. His years in Ottawa as leader of the Alliance and the Conservatives had given him a clearer understanding of how Quebeckers view themselves and their place within Canada.

The motion was supported by all parties, with the Liberal caucus divided on the issue – another happy consequence, as far as the Conservatives were concerned – and widely praised both inside and outside Quebec. Westerners who might have objected to the special treatment that Quebec was once again receiving mostly held their tongues. Harper's bona fides on the issue were impeccable; if he felt this had to be done, they could live with it. But there was one person who couldn't live with it. As he had warned Stephen Harper he would, Michael Chong abstained on the vote and resigned from cabinet. He promised Harper he would cause no trouble, and he kept his word. Michael Chong as a backbencher has never backbitten his leader on or off the record, though he has campaigned persistently to restore the traditional powers of Members of Parliament to hold the government (even if their party forms it) to account. But just as Harper could not tolerate authority when he was a subordinate, so too he could not tolerate dissent when he was in charge. Michael Chong, by behaving the way Harper used to behave when he served under Preston Manning – obstinate, principled – had doomed his career. Stephen Harper would never hire Stephen Harper.

Nonetheless, the prime minister badly mismanaged the affair. Chong was never a major player in cabinet or in caucus, but he was young and partly of Chinese ancestry, and he held an exurban riding outside Toronto, the kind of riding that the Tories prized. He was everything Harper wanted the Conservative Party to appeal to: professionals from ethnic minorities living in the 905. Harper could have kept Chong in cabinet by reaching out, consulting him, exercising his formidable powers of persuasion. Instead he ignored, and then lost, his minister of intergovernmental affairs. It was poor caucus management. But it was also typical of a man who had already established a reputation as the most controlling prime minister in Canadian history.

THIRTEEN

Control

In early February 2006, Derek Burney sat across a desk from Stephen Harper, who was reading the mandate letters Burney had prepared for the new cabinet. Each letter was three pages. The first reminded the new minister of the Conservatives' governing priorities: tax reduction, the child care benefit, the Accountability Act, reducing patient wait times, criminal-justice reform. The second page outlined the minister's particular responsibilities. The third page contained what Burney called the "mother of God" paragraphs, reminding the minister of his or her duty to act with integrity, to avoid conflicts of interest, to adhere to directives coming from the Prime Minister's Office, and to be prepared for instant dismissal if the minister committed any act that tarnished the image of the government, the party, or, especially, the prime minister. Burney had routinely prepared these documents when he was chief of staff to Brian Mulroney, who paid little attention to them. Now Burney sat silently as Harper went through each letter, line by line. By the time he had finished, the pages were festooned with changes. "I don't agree with this," Harper explained to Burney, or, "This isn't in our election platform." Burney shrugged. "It's your government."[1] Yes it was. This is how Stephen Harper would govern for the next decade.

Some leaders like to micro-manage; others prefer to delegate. Each approach has its strengths and weaknesses. But Harper's determination to grasp all of the levers, and even the widgets, of the federal government is matched by an equal determination to control the flow – or rather, the trickle – of information coming out of the government. Bureaucrats, as mentioned, are prohibited from speaking to reporters. Scientists are prohibited from releasing the results of their research. Ambassadors have been ordered to obtain permission from the Centre before representing Canada in meetings. (The mantra from the PMO, as diplomats bitterly put it, is: Do nothing without instructions. Do not expect instructions.) Access to Information requests are routinely held up for so long that by the time the information is released, it's no longer of any use, and the pages are mostly blacked out in any case.

Although they are in fact separate issues, this general air of secretiveness gets mixed up with the Conservatives' willingness to demonize opponents. In fact, the Tories don't have opponents; they have enemies. The leader of the Liberal Party is an enemy. Judges who strike down their legislation are enemies. Union leaders are enemies. Authors and other artists who criticize the Conservatives are enemies. Journalists who cast a more-than-occasional critical eye on the government are enemies. And toward his enemies Stephen Harper bars no holds. From the attack ads outside the writ seeking to discredit the Opposition leader before voters have even gotten to know him, to the derisive approach to the opposition in Question Period; from turning Members' Statements – once innocuous declarations of praise for the success of the local fall fair – into yet another platform for deriding the opposition, to using "push polls" that sully an opponent's reputation, the Tories have plumbed depths that not even the Liberals were prepared to sink to, something that didn't seem possible in the Chrétien and Martin years.

The Conservatives' autocracy, secretiveness, and cruelty, critics accuse, debase politics to a level that threatens the very foundations of Canadian democracy. "Hardly anything in this world hints of Putinism more than Harperism," columnist Ralph Surette of the Halifax *Chronicle Herald* opined.[2] Journalist Mark Bourrie, in his scathing indictment of the Harper government's relations with the press, warned, "If all goes his way, the government and the country itself will belong to a clique of professional political insiders who serve at Stephen Harper's pleasure . . . he'll have created a new, undemocratic way of ruling Canada . . . with sham elections maintaining the myth that democracy is the same thing as regular elections."[3]

Let's consider the bill of indictment, starting with the accusation of autocracy. Over the course of the past ten years, this government has had repeated run-ins with Elections Canada. The biggest was an in-and-out money shuffle, which involved sending funds from the national office to ridings during the 2006 election; the ridings then used the funds for, in effect, national campaign advertising, thus doing an end-run around the spending limits. Elections Canada laid charges against campaign chair Doug Finley and others, but the matter was dropped after the party pleaded guilty and paid a $230,000 fine. And then there was the robocalls affair,* which badly tarnished the government, even if it turned out that voter fraud had been limited to the riding of Guelph. The Tories' response: the 2013 Fair Elections Act, which, among other things, limited the power of Elections Canada to investigate allegations of election fraud and to promote voter turnout. (Conventional wisdom holds that marginal voters, if they do vote, rarely vote Conservative.)

The Conservatives summarily eliminated long-standing agencies and programs, such as the Court Challenges Program, which offered government funding to organizations seeking to launch legal challenges against the federal government, and the International Centre for Human Rights and Democratic Development (better known as Rights and Democracy), an agency that promoted democratic governance and the rule of law overseas. The Law Reform Commission, which studied the intersection between law and society, was axed, along with – no surprise here – the National Roundtable on the Environment and the Economy.

Twice the Conservatives prorogued Parliament for partisan political reasons: the first time to avoid defeat at the hands of the opposition parties in 2008; the second, to shut down an inconvenient inquiry into Afghan detainees. But there were many other, less egregious offences, such as the secret two-hundred-page handbook issued to committee chairs on how to

---

* Many of the events described in this chapter will be dealt with more fully in future chapters.

prevent opposition politicians from dominating parliamentary committees, and how to shut down the committees' business if they succeeded.

Many people consider the government move to strip political parties of public funding anti-democratic, though it could also be argued that taxpayers should not be forced to support partisan political activity. Having created the Office of the Parliamentary Budget Officer, the Tories then slashed its funding, once it became clear that Kevin Page, its first incumbent, was showing an alarming streak of independent thinking.

The government fell early and often into the habit of introducing massive omnibus bills, attached to the federal budget, knowing that the opposition would not be able to vote against them without voting against the budget itself, forcing an election. In majority government, the Conservatives continued the practice, seemingly out of sheer habit. Bill C-51, which granted major new powers to the security services to detect and deter terrorist threats at home, was forced through Parliament in spring 2015 with unseemly haste, despite well-grounded concerns that the bill threatened civil liberties.

There were the arbitrary cuts to environmental programs, the relentless attack ads between elections, the egregious use of government funds for what were, in effect, partisan Conservative advertisements. There was the with-us-or-with-the-child-pornographers legislation (fortunately withdrawn) that would have allowed police to track Internet activity without a judicial warrant. There was the stacking of the Senate with patronage appointments. There was the government's open attack on the integrity of Supreme Court Chief Justice Beverley McLachlin over the Marc Nadon affair. There was the sudden, suspicious wave of audits by the Canada Revenue Agency into charities that just happened to oppose Conservative government policies. (The CRA insists there was no connection.) Worst of all, in the eyes of its critics, the Harper government became the first in the Commonwealth to be declared in contempt of Parliament, for refusing to fully disclose the costs of the F-35 jet fighter program, among other items.

As for the Harper government being secretive, that puts the matter charitably. A few examples: Among other efforts to muzzle government scientists working on environmental issues from presenting their research, Environment Canada scientist Mark Tushingham was prohibited from speaking publicly about a novel he had written that centred on climate change. Along with its notorious reluctance to reply to Access to Information requests, the government eliminated the Access to Information database (the Coordination of Access to Information Requests System), which had listed every request for access to information, citing a lack of demand for its contents. Further, the government sought to vet the press releases even of such independent agencies as the auditor general. In his most public act of secrecy, Stephen Harper simply refuses to talk to the media more than he absolutely must, and he rarely must. His ministers also avoid the press. And of course, who could forget Nigel Wright's secret cheque to settle the accounts of Senator Mike Duffy?

Lastly, how cruel is the Harper government? Vic Toews labelled Louise Arbour, the former United Nations commissioner for human rights and Supreme Court judge, a "national disgrace" because of her concern over civilian casualties when Israel entered Lebanon in 2006. And Chris Alexander, as immigration minister, stripped access to public health care from refugee claimants whose claims had been denied.

When confronted by an official who contradicts the government, the government's first response is to fire the official, or, if that's not possible, to debase his or her reputation. This includes Linda Keen. The former head of the Canadian Nuclear Safety Commission ordered the nuclear reactor at Chalk River shut down, citing safety concerns. This led to a critical shortage of medical isotopes. The government fired Keen and ordered the reactor reopened. It includes Paul Kennedy. When the former head of the Commission for Public Complaints Against the RCMP tried to acquire more power and greater independence for the commission, the government responded by refusing to renew his contract.

It emphatically includes Richard Colvin. The public servant testified that he had warned government officials of possible complicity by Canadian Forces in the torture of Taliban prisoners. The government did everything in its power to discredit his testimony. It even includes Diane Ablonczy, who goes back with Harper as far as the earliest days of Reform, and who helped Laureen and Stephen get together. After Ablonczy, as a minister of state, used a tourism fund to help finance Toronto's Gay Pride festival, she had control of the fund taken away from her. (The government insisted there was no connection.)

The Conservatives' treatment of Omar Khadr might also be described as simply cruel. Captured in Afghanistan in 2002 and accused of killing an American soldier, Khadr was sent at the age of fifteen to the Guantanamo prison, where he languished in legal limbo until 2010, when he pleaded guilty to war crimes. Neither Liberal nor Conservative governments pressed for a resolution to his case. The Harper government only reluctantly accepted Khadr's return to a Canadian prison in 2012 and refused to allow him to communicate with journalists. It also fought to prevent him from being released on bail.

As for the Conservative government's plethora of cuts to government departments, agencies, and programs, including the national parks, the CBC, Canada Post, and VIA Rail; its decision to eliminate the mandatory long-form census; its refusal to hold a public inquiry into missing Aboriginal women; its failure to support veterans returning from Afghanistan; and its efforts to recriminalize prostitution rather than supporting workers in the sex trade – classifying these measures as autocratic, secretive, or cruel is a pointless distinction.

Taking it in sum, the columnist Lawrence Martin concluded in a 2012 column that, because of these and other abuses, "technically we might still call [Canada] a democracy. In practice it's a democracy in name alone."[4] John Ralston Saul went even further. The public intellectual and spouse of former governor general Adrienne Clarkson is particularly incensed by the omnibus bills, which he called "a direct negation of our democratic system." ". . . Napoleon would have approved," he wrote. "Mussolini would have been jealous. Peron would have been filled with admiration."[5]

So what to make of it all?

First off, claims that, under the Harper government, Canada has ceased to be a democracy are nonsense. Saul's invocation of Mussolini and Peron is positively offensive. The comparison of Stephen Harper to Vladimir Putin belongs to the same kind of mindset that considered the United States and the Soviet Union morally equivalent during the Cold War. By any objective comparative standard, Canada remains, today, one of the freest nations on earth. The *Economist* considers it the freest in the G8.[6]

As for freedom of the press, Reporters Without Borders ranks Canada the eighteenth-freest nation on earth, which sounds mediocre only until you realize that Canada, by this organization's measure, ranks far ahead of Great Britain (33), France (39), or the United States (46).[7]

But have the three Harper governments been autocratic, secretive, and cruel? The answer is yes, sometimes. At other times they have exhibited other traits. At all times, they have reflected the qualities of Stephen Harper and the circumstances he confronts.

From his boyhood in Leaside, Harper learned not to trust those beyond the inner circle of family and close friends. That circle is not much larger today. Relations with those outside the wall can be cordial, but they are rarely based on implicit trust, an emotional resource that Harper invests in only a very few. And his encyclopedic memory includes not only the history of maritime border disputes, or who starred in what film; it also includes every act by every person who has slighted, offended, or betrayed him. Such acts are never forgotten and only rarely forgiven. Stephen Harper holds grudges.

He has never successfully cultivated the social skill of pretending to connect. He has difficulty feigning interest. His associates talk of him sometimes simply turning his back and walking away from them while they are in mid-sentence. He rarely displays much ability or desire to be collegial, or even polite. This tendency toward abruptness gets worse when he is tired or under stress.

Politics involves the exercise of power. There are a great many people who seek to take advantage of that power, or to take it away. Harper's reluctance to trust has served him well in his climb to power and his decade of exercising it as prime minister. But because his suspicion of the intentions of others is so overt, those who serve under him inhabit an environment of suspicion, and are, or become, suspicious as well – the culture of paranoia that Tom Flanagan observed when he worked for Stephen Harper. The reservoir of goodwill in the Prime Minister's Office is shallow and quickly drained.

The government reflects Harper's style of decision making. Stephen Harper is not a leader who invites a bunch of people in to debate an issue while he listens quietly. He feels no imperative to forge consensus. He is his own consensus. He prefers written briefings to oral. When a large decision looms, he likes to gather together all the information he can, read it over, process the information, think about it, and then think about it some more. He has no hesitation about delaying a decision for as long as it takes until he has made up his mind. Once his mind is made up, he announces his decision and expects it to be acted on. In other circumstances, he will come quickly to a point of view and argue it fiercely, only to quietly change his position after reflecting on the counterarguments. And, needless to say, Harper brooks no dissent within his own office. Anyone who opposes his views or style of management is welcome to work elsewhere. To repeat, Stephen Harper would never hire Stephen Harper.

In short, the government is autocratic and secretive because it reflects the personality and world view of the prime minister. With Harper and his administration, what you don't see is what you get.

That said, if Harper is suspicious about the world around him, he has reason to be. As Joseph Heller famously said, "Just because you're paranoid doesn't mean they aren't after you." Harper sees himself as an outsider because he *is* an outsider. He is from the West, but most of the country lives near the Great Lakes or St. Lawrence River. He is from the suburbs, but the Laurentian elites generally live downtown. Harper is hostile toward these elites, and they are hostile toward him. He is contemptuous of progressive academics, and they reciprocate. He distrusts the judiciary, and the judiciary has vindicated that distrust by striking down parts of his law-and-order agenda. The gala-goers he derides spit out his name in the foyer at intermission. When Stephen Harper rejected the University of Toronto, when he rejected the life of a Tory political aide in Ottawa, when he embraced the West, he fled from the commanding heights of the Central Canadian academic, cultural, and political landscape. He is the embodiment of alienation. But in Western Canada and even in parts of Central Canada, there are millions who feel equally alienated. They tend to live in suburbs or in towns or on farms. And they tend to vote for him.

Relations with the Parliamentary Press Gallery are particularly fraught. From the day of the *Winnipeg Free Press*'s cartoon, captioned "Join Preston Manning's thump for Jesus"; through the years in which Reform was depicted as a bunch of rednecked racists; to the 2000 election, during which commentators poured derision on Stockwell Day; through the years when Harper was dismissed by Central Canadian columnists and editorialists as a Western radical conservative who would never be elected prime minister, this prime minister has loathed the press. Particularly traumatic was the day during the 2004 election when the Tories went off the rails with their release accusing Paul Martin of being soft on child pornography. Yes, the release was foolish, and yes, Harper should have retreated rather than doubling down. But those on the Tory bus that day witnessed a pack of reporters in a frenzy, convinced they had finally found a stick with which they could beat the Conservatives into defeat.

Harper had also watched what he considered the Martin government's self-immolating approach to the media. The former prime minister's advisors had spent so much time cozying up to journalists with slanders about Jean Chrétien that they had difficulty breaking the habit. Reporters grilled ministers and sometimes the prime minister as they left cabinet each week. It was a matter of course for ministers, deputy ministers, and senior staff to respond to queries from senior journalists on the Hill. Lunch in the parliamentary restaurant with a minister or senior aide was a very pleasant way of obtaining a good story or column for the next day. Life was good.

Harper's determination to put a stop to all of this hardly endeared him to the fourth estate. Ministers and senior bureaucrats suddenly became unavailable. Access to senior staff was also strictly controlled. Harper rarely spoke to the press, and when he did, Deputy Press Secretary Dimitri Soudas insisted that reporters apply to have their names put on a list. Reporters refused, and began boycotting "avails," as they're called, with Harper. The boycott eventually collapsed. It hardly mattered anyway. By his third government, Harper routinely went for weeks at a stretch without ever speaking to the press.

But though it's ludicrous for the Conservatives in their fundraising appeals to speak of the "Ottawa media elite" as though it were some conspiratorial cabal, the press has polarized into pro- and anti-Harper factions, and it's human nature to consider the people who agree with you balanced and fair, and the people who disagree with you biased and filled with ill will. The Conservatives take for granted the unswerving loyalty of the *Sun* newspaper chain and recently deceased Sun TV, and obsess over the diatribes of

Heather Mallick in the *Toronto Star*. They take for granted the thoughtful defence of their policies that can often be found in the pages of the *National Post* and seethe at Rick Mercer's CBC rants. But truth be told, the *Toronto Star* does detest this government, stem to stern, and the CBC's Laurentian world view is so deeply entrenched that those who work there don't even know it exists. That doesn't excuse the Tories' obsession with controlling and limiting information, but it helps to explain it.

There are other reasons for this government's behaviour. History is part of it. As we've seen, the Conservative coalition in the twentieth century never made any sense. It typically consisted of nationalist Quebeckers angered by the centralizing Liberal tendency, populist conservatives in the West, Red Tories in Ontario and Atlantic Canada, and Liberals who had gotten sick of always voting Liberal. That's why the Bennett, Diefenbaker, and Mulroney governments ended so badly. Harper is determined to forge a stronger conservative coalition, by convincing suburban voters in Ontario that their self-interest lies in making common cause with Western conservatives. To forge and maintain such a coalition requires intense discipline. Including message discipline.

Historical acceleration is also a factor. For about 250 years, events have been happening faster, thanks to a perpetual revolution in travel and communications, forcing governments to become more disciplined in responding to those events. The nineteenth century – transformed by the invention of the steam engine, the telegraph, photography, the modern newspaper – witnessed the emergence of political parties and the whipped vote. Powerful cabinets and bureaucracies emerged in the middle of the twentieth century, along with radio and the news reel. Power began shifting to the executive in the 1960s and '70s, with the arrival of television. The information revolution brought about by the Internet and mobile phones has accelerated that shift. In a world of proliferating news sources and social media, one indiscreet tweet can bring a world of hurt. All governments everywhere are centralizing and limiting the flow of information. Yes, this makes government less democratic, and yes, this is a real problem. It's a problem in France and in Great Britain and in Germany and in the United States and in Australia. And in Canada.

Some of what critics call autocratic, secretive, and cruel in the Harper government is actually just conservative. Harper cancelled the Court

Challenges Program, for example, because no genuinely conservative administration would give people money to take the government to court, with the taxpayers paying the costs of both plaintiff and defence, and with some expensive new program the likely outcome. The Law Reform Commission, Rights and Democracy, and the National Roundtable on the Environment and the Economy were eliminated because they clashed with the government's priorities. A conservative government will seek to limit the influence of the bureaucracy because bureaucracies by their nature seek to expand their mandate in order to justify their enlargement. The Conservatives order environmental scientists to keep their work confined to their hard drives because they suspect much of that government research is agenda-driven.

One of the fundamental priorities of the Harper government is to shrink the size of the state. Permanently. Shrinking the size of the state is Harper's single greatest imperative. It is what makes him a genuinely conservative prime minister, and this Conservative government the first truly conservative government in Canada's history. When he cuts the GST and lowers corporate taxes, he shrinks the size of the state and makes it hard for his successors to increase it. (Note the great reluctance of the Liberals to increase personal taxation. Even the NDP is willing to leave the GST alone.) When he transfers funds to the provinces without attaching any preconditions, he shrinks the size of the state, at least at the federal level. When he cuts funding for scientific research, he shrinks the size of the state, since that research invariably leads to calls for increased government funding to implement the results of that research. On Stephen Harper's watch, no program is funded that could lead to pressure for increased government activity. It is perfectly reasonable to object to all of these measures. But it is not reasonable to expect a conservative government not to act like a conservative government.

Finally, part of the allegation that the Harper governments have been autocratic, secretive, and cruel is simply false. For one thing, over time, Harper has increasingly delegated authority within the Prime Minister's Office, according to those who have worked in that office. Ever since Tom Flanagan took him to the woodshed back in 2005 for gumming up the works by trying to control everything, Harper has been learning to gradually, reluctantly let go. He was also able to let go because people got better at their jobs. In the early months of the first government, the inexperience of staff led to endless mistakes, most of which the public never got to see. As people grew into their responsibilities and the organizational flow charts began to make sense, Harper was prepared to delegate more.

And not all ministers are in thrall to the Centre. Jason Kenney created his own, separate power base at Immigration. Jim Flaherty and Stephen Harper collaborated on what went into the budget, and that collaboration was real. Tony Clement tweets up a storm, without ever asking permission. John Baird, whether at the Treasury Board, Environment, or Foreign Affairs, enjoyed considerable autonomy and influence, because of his track record of success. Peter MacKay has let it be known when he disagrees with government policy. James Moore, when he was at Heritage, defended the arts and even the CBC from internal attacks. In recent years, Transportation Minister Lisa Raitt has demonstrated not only her competence, but her confidence in handling the press. Cabinet can be divided into what could be called frightened ministers and not frightened ministers. The names above are not frightened.

The government is not so secretive as some perceive it. Yes, the Conservatives tried to limit the activities of the parliamentary budget officer, but they created the office in the first place. They also created the conflict of interest and ethics commissioner, and the public sector integrity commissioner, and the commissioner of lobbying. Under the Conservatives, auditing activity has actually increased. And the Open Data pilot project is making it easier for citizens to access at least some government documents.

Legislatively, the Conservatives have hardly been cruel. Social transfers have been protected. Billions of dollars have been spent on infrastructure. Spending on Aboriginal programs has increased, and would have increased by even more, had Aboriginal leaders not vetoed education reform. There have been big new programs in the Far North. And there has been a plethora of tax credits on everything from music lessons to tools for tradespeople – to the chagrin of fiscal purists. Some of the anti-Conservative rhetoric is just that: rhetoric.

But it remains an unalterable fact that the face of the Harper government is Stephen Harper's face. That face is stern and cold. It is also intelligent and perceptive. Yes, it can be cruel, but I do not believe that Stephen Harper is, at his core, a cruel man. Just a very tough one.

It might be fair to say this: If you decided that, despite its accomplishments, the Harper government has left the public service so cowed, the flow of knowledge so impaired, and Parliament so weakened that it doesn't deserve your vote, that would be a reasonable call. If you decided that democratic institutions remain robust and the government should be judged on other aspects of its record, that too would be a reasonable call.

During his tenure, a compact has seemed to form between the people and Stephen Harper. He promised to run the country's finances well, to protect people's jobs and keep their taxes low. He promised to strengthen the military and assert Canada's interests overseas. Most important, he promised not to do much else. He has avoided the trials and traumas that have roiled the country since the days of the Quiet Revolution. He hasn't asked for the people's love, which is just as well, because the people haven't been inclined to bestow it. But at his peak in popularity, about four Canadians in ten said they preferred to have him running the shop, even as they shook their heads at some of his antics. As for the remaining six, we'll never know how many of them refused to vote for the Conservatives but have been quietly relieved to have them in power.

It has been a comfortable arrangement. It has lasted a decade, which, when you think about it, is quite remarkable, given that this government is famously autocratic, secretive, and cruel.

By late November 2006, it had become perfectly clear that the Liberal Party was going to meet in Montreal to choose the wrong person as leader. Who would that leader be? It didn't matter. All the major candidates were fatally flawed.

Michael Ignatieff had been in the lead through most of the campaign. A troika of Liberal strategists – Alfred Apps, Ian Davey, and Dan Brock – had recruited the tall, hawk-nosed public intellectual from Harvard, where he was teaching at the Carr Center for Human Rights Policy. The original plan had been for Ignatieff to win a seat in Toronto in the 2006 election, move into the Martin cabinet in some senior portfolio, and then run for leader when Martin stepped down. No one had factored in the possibility that Martin might actually lose the election. Now Ignatieff and his cabal were running a strong campaign, reminding party members that outsiders had often been brought in to lead the party, most notably Trudeau and Pearson. But Ignatieff hadn't just been outside the party; he'd been outside the country, from 1978 until 2005, almost thirty years.

His chief rival was his former friend from his college days, Bob Rae. Rae had a great deal of experience in politics and government. His problem was that he had obtained that experience as a New Democrat, and the government he had led, at Queen's Park in the 1990s, had turned out to be the most unpopular in the province's history. Rae switched to the Liberals in 2006 and promptly started running to replace Martin. Weren't there any Liberals willing to lead the Liberals?

There was one: Stéphane Dion. But the bookish university professor spoke English with a strong and not always intelligible French accent, and his support for the Clarity Act had not won him many friends in Quebec. It was hard to figure out where his political base was to be found. Gerard Kennedy had a political base: in Ontario, where he had served in Dalton McGuinty's government. But Kennedy had little national profile, and was said to have been disliked by his own cabinet colleagues. It was highly noticeable that Greg Sorbara and George Smitherman, two of those cabinet colleagues, were running Bob Rae's campaign. None of the other candidates had any realistic hope of victory.

The Liberal leadership convention that climaxed with voting on December 2, 2006, was the last delegated leadership convention held at the federal level. All three major parties have now switched to a direct leadership vote by members or supporters. Though delegated conventions – in which members in each riding choose delegates to vote on their behalf – can be very exciting, they are also unpredictable, as the Liberals discovered to their eternal regret. With Ignatieff in first place but stalled, and Rae unable to build momentum, delegates stampeded to Stéphane Dion on the fourth ballot. Within weeks of Dion taking over, the Tories released their first attack ad, right in the middle of the Super Bowl broadcast. It was taken from a leadership candidates' debate, in which Dion woefully failed to defend his record of inaction on climate change when he was environment minister. "Stéphane Dion is not a leader," the ad proclaimed. The Conservatives had actually intended to run attack ads earlier, but Dion was such a long shot that they hadn't bothered to prepare anything in advance.

The Liberals had decided to confront a cold, dull, academic prime minister with a cold, dull, academic leader of the official opposition. They had chosen someone who was as reluctant as Harper to take advice, as unwilling to compromise as Harper had been in his earlier years. What Harper had that Dion lacked was political street smarts. Before long, there were stories of dissent within the Liberal caucus. The party lost a by-election in the Montreal riding of Outremont, which should have been one of its safest seats. Worse, they lost it to the NDP, bringing Thomas Mulcair, a former cabinet minister in Jean Charest's government, to Parliament. Mulcair would become a new and increasingly powerful voice for the New Democrats, who were serious about making real gains in Quebec.

Harper had hopes for gains in Quebec as well. The 2007 budget, along with cutting the GST another percentage point, laid out the Conservatives' plans for fixing the so-called fiscal imbalance. Generally speaking, federal revenues were too high, leading to massive budget surpluses, and provincial revenues were too low, leading to repeated deficits. The Conservatives tackled the problem by recalculating the equalization program to increase federal transfers. That, and the cuts to the GST, pretty well eliminated the surpluses. But anyone who looked closely would notice that almost half of the increase in equalization payments went to Quebec.

Liberal premier Jean Charest, who was in a tough election fight against the upstart Action démocratique du Québec, led by the young and handsome Mario Dumont, announced he would use the federal transfers to cut taxes. Harper should have been pleased; he was all about cutting taxes, and Quebec's taxes were too high. But the prime minister saw it as a betrayal. He was increasing transfers to redress a fiscal imbalance, not to finance a provincial tax cut. Relations between Harper and Charest chilled instantly. Neither would lend a hand to help the other in elections to come, which didn't help Tory ambitions in Quebec.

The "fiscal imbalance" that the 2007 budget addressed has long been forgotten by almost everyone. But it signalled a shift in relations between Ottawa and the provinces that stands as one of the Harper government's signal achievements. In fact we might call it the First Big Thing that Stephen Harper accomplished as prime minister. In this move, Harper eased seventy years of federal–provincial tensions and contributed in no small way to the collapse of the sovereigntist movement in Quebec.

Up until the Second World War, the federal and provincial governments more or less raised the money that they needed to operate. But during the war, everyone agreed that Ottawa needed complete control over everything, and so in 1940 the provinces "rented" their authority to raise personal and corporate income taxes to the federal power. After the war, Ottawa decided it needed to hold on to its newfound taxing power in order to construct the social safety net: universal public health care, near-universal public education, welfare and subsidized housing for the poor, and so on. The problem was that these were all areas of provincial jurisdiction, but Ottawa had all of the money. So Liberal governments offered to fund a portion of the costs of the programs, in exchange for common standards in administering them. Provinces also returned to taxing income and imposed sales taxes. Quebec routinely opted out, established its own programs, and received federal compensation. Poorer provinces that couldn't raise enough money to run their own programs received additional federal funds through an equalization program, which meant taxpayers in wealthier provinces were subsidizing governments in poorer provinces. Things became very, very complicated.

If that weren't bad enough, the country spent about thirty years on the brink of falling apart. The Quiet Revolution of the 1960s spawned the militant FLQ (Front de libération du Québec) and the moderate Parti Québécois. Lester Pearson, Pierre Trudeau, Brian Mulroney, and Jean Chrétien all struggled to accommodate Quebec's aspirations while containing the threat of separatism. The Victoria Charter. The PQ victory in 1976. The first referendum on sovereignty. The patriation of the Constitution. Meech Lake. Charlottetown. The second referendum. The Clarity Act. For a third of a century, Canada had a headache.

In 1995, as part of its campaign to eliminate the federal deficit, the Chrétien government slashed funding to the provinces, creating the so-called fiscal imbalance. Once the books were balanced, rather than giving the money back, Jean Chrétien tried to attach conditions. It was embedded in the Laurentian genetic code that the federal government should promote unity by using its spending power to convince or coerce provincial governments to adopt shared national standards set and enforced by Ottawa. Only by now the provinces were having none of it. They'd been hoodwinked once too often by governments that established shared-cost programs and then cut the federal funding down the road, leaving them holding the bag. As we saw, when Paul Martin tried to tie national standards of accountability to his health care accord, the premiers threatened to walk away from the table. Martin caved. While the 2004 health care accord spouted the language of accountability, the provincial governments were free to spend the new money any way they saw fit, and they did.

Stephen Harper watched all of this with growing alarm (in his teens), disdain (in his twenties), and anger (in his thirties). That anger culminated in the rant to the *National Post* after the 2000 election and the Firewall Letter. Anger was replaced by resolve when, as Opposition leader, he watched the premiers pummel Paul Martin. Harper had vowed the fiasco would never be repeated on his watch, and he kept his word.

The prime minister had dinner with the premiers three weeks after taking office. They were in town for a meeting of the Council of the Federation (which is what the premiers call themselves when they meet without the prime minister) and it seemed appropriate to introduce himself. But the prime minister resolutely low-bridged the affair: dinner at 24 Sussex Drive; no agenda, no press conference or communiqué afterward. He met with the premiers twice more, on November 10, 2008, and January 16, 2009, to discuss the state of the economy. And that's it. Harper has had hundreds of meetings and phone calls with individual premiers. His ministers join ministerial conferences on finance, health, and the like. But the grand gesture of a conference of first ministers is a gesture he prefers to avoid.

Partly it's a question of temperament. Harper is uncomfortable in elaborate ceremonial gatherings. For example, state dinners with foreign leaders have been rare on his watch. Dignitaries visiting Canada are told that the prime minister prefers private working dinners to the formal spectacle of a five-course meal with music and multiple toasts. First ministers' summits, with Harper perched at the head of a conference table, with little of the negotiating done in public and most of it behind closed doors, with coalitions formed and dissolved, with the prime minister jockeying to swing recalcitrant premiers to his side – that is not Stephen Harper's way. Building a coalition one phone call or person-to-person conversation at a time is what he prefers.

But Harper's reluctance to convene first ministers' meetings is also part of a three-pronged strategy that he has pursued diligently to lower the temperature in federal–provincial relations. The first prong was to transfer at least part of the money that Ottawa had taken during the Second World War back to the provinces. There was nothing formal about it, no transfer of tax points or any other elaborate scheme. Ottawa flowed the money to the provinces by honouring the health accord that Paul Martin had negotiated, by redressing the fiscal imbalance through a rejigged equalization program, by limiting increases in government spending (once he had a majority government and the recession was over) to inflation and population growth, and by cutting the GST and other taxes. The overall effect was to drastically reduce the federal fiscal imprint. By the end of Harper's third mandate, federal revenues as a share of GDP were at 14.1 per cent, their lowest level since at least 1958.[8] Under Pierre Trudeau, they peaked at 19.5 per cent. And as Ottawa lowered its taxes, provincial governments raised theirs, in what amounted to one of the largest shifts in taxing power in Canadian history. And hardly anyone even noticed.[9]

The second prong was to get Ottawa out of the provinces' face. Stephen Harper co-authored the Firewall Letter as a protest against federal intrusion into Alberta's affairs. Then, he thought the solution was greater autonomy for Alberta. As prime minister, he thought the solution was to eliminate the irritant. During Harper's decade in power, Ottawa avoided any new initiatives in health care, education, social assistance, or any other area of provincial jurisdiction. (One exception to this rule, the national securities regulator, we'll take up further on.) The most conspicuous example of this approach arrived with the 2014 expiry of the Martin health accord.

Everyone anticipated an epic round of bargaining as the agreement approached its end. Ministers would shuttle between the federal and provincial capitals. Terse communiqués and accusatory press conferences would ratchet up the tension. Quebec would seek allies in angrily rejecting Ottawa's demands, while simultaneously insisting on higher increases. With any luck, reporters would get to camp out in front of the Government Conference Centre for days on end, as word filtered out of an encouraging new proposal from Saskatchewan.

Instead, on December 19, 2011, three long years before the accord was set to expire, after most MPs had headed home for the holidays and most people in the capital were recovering from the weekend Christmas Party, Finance Minister Jim Flaherty presented the provinces with a take-it-or-leave-it announcement (actually, leaving it wasn't an option) at a finance ministers' meeting in Victoria. Once the Martin accord expired in 2014, increases would continue to rise by 6 per cent for two years. Future increases would match the nominal increase in the GDP (inflation plus real growth) but would never drop below 3 per cent. The new deal would expire in 2024, which in political terms means eternity.

Afterward, Ontario finance minister Dwight Duncan explained what had happened in the room. "[Flaherty] put the document in front of us and said, 'This is the way it's going to be,'" Duncan told reporters. "We all kind of paused; we all looked at each other."[10] Many of the finance ministers and premiers denounced the deal as arbitrary and inadequate. But there was no steam in their protests. The federal government wasn't asking for anything in return. For most people, increases that covered off both inflation and growth seemed pretty reasonable. Anyway, it was Christmas.

There was a third prong to the Harper government's approach in intergovernmental relations: an end to equalization by stealth. The health care funding increases that Flaherty announced were to be disbursed on a strictly per capita basis: Each province's grant was based on the size of its population. In the past, Ottawa had built an equalization component into program spending. This was above and beyond the actual equalization program itself. Typically, if the federal government was dispersing funds for, say, scientific research at universities, the poorer provinces would receive a bigger grant, per capita, than they were entitled to. But on the Conservatives' watch, there was to be no equalization outside equalization. The ten-year health care announcement would be paid out according to population numbers and nothing else. Not fair! British Columbia complained; our population is older on average (all those retirees in Victoria) and our needs are greater. Not fair! Quebec fumed; our tax base is weaker than Alberta's and we're less able to pay our own way. (Though no Quebec premier ever put it like that.) Not fair! complained the Atlantic Provinces; we're even poorer than Quebec. (They don't put it like that either.) It didn't matter.

The Conservatives went even further in the 2012 budget. Employment Insurance – another equalization program in all but name, since benefits are higher in areas of high unemployment – was tightened up. Workers would have to accept a job at less than their previous wage, and within a one-hour commute of where they lived, or pogey would be cut off. Again the premiers of Quebec and the Atlantic Provinces raged: their economies relied on seasonal workers; without EI people would be forced to move away. Again the protests went nowhere. The majority of the population in Ontario and the West was of the opinion that they should not have to work harder and longer to pay for people in the East not to work at all.

This three-pronged approach – reducing the federal fiscal footprint, transferring funds to the provinces without strings, and stripping equalization out of programs other than equalization – worked wonderfully well, most of the time, in most parts of the country. Unquestionably the changes to EI will hurt the Conservatives in Atlantic Canada in the next election. But for ten years, Canada has enjoyed something it hadn't experienced since the 1950s: quiet. No roiling constitutional disputes. No protracted negotiations over this grand scheme or that. No cries of regional alienation or pleas for new initiatives to unite a fractured country. The country isn't fractured. In fact, after a decade of what could be called passive federalism, Canada is more united than at any time since the Second World War.

Harper obsessed on fiscal transfers. It was a file he micro-managed even more than the others. His personal briefing materials on the fiscal imbalance filled an entire filing cabinet in his office. Here was a situation in which Preston Manning's policy advisor could personally engineer a key priority of the old Blue Book, by shrinking the federal government, increasing the fiscal capacity of the provinces, and generally lowering the level of aggravation between the two. Jean Chrétien largely left Paul Martin alone as his finance minister engineered his own downsizing of government. But Jim Flaherty had an intimately engaged collaborator in Stephen Harper, whether he wanted one or not.

In the 2011 election, a surging New Democratic Party shattered the Bloc Québécois' hold on Quebec, reducing the separatist party's tally to four seats. We'll look at the details of that transformation later; what matters here is that, almost twenty years after the Bloc first emerged as the voice of an alienated Quebec, that voice was silenced. By 2015, with defections among its remaining MPs and little public support, the Bloc appeared to be on the verge of extinction. In desperation, the party turned in June 2015 to Gilles Duceppe to lead it once again – the longest of Hail Mary passes to prevent the party's complete demise.

The hopes of sovereigntists were rekindled in 2012, when Pauline Marois led the Parti Québécois to a narrow victory over Jean Charest's Liberals in the provincial election. Marois intended to inflame tensions between Quebec City and Ottawa by demanding greater control over culture and other files. But Harper simply refused to have the conversation. To every demand, the answer was: We're focused on the economy; we suggest you do likewise. Because Harper had launched no grand national schemes, there was nothing for the PQ to push back against. In spring 2014, gambling that circumstances were right for a majority government that would be followed by a referendum, Marois called an election. She was handed a humiliating defeat. Commentators in Quebec began to wonder whether the sovereignty movement was a one-generation phenomenon, doomed to extinction as middle-aged and older separatists gradually disappeared.

It would be grossly inaccurate to accord Stephen Harper most of the credit for the collapse of the sovereigntist cause. But he deserves at least *some* of the credit. After all, it happened on his watch. Critics warned that a Conservative Westerner would be ill-equipped to handle a rising tide of separatism in Quebec. But there was no tide. In part that was because the federal government offered the separatists nothing to rage against. Harper treated Quebec with respect; he offered it a role in UNESCO, recognized the Québécois as a nation, and redressed the province's fiscal grievances. And then he left Quebec alone, just as he left all the other provinces alone. Passive federalism wasn't very exciting, but it turned out to be enormously successful. Under the Conservatives, there have been fewer major federal–provincial disputes than at any time since Louis St. Laurent was prime minister.

There were exceptions, of course. Jim Flaherty sniped at the deficits and energy subsidies that Dalton McGuinty racked up in Ontario. As a former Ontario finance minister himself, the Irish pugilist just couldn't help weighing in. Kathleen Wynne, McGuinty's successor, complained that the prime minister wouldn't even meet with her. She had reason to complain; Harper saw the Wynne government as a virtual extension of the federal Liberal Party, since many of Justin Trudeau's advisors had worked for McGuinty at Queen's Park. But then, Harper was one to talk; his own government was in many ways a federal extension of Mike Harris's government from the 1990s.

Danny Williams caused grief. When Paul Martin refused to give him what he wanted on equalization, the populist premier of Newfoundland and Labrador ordered Canadian flags lowered to half-staff on government buildings. When Stephen Harper refused to give him what he wanted on equalization, Williams organized an Anything But Conservative campaign that cost the Tories seats in the 2008 election. As well, the Newfoundlanders pushed for more compensation once they read the fine print of the free trade agreement with the European Union.

But in the grand scheme, these were local squalls.

Not everyone approves of passive federalism. There are still those who long for new national programs to address pressing concerns and to unite the country. One example: In August 2014, the new head of the Canadian Medical Association, Chris Simpson, called on the federal government to lead a pan-Canadian initiative on improving health care for seniors. Canadians "are tired of excuses as to why the federal government can't take action," he warned. "The constitutional construct we have has for too long served as an excuse for the federal government to be absent from the table."[11]

Such a strategy would doubtless involve increased federal funding. It would require provinces to meet standards in exchange for receiving that funding. Quebec would almost certainly demand to be allowed to opt out of the program and set its own standards, while still receiving funding. This time, Ontario, British Columbia, Alberta, and Saskatchewan might demand the same. Things would become very, very complicated. Nonetheless, as a *Toronto Star* editorial opined in December 2014, "If we believe that some things – say, child care, home care, pharmacare, medicare, income security – are so fundamental to citizenship that they should be guaranteed for all Canadians, wherever they live, Ottawa has a crucial role to play."[12]

Dr. Simpson and the *Star* offered a powerful alternative vision of federalism: one more activist, socially progressive, and Ottawa-centric. The question is whether Canadian voters want to return to that model of running the country, with all of its messiness, increased tension, and threats to national unity. Future federal elections will be fought over this issue. Should Ottawa respect provincial jurisdictions, as the Conservatives have done, or should it champion national programs in health care, education, and social services, as the Liberals and New Democrats propose? In that debate, someone might remind Dr. Simpson that he took an oath: First do no harm. Canada's twenty-second prime minister can fairly claim that, on the issue of national unity, he upheld that oath.

FOURTEEN

Crisis

On top of everything else – which included a cold and remote demeanour, troubles with English pronunciation, a divided caucus, and a general lack of political acumen – Stéphane Dion had no understanding of how voters worry. People need to worry. It's in our bones. We worry about whether our jobs are secure. If we're not worried about work, it's whether the kids are getting a good education, or how we'll cope with our aging parents or our aging selves. And if our jobs are safe, our health care adequate, and our kids in good schools, then we might worry about the environment.

At the beginning of 2007, few people were aware of the subterranean shudders that threatened an economic earthquake. Unemployment and inflation appeared to be under control. In Canada, the federal and most provincial governments had enough money to meet demand and still post a surplus. For most people, life seemed good. But Al Gore and a bevy of scientists were warning that the environment was at risk of massive damage thanks to global warming caused by hydrocarbon emissions. Stéphane Dion honestly and passionately believed that fighting climate change was the most important duty of government. It took him more than a year, but he finally unveiled his solution in June 2008. The Green Shift proposed a tax on carbon that would be offset by tax reductions elsewhere. There were two problems with the Green Shift. First, no right-minded person believes any politician who promises to offset a tax hike with a compensating tax cut. Second, any pollster will tell you that the environment is a placeholder issue: it's what people worry about when there is nothing else to worry about. Once the economy emerged as a major issue in autumn 2008, the environment all but disappeared as one. The Green Shift might have been sound policy, but the timing was lousy.

If you talked to any senior Liberal in those days, anyone who wasn't a paid employee of the leader, you generally heard the same story. Dion was a disaster. He wasn't connecting with voters. His staff was weak and disorganized. The Conservatives were outfundraising the Liberals three-to-one. The only reason the Liberals continued to prop up the Conservatives, after more than two and a half years in power, was fear of the magnitude of the defeat that awaited them. These senior Liberals wanted an election anyway. Get it over with, they argued, then find a new leader. It should probably be Ignatieff. Not picking him the first time had been a horrible mistake.

Dion spent the summer of 2008 selling the Green Shift, and finding few buyers. The Conservatives released a series of ads that featured Harper in a navy blue sweater vest, perched on the edge of an armchair, talking about his children, about how important immigrants were to the country, about how his tough-on-crime legislation was making Canada a safer place. The party was trying to soften its leader's image, humanize him, make him seem comfy. Like that was going to work.

In June, Harper was telling senior staff that he wanted to avoid an election. But over the course of the summer, his thinking changed. Officials in Finance were starting to get seriously worried about the wobbles in the U.S. economy. The housing boom there might actually have been a bubble. If it burst, the United States could go into a recession, taking Canada with it. The Tories would be blamed for the bad times that followed. As Ottawa sweltered in the August heat, Harper started whistling a new tune. At a caucus retreat in Lévis, Quebec, he complained that the opposition parties were gumming up the legislative works in parliamentary committees, and that maybe it was time for an election. Two weeks later, Dion obliged by warning that he might be ready to bring down the government. Harper had no intention of letting Dion control election timing. On September 7, he visited Rideau Hall, and the election date was set for October 14. Despite all of this advance notice, it took the Liberals three more days before they were able to charter a campaign plane. Things were that bad.

They got worse. The Liberals were ten points back on overall popularity. Then they were behind fifteen points. With gas prices through the roof – they peaked at $1.49 a litre in July – the last thing people wanted was a new petroleum tax. The Green Shift was a millstone that threatened to drag the Liberals to the bottom of the sea.

But the situation was much more precarious for the Conservatives than it seemed, and the strategists in the Tory war room knew it. Team Harper wanted the election to be about leadership and nothing else. But when Lehman Brothers, the large American investment bank, collapsed on September 15, right in the middle of the election, suddenly the economy was front and centre.

As we've seen, when confronted with a problem, Harper likes to retreat into solitude, think about the problem until he has it figured out, and then announce his solution. This has worked well for him in government, but he didn't have the luxury of time in this instance, and he's lousy at improvisation. Unfortunately for Harper, the volatile weeks of a federal election are all about improvisation. We've seen before the dynamic of an election campaign shifting and Harper failing to respond: the brouhaha over the child pornography press release in 2004; his accidental musing about the Conservatives' majority government in 2006. Now, once again, the Tories' carefully planned election campaign script was garbage. Once again, Harper froze. Forced to improvise, he failed.

Some observers have described Harper as a masterful political strategist and tactician. That's only half true. Harper's long-term strategic sense is often brilliant. As far back as the 1980s he was insightfully diagnosing the Canadian political landscape and how a conservative party could exploit the terrain to its advantage. But in making day-to-day tactical decisions, he is prone to misfire, misreading the public mood and his opponents' intentions while leaping and sticking to bad snap judgments. Harper has survived in politics as long as he has because of his superior strategic skills. As for tactical prowess, more than anything else he's been lucky to get away with his many mistakes.

The Conservatives didn't have much of an election platform. They didn't feel they needed one. After all, this election was about whether people wanted Harper or Dion as leader. It was not supposed to be about rescuing the Canadian economy from the consequences of an unexpected financial crisis. So when the Tories finally released their platform on October 7, a week before the election, the first and only thing that everyone noticed was that there was nothing in it to combat the accelerating economic crisis. That's because there wasn't a crisis, Harper told reporters, just a temporary panic that would blow over.

"I think there's probably some great buying opportunities emerging in the stock market as a consequence of all this panic," Harper said. "There's a lot of panic but a government can't panic."[1] He repeated and expanded on the remark that night in an interview on CBC with host Peter Mansbridge. Dion promptly ditched the Green Shift and his teleprompter and let loose, accusing the Conservatives of ignoring the suffering millions whose jobs were suddenly at risk. He had no plan to save those jobs either – the crisis surprised the Liberals every bit as much as the Conservatives – but that didn't matter; the economy was Harper's shtick and he was clearly in denial about the scope of the crisis.

This was not Harper's only problem. Back in the third week of September, he had responded to criticism from Layton and Dion over forty-five million dollars that the federal government had cut from arts funding – a picayune amount in the scheme of things – by saying, "I think when ordinary working people come home, turn on the TV and see . . . a bunch of people, you know, at a rich gala all subsidized by taxpayers claiming their subsidies aren't high enough when they know those subsidies have actually gone up – I'm not sure that's something that resonates with ordinary people."[2] Quebeckers take their culture seriously, and the Tories saw their support plummet in that province. Now polls began to tighten in the rest of the country. Between Harper's comments on culture and the economy, he was at risk of throwing away the election. In the Tory war room, concern morphed into fear. Harper's "buying opportunity" stumble had cost the party ten points. Never mind saying goodbye to a majority government: internal polling numbers revealed that Harper might actually lose.

And then Stéphane Dion handed the election back to Harper in one of the most ethically questionable acts in the history of Canadian journalism. On October 9, five days before the election, Dion appeared on ATV's suppertime news show from Halifax, hosted by Steve Murphy, a fixture in Atlantic Canadian broadcasting. The interview was pre-taped, and it began with Murphy asking Dion a reasonably straightforward question: "If you were prime minister now, what would you have done about the economy and this crisis that Mr. Harper has not done?" Straightforward, that is, if you are a native English speaker familiar with the subjunctive mood. The question left Dion completely at sea.

Dion: If I would have been prime minister two and a half years ago?

Murphy: If you were the prime minister right now.

Dion: Right now?

Murphy: And had been for the last two weeks.

Dion: Okay, no. If I'm elected next Tuesday, this Tuesday, is what you are suggesting?

Murphy: No, I, I'm saying if you, hypothetically, were prime minister today.

Dion: Today.

Murphy: What would you have done that Mr. Harper has not done?

Dion: I would start the 30/50 plan that we want to start the moment that we'll have a Liberal Government. And the 30/50 plan, uh, the 30, in fact, the plan for the first 30 days, I should say, the plan for the first 30 days once you have a Liberal Government. Can we start again?[3]

They started again. Again Murphy asked the question, and again Dion stumbled trying to answer it. Again Murphy asked the question. Again Dion failed to answer it. On the fourth try, Dion simply ignored the question and told Murphy what he would do once he became prime minister.

So what could we learn from this, apart from the fact that Dion's English is not idiomatic? Well, for starters that he had no clear idea of what he would have done differently had he been in charge when the economic crisis hit. That he is not a natural politician – Jean Chrétien, whose English syntax is also uncertain, would have swatted the question away. And that Dion was more trusting of the CTV television network, to which ATV belongs, than he should have been.

In fact, CTV aired the entire interview, including Dion's repeated requests to start again. And then Mike Duffy aired the exchange on his national cable news program. And then Stephen Harper rushed to the microphones. "When you're managing a trillion-and-a-half-dollar economy, you don't get a chance to do do-overs, over and over again," he reminded voters.[4] For the Conservatives, Dion's Halifax flub was golden. They had wanted the election to be about a choice of leadership: Harper versus Dion. Instead, it had become about Harper's handling, or mishandling, of the economic crisis. Now, it was about leadership again, thanks to Dion himself, with a little help from Steve Murphy and Mike Duffy.

In April 2009, the Canadian Broadcast Standards Council ruled that CTV had violated the council's code of conduct in broadcasting what Dion thought were outtakes of the interview. "Such outtakes . . . are very common, even absolutely routine," the council's panel concluded. "The Panel does not, therefore, even find it a modest stretch to have a person in authority agree to a restart, or even more than one restart."[5] But by then it was all ancient history.

On Election Day the Conservatives pushed their popular support up marginally – by 1.4 percentage points to 37.7 per cent – and their seat count up substantially from 127 to 143 seats. That meant it would take the combined vote of all three parties to bring the government down. But it was still short of a majority. Harper's decision to wait on calling an election, and then his decision to force it, compounded by his paralysis in the face of an accumulating economic catastrophe, had cost him a majority government. It might have cost him even more, had his opponent not self-immolated on national television.

For Dion, the result was devastating. Like John Turner in 1988, he seemed to have caught the wind in his sails after a difficult start, only to watch his momentum flag at the end. But in this case, the letdown was far more severe. The Liberals lost 18 seats, and recorded their lowest popular vote in the party's history up to then, 26 per cent. After mulling the situation for a few days, Dion announced he would step down as leader as soon as the party could choose a successor.

Four weeks later, Stephen Harper stood on a stage in Winnipeg and rewrote history. In a further demonstration of just how well oiled the Conservative Party machine had become, he had ordered up, and the party had delivered, a policy convention within a month of the election. "The Conservative Party is Canada's party," he declared.[6] Reaching back into history, and then rewriting it, he welded the party that he led to the party of Macdonald. "It was Conservatives who founded the Confederation in 1867, creating one of the most durable political arrangements anywhere in the world," he claimed. Joe Clark and many others believed the party of Macdonald expired the day the Progressive Conservatives merged with Harper's Canadian Alliance. But Harper had no intention of following that script. He had a new script. He was the leader of the party of Confederation, the party that built the Canadian Pacific Railway and extended voting rights to Aboriginal Canadians, the party under whose banner Canada elected the first Chinese-, black-, Japanese-, Muslim-, and Hindu-Canadian Members of Parliament. "We are the party with the first female cabinet minister, the first Aboriginal senator," and the party of John Diefenbaker's Bill of Rights. "This is our history. This is the truth, past and present. No other party has a better record for bringing Canadians together and of standing up for their country's interest – because the Conservative Party is Canada's Party."

It was an audacious bit of historical revisionism. But it was necessary, even vital. Harper was determined to make the Conservative Party a broad, national conservative alternative, not to the Liberal Party, but to the progressive coalition in its entirety. His goal was nothing less than to make the Conservative Party the new natural governing party for a Canada that would be more conservative in this century than it had been in the past. The country would be more conservative because its conservative centre – the West in general and Alberta in particular – were growing faster than the rest of the country. And it would be more conservative because, for a decade and a half at that point, the country had been bringing in 250,000 people every year – from parts of the world such as China, India, and the Philippines – who were more conservative in outlook than the native born.

Election stumbles notwithstanding, this was Stephen Harper's great achievement. He had created a new Conservative coalition by marrying suburban voters in Ontario – especially aspirational immigrant suburban voters – to the traditional base of populist conservatives in the West. It was an enormous accomplishment that promised to reshape the very architecture of federal politics in Canada.

Two weeks later, he would come within a hair's breadth of throwing it all away.

APEC[7] summits typically accomplish little, other than bringing leaders together to be photographed in colourful native garb, a longstanding APEC tradition that the rotund prime minister would happily have foregone. The 2008 summit, in Lima, Peru, coincided with final preparations for the Canadian federal government's annual autumn fiscal update. The recent election victory had handed Harper a mandate to govern, and he intended to use that mandate. Given the worsening global economy, the update's forecasts and prescriptions would be closely watched. But an enormous wrench got thrown into the works. Unknown to anyone, on the flight to Lima, the water in the ice cubes on CF-01 was tainted. Harper, you will remember, prefers Coke to coffee. He and much of the Canadian delegation became sick as a dog.

This was the worst possible time to make two crucial decisions, but Harper made them anyway, and they were both horribly bad. The first, known as "the nuclear option," was the decision to eliminate the public subsidy for campaign finances. As we've seen, Harper placed a huge emphasis on identifying, cultivating, and expanding the donor base that he had inherited from the Reform Party. The CIMS database was well on its way to becoming a sophisticated mechanism for identifying, tracking, and soliciting funds from everyone who inclined toward that party. Now, if he could only eliminate the $1.95-per-vote public subsidy that the Chrétien government had put in place to compensate for eliminating corporate donations, the Conservative leader figured he could force all parties to live exclusively off their fundraising from individuals, at which his party excelled and the Liberals, especially, were dismal.

Tory MPs enthusiastically supported the idea when he raised it with them in caucus. His staff was behind it. Guy Giorno, especially, supported the move. The previous July, Giorno had replaced Ian Brodie as chief of staff. Devout, intense, and intensely partisan, Giorno had served as Mike Harris's chief of staff; he was another of the imports from Queen's Park who had shaped the Harper government. Among other qualities, he displayed a take-no-prisoners approach to anyone, be it an opposition politician or an obstreperous bureaucrat, who crossed his boss or interfered with the government's agenda. In Giorno, far from having a senior lieutenant who might temper Harper's more partisan instincts, the prime minister had an aide who egged those instincts on.

Most people who knew of the plans to cancel the subsidy assumed that it would be phased out over several years. Instead, the word came down from Lima to the finance department: the upcoming economic statement will eliminate public subsidies entirely, immediately. The opposition parties, Harper reasoned, would have no choice but to submit. The Liberals were demoralized and in the middle of a leadership campaign. What else could they do? Bring down the government just weeks after an election? They wouldn't dare.

Compounding this folly, Harper and Finance Minister Jim Flaherty decided to deny that there was an economic crisis in Canada. Looking back, the decision seems beyond stupid, especially considering those involved, who should have known better. After all, it was boldface clear by November 2008 that the global economy was cratering, taking the Canadian economy with it. The country was almost certainly already in recession, and that recession threatened to be long and severe. At an emergency G20 meeting in Washington on November 15, Harper had committed with other world leaders to massively stimulate their economies to combat the recession. (We were all Keynesians again.) During his speech to APEC, Harper had repeated that commitment to stimulus spending.

But Jim Flaherty loathed the thought of going down in history as the finance minister who sent Canada back into deficits. He had never run a deficit as Ontario finance minister, and he didn't want to run one as federal finance minister. In any case, it made sense to hold off on specific commitments until the 2009 budget, when the scope of the crisis would be clearer.

Maybe, just maybe, Canada could escape the worst effects of the recession without having to go too deeply into the red.

Harper was sick. He wanted to go after the voter subsidy. He was thousands of miles from Ottawa. Flaherty didn't want to admit there would be a deficit, and wanted to keep his powder dry. Harper and Flaherty weren't communicating properly. Guy Giorno, who was acting as liaison, was recommending that both sides take a hard line. The trade-off: Put in the cut to the voter subsidy, Harper's priority. Avoid any mention of the deficit, Flaherty's priority. Two disastrously wrong decisions, each reinforcing the other. "Canada's financial system is mature, sophisticated, well managed and able to withstand sizeable shocks," Flaherty comforted, quoting from an International Monetary Fund report, when he rose in the House on November 27.[8] The budget, he declared, remained in balance, though the finance minister acknowledged, "a further deterioration in global economic conditions could result in a deficit."

Along with the immediate elimination of the per-vote subsidy for political parties, the fiscal statement also imposed a wage cap on public servants and took away their right to strike, which poked a stick in the eye of the NDP. What Harper didn't know – what no one in the Conservative camp knew – was that Jack Layton had talked with the Liberals during the election about the possibility of a Liberal–NDP coalition in the next Parliament. In the event, the Liberals lost so many seats that it would take support from the Bloc to defeat the Conservatives and form a coalition government, something Dion wasn't prepared to consider. But that was then. Now, with the survival of his party at stake over the loss of the public subsidy, Dion marched out of the Chamber as soon as Flaherty had finished his speech and announced that the Liberal Party would vote to defeat the government at the earliest opportunity. That opportunity would come Monday, when the opposition parties would be able to put forward a motion of their choosing.

Flaherty delivered his statement on a Thursday. The next day, Friday, November 28, the government retracted its decision to eliminate the public subsidy for political parties. On Sunday, the government recanted on eliminating the right to strike and on a provision to inhibit payment equity complaints. In essence, Flaherty had jettisoned his entire fiscal statement in only three days. It didn't matter. Jack Layton and Stéphane Dion were resolved to forge a coalition government, and Gilles Duceppe was prepared to support them. Stephen Harper, it appeared, had managed to engineer his own defeat.

When senior staff met on Monday morning, the faces around the table mixed horror with resignation. They had hoped that jettisoning the toxic elements of the financial statement would defuse the crisis. But the opposition parties continued to hang together. The government appeared doomed. Harper came into the room. He was still sick. And he was already resigned to losing office. Let them take power, he told staff; they'll make such a hash of it that in a few months we'll be back into an election. This did nothing to improve the mood.

Later that morning, Harper met with senior ministers. Tony Clement, who was now industry minister, was there, along with Quebec lieutenant and foreign minister Lawrence Cannon and Marjory LeBreton, government leader in the Senate, among others. LeBreton's maternal persona masks a sharp political mind and a calculating disposition. She and Cannon had a recommendation: the government should have Parliament prorogued – that is, suspended for several weeks and then brought back into session. Prorogation is a routine procedure, used by heads of governments in parliamentary democracies to clear the order paper and prepare for a new session. It's something a prime minister or premier might do halfway through a mandate, to prepare for a cabinet shuffle and Throne Speech. But to prorogue Parliament mere weeks after the return of Parliament, and for the clear intent of avoiding defeat in the House – that would be an audacious move. There was some question as to whether it was even constitutional, or whether Governor General Michaëlle Jean would approve the request.

Harper shook his head. He was inclined to let the coalition form, and then work for its defeat. Clement also urged prorogation, warning that if the other side took power, even briefly, they would use it to demonize the Conservatives, just as Dalton McGuinty had successfully demonized the Harris government after the Liberals won the 2003 election in Ontario. But the PM had made up his mind to let the coalition form.

Later that day, cabinet ministers Jim Prentice, James Moore, Tony Clement, and Jay Hill came straight from the Operations Committee to meet with Harper and urge prorogation.[9] Harper was still inclined to let the coalition govern, and then take the case to the people in the next election. Bad idea, James Moore maintained. The Conservatives themselves knew from experience that the longer a party – or a coalition – governed, the more legitimate it would appear in the eyes of voters. Clement repeated his warning that the coalition would try to rebrand the Conservatives as toxic, and likely succeed. But the most telling argument came from Jay Hill, who was government House leader. He warned Harper that if he didn't shut the coalition down, he would lose the support of the caucus. That got Harper's attention.

Though Harper didn't immediately realize it, the situation had already started to shift in his favour, even as he contemplated his defeat. Dion and Layton were making a fatal mistake of their own. At a press conference that afternoon announcing the creation of the new coalition, three figures sat at the table: Dion, Layton, and Gilles Duceppe. There was no reason for this. The Bloc Québécois was not part of the coalition. There would be no Bloc MPs in cabinet. Duceppe had simply agreed to vote in support of the coalition in the House of Commons for a period of time, provided he was properly consulted. Yet there he was, acting for all the world like a member of an incoming coalition government, rather than the leader of a party committed to breaking up the country. He even signed a piece of paper, a for-show declaration of the coalition's intent. Brian Topp, who chaired Jack Layton's 2008 election campaign and then helped negotiate the coalition, later wrote a book about that week. The press conference, he acknowledged, was a fatal mistake. "As a political proposition," he wrote, "the coalition essentially died during its very first step out of the gate."[10]

That night, before he was to address the Conservative caucus at its annual Christmas Party, Harper was standing in the kitchen of the Westin Hotel with Laureen, Ray Novak, and press aide Dimitri Soudas. It was quiet, glum, the four of them enveloped in a fog of defeat. That fog also enveloped the room where the Tory MPs stood about, wondering what had happened. They had won an election. How could they be about to lose the government?

Just as her husband was about to go onstage, Laureen Harper took his arm and whispered into his ear. What she told him only they know. You're a fighter, she might have said. You are never going to be defeated by a separatist, a socialist, and the losingest leader in the history of the Liberal Party. Or maybe she just said she loved him. Whatever it was, it transformed Harper. His head went up, he threw his shoulders back, and he stormed into the room, where he gave the caucus what they needed above all: a shot of hope, mixed with a stiff dose of outrage.

A revived Harper also showed up the next day at Question Period. Gone was his previous hangdog, stumblebum, can't-you-see-I'm-sick performance of the previous sessions. "This deal that the leader of the Liberal Party has made with the separatists is a betrayal of the voters of this country," he thundered, "a betrayal of the best interests of our economy, and a betrayal of the best interests of our country. And we will fight it with every means that we have."[11]

Actually, he only needed one means. On Thursday morning, Harper visited Michaëlle Jean at Government House and asked her to prorogue Parliament. After receiving that request, Jean left the room, and left the prime minister to cool his heels for two hours, as a sign of her displeasure. But there was never any doubt about the outcome. The Conservatives had received the greatest number of seats in the House of Commons in the last election. The Conservatives had been the government in the previous Parliament. Following constitutional precedent, Jean had invited Stephen Harper, as leader of the Conservative Party, to form a ministry. That ministry had met the House, presented a Throne Speech, and the House had voted confidence in that Throne Speech. From that vote on, the prime minister had absolute authority to govern, which included asking the governor general to prorogue Parliament. Had she refused, Jean would have been exercising authority that the governor general, who is effectively appointed by the prime minister of the day, simply does not have. In 1925, Lord Byng erred in refusing Mackenzie King's request to dissolve Parliament and call an election. Had Jean followed Byng's precedent, she would have compounded the error. This was the consensus of the constitutional scholars who advised her in the hours leading up to her decision. She took their advice.

Articles and books have been written arguing that the coalition would have been entirely legitimate and that the attempt to create it failed in large measure because the Canadian public didn't understand how parliamentary democracy works.[12] Humbug. The iron law of coalition government is this: coalitions are legitimate if they are legitimate, and illegitimate if they are illegitimate. The agreement that the Liberals and NDP reached in Ontario in 1985 to topple the Conservatives was legitimate because David Peterson's Liberals had come within a whisker of defeating Frank Miller's Conservatives, and the idea of the Liberals and NDP replacing the ancient regime was popular with voters. This coalition, in contrast, would have been led by an outgoing Liberal leader who had just lost an election (badly), would have had NDP MPs in cabinet, and would have been propped up by separatists. Michael Ignatieff described it as "a coalition of losers."[13] Illegitimate. End of story.

At 11:30 a.m. on Thursday, December 4, Harper met with reporters to announce that the House of Commons stood adjourned until January 26. The government would live to fight another day. As it turned out, that day would last for almost seven years.

FIFTEEN

Prorogue

It had been a month since Harper picked up that bug on the way to Lima, and he still felt lousy. And after rallying to defeat the coalition, he was back in the dumps again, this time over a new threat. Michael Ignatieff had been the very last Liberal MP to sign a declaration of support for Stéphane Dion's coalition proposal. Most Liberals had concluded that the convention made a mistake when it chose Dion in 2006. The Monday after prorogation, the first Liberal leader since Edward Blake in the nineteenth century never to become prime minister announced he would step down as soon as an interim leader could be found. He had no choice: caucus was furious with, among other things, a botched video that Dion had released responding to Harper's address to the nation during the coalition crisis. They were appalled by polls showing that voters preferred Harper as prime minister to Dion by measures of two to one. By Wednesday, Ignatieff was interim leader. And within days, Bob Rae and New Brunswick MP Dominic LeBlanc had abandoned their leadership campaigns in favour of the latest white knight.

Stephen Harper now faced a new, popular, and potentially more formidable opponent. The Conservatives would have to present a budget when Parliament returned, and survive the vote on that budget. If the opposition combined to defeat the government, then the coalition could yet take power. The very fact that Ignatieff had not been Liberal leader in the last election might make him more credible in the eyes of voters. But the coalition would never happen, Harper vowed. He told senior staff that he intended to have Michaëlle Jean dissolve Parliament if the government were defeated on the budget. Could Harper defeat Ignatieff in an election? The polls suggested the new Liberal leader might win.

Once again, Harper was misreading the situation. This had become a chronic problem: he had almost defeated himself in the election by dismissing the economic crisis as a splendid investment opportunity; then he gambled that he could push draconian measures through the fiscal update, which brought on the coalition crisis; then he had to be talked out of allowing the coalition to take power; now he was predicting his government had only weeks to survive. His political radar had never been this consistently faulty.

The truth was that Michael Ignatieff didn't want to become prime minister in a coalition government, and was signalling as much. "Coalition if necessary but not necessarily coalition," he told CTV News even before he was appointed leader.[1] The Liberals, he maintained, should look at the January budget before deciding whether to join with the NDP – who still wanted to form the coalition – and the Bloc – who were still willing to support it – to bring the government down. So the right budget would keep the government alive. Harper didn't realize that Ignatieff, though deputy Liberal leader, had been excluded from the coalition talks. The former Harvard academic saw the proposed Dion government as "a desperate leader clinging to power by any means, resorting to a *coup de théâtre* to survive."[2] And the coalition, in Ignatieff's view, was illegitimate.

Flaherty and Harper were back on the same page. Both economic necessity and political survival dictated going heavily into deficit in order to stimulate an economy gripped by recession and to survive a confidence vote. But the deficit, they agreed, should be temporary and non-structural – that is, none of the spending measures should become entrenched, making it harder for the government to return to surplus once the recession ended. When Parliament returned in January, the finance minister presented a budget that would put the federal government fifty-eight billion dollars in the red, to fund a sixty-billion-dollar infrastructure program over two years with an emphasis on "shovel-ready" projects that could be underway within two years. As well, Employment Insurance benefits would be extended, and there would be the temporary (and highly popular) Home Renovation Tax Credit and an energy-efficiency retrofit program.

Stimulus spending can go awry in two ways. It can take so long to get the money out the door that it does no real good, and/or governments may tilt the spending in favour of ridings they hold or want to hold. But a 2011 auditor general's report found that, for the most part, the money had been spent wisely and well. The infrastructure program "largely achieved the Economic Action Plan objective to spend federal funding in a timely manner," Interim Auditor General John Wiersema concluded.[3] For that stern guardian of the public purse, this was rapturous approval.

While it wasn't easy to monitor exactly where the money had been spent and on what, the *Globe and Mail* was able to analyze data from one program dedicated to new recreational facilities in Ontario. Although there was some evidence that money flowed disproportionately to ridings held by Conservatives, NDP-held ridings also benefited, while Liberal-held ridings suffered in comparison. "Conservative MPs have been working very hard, obviously, in many cases securing projects for their ridings," Harper told reporters, unapologetically. "I would encourage the other parties to work equally hard."[4]

Ignatieff decided to support the budget. He preferred to bring the government down later, when the economic crisis had subsided, rather than plunge the country into an election in the midst of that crisis. Besides, he didn't believe his own prime ministership would be legitimate. "I turned down the coalition, not knowing as I did so I had just given up my one chance to be prime minister of my country," he later reflected, ruefully.[5] In exchange for their support, the Liberals insisted that the Conservatives present quarterly updates on how the money was being spent. Harper was delighted to oblige; the updates turned into promotional events celebrating the many wonderful ways in which the Economic Action Plan, as the budget/stimulus program billed itself, was benefiting Canadians.

By February 2009, Harper had every reason to believe that he had dodged a firing squad's worth of bullets. He hadn't. The audacity – and the stupidity – of his decision to turn the November 2008 economic update into an assault on party financing exploded the status quo in Ottawa, forcing the PM to make a host of day-to-day decisions that normally he would have thought about for weeks before acting on. Harper, as we know, is at his best when he takes a complex, seemingly intractable problem, studies it, works it over, and looks at it from every angle. This tendency is illustrated perfectly by an example from several years further on in his mandate. In 2012, Harper personally took charge of the vexed challenge from the Chinese state-owned firm CNOOC (China National Offshore Oil Corporation) when it sought to acquire the Canadian petroleum firm Nexen. Sidelining Industry Minister Christian Paradis, Harper worked on the issue for weeks, before finally deciding that the acquisition could go ahead but that any future takeovers from state-owned enterprises would almost certainly be rejected. (By the way, the press conference in which Harper personally explained the decision at length was masterful, suggesting he really should have done more of them.)

But the coalition crisis forced Harper to make a series of rapid, convulsive decisions. The most obvious was to ask the governor general to prorogue Parliament. There was, however, another that would have far more calamitous consequences down the road. Since coming to office in February 2006, Harper had failed to appoint any senators.[*] The Reform legacy of the Triple-E Senate lingered in his political DNA. Senate reform would demonstrate to the Reform base of the party that he was still one of them, still the Stephen Harper of the Winnipeg Conference of 1987 and the Saskatoon Conference of 1991, of the Blue Book that he had largely written himself.

He proposed that senators should be elected, with a term limit of eight years, and sent the Senate legislation to implement the change. Critics warned the bill was unconstitutional – as the Supreme Court in 2014 declared it was – and in any case senators themselves had no intention of passing it. But at least it mollified true believers. In the meantime, Harper refused to fill any vacancies. Senators were becoming thin on the ground.

In the midst of the coalition crisis, word got out that Stéphane Dion

---

[*] With the exceptions of Michael Fortier, whom he had put into cabinet, and Bert Brown, who had won a senatorial election in Alberta.

intended to fill the eighteen seats that Harper had left vacant with Liberal senators once he became prime minister. Such a move would secure a continued Liberal majority in the Red Chamber for many years. Harper was determined never to give the Liberals that chance. With Parliament prorogued, on Christmas week 2008 he appointed eighteen new senators, all Conservative. Some were reminiscent of so many appointments in the past: party bagman Irving Gerstein, failed Conservative candidate Fabian Manning. Some were commendable, such as former Olympic champion Nancy Greene Raine. And there were three that appeared commendable at the time. Patrick Brazeau was head of the Congress of Aboriginal Peoples, which had been more supportive of the Tories' Aboriginal policy than the Assembly of First Nations had. Pamela Wallin was a former broadcast journalist whom Jean Chrétien had appointed consul general in New York, where she had served ably. Mike Duffy was a popular TV talk show host. It probably didn't hurt Duffy's chances at a Senate seat that his airing of the Stéphane Dion do-overs in the 2008 election spread the Liberal leader's embarrassment from sea to sea. These three seemed like good appointments. We know now how bad they actually were.

Had Harper taken more care in appointing senators by making those appointments less partisan; had he pushed provincial governments to hold senatorial elections; had he just given each appointment more careful thought; had he not appointed them in one fell swoop – he might have survived one potentially fatal crisis without sowing the seeds of the next one.

As the coalition crisis faded, Harper started remembering again why he loved the job of prime minister so much. And he did love it; to repeat the old saw, your worst day as prime minister is better than your best day as leader of the opposition. A good prime minister needs to be on top of his files, and even the most suspicious bureaucrats acknowledged that Harper knew his briefs cold. He sometimes delighted in questioning an obscure point at the back of some policy document to see if a deputy minister was as well versed on an issue as he was. Travel was a drag, but it did afford an opportunity to engage in a top-flight policy discussion with, say, the other leaders of the G8. The university student who liked to sit around the table at parties, earnestly discussing politics or economics or hockey, now sat at very different tables. Back home, there were officials to appoint and remove as the Conservative prime minister slowly shifted the senior ranks of the public service, filling available slots with mandarins closer (if rarely close enough) to his way of thinking. Over time, this became frustrating for him: Harper chose seven of the nine judges currently sitting in the Supreme Court. But unlike the legal establishment in the United States, Canada's is broadly consensual, and the Harper-appointed court showed no hesitation in striking down Harper government legislation. Harper became increasingly upset with his inability to locate a genuinely conservative judge for the court. But still, better to appoint a judge than to let someone else appoint a judge.

The second Harper government was very different in tone from the first, because of its stronger mandate, because of Harper's increasing comfort in his job, and because of two key changes at the top. Guy Giorno we have already met. As chief of staff, he set the tone for the Prime Minister's Office, and that tone was very different from the one set by Ian Brodie. Though Giorno and Brodie were equally committed conservative ideologues, and equally practical political operators, they were very different men serving at very different times. Though he could be more than blunt if he was unhappy with a situation or the performance of a subordinate, Brodie showed an affable face to the world, and sought to build bridges with the public service in an effort to shore up a rookie minority government that, it originally seemed, could fall at any time. But Giorno's approach was, as we've seen, more confrontational. As a young aide to Mike Harris, he had helped design and implement the Common Sense Revolution, with its tax and spending cuts, welfare reforms, and restructuring of education and municipalities. The social upheaval that followed left the province deeply polarized, and Giorno a fierce warrior on the conservative side of the divide.

Harper's new chief of staff was far more suspicious of the bureaucracy than Brodie had been, and more comfortable with running as much of the government as possible out of the PMO. Meetings with Kevin Lynch, clerk of the Privy Council, became less frequent. Nor would the bureaucracy be able to access the PM directly in writing. All memos and reports, whether from Lynch or from anyone else, first had to pass through Giorno or another authority in the PMO, who would attach a commentary offering his or her views of the policy and political implications. Giorno wanted to distance Harper from a bureaucracy that he felt often didn't have the prime minister's or his government's best interests at heart. Just like his boss, Giorno had a less-than-trusting nature.

The new chief of staff also advocated an even more bare-knuckles approach to attacking the Liberals. If Brodie worked more comfortably with the Jekyll in Stephen Harper, who had to keep his inner Hyde suppressed during the first administration, Giorno encouraged Hyde to come out, and Harper was happy to let him out.

The changes soon led to Lynch's departure as clerk. He had served ably and with devotion; if anything, he was even more of a workaholic than Harper. (The joke in the senior suites was that Lynch had once convened a seminar on managing work/life balance on a Saturday morning.) But Lynch grated on Harper at times. The clerk thought he was the smartest person in the room, and the prime minister tended to disagree. In June 2009, Harper replaced him with Wayne Wouters. While as accomplished as Lynch, and as willing if need be to challenge his prime minister, Wouters saw himself essentially as an enabler of the government's agenda.

With a more accommodating clerk, and a more militantly partisan chief of staff, Harper was ready to take on a world of opposition. His first task was to cut Michael Ignatieff down to size.

In the spring of 2009, the Tories launched a series of attack ads for television and radio that claimed Michael Ignatieff was out of touch with Canadians because he had been out of the country for twenty-seven years. "Michael Ignatieff: Just visiting" was the kicker. Running attack ads so far out from an election was a testament to the success of the Conservative Party's fundraising efforts and to their determination to define the new leader on their terms before he was able to define himself. The ads were devastating. Although Ignatieff had enjoyed a bump in the polls in the early months of his leadership, by summer 2009 the Conservatives were ahead once again. Ignatieff, concerned about further erosion, declared at an early-September caucus retreat in Sudbury, "Stephen Harper, your time is up." He was going to bring the government down as soon as the House returned in September. But unlike Paul Martin, who saved his government for a few months by wooing Belinda Stronach to his side, Ignatieff couldn't count. With his strengthened minority, Harper needed the support of only one opposition party in the House to survive a confidence vote. All Harper had to do was work out a deal with Jack Layton.

Layton had failed to forge a coalition with the Liberals, simply because Stéphane Dion was too inept. Now, with yet another seemingly weak leader in charge of the official opposition, Layton was increasingly sympathetic to an argument Harper had been making for years: that it was in the interests of both the Conservatives and the NDP to squeeze the Grits. Harper had been convinced of this ever since he wrote the 1989 memo to Manning about how Quebec had prevented Canadian politics from evolving into a two-party system. Layton wanted to make the NDP the natural home to Quebeckers who wanted social democracy but who weren't separatists. He had made a good start with the arrival of Thomas Mulcair. Now he wanted to build on that foundation. And he wanted to replace the Liberals as the default party for progressives in downtown Toronto, downtown Vancouver, downtown Winnipeg, downtown wherever.

In Stephen Harper, Jack Layton saw a dour reflection of himself: a skilled strategist willing to do whatever it took to dominate his political side of the fence, at the expense of the mushy middle. So it was an easy thing to sit down with Harper and secure some concessions on enhanced Employment Insurance benefits from the government in exchange for NDP support. Ignatieff's motion of non-confidence was easily defeated. (Harper had already learned painfully in 2005 not to introduce a motion of non-confidence unless you know you will win it.) The Harper–Layton agreement made Ignatieff look politically out of his league, and perhaps he was. By Christmas, the polls were so alarming that the Liberal leader fired his senior staff.

Former Harper aide Bruce Carson insightfully observes that as Harper settled into his second term, he realized that he had a majority government in all but name. Harper "was figuratively saying to the opposition: If you want to bring down the government and face the consequences of a general election – fill your boots," Carson wrote. "Most commentators, who decried the so-called high-handed actions of the government on matters like the long-form census, Afghan documents, and the costs of various initiatives missed that backdrop."[6] The Conservatives had spent much of the first mandate trying to establish themselves and their agenda. Now they were in charge. Harper was more trusted as a leader; the Conservatives were more trusted on the economy. They didn't exactly encourage a thousand democratic flowers to bloom. But Harper was immune to the complaints of stonewalling, philistinism, and contempt. Most people, he was convinced, just didn't care about these issues, as long as the Tories were seen as properly managing a difficult economy.

Take detainees, for instance. For as long as the Conservatives had been in power, people had been questioning the treatment of prisoners captured in Afghanistan after they were handed over to local Afghan authorities. Were the Afghan detainees, as some suspected, being tortured by Afghan jailers? If so, then the Canadian military police officers who handed over the prisoners might be complicit in war crimes. Everything is fine, insisted Defence Minister Gordon O'Connor: the Red Cross and Red Crescent monitor the situation. But when he was forced to apologize to the House for misrepresenting the role of the Red Cross, Harper was in turn forced to move O'Connor, a former army general whom Harper liked and respected, out of Defence. This angered Harper. O'Connor was the kind of stoic, square-jawed, up-by-the-bootstraps soldier (he entered the army as a second lieutenant and retired a brigadier general) whom the Harper family had always admired – the very best of the military tradition that Harper's father had honoured by chronicling the army's military insignia. And now some political midgets had forced Harper to cashier an honourable man over concerns for the fate of men who, as Stockwell Day put it, "are the guys who are trying to kill our guys."[7] The alleged victims weren't Afghan, in Harper's eyes, they were Taliban; they weren't detainees, they were prisoners; they weren't soldiers, they were terrorists. The prime minister really wasn't very concerned about what happened to them.

So when the Military Police Complaints Commission began investigating the allegations in February 2007, the government responded by refusing to hand over to the commission any of the documents requested, citing national security concerns. When a federal bureaucrat, Richard Colvin, testified to a parliamentary committee in November 2009 that he had warned of possible detainee abuse when he was stationed in Afghanistan, the Conservatives accused Colvin of having been "duped" by the Taliban.[8] And when the heat of opposition attacks started to singe the Conservatives' popularity, Harper had Parliament prorogued again at the end of 2009; it would remain suspended through most of the winter of 2010.

The second prorogation backfired. True, most Canadians didn't know much or care much about the arcane rules of Parliament, and maybe they didn't care much either about the fate of Taliban prisoners once they were in the hands of their Afghan jailers. But they did know that Stephen Harper had shut down the House of Commons to avoid defeat in December 2008. Now, only a year later, he had done it again, to avoid awkward questions from the opposition. The demonstrations against the government spanned the breadth of the country and there were even a few gatherings overseas. Once again, the Tories' popularity dropped while the Liberals' rose. Harper was confirming in the public mind the accusations of his critics. He would play fast and loose with democratic processes in order to cling to power. Autocratic. Secretive. Cruel.

Things got worse when the House finally returned in March. Speaker Peter Milliken warned the Conservatives that, by refusing to release documents on Afghan detainees to a parliamentary committee, they were risking a citation of contempt of Parliament. The government reluctantly handed over the documents but managed to tie up the actual release in such national security bubble wrap that nothing much ever came out publicly.

It would have been much, much easier just to cooperate. But Harper was bound and determined not to cave in to the demands of people who, it seemed to him, worried more about the prisoners Canadian soldiers captured than they did about the soldiers themselves. Besides, he was convinced he was politically immune. Even if Michael Ignatieff were able, did he really want to engineer the defeat of the Conservatives over the question of Taliban prisoners? Harper would happily fight an election on the issue. Or rather, Harper would fight the election on leadership and economic management and let the Liberals try to make mistreating the Taliban the ballot question.

In the end, it was all smoke, no fire. "The Commission finds the allegations made by AIC [Amnesty International Canada] and BCCLA [British Columbia Civil Liberties Association] against the eight subject officers in the June 12, 2008 complaint to be unsubstantiated," the Military Police Complaints Commission's final report concluded in 2012. "Viewing the evidence as a whole . . . the Commission finds their actions under the circumstances prevailing at the time met the standards of a reasonable police officer."[9] But again, the final report went virtually unnoticed. It had never been about the prisoners, or even the troops. It had always been political.

———————

In late autumn 2009, Munir Sheikh, Canada's chief statistician, sent a memorandum to Industry Minister Tony Clement, outlining plans for the 2011 census. Following the time-honoured ritual for approving the once-in-five-years tally of the state of the nation, the memorandum would be forwarded to the Prime Minister's Office for approval by cabinet. As always, there would be a short-form census for most households to fill out, with questions on how many people lived in each household, their ages, their relationships to each other, and the languages spoken in the home. The long-form census, which would be sent to a random 20 per cent sample of households, would probe further, with questions about matters such as place of birth, citizenship status, ethnic background, previous residences, education, household activities (such as who does the housework and who handles child care), disabilities, employment, commuting habits, income levels, type of housing, transportation used, and others. With the memo dispatched, Sheikh waited for approval. And waited. And waited.

Since 1971, the mandatory census, in both its forms, had provided vital data for, among many others, the federal, provincial, and municipal governments, who used the information to decide how well immigrants were integrating into Canadian society, which cities were growing and which were in decline, where to locate new schools and hospitals, who was moving where, how families were coping with economic and social challenges.

Without reliable data, rational planning would be replaced by educated guesses. As boring and mundane as the census may seem, it is vital to the life of the nation.

But libertarians had long complained that the requirement for citizens to tell the state about their ethnicity, education, employment, income, and other personal details was intrusive, and in his heart, Harper is more libertarian than conservative, more interested in minimizing the size and intrusiveness of government than in preserving ancient ways. David Cameron's Conservative government scrapped the traditional census in Great Britain, and many Republicans vocally oppose the U.S. census. Both libertarians and conservatives also harbour dark suspicions that bureaucrats and progressive politicians use census data to justify expensive new programs. Starve the beast of data, the theory goes, and government will be less able to tax and intrude, because it won't know enough to justify the tax or the intrusion. Harper's ornery distrust of bureaucrats and his unwillingness to make their priorities his priorities caused him to push back against the census. Besides, he believed, the census itself was an antiquated idea. In an age of data mining, surely there were better and less intrusive ways to draw up a picture of the nation.

In January, the word arrived: The prime minister wanted to see options for a voluntary survey. Dismayed by the request – because such a survey would be a poor and inaccurate substitute for a proper census – Sheikh and his crew at Statistics Canada nonetheless came up with several options and sent them to Clement. Sheikh also warned that the cost of the alternatives would be higher by millions than the cost of the census because of the larger sample size, the resources required to process the responses, and the need for increased follow-up. And he repeated that a proper long-form census was the only viable option in the eyes of Statistics Canada.

In June, word came back: Replace the census with a National Household Survey, which would be sent to more households in an effort to partially compensate for the lower expected response rate. The matter was never raised in cabinet. The decision was Harper's alone. The government posted the news in the *Canada Gazette* on June 26. The Canadian Press broke the story on June 29. And all hell broke loose.

The problems with the household survey are many: first, some groups are more likely to fill out the survey than others. People with little education, those without jobs, ethnic minorities, and those with low incomes, among others, might be disinclined to take the time needed to fill out the form, skewing the results. Second, there would be no baseline, no anchor, to compare the survey against, making it more difficult for it to provide accurate information. Third, because the survey was methodologically a different instrument than a census, its results could not be compared with past censuses, since this would amount to comparing apples with oranges, which is why Ontario, Quebec, and several other provincial governments publicly protested the decisions. So did scores of other governments and organizations, including municipalities, universities, school boards, NGOs, societies representing francophones outside Quebec, think tanks (including the conservative C.D. Howe Institute), business groups, and many, many economists. Against this wave of dissent, the government could cite only two complaints from citizens bothered by the long-form census on privacy grounds.

Through all this, Sheikh kept quiet, even though he was being inundated by hundreds of emails of protest, including a public comment from a previous chief statistician who claimed he would have resigned over this issue. But Sheikh had been a public servant for thirty-five years. It was his job to advise and then implement. One thing, however, that did alarm him were comments coming from Clement claiming that Statistics Canada had assured the government the new survey would be the equal of the old census. Statistics Canada had said no such thing, because it wasn't true and anyone who knew anything about the census knew it wasn't true.

Sheikh sounded the alarm about Clement's comments to his superiors. Saying that StatsCan believed a survey was as good as a census was not only false, it damaged the reputation of one of the world's most respected statistical agencies. By now, there was virtually a lineup of Statistics Canada employees outside the door of the chief statistician, demanding an explanation for what was going on. Sheikh called a town hall meeting for July 21, to give everyone a chance to ask questions or simply to vent. But the meeting never took place. That morning's edition of the *Globe and Mail* had Clement upping the ante by saying that the chief statistician himself had assured him the new survey would be as accurate as the old long-form census. Sheikh handed in his resignation.

None of this bothered Stephen Harper. He was on holiday during most of the brouhaha, relaxing at Harrington Lake. But it should have bothered him. As an economist, he knew the value of accurate, empirically tested data, and the price that researchers paid for not having it. He should not have been surprised – no one else was – when the results published in 2013, as well as subsequent research, revealed that the voluntary survey's information was badly compromised. Cancelling the long-form census was one of the Conservative government's most discreditable and puzzling acts.

There was another, better, way to handle the situation: commit to the mandatory long-form census for 2011, while announcing that this would be the last one and convening a commission to look at international best practices for obtaining a reliable survey through less intrusive means. But neither side wanted to compromise on this issue. The more experts complained, the more Harper dug in his heels and thumbed his nose. By the time of the 2015 election, he was taking active, positive pleasure at Laurentian fury over the lost census. He took a particularly grim satisfaction in the *Globe and Mail* editorials and columns slagging him over the census. If you want Stephen Harper to do something, there's a sure and simple way: convince the *Globe*'s editorial board to recommend the opposite.

––––––––––

The government took a similarly secretive and uncooperative approach toward providing data on the cost of the new F-35 jet fighter, to replace the aging fleet of CF-18s. The Chrétien government had committed Canada to acquiring the Lockheed Martin fighter as part of a consortium of nations that shared the development costs of the new plane. In 2010, the Department of National Defence under Peter MacKay confirmed that commitment. But delays were endless, costs kept climbing, and other nations, not just the Canadian political opposition, started questioning the wisdom of the purchase. That didn't prevent the DND from estimating a total cost for the jets of only nine billion dollars.

Parliamentary Budget Officer Kevin Page thought that number was low. Page had been appointed PBO under the Accountability Act. But he reported to the librarian of Parliament rather than to Parliament itself, and his mandate was limited more or less to providing advice to MPs who wanted information about the costs of proposed or existing programs. Page decided to interpret that mandate liberally. He wanted his office to become more like the U.S. Congressional Budget Office, which provided Washington with impartial estimates of the costs of proposed programs. He began doing his own analyses of numbers coming out of Finance and other departments. Those analyses were often embarrassing for the government – especially the one warning that the Conservatives' tax cuts had created a structural deficit that would have to be eliminated by cuts to spending.

Alarmed by what they considered a rogue public servant, the Conservatives tried to cut Page's funding, backing down only in the face of a public outcry. No matter. They would simply starve Page of information by stonewalling all requests for any. But Page was resourceful. In the case of the F-35, he relied mostly on American estimates. His conclusion: the plane would cost twenty-nine billion dollars over a thirty-year lifespan. The DND countered with a new estimate: fifteen billion dollars over a twenty-year lifespan. The auditor general weighed in, observing that the original DND estimates didn't include operating and personnel costs. Her figure: twenty-five billion. So Page was on the money. The DND replied by commissioning the consulting firm KPMG to draw up its own estimate. The firm came back with forty-five billion dollars over forty-two years.

Much of the discrepancy had to do with what was included and what was left out, and what time frame was being factored in. But it didn't matter. National Defence had clearly low-balled the costs of the plane in order to secure approval. And as far as the opposition parties were concerned, this was further proof that the Harper government was misleading Parliament by refusing to produce accurate estimates. Why, it's something that might be worth fighting an election over.

Harper rejected the opposition's demands for information because he saw no reason why he should help his many opponents by giving them what they wanted. Instead, he would give his conservative base what they wanted: an end to funding for the mandatory long-gun registry, an end to the long-form census, and some day even an end to the Wheat Board monopoly – all of them intrusions of the state into the lives of individuals.

A reliable census is vital. It helps us to know ourselves, and to spend wisely. The F-35 fighter program was and is troubled, with costs rising and reliability uncertain. Police forces used the long-gun registry to find out if there were guns in houses they had to visit in the course of duty. The Military Police Complaints Commission investigated the Taliban prisoner exchanges in part to protect troops on the ground from possible charges of war crimes. Harper neither needed nor wanted to distinguish his political and ideological opponents from people who were just doing their jobs, or who genuinely supported a more open and accountable government. They opposed him, and that was all that mattered.

Stephen Harper was not only prepared to stonewall, blindside, and generally defy his opponents. He was also willing to stonewall, blindside, and generally defy the world – at least when it came to climate change. In the first mandate, when the government was weak, the economy was strong, and the public was worried about global warming, the Conservatives saw the environment as a shield issue. (Sword issues are used to strike blows against your opponents; shield issues are ones in which you seek to shield yourself from political damage.) The Conservatives would never win votes for their stand on the environment, but they couldn't afford to lose too many votes either. So when Environment Minister Rona Ambrose couldn't come up with a climate change plan that satisfied the more reasonable critics, she was replaced by John Baird, who was brought in to put out the fire by promising a series of caps that would limit carbon emissions sector by industrial sector.

When the recession struck and climate change receded as an issue, so did Harper's interest in it. The government now promised to match any moves made by Congress and the new Obama administration to limit climate-changing emissions. But since Congress had no intention of acting on Obama's urgings, that meant Canada would do little or nothing. The difference between Canada and the United States, though, was that Canada ratified the Kyoto Protocol on climate change, promising to reduce emissions to below 1990s levels. The Americans ratified nothing. Faced with a choice of making draconian cuts to emissions or abandoning its commitments, on December 11, 2011, Canada withdrew from the Kyoto Protocol, the first time in this country's history that it had withdrawn from a treaty.

In private, Harper frankly acknowledges that human industrial activity is dangerously warming the atmosphere. But he can't understand – which is to say he completely rejects – the argument that Canada should act on its own to reduce emissions. This country, even with the oil sands going at full tilt, contributes less than 2 per cent of global emissions. As he sees it, curbing expansion of the oil sands in Alberta, imposing a carbon tax on industrial production in Ontario, or any combination thereof would damage economic growth, increase unemployment, and make everybody everywhere in this country poorer. And it would accomplish little, because the United States, China, and India account for more than 40 per cent of emissions, and they've signed nothing (although the Americans and the Chinese did reach a tentative agreement in 2014 that would let China continue to increase emissions until 2030). The better strategy at this point, he believes, is to focus on preparing the population for the effects of climate change. Preventing it was never really on the table.

That's the reasoned side. Then there is Harper's visceral contempt for environmental activists, as one element in the coalition of free riders who attack, like viruses, the institutions and businesses that sustain the country. They belong to the political class, as Harper defined them in his 1989 memo to Manning. They work in universities, or the public service, or non-profits. Their jobs don't depend on businesses making profits. (In the grand scheme, their jobs actually do depend on such profits, but they don't see it that way.) Most important, they raise their children to inhabit the world they inhabit. Few sociology professors raise future investment bankers, or even store owners.

This, at least, is how Harper views this class. It's no skin off their upturned noses if the oil sands are forced to scale back, or heavy industry to shut down. They have the luxury of worrying about the environment because they are immune from the economic consequences of fighting climate change. They are environmental activists because they can afford to be, just like the professional who spends forty thousand dollars on a hybrid car and then argues that everyone else should pay a carbon tax. They aren't Stephen Harper's kind of people and he isn't their kind of prime minister.

———————

Against this litany of obstruction, mendacity, and philistinism — at least in the eyes of his many critics — what could Stephen Harper possibly offer voters as 2010 drifted into 2011 and a seemingly inevitable election? Quite a lot, actually. Corporate taxes were down, sales taxes were down, boutique tax credits abounded. Despite the inevitable loss of revenues from all those tax cuts, the recession-induced deficit was already on the mend, with the budget scheduled to be back in balance by mid-decade. The jobs lost to the recession had been replaced, and unemployment levels were slowly coming down. Trade talks were underway with the European Union and India, with a goal of lessening dependence on the troubled American giant.

Harper's management of the economy, especially during the recession, deserves to be counted as his Second Big Thing. To be sure, he was heir to two decades of enlightened fiscal and monetary policy. Brian Mulroney laid the foundation for Canada's recovery from stagflation and deficits by negotiating the free trade agreement with the United States and imposing the Goods and Services Tax, even as the Bank of Canada finally wrestled inflation to the ground (a promise Pierre Trudeau had conspicuously failed to deliver). Though the tax severely damaged Mulroney's popularity, it also generated the revenue needed for the next step. Jean Chrétien and Paul Martin took that next step, by slashing federal spending to eliminate the deficit, while also putting the Canada Pension Plan on a firmer foundation by raising contributions and at the same time maintaining tight controls on the banks. Once the books were balanced, the Chrétien Liberals began a phased approach of debt reduction, tax breaks, and increased spending. The Conservatives inherited and continued that approach.

But it was Stephen Harper who faced the whirlwind of a recession that threatened to become a depression. After the near-disastrous false start of the November 2008 economic update, he and Finance Minister Jim Flaherty acted decisively and effectively. The stimulus program was the right size – roughly sixty billion dollars over two years; properly targeted – infrastructure and home renovations; and then quickly reined in to prevent the structural deficit that Kevin Page had warned about. And the tax cuts of 2006 and 2007 turned out, inadvertently, to be recession-fighting measures of their own, leaving more money in consumers' pockets at a time when money was scarce. Effective management of the financial crisis, coupled with sound management of the economy generally, must count as one of the greatest achievements of the Harper government, especially the second one.

But it wasn't just the economy, stupid. The Conservatives had successfully entrenched and expanded their coalition of Western and Ontario suburban voters. Ted Morton, the Calgary School professor who ended up as Alberta's finance minister, remembers a popular Alberta bumper sticker: "Defend the West. No Kyoto. No Wheat Board. No gun registry." "He ticked those three boxes," Morton points out. "That counts for something."[10] The government's sound economic management and strong law-and-order emphasis was also increasingly attractive to suburban, middle-class voters, especially in Ontario and especially new Canadians, making the Harper Tories the only conservatives in the developed world popular with immigrant voters.

Overall, despite critics' howling over the environment and contempt of Parliament and mistreatment of detainees, the Conservatives appeared to be managing the challenges of governing well. The wars south of the border over the Affordable Care Act ("ObamaCare") and the perpetual near-disaster known as Europe only made the Canadian Conservatives look better, at least in the eyes of their supporters and the Persuadables.

About a third of the electorate looked at the world the way Stephen Harper looked at it. Farmers and hunters celebrated the fact that the long-gun registry was out of their lives. Westerners were delighted to see one of their own finally in charge in Ottawa, determined to promote the oil sands and other natural resources on which the Western economy depended. Small business owners celebrated the steady lowering of corporate taxes. Immigrants living in the endless tracts of suburban housing on the edges of Toronto, who thought their adopted country was far too soft on criminals, supported the

Tories' law-and-order agenda. Some just liked the fact that, under Stephen Harper, the federal government left people alone. These were the 30 per cent of voters, give or take, who had been with the new Conservative Party since day one, or who had gravitated to it in recent elections.

And there were those who might be neither a supporter nor an opponent of Stephen Harper, the 10 per cent of voters who voted Conservative last time but without enthusiasm, or who didn't vote Conservative last time but were thinking about it now. These were the Persuadables, who liked the job the Tories were doing on the economy but didn't like the arrogance of the party; who didn't mind seeing punishments for offenders toughened up, so long as the government didn't go too far; who still worried about a possible hidden agenda that would bring back abortion legislation or limit gay rights. They considered Stephen Harper the coldest fish they'd ever seen, but they worried that Michael Ignatieff simply didn't understand their suburban, doing-okay-but-could-do-better, middle-of-the-road-in-everything world. And Jack Layton, although quite likeable, was a New Democrat, after all. Stephen Harper dedicated his government to earning these voters' support.

Harper had brought on side a few of the Persuadables in 2004, but not enough. He had persuaded more of them in 2006, and more still in 2008. But to win a majority government, he needed almost all of them, almost all of that 10 per cent of the electorate that, combined with his base of 30 per cent, would take him to a majority government. Beyond that are the 60 per cent of voters who wouldn't cast a Conservative ballot to save their children. Harper cares little about what they think, and it shows. There has never been a prime minister as utterly contemptuous of people outside his voting coalition as Stephen Harper. And the more they rage, the less he cares.

SIXTEEN

Fulfillment

As the second mandate tottered toward its inevitable end, people seemed to have gotten used to Stephen Harper as prime minister, and Harper had gotten used to it as well. Being Canada's CEO meant making decisions, mostly small, a few large, each and every day. The longer you served, the more decisions you got to make. The longer you served as the most conservative prime minister in the country's history, the more conservative the country might become.

There were other compensations. Both Stornoway and Sussex Drive had good pianos, and Harper had never given up practising. At home in the evening after work, or between briefing binders, he would practise playing popular tunes. He hooked up with a local Ottawa band, Herringbone – three guys with day jobs who were friends and who liked to play pop, folk, and Celtic music together after work – who would come over to 24 Sussex Drive for jam sessions. He was proficient both on the keyboard and as a vocalist. This gave Laureen Harper an idea. She was helping organize a gala at the National Arts Centre – a Brutalist chunk of concrete bequeathed to Ottawa for better or worse by Pierre Trudeau, with a hideous exterior but good acoustics inside – that would feature the National Arts Centre Orchestra and famed cellist Yo-Yo Ma. At a G20 event in Pittsburgh where Ma was present, Laureen Harper asked the cellist whether he would agree to play with her husband if she could rope him into it. Happy to, Ma replied. The organizers of the gala were enthusiastic. All that remained was convincing Stephen. "I've been married to him long enough to know when a 'no' means 'maybe' and 'maybe' means 'yes,'" she recounted later.[1] On October 4, as the NAC concert was wrapping up, out onto the stage walked Stephen Harper, with Ma and members of Herringbone. He played and sang a credible rendition of the Beatles' "With a Little Help from My Friends." The audience, many of whom were no friends of this art-funds-cutting prime minister, were seduced, and gave him a standing ovation.

He had another pastime besides the piano. As we've seen, as far back as his years in Leaside and Etobicoke, Harper had obsessed over hockey statistics. And he had always searched for after-hours activities that took his mind off work. If it wasn't the piano, it was his book on the early years of hockey, which he started in 2004 as Opposition leader and finished in 2012 – which is a long time to spend on a book. But he did have a day job. "I had become unusually interested in hockey history as a youngster growing up in Toronto," he wrote. "As a studious and rather unathletic boy, this pastime helped to compensate for my conspicuous inability on the ice."[2]

The book is a love letter to the game, and to the Maple Leafs, who broke his heart as they continue to break the hearts of so many. But it is also political. *A Great Game* describes a burgeoning Toronto at the turn of the last century, straining to dominate English Canada as thoroughly as Montreal – by far Canada's largest city – dominated Quebec. It chronicles, as well, the bitter contest for control of the game by two groups. The upper-class anglophilic Tory elites who dominated the power circles of Hogtown wanted the game to be kept strictly amateur, since, as Harper wrote, "without money, sport was regarded as a noble calling in which the young man nurtured heroic qualities – endurance, courage, self-sacrifice for the team – all to attain the glory of the championship."[3] But that generation's edition of the Family Compact found its control over the game undermined by more common men looking to make a buck off their athletic skill and organizing ability. The Tories loathed these rabble, believing that "once paid, the athlete was socially disreputable, morally deviant and . . . even disloyal to the nation."

In the book, Harper's loyalties are clearly with the subversives who wanted to take hockey away from the old boys with their stiff upper lips and make it a professional sport that paid its workers and charged its customers the market clearing price. There is more to his argument than an economist's and a hockey fan's understanding of the forces at work on professional sport. There is the ingrained hostility to the control of culture by affluent elites. Professional hockey was a populist reaction against the insufferable moral superiority of the ruling caste. Harper supported that historical struggle so enthusiastically that he wrote a book about it.

Harper shares another passion with Laureen: cats. Laureen loves cats more than dogs, which she has always considered farm animals that stay outside unless the temperatures descend below minus thirty. But cats are different – imperious but loveable companions that she has kept as pets throughout her adult life. When Stephen married Laureen, he also inherited Cabot and Cartier, later known within the family as the two founding cats. Harper fell for both of them. Despite his asthma and his reserve, he has a soft spot for anything furry. Cats became part of the family, with Harper so attached to them that when one of the cats was run over while the family was living at Stornoway, Laureen had it buried before the leader of the Opposition got home, because she feared the sight would have upset him so much. (According to a lawsuit by a disgruntled former cook, it was the cook who buried the cat. According to a family friend, it was Ray Novak.)

At 24 Sussex Drive, Laureen created a third-floor cat room, where she fostered rescued animals from the Humane Society until they could find a home. Several hundred kittens and cats stayed at 24 for varying periods over the decade, as well as Charlie the chinchilla, who made it onto a family Christmas card. The PMO happily tweeted photos of Harper reading and eating breakfast with a cat lounging nearby. When Laureen is away, Harper is expected to tend to the kitty litter himself, proving the adage that dogs have owners and cats have staff.

———————

Around the time Laureen talked Stephen into delivering his surprise performance at the NAC, the couple found themselves the subject of rampant rumours. The Harper marriage is in trouble, went the story. Laureen Harper has been having an affair with a member of the family's security detail. It was a male RCMP officer. No, it was a female. Laureen has moved out. She is staying with friends in New Edinburgh (a mostly-swank Victorian-era neighbourhood that surrounds the grounds of Rideau Hall and includes 24 Sussex Drive). No, she's staying at the Westin Hotel. Or maybe it was the Château Laurier – obviously to be as inconspicuous as possible.

Every major news organization with a parliamentary bureau investigated the rumours. Journalists sidled up to people in bars who knew people who knew the Harpers. Bureau chiefs dispatched hapless reporters to hang out in hotel lobbies hoping for a sighting. Yes, the Harpers were entitled to a private life, but if the marriage was over, then that was a matter of public interest, and it was every newspaper's and network's obligation to report the situation – if possible, before the other guy did. No one ever found anything to corroborate the gossip. Three different individuals who are either close to the family or to the government offered essentially identical explanations for the rumours: They are false. They spring from a bitter clash among those guarding the prime minister, and perhaps from something very dark in the psyche of the Laurentian elites.

For many years, the Prime Minister's Protection Detail was known as Club Med, a place where RCMP officers in the twilight of their careers could semi-retire while racking up thousands of dollars in overtime and thousands of travel points as they escorted the prime minister of the day to exotic locales. The staggering inefficiency of the PMPD was revealed in 1995, when a would-be assassin climbed over the gate and onto the grounds of 24 Sussex Drive late one night, broke into the residence, and confronted Aline Chrétien in a hallway with a long knife. Mrs. Chrétien retreated into the bedroom, locked the door, woke her husband, and called the RCMP detail at the front gate. But it took them thirty minutes to get into the house because they didn't have the right keys; all the while, the couple waited for rescue, the prime minister brandishing a soap stone carving. Chrétien was furious that he and his wife had almost been assassinated while security slept, and was even angrier when the RCMP blithely informed the public that the couple had never been at any risk. But nothing got better, even after the attacks of September 11 and Canada's increasing involvement in Afghanistan put this country in the crosshairs of any Islamist terrorist group or person looking for a target.

The Harpers were no more impressed than the Chrétiens with the quality of their protective detail. There was, for example, the time a female officer assigned to protect Laureen Harper was so hung over she didn't show up on the job until noon. It seemed to take an hour and a half for guards to change shifts, during which time the Harpers had to cool their heels. Laureen is an enthusiastic hiker and Harrington Lake is perfect for such things. But on her hikes, the guards often insisted she had gone far enough for her personal safety or their convenience. All of this would only have been annoying, but Ben and Rachel were also the responsibility of the PMPD, and the parents were keenly aware that Stephen Harper's job put their children at risk.

Things changed with the arrival of Bruno Saccomani as head of the PMPD in 2009. The RCMP assigned Saccomani the job of professionalizing the prime minister's security. That meant, as it turned out, doubling the budget and increasing the size of the force. It meant new and better SUVs and other protective cars. It meant new, younger officers. And it meant internal tensions, between the new guard and the old guard, leading to an internal management report and other complaints and counter-complaints that offered further proof of a split within the ranks of the security detail.[4]

Laureen Harper particularly liked two of the younger new arrivals, who were willing and able to keep up with her on her hikes and other excursions. (Stephen Harper also goes for walks, virtually his only form of exercise. Residents of New Edinburgh will occasionally see him tromping past their houses, with the security detail leading the way and following behind.) The two RCMP officers became popular with the Harper family, which led to complaints from within the PMPD that the officers had become too close to the people they were supposed to be protecting, compromising their professionalism. The two, a man and a woman, were eventually transferred out of the detail. But before long the story was being embellished – nudge, nudge, wink, wink – to include a non-existent affair.

Bruno Saccomani carried on, despite internal complaints, until a grateful Stephen Harper appointed him ambassador to Jordan in 2013. The patronage appointment caused considerable offence within the foreign service, who wondered why a bodyguard, as they derisively called him, was getting a plum diplomatic assignment. He got it because Harper knew and trusted Saccomani, and because he valued his service more than he worried about offending diplomatic sensibilities. And then some.

Former aides to Brian Mulroney tell of vile and false rumours about his marriage to Mila that circulated while he was prime minister. Similar baseless claims were made about Mike Harris and his then wife Janet, when he was premier of Ontario. It seems that when conservatives are in office, it isn't simply enough to disagree with their policies; their mere presence is objectionable, a disturbance in the natural order. If they can't be discredited at the ballot box, then rumour and innuendo about their private lives are the next best way to prove – at least to those who can't get by without such proof – that conservative leaders are illegitimate. Not One of Us.

If you were a politically engaged Canadian in the spring of 2011, you might have thought Canada had endured more than five years of Conservative misrule that the voters needed to end here and now. While grudgingly acknowledging that the Tories had managed the recession well – though any competent Liberal finance minister could have done the job better – you were appalled by the arrogance and secrecy of the Harper government over the true costs of the F-35 fighter contract, among many other things. You were alarmed by the government's thick-necked measures to toughen penalties for criminals, its empty-handed belligerence overseas, its neglect of the environment, and its utter contempt for Parliament. You wanted an election.

Stephen Harper liked such thinking because he also wanted an election, but he wanted the opposition to force it, and such impatience served his ends. He knew 60 per cent of Canadians would never vote Conservative. Unfortunately for the progressive side of the fence, the vote was split. Some thought Liberal leader Michael Ignatieff had the gravitas and global experience to get the job done. Others preferred the sunny smile and soft social democracy of NDP leader Jack Layton. Many Quebeckers were attracted to the sovereigntist rhetoric of Bloc Québécois leader Gilles Duceppe. A few, placing the environment above all else, supported Green Party leader Elizabeth May. All of these like-minded, anything-but-Conservative voters simply couldn't come together on who should replace Harper as prime minister.

Ignatieff's situation was particularly dire. The Conservatives were out-fundraising his party by a ratio of greater than two-to-one. (In 2011, according to Elections Canada, the Conservatives brought in $22.8 million from 110,000 donors, while the Liberals brought in $10.1 million from 50,000 donors.)[5] The Conservatives had used the money raised to run a devastating series of negative ads highlighting the transient nature of the Liberal leader's tenure. "Michael Ignatieff: Just visiting." "Michael Ignatieff: He didn't come back for you." And the painful truth was that Ignatieff had indeed been out of the country for more than two decades. It is hard to envision an American running for president or a Briton for prime minister with that kind of gap in his or her resumé. In any case, the Liberals had neither the money nor the method to counter such negative branding. Polls showed the Conservatives hovering close to majority-government territory, with support in the high 30s, the Liberals at around 30 per cent, and the NDP another 10 per cent or more back. These were not numbers that should prompt any Liberal to want an election.

Still, there was no reason to think the situation would get any better. And on March 9 Peter Milliken ruled that there was apparent evidence that the government was in contempt of Parliament for failing to disclose the costs of the F-35 program and other spending priorities. A parliamentary committee dominated by opposition members soon found the government guilty as charged. If that weren't enough, International Development Minister Bev Oda was also in trouble for – well, it had something to do with her inserting the word *not* into a memo, then denying she wrote it, but nobody really understood what the fuss was all about. What mattered was that the Conservatives were going to be found in contempt of Parliament by a vote in the House of Commons – the first time any Commonwealth government had been so censured. It was just what the Liberals wanted. They'd have impeached Harper if the rules allowed it.

And the NDP was also ready to pull the plug. This appeared to make no sense at all. Jack Layton was not a well man. A year before he had announced he had prostate cancer. A year later, after hip surgery, he was walking with a cane and sometimes sweating profusely when forced to stand for long scrums with reporters. He was clearly in pain and in no shape to fight an election. But Layton also realized that the Liberals were vulnerable. If the NDP were going to make serious gains at their expense, now was the time to seize the opportunity.

Stephen Harper had been prime minister for more than five years. The contempt of Parliament citation was as clear an indictment of Conservative perfidy as anyone would ever come up with. Jim Flaherty had just presented a budget that promised a return to balance, along with another round of boutique tax credits aimed directly at the Persuadables. If the budget passed, and if the opposition didn't bring the Conservatives down now, then Harper would enjoy another year in power, giving his second government virtually a full four-year mandate. Besides, having found the Tories in contempt of Parliament, how could any self-respecting opposition party let it carry on?

The question was whether the Persuadables cared more about the health of parliamentary democracy or about tax cuts. Harper was convinced – and the party's internal polling confirmed it – that taxes mattered more. He kept telling everyone around him that he couldn't believe the opposition would bring down the government over something as arcane as parliamentary procedure. But he also knew the calculus that would force them to do exactly what he wanted them to do. He was right. On March 25, the opposition combined to find the government in contempt and brought it down. Election Day would be May 2.

For Stephen Harper, winning a third minority government wouldn't be enough. Another minority win would likely mark the end of his career as leader of his party. If he couldn't deliver a majority for the Tories with the Liberals as weakened as they now were, then many in the Conservative Party would be anxious to give someone else a try. Besides, the opposition had temporarily united in 2008 in an effort to replace his government with a coalition; there was no reason to believe they wouldn't do it again in 2011. And that would be the theme of the campaign. Canada needs a "strong, stable, national, Conservative majority government," as Harper said on the hustings, over and over and over again. The alternative, he warned, would be a Liberal/socialist coalition, propped up by the separatists. Voter, which option would you prefer?

The team was, by now, finely honed. Doug Finley, fighting cancer, handed management of the campaign to the ferociously intense Jenni Byrne, with Guy Giorno as campaign chair. This time, the Tories would not try to find a path to a majority through Quebec. Instead, they would focus on the suburban ridings surrounding Toronto and Vancouver, including the immigrant voters who dominated many of those ridings. Even within Toronto itself, where suburban voters had put right-wing rebel Rob Ford into the mayor's office the previous fall, there might be seats available. If they could be persuaded that a majority Conservative government was in their best interest, then a majority might be possible. Harper, in essence, was going back to his 1989 memo to Manning. Forget Quebec. Focus on suburban English Canada, especially immigrants.

The Conservative leader was also determined not to undermine his own election campaign the way he had undermined it so often in the past. This time every single day of the campaign was tightly scripted, and the speech varied little from week to week or town to town. Canada was an island of prosperity in a sea of economic troubles, Harper insisted, but those troubles could overwhelm the country if an irresponsible coalition of socialists and separatists propping up a Liberal Party led by a "visiting" Harvard intellectual ever came to power. Only a Conservative majority government could stem the tide.

Ignatieff had three big advantages over his predecessor, Stéphane Dion: first, he wasn't encumbered by the promise of imposing a carbon tax; second, his campaign team, headed by chief of staff Peter Donolo, a former Chrétien aide, was vastly more professional than those who had led Dion to his debacle; third, Ignatieff had spent much of the previous year barnstorming the country, learning to become comfortable in town hall settings where he dropped his g's and answered questions from the crowd on everything from agriculture subsidies to the war in Afghanistan. He loved the town halls and had become very good at them.

But he was off script from the first day of the campaign, when reporters repeatedly asked whether he would form a coalition government if the Tories failed to obtain a majority and were defeated in the House. Reporters also grilled Harper about his own letter from 2004, in which he informed the governor general along with other opposition leaders that the Conservatives might be willing to form a coalition of their own. It didn't matter. The talk was about coalitions, and coalitions were what the Conservatives wanted to talk about, so this suited them fine.

Front-running candidates usually campaign in a bubble, protected from reporters and potentially hostile members of the public by being confined to environments that are carefully vetted, with speeches that are equally carefully scripted. But no one had seen a bubble the likes of that surrounding Stephen Harper in 2011. He had prepared long and hard for this campaign, and by God, he wasn't going to torpedo it by saying something stupid again. Each morning, he reannounced part of Jim Flaherty's budget-that-could-have-been. Then he took five questions from reporters, no more. No supplementals. In the evening he appeared at a rally, with the same set speech from the day before. Canada was doing well but "a sea of troubles is lapping at our shores." The crowd was carefully pre-screened to weed out potential disruptors. Reporters on the bus were incredulous at a campaign with so many hatches battened down. But Jenni Byrne agreed with her boss: As *Maclean's* columnist Paul Wells wrote in his book on the Harper governments, in certain unscripted moments Harper either turned into "Angry Stephen," as he did during the 2004 campaign when he accused Paul Martin of being soft on child predators, or "Professor Stephen," as when he talked in 2006 about the Liberal dominance of the courts, Senate, and public service, or when he described the 2008 economic meltdown as "an excellent buying opportunity."[6] There would be no Angry Stephen or Professor Stephen this time. There would only be Prime Minister Stephen Harper, answering four questions a day from the boys and girls on the bus, plus one from the local press.

In most elections, the campaign boils down to a single question: Who do you trust to mind the store? This election was no different. Who do you trust to mind the store, Stephen Harper or Michael Ignatieff? Never mind the details of the Family Pack of benefits that the Liberals were offering. Never mind the targeted tax credits in Jim Flaherty's budget. Never mind what Jack Layton or Gilles Duceppe or Elizabeth May said. Forget about that F-35 unpleasantness. Stephen Harper or Michael Ignatieff: Choose. In the televised debates, Harper ignored his opponents and talked directly into the camera, his words quiet and reassuring. Ignatieff tried to engage him, but failed. Instead, he got clobbered by smiling Jack Layton, who lampooned the Liberal leader's high rate of absence from the House, which was the price of criss-crossing the country doing town halls with voters. "You know, most Canadians, if they don't show up for work, they don't get a promotion," Layton skewered.[7] Ignatieff had nothing to come back with. The NDP now knew that success for them lay not in taking on the Tories but in taking on the Liberals, their true political enemies.

To contrast his open style with Harper's shrink-wrap campaign, Ignatieff hosted a daily Open Mike session, when people in the crowd could ask him anything. Reporters covering the campaign admired his courage and frankness. But seminars in public policy don't make for good TV clips, and so the networks ignored the Open Mikes. Meanwhile, the Conservative campaign beat the drum: Harper or Ignatieff. Choose.

And in the final week of the campaign, the voters did choose, though the choice was a shock for both Liberals and Conservatives. Jack Layton's NDP surged into first place in Quebec. Gilles Duceppe had gone to the well of nationalist resentment once too often. Outside Quebec, the NDP made substantial gains in Toronto and Vancouver. First one poll, then another, showed the Liberals sliding into third place. And the NDP was gaining rapidly on the Conservatives, something that Stephen Harper had never considered. Was the campaign going to be torpedoed in the final week once again? Was Harper to be left once more staring at the cameras without a script?

No, as it turned out. Because the orange wave was mostly confined to Quebec, it failed to eat into Tory support. Instead, NDP surges siphoned Liberal support in tight races outside Quebec, especially in the 905, allowing the Conservatives to come up the middle. A so-called exposé from the Sun News network, reporting that Layton had been found in a massage parlour back in 1996, probably didn't hurt the NDP much, but it certainly didn't help them. By election night, Harper knew he had won, though he didn't yet know if he had his majority. At a sound-check rehearsal at Calgary's Telus Centre on the afternoon of Election Day, a rather goofy Stephen Harper refused to rehearse his speech, instead doing one impersonation after another – his Joe Clark was particularly fine – while Ben, embarrassed as only a teenaged male can be embarrassed by his father, pleaded, "Read the speech, Dad, read the speech."[8]

Everything he had ever dreamt of came true that night. A solid majority government, with 40 per cent of the vote. Though the Tories took only five seats in Quebec, they swept the 905 in Ontario and the Lower Mainland outside downtown Vancouver. The NDP dealt the separatist threat a mortal blow, at least at the federal level, with the Bloc reduced to four seats. Jack Layton had taken the NDP to an astonishing 31 per cent of the vote, making it the official opposition. The Liberals were reduced to 19 per cent, a paltry thirty-five seats. The 1989 memo had fulfilled itself: Canada was cleaving into a party of the left and a party of the right, with the Canadian Liberals belatedly fated to follow their British predecessors into oblivion, or so it seemed at the time.

In Calgary that night, Harper told Laureen, "I can never adequately express my love," as she wiped tears from her eyes. He apologized once again to Ben and Rachel for being away so much. And to Canadians, including the majority who would never, ever cast a ballot for him: "We are intensely aware that we are and we must be the government of all Canadians, including those who did not vote for us."[9] Anyone who had been around the political block knew that wasn't true, but on that night of nights, it didn't matter. Stephen Harper had it all.

SEVENTEEN

Foreigners

In the early days of his prime ministership, Stephen Harper was most surprised by the time he spent on foreign affairs. Unlike the United States, where the issue of how to run the world regularly crops up during election campaigns, politics in Canada is almost entirely domestic. Governments are elected or defeated on how they manage affairs at home. During the 2006 election, Canada's mission in Afghanistan was not mentioned once in the debates, even though our country was effectively at war.

But Harper shouldn't in fact have been surprised that foreign policy ate up much of his day. In the Canadian federation, the things that really matter to people's lives – the schools their children go to, the hospitals that care for their parents, the freeways they sit parked on during the morning commute, the buses they catch, the minimum wage that their daughter earns in the job after school, the university she hopes to get into, the police who keep them safe and the jails that house minor offenders, are managed by provincial and municipal governments. When it comes to domestic policy, the federal government operates largely behind the scenes: transferring money to the provinces to pay for all the above, setting air quality and water quality and food inspection and fuel emission standards, sending pension cheques, guarding the border. Most people hardly think about copyright protection, will never break a federal criminal law and end up in a federal penitentiary, don't know and largely don't want to know about what the security services are doing to keep them safe, and rightly assume that someone is looking after aviation safety and bank regulation. They haven't been to Ottawa since the school trip in grade eight. They've never set foot inside a national museum. They were born here rather than overseas, and so have never come in contact with the immigration system. They're never going to apply for a research grant. They don't farm and they don't live on a reserve. They've never served in the military. They don't distinguish between federal and provincial parks – why should they? They rarely watch the CBC. They've given up on the post office.

Because Canada is one of the world's most decentralized federations, Ottawa matters little in the life of the people. Previous federal governments tried to make it matter more, by creating national programs jointly funded by Ottawa and the provinces. But Stephen Harper doesn't believe in such programs. He feels strongly that Ottawa should keep out of the provinces' hair and jurisdiction. In terms of domestic policy, that leaves him with little to do.

The federal government is, however, in charge of foreign affairs. And Canada is a large medium power – part of the G7 and the G20 (which Paul Martin helped to invent), the Commonwealth, La Francophonie, the United Nations, NATO, APEC, the Arctic Council – well, you name it, we're in it. In terms of foreign policy, there was much to do.

Harper had strong opinions about the state of Canadian foreign policy when he came to office. He thought it was all wrong, and he aimed to fix it. In fact, Stephen Harper's reorientation of foreign policy stands as the Third Big Thing that the Conservatives have accomplished. Experts hotly debate whether the Conservative break with the past is a good thing or a bad thing. But everyone agrees it's a thing. Under Stephen Harper, Canada speaks with a different voice in the world. Before he came to power, foreign policy was more outward-looking. After he came to power, it became more inward-looking. Before him, it was nuanced; under him, it became blunt. Before him, diplomacy was mostly multilateral; under him, it became more unilateral. Before him, process mattered as much as results; under him, results were all that counted.[1]

It all goes back to Joe Harper. When he impressed on his oldest son the importance of standing up for Israel – a democracy surrounded by hostile autocratic states, a legacy of the Holocaust, a refuge for Jews in a world still gripped by anti-Semitism – Joe burned into Steve Harper the notion that foreign policy should be guided by values. Neither father nor son probably realized that this approach to the world contradicted Canada's proud Pearsonian tradition of non-partisanship in foreign affairs. Louis St. Laurent laid the foundation for that tradition in a speech he delivered in 1947, when he was foreign minister under Mackenzie King. In that speech, St. Laurent declared that Canada should make a point of joining and supporting the plethora of new multilateral institutions that were emerging in the wake of the Second World War. "Our geography, our climate, our natural resources, have so conditioned our economy that the continued prosperity and well-being of our own people can best be served by the prosperity and well-being of the whole world," he observed. "We have thus a useful part to play in world affairs, useful to ourselves through being useful to others."[2]

Being useful to others meant avoiding strongly partisan stands. Yes, Canada would support Israel, but it would also reach out to Arab states, understanding and sharing in their concerns over regional instability and the plight of the Palestinian people. Although St. Laurent committed Canada to war in Korea, it was under the flag of the United Nations; elsewhere and later, the emphasis was on peacekeeping, more or less invented by St. Laurent's successor as foreign minister, Lester Pearson. In fact Canadian foreign policy from the end of the Second World War until Stephen Harper became prime minister followed what was called the Pearsonian tradition: balanced, helpful, cooperative, seeking collective security through collective action, respectful of the United Nations, firmly allied with the West but a helpful back channel in relations between the United States and the Soviet Empire and then Russia, gentle in its criticism of Chinese human rights abuses, sympathetic to the aspirations of the least developed nations.

At its best, the Pearsonian tradition helped lower temperatures in the Suez dispute, kept Greeks and Turks from killing each other in Cyprus, aligned the Commonwealth against apartheid South Africa, contributed to a peaceful end to the Cold War, helped form the International Criminal Court, and led the way on the global landmines treaty. But by the time the Conservatives came to power, the policy had already begun to unravel.

One problem was lack of money. Under St. Laurent, Canadian defence expenditure consumed 7 per cent of GDP, as Canada bulked up to take on its NATO responsibilities and sent a battalion of troops to fight the Korean War. By the time Jean Chrétien left office, military spending had shrunk to 1 per cent of GDP (the United Kingdom spends 2.5 per cent and the United States 4.3 per cent) and Canada had gone from being the largest contributor of forces to peacekeeping to being one of the smallest. Canadian troops were exploited as hostages in Kosovo, and they watched helplessly as Rwanda descended into genocide.

Another problem was incompetence. Confusion and politicking led the Chrétien government to agree to drastic reductions on carbon emissions when the Kyoto Protocol to fight global warming was signed in 1997. Chrétien was determined that Canada's commitment would be more aggressive than the Americans', but the U.S. set its ambitious target knowing there wasn't any chance of Congress ratifying it. By the time Stephen Harper came to power, it was already becoming clear that Canada would never meet its Kyoto obligations. Humiliation lay ahead, one way or another. As well, to compensate for refusing to join the war in Iraq, Canada had expanded its commitment in Afghanistan. But by the time the Martin government actually turned commitment into action, the only available theatre of operation was Kandahar province, which turned out to be the bloodiest front in the war. Further, Canada's devotion to multilateralism led us to put most of our trade eggs in the Doha basket of trade talks, launched by the World Trade Organization in 2001. But Doha failed, mostly because Canada and other nations were unwilling to surrender agriculture subsidies.

Meanwhile, trade talks with South Korea and Singapore foundered, as the Liberals surrendered to local protectionism. The United States slapped tariffs on softwood lumber, carried a grudge over Chrétien's refusal to support the mission in Iraq (though Canadians loved him for it), and was furious when Paul Martin first supported, then rejected, participating in the ballistic missile defence program, George W. Bush's ambitious shield to protect the United States and its NATO allies from missile attack.

Canada had angered the Americans, squandered trade opportunities, made global-warming promises the nation couldn't possibly keep, abandoned peacekeeping, and sent an expeditionary force to the worst quagmire in Afghanistan. Foreign policy under the Liberals had become mostly incoherent by the time Stephen Harper took office. His task was to make it make sense again, which turned out to be a long row to hoe.

As far back as the 1988 Blue Book, Harper had laid out Reform's vision for foreign policy. Under Brian Mulroney, he wrote, "Canada's role in international bodies is seen as simply adjusting and fitting into the views of foreign governments, rather than vigorously promoting Canadian values and Canadian interest," while under Trudeau "Canada had become distrusted by our natural allies and a hero to those governments with which Canadian values have little in common."[3] Like the other values and beliefs that he forged in the 1980s, Harper carried those beliefs into office. In terms of foreign policy, that meant exploiting the fact that there were conservatives in office on both sides of the border, in order to restore trust in the Canada–United States relationship. It also meant cooling down the fervour of the Chrétien and Martin governments' embrace of China – which was, after all, a crypto-Communist dictatorship. It meant reorienting Middle Eastern policy more firmly in favour of Israel, the only real democracy in the region. And it meant pursuing trade deals more aggressively.

Harper didn't wait long to act. As he was travelling to the 2006 APEC meeting in Vietnam, he laid down the gauntlet. "I don't think Canadians want us to sell out important Canadian values," he told reporters. "They don't want us to sell that out to the almighty dollar."[4] To make sure the Chinese understood that this message was intended for them, Harper met with the Dalai Lama (whose struggle for an independent Tibet is one that most Canadians support) in his office, with a Tibetan flag displayed on the prime minister's desk, which a spokesperson for the Chinese Foreign Ministry described as "disgusting conduct."[5] Just in case the Chinese didn't get the point, four Conservative cabinet ministers attended that year's National Day celebrations in Taiwan. And Harper boycotted the Beijing Olympics.

The Harper government was particularly incensed with how China handled the case of Huseyincan Celil, a Uyghur who holds both Chinese and Canadian citizenship. In 2006, Celil was arrested in Uzbekistan and extradited to China, where he was convicted of terrorism-related offences and sentenced to life in prison. To the Conservative government, having a Canadian citizen extradited from a third country to face Chinese justice was an affront, and both Harper and Foreign Affairs Minister Peter MacKay protested loudly and publicly.

Harper also didn't care if he offended Arabs in his stalwart defence of Israel, something Joe Harper had instilled in him that, as an adult, he fervently embraced on his own. On one of his first visits abroad, to the G8 summit in St. Petersburg in July 2006, he stoutly defended the Israeli incursion into Lebanon – "Israel has the right to defend itself . . . Israel's response under the circumstances has been measured"[6] – even as fellow NATO members accused the Israelis of overreacting to the kidnapping of two soldiers by Hezbollah. Reporters on the plane assumed the rookie PM had stumbled. But it was no stumble. Harper would always come to Israel's defence, even when George W. Bush or Barack Obama weren't prepared to.

Harper was active in other fields as well. He cut back on the number of countries receiving foreign aid (though not on the overall aid budget). He beefed up the military budget, in part as a matter of principle and in part to respond to the military challenge in Afghanistan. And he went north. The new prime minister had always had a *Boy's Own* fascination with the Canadian Arctic, a place he had never visited. A history buff since high school, he had carefully studied the doomed Franklin expedition. What had happened to the men, and where lay the wreckage of the ships? He had embraced John Diefenbaker's vision of the Far North as a new Canadian frontier that should be developed and defended. In the summer of 2006, Harper made his first visit to the Arctic, a journey he has repeated each year of his prime ministership. When up there, he seemed to regress in a most delightful way.

On the 2010 expedition, when foul weather made it impossible to get out of Churchill, Harper invited reporters to lunch at his hotel, to their general astonishment. During the off-the-record gathering, he was expansive and very funny. He talked about how much he and the family loved Harrington Lake, where he often took long walks in the woods. "The only thing is, you see a lot of bears," he told his bemused audience. "But when you do, the best thing is to run at them, yelling and waving your arms. It always scares them away."

"Prime Minister, are you telling us that you routinely run toward bears in the woods, yelling and waving your arms?"

"Sure." Pause. "Of course, there are guys right behind me with guns."

In Tuktoyaktuk, on that 2010 trip, just as everyone was boarding the Hercules transport to fly south, Harper broke away, got on an all-terrain vehicle, and booted it down the runway, to the consternation of the RCMP. And he danced with children in Inuvik, even donning seal-skin mittens – Harper at his most unHarperish, unscripted and with no purpose other than to have some fun.

He had a vision for the Canadian North that could become part of a new Conservative myth of Canada. All the other myths were Liberal: the flag, public health care, the peacekeeping tradition, multiculturalism. The Canadian myth was red; Harper wanted to turn it blue. The North could be a key to that. It was an area Liberals had ignored and neglected, but now with global warming, the Northwest Passage might one day be open to shipping. There were oil and gas reserves, and other nations were staking their claim to vast territories. Well, Canada would stake its claim, too, and back up that claim with a new deepwater port, a state-of-the-art icebreaker, patrol ships, and a stronger military presence. Harper's government would even help fund a search for the ships of the Franklin expedition.

Canada, as reimagined by the Conservatives, would be a winter country. It would be the country that repeatedly went to war in defence of freedom; the country that prevailed at Vimy Ridge. (Under Harper, the Vimy Memorial replaced the sculpture *The Spirit of Haida Gwaii* on the twenty-dollar bill.) The Museum of Civilization under the Conservatives would become the Museum of Canadian History. The new citizenship guide would portray a more robust, assertive Canada. And in this reimagining, Canadian foreign policy would also be aggressive and assertive in defence of Canadian values and Canadian interests.

But it all came a cropper. Harper was forced to reverse or recalibrate on one foreign affairs file after another. Liberal incoherence was replaced by Conservative incoherence, as Harper struggled to master the complexities of global statecraft.

The icebreaker and the patrol vessels and the deepwater port still exist mostly in blueprints, victims of the government's commitment to balance the budget by 2015. Though the government did fund a highway that improved Arctic links south to north and east to west, most of the Conservatives' grand schemes were undermined by recession, deficits, and budget cuts. The new northern myth remained largely that – a myth.

Harper made a total hash of things with China. He thought that he could snub the Chinese over the Dalai Lama, Taiwan, and the Olympics, even as Canadian businesses continued unabated to invest in the rising Asian giant. Wrong. China may be a strange mixture of Communist ideology and capitalist reality, but that capitalism is state-controlled. The big banks, oil companies, and other firms are under the sway of the Party and its favoured sons. As the Canadian government snubbed the Chinese government, trade with China suffered. Word came from the office towers in Toronto and Calgary and Vancouver that Harper's principled stand was bad for business.

And Harper's policies on China were hurting the Conservatives' popularity among Sino-Canadians. In the 1990s, many Chinese immigrants came from Hong Kong and were naturally hostile to a regime in Beijing that threatened their financial security. But later arrivals were from the mainland. While they might not love the Chinese government, Harper's rhetoric sounded to them not like Communism-bashing, but like China-bashing, or even Chinese-bashing. All the progress the Conservatives had been making among immigrant voters was being put at risk, at least as far as Chinese immigrants were concerned, and most years they made up the biggest single group of immigrants coming into Canada. So the government's principled approach to an emerging economic superpower was costing the economy money and the Conservatives votes.

Stockwell Day also weighed in. Since losing the Alliance leadership to Harper, Day's behaviour had been impeccable. Unlike Conservative and Liberal leadership losers, the former Alliance leader made no effort to cultivate a cabal, waiting for the moment of weakness to launch an insurgency. Instead, he served faithfully and well. Day's anti–Communist China credentials were impeccable, and he was still respected by the Christian conservative wing of the party. So when, as international trade minister, Day came back in April 2009 from a nine-day visit to China with his eyes opened to the giant tiger's burgeoning growth and with a warning to the boss that both of them were all wrong on China, Harper listened. The place is growing like Topsy, Day reported, and we're missing out. Harper knew that his former rival could be counted on to sell any switch in the government's China policy to the base. The final impetus to change arrived in the form of the financial crisis. By autumn 2009, it was clear that the Great Recession had crippled the American and European economies, while barely slowing the onrushing Chinese and Indians. It was time to recalibrate.

The cold messages were replaced by a warm embrace. Other cabinet ministers made their way to China, to smooth ruffled feathers. The government promised to open new trade missions across the country. And in December 2009, Harper visited China himself, where he learned that the Chinese do not easily forgive. After the pomp and circumstance of a marine band and a guard of honour in the Great Hall of the People, Harper and Premier Wen Jiabao repaired to a side room for private discussions, with a pool reporter listening in on the opening remarks and reporting back to the rest of the media in a nearby hotel.

But instead of the boilerplate that invariably accompanies such grip-and-grins, the premier offered the prime minister a stern rebuke. It had been five years since a Canadian prime minister had visited the Middle Kingdom, he observed. "Five years is too long a time for China–Canada relations and that's why there are comments in the media that your visit is one that should have taken place earlier," he said, as jaws dropped.[7] Such public criticism, especially at an innocuous ceremonial event, was unheard of in diplomatic circles. There was more to come, though the accompanying media didn't realize it at the time. Throughout the trip, Harper was subtly snubbed by his hosts. At dinners, he was not seated at the place of honour. Arriving at an airport, a second-tier official was on hand to meet him. This was the fruit of Harper's principled stand toward the godless Communists in Beijing: complaints from Bay Street, anger among Sino-Canadians, and ritual humiliation in China.

But it wasn't just the Chinese that Harper crossed swords with. The Canadian prime minister was an early and fervent critic of Russian strongman Vladimir Putin. The two men started off on friendly enough terms, with promises of encouraging business investment and cooperation in the Arctic, when the two met in 2006 at the G8 St. Petersburg summit. But things soon changed. Canadian businesses remained wary of investing in oligarchic Russia. Harper condemned Russia's 2008 invasion of Georgia, considered Russia an aider and abettor of Iran's nuclear weapons program, condemned Russian support for the Assad regime in Syria's civil war, and protested Russian laws that persecuted gays and lesbians. Needless to say, Harper didn't show up at the 2014 Olympic Winter Games in Sochi, and at the June 2013 meeting of the G8 in Enniskillen, Northern Ireland, Harper courted controversy by declaring that Putin didn't belong in the G8. "I don't think we should fool ourselves," he told reporters. "This is G7 plus one."[8]

All that, of course, was mere prelude to the utter condemnation by the Harper government of Putin's actions in Ukraine. Foreign Minister John Baird stood with protesters in Kiev's Maidan square while the Yanukovych regime was still in place – a simply unprecedented insult directed toward Russia. After the regime fell and Yanukovych was sent scurrying to Moscow, Harper was the first Western leader to visit Ukraine and endorse the new government. He ordered Canada's ambassador to Russia back home for consultations after the invasion of Crimea, led the charge to have Russia expelled from the G8, and made headlines around the world in November 2014 when he greeted Putin at the G20 summit in Australia with the words, "I guess I'll shake your hand but I have only one thing to say to you: you need to get out of Ukraine."[9]

"That's not possible, because we're not there," Putin replied.

"That's why I don't talk to you," Harper retorted, and walked away.[10]

Such blunt talk was utterly at odds with the Pearsonian tradition, which would have emphasized more temperate language accompanied by back-channel efforts to establish a dialogue between Moscow and Kiev.

Christopher Westdal, former Canadian ambassador to both Russia and Ukraine, believed Harper was simply pandering to the 1.3 million Canadians of Ukrainian descent. "Diasporas are a huge problem in foreign policy," he observed.[11] They were causing the Harper government to abandon dialogue and bridge-building in favour of a naked play for domestic votes. Though Westdal was referring to Ukraine, the charge could just as easily be made about Israel. After all, four-square Conservative support for Israel has resulted in several ridings with large Jewish populations switching from Liberal to Conservative in recent elections. But it has damaged Canada's reputation for even-handedness in Middle Eastern relations.

Vacillation and incompetence produced Canada's worst international embarrassment in years, when the members of the UN General Assembly failed to support this country's bid for a seat on the Security Council in October 2010. How could it have happened? Well, Germany and Portugal were also in the running, and the European Union was going to back its own. The Harper government's staunch support for Israel had alienated Arab states, and the cutbacks to the number of nations receiving Canadian foreign aid had angered some African states. Harper himself didn't know what he wanted – first directing that the embassy staff in New York must offer no concessions for votes and then, realizing the prestige of the seat and the blowback of rejection, ordering a full-court press. Too little, too late; we were whupped by the Portuguese.

There is one relationship for any Canadian prime minister that matters more than all others combined: the relationship with the American president. And if there was one thing that frustrated Stephen Harper more than anything else, it was his tortuous and often futile effort to get anywhere with Barack Obama.

Harper was saddened by his visit with Margaret Thatcher in 2006. She had come to his London hotel, where he was staying on his way to the G8 summit in St. Petersburg. Ill health had slowed the Iron Lady, who spoke in carefully rehearsed sentences that she sometimes repeated. But one point she did emphasize, with some of her former firmness: Stick close to the Americans above all. That's what matters most.[12] Harper agreed, although he knew it wasn't easy.

The debacle in Iraq had destroyed George W. Bush's presidency. No weapons of mass destruction to be found. A vicious insurgency, mounting casualties and costs, out-of-control deficits. Most Canadians outside Alberta are generally suspicious of Republican presidents; getting too close to the greatest failure in the White House since Hoover presided over the Depression could be fatal. Which was too bad, because the two men got along well. The transplanted Texan and the transplanted Albertan shared a similar world view and found themselves comfortable with each other. The two administrations were able to sort out the softwood lumber dispute, and Bush travelled to Montebello, Quebec, for the Three Amigos summit with Mexican president Felipe Calderón in 2007. Other than that, Harper could do little but keep a friendly distance – publicly, emphasis on the noun; privately, on the adjective.

Barack Obama's insurgent campaign to steal the Democratic presidential nomination from Hillary Clinton offered new opportunities for the Harper government. Polls showed that Canadians loved the African American senator more than they loved any Canadian politician, living or possibly dead. Mother from Kansas, father from Kenya, raised in Indonesia and Hawaii, educated in California and New York: he was the multicultural Canadian prime minister that Canada had never had.[13] Harper was enough of a student of American politics to realize that, by March 2008, Obama had the nomination locked up, and probably the presidency. An Obama presidency would offer a tantalizing opportunity for collaboration in areas that otherwise might provoke a storm of nationalist backlash. But first, Harper needed to rebuild the bridge that Ian Brodie had inadvertently burned.

In spring 2008, with Obama and Clinton locked in a battle over the upcoming Texas and Ohio primaries, Brodie had let slip during an off-the-record talk with reporters that Canada had received back-channel assurances that Obama's protectionist rhetoric about reconsidering the North American Free Trade Agreement was just campaign folderol. (Brodie actually attributed the remarks to the Clinton camp, who were saying the same thing, but reporters eventually sorted it out.) When the Canadian media broke the story, the American media picked it up, damaging Obama's credibility.[*]

Nonetheless, Obama never publicly mentioned the matter and travelled to Ottawa on his first foreign visit as president. The two men discovered they had things in common: both had two children of about the same age and were grappling with the challenge of raising a family in a famous house; both were policy wonks, and each knew a lot about the other's country. Obama's sister Maya had married a Canadian doctor, and Obama had visited north of the border several times. So when Harper proposed that the two administrations work on creating a continental security perimeter that would entail a remarkable degree of joint customs inspection, Obama agreed. The proposal would improve security while easing cross-border irritants, and Harper could commit to a degree of security cooperation that would have had the Canada-firsters in the streets had it involved any other president.

The Beyond the Border program was finally unveiled in 2011, and didn't amount to much, mostly because the Americans lacked the money to implement the needed infrastructure, but also because by then the relationship between the two leaders had seriously started to cool. Obama, Harper concluded, simply couldn't make up his mind about anything, and once he made it up, was inclined to change it. The president reacted to domestic pressures he should have ignored, Harper believed, while instead ignoring vital national interests. His indecisiveness strengthened America's enemies abroad, especially Vladimir Putin's Russia. Obama was an inconstant ally and uncertain friend. Personally, Stephen Harper still liked Barack Obama and enjoyed the prestige of being listened to by the president of the United States. But on a professional level, he lost all respect for him.

That lack of respect was partly ideological, of course. Harper is an Albertan Conservative, and instinctively suspicious of liberal Democrats like Obama. The prime minister would have been much happier with

---

* I covered the 2008 primaries, and in the midst of the brouhaha I received a phone call in my Cleveland hotel room from a senior Obama aide asking if I knew Ian Brodie and why I thought he was trying to sabotage the Obama campaign in Ohio. Brodie, of course, was trying to do no such thing, but the damage was done.

John McCain or Mitt Romney in the White House. Some of what Harper considered inconstancy was really Obama trying to pivot America away from old conflicts, such as the Middle East, so that it could face new challenges and opportunities in the Pacific. There was also, as we'll see, Obama's frustration with Harper over the prime minister's belligerent approach to the crucial Keystone XL pipeline. Part of it was simply unfair: Harper knew, or should have known, that Obama was constrained by a hostile Congress, including Blue Dog Democrats in his own party, and that his determination to implement health care reform trumped all other considerations. But Harper was also right.

Things were already tense thanks to the Buy America program, in which Congress prohibited Canadian firms – even American firms with strong Canadian connections – from bidding on government contracts. And the situation got worse at the 2010 G20 summit, which Harper hosted in Toronto. With the worst of the recession over, the prime minister, backed by Germany's Angela Merkel, wanted global leaders to commit to shifting away from stimulus spending and toward deficit reduction. Pressured by Congress to reduce America's trillion-dollar deficit, Obama was initially willing to go along. But as the summit approached, he began to waffle, influenced by economists such as Paul Krugman, who argued that it was too early to turn off the spending tap. It took a lot of arm-twisting to get Obama and the other eighteen leaders to all agree on a target of halving government deficits by 2013.

Relations between the two countries took another potentially dangerous turn at the Summit of the Americas in Cartagena in 2012. Argentinean president Cristina Fernández de Kirchner wanted summit leaders to support her country's claim to the Falkland Islands, which Argentina calls the Malvinas. Harper had never admired Margaret Thatcher more than when she sent what was left of the British fleet into the South Atlantic in 1982, accompanied by an expeditionary force, to expel the Argentineans after they invaded the islands. He was never going to countenance such a claim. And the United States, though officially neutral in the conflict, had vetoed similar resolutions at previous summits. But Obama was anxious to improve America's reputation in the southern hemisphere, and inclined toward neutrality. Harper confronted him personally: This is a question of human rights, he told the American president. Neither of us should ever be neutral when it comes to defending the right of a free people to choose their form of government. Ultimately, Obama swung the American vote behind Canada, and the motion failed.

"This is pointless. Why did I even come here?" Fernández de Kirchner fumed as she marched out of the conference.[14] The British were deeply grateful to Canada, but Harper was starting to have grave doubts about Obama's spine. Those doubts worsened in 2013, after Obama warned Syrian president Bashar al-Assad that he considered the use of chemical weapons in that tragic civil war "a red line" that the regime must not cross. When it became clear that Assad had in fact used chemical weapons, Obama waffled again, ultimately agreeing to a Russian proposal to have the weapons removed. How can anybody do anything anywhere, Harper fumed to aides, when Obama issues an ultimatum and then doesn't act on it? If that weren't bad enough, the president failed to offer Ukraine the resolute support that the prime minister believed it deserved.

Harper had an ally and friend in Israeli prime minister Benjamin Netanyahu. Obama was disappointed when the arch-conservative Likud leader won the 2009 election, and over the years their relationship went from cool to heated to hostile to barely on speaking terms, as the president pressured the prime minister to stop housing construction on land claimed by the Palestinians and to accept a two-state solution to the Palestinian–Israeli standoff, measures that Netanyahu emphatically rejected. Meanwhile, Netanyahu warned that the administration was guilty of Munich-like appeasement toward Iran. (U.S.–Israel relations reached a low ebb when the Israeli prime minister said as much in an address to Congress in March 2015.) Obama knew that Harper was four-square behind Bibi, as Netanyahu is known, and as relations deteriorated between Washington and Tel Aviv, they deteriorated between Washington and Ottawa as well. When Harper and Netanyahu talked to each other, which was often, they could only shake their heads in mutual bewilderment at what they saw as that dithering man in the White House.

But Keystone trumped everything. The Keystone XL pipeline was supposed to ship bitumen from the Alberta oil sands to refineries in the Gulf of Mexico. Because the pipeline crossed the Canada–United States border, it required the president's approval, which Harper insisted to an American reporter in 2011 should be "a complete no-brainer," given that "the economic case is so overwhelming. The number of jobs that would be created on both sides of the border is simply enormous. The need for the energy in the United States is enormous."[15] But Hollywood actors and other assorted environmentalists were pressuring Obama not to accept Canada's dirty oil. (They preferred Venezuela's dirty oil.) In the lead-up to the 2012 election, Obama needed the support – and dollars – of the environmental lobby and California's cultural elites. The administration also wasn't impressed with the Canadians' aggressive and highly public lobbying in Washington, which embarrassed the administration and provided fodder for Republican opponents.

With even the Republican governor of Nebraska opposed to the pipeline, which would travel over a sensitive aquifer, Obama phoned Harper on November 10, 2011, to tell him he wouldn't be approving Keystone in its current form. There would have to be changes.[16] Harper was furious. He had billed Canada as a new emerging energy superpower. And now Obama was undermining that claim by stymieing development of the oil sands. At the APEC summit in Hawaii, a few days later, the two leaders walked side by side, jackets over their shoulders, and then sat at a picnic table. Neither held back. The relationship between the two leaders had cooled and would never warm up again.

At the next meeting of the Priorities and Planning Committee, Harper ordered a full-court press to find alternatives to Keystone. The preferred option appeared to be the Northern Gateway proposal, which would ship oil from the oil sands through B.C., to Kitimat, then on to China and other parts of Asia. Not only would it provide alternative markets for oil sands oil, it would show the Americans that they weren't the only game in town. To prevent the proposal from being hung up for years in environmental hearings, Harper ordered changes to streamline environmental assessments, and sent Natural Resources Minister Joe Oliver out to warn the public about "environmental and other radical groups" who sought to cripple natural resource exports by undermining pipeline and other proposals.[17]

But of course, it wasn't foreign radicals the Conservatives had to worry about when it came to Northern Gateway; it was First Nations in B.C.

resolutely opposed to the pipeline, which they saw as an invitation to a cat-
astrophic oil spill either on shore or off the coast of B.C. Focus shifted back
to Keystone. The Nebraska governor was now onside with a rerouted pipeline and the State Department had given the go-ahead. Still Obama refused
to decide, one way or another. Now it was the 2014 mid-term elections that
he had to worry about. And in February 2015 he vetoed an attempt by the
Republican-dominated Congress to push through approval of the pipeline.
It was his decision to make, he insisted, and he would make it when he
made it, if he bothered to make it at all.

By 2014, the Trans-Pacific Partnership had become a fresh irritant.
Canada had initially refused to join the talks among a group of Pacific
nations who were determined to create a cutting-edge free trade agreement
that tackled agriculture subsidies, intellectual property, and government
procurement. Such an agreement could put Canadian protection of dairy
and poultry at risk, so the government took a pass. But then the United
States joined the talks in 2010, and suddenly Harper wanted Canada at the
table. The recession had convinced him that Canada's trading future lay
in the Pacific. And anyway, Mexico was in on the talks, which meant they
could supersede NAFTA.

Getting to the table required American approval, and Harper was
shocked by the American demands. Even before taking part in the negotiations, Canada had to declare a willingness to, if required, abandon
every protection, including supply management and intellectual property.
(The intellectual property issue went away with the passage of the new
Copyright Act.) Ultimately, we agreed and they agreed – Canada could
always argue to protect dairy and poultry once at the talks – but Harper
was bruised by the callousness of the American approach. Friends and
allies don't treat friends and allies the way the Americans treated us, he
told those around him.

By the end of the third Harper mandate, Canadian relations with the
United States were in worse shape than they'd been when he arrived a decade before. The Obama administration still hadn't approved Keystone, and
the Conservatives now waited and hoped for a Republican in the White
House who would give the go-ahead. Obama and Harper were correct but
cool in their conversations. Nothing was going to get done until there was

a new prime minister and/or a new president. It was time for another reset.

History will judge whether Barack Obama was prudent or merely timid; a friend of the environment or a useful idiot for bleeding-heart movie stars; the president who extricated the United States from its Middle Eastern morass or the president who allowed the United States to get drawn back in; Putin's bane or Putin's poodle. But one thing is beyond dispute: The relationship between the president of the United States and the prime minister of Canada is asymmetrical. The United States matters more to us than we to them, by a factor of about ten. It is the prime minister's job to keep the relationship productive. It's Stephen Harper's job.

But because of that asymmetricality of power, the Canadian prime minister is subordinate to the U.S. president. And as we have seen time and time and time again, Stephen Harper simply cannot stand being told what to do. All his life he has chafed against authority. People who think they know more than he does annoy him. He cannot defer. And that may well be part of the reason for the dysfunctionality of the relationship between the Langevin Block and the West Wing during the Harper–Obama years. Barack Obama simply wouldn't do what Stephen Harper wanted him to do. And there was nothing Harper could do about it. He hates that.

By 2015, Stephen Harper's foreign policy didn't look at all like what he'd hoped for in 2006. He had been forced to reverse himself on China, and his relationship with the United States was worse than when he arrived. All of this and more led University of Ottawa professor Roland Paris, one of many critics of the Harper government's foreign policy, to conclude that this policy was "incoherent," that it sought to reverse decades of time-tested foreign policy prescriptions, based on multilateral engagement, participation, and peace-seeking, with its polar opposite. "With the exception of a few areas and a few relationships and a couple of issues, it's been more defined by neglect and a lack of attention to how the little pieces the government is focused on fit together," he complained.[18]

Paris is not alone: critics of Harper's foreign policy include both Brian Mulroney and Joe Clark (who wrote a book about it)[19] as well as former diplomats Paul Heinbecker (who wrote another book)[20] and Robert Fowler, among many others. Collectively, they see the Harper government's foreign policy as a betrayal of honourable tradition, as a ham-fisted attempt at conservative revisionist history, as a waste of the talent and resources of the diplomats at Foreign Affairs (now renamed Foreign Affairs, International Trade and Development – pronounced "D-FAT-D" or, more commonly, "DEFEATED"), as vulgar.

That's one way of looking at it. But there's another.

The Harper government's foreign policy has failed at everything except results.

Four months before Canada lost its bid for a seat at the United Nations, Harper hosted the G8 leaders in Huntsville, Ontario, and the G20 in Toronto. As we've seen, Harper was effective in establishing a strong consensus on deficit reduction at the G20, even though it was overshadowed by demonstrations, police tactics, and the one-billion-dollar bill. But equally important, at the G8 meeting (which was accompanied by stories of Tony Clement's lavish spending in his Parry Sound–Muskoka riding that had nothing to do with the summit) Harper corralled his fellow G8 leaders into funding a global maternal health initiative that poured $7.3 billion into protecting the health of vulnerable mothers and their children.

The Muskoka Initiative was a major boost in the global effort to cut the infant mortality rate in half between 1990 and 2015. "[Harper] could have chosen so many other issues at the time he hosted the G8," Rosemary McCarney, of the Canadian Network for Maternal, Newborn and Child Health later pointed out. "He could have chosen a trade issue, or a fiscal policy issue, but he chose this issue."[21] He also chose to prohibit Canadian funding for abortion services as part of the program, which earned him plenty of criticism at home and a tongue-lashing from U.S. secretary of state Hillary Clinton. But the fact remains: At the 2010 G8, Harper convinced world leaders to seriously fund a push to meaningfully improve maternal health and reduce infant mortality. He succeeded and the maternal health initiative has succeeded. When Harper committed Canada to a further $3.5 billion over five years in 2014, Melinda Gates of the Bill and Melinda Gates Foundation declared, "Canada has earned a global reputation for driving the agenda when it comes to women and children. The Muskoka Initiative rallied the entire world around saving mothers and their babies."[22]

The diplomats at Foreign Affairs who first sent in a proposal for an initiative on maternal health never expected any response from Harper other than a curt no. Why did he grab the idea and run with it? No credible explanation has been offered other than a deep-seated and powerful revulsion on both his part and Laureen's at the thought of children suffering. Harper can become quite emotional when he hears about tragedies involving children.

The Muskoka G8 and Toronto G20 also marked Harper's evolution as a global statesman. In the early years of his prime ministership, the plain truth was that he was an amateur on the world stage. Shy by nature, uncomfortable with travel, useless at the gossipy back-and-forth that greases the wheels of summit diplomacy, Harper was ill-suited to represent Canada abroad. Diplomats winced as they watched him in action. But he got better at it. By 2010, he was negotiating comfortably with other world leaders. He discovered he rather liked Angela Merkel, the equally wonkish German chancellor who became something of a friend and ally during trade negotiations and at international summits.

And as Harper gradually brought coherence to aspirations, his thinking and actions became clearer and more consistent. Under the Conservatives, Canadian foreign policy actually does serve Canadian values and interests. Not international aspirations toward collective security, not multilateral forums in search of environmental security, not the implausible targets set at talking shops that are never met. Canadian values. Canadian interests. The Canadian trading relationship. Canadian national security. Canadian human rights priorities.

One close observer described the Harper Doctrine – if that's what it is – as "simpler, less nuanced, seen in black and white, good and evil terms, results-oriented, ruthlessly guided by Canada's self-interest, and reflective of core Conservative perceptions and values."[23] There may be no better description, with the maternal health initiative the largely altruistic exception.

Timing also began to work in Harper's favour. Pearsonian internationalists trumpet the importance of soft diplomacy, in which countries influence global affairs by their example rather than through actual or implied force. The recession was a soft-diplomacy triumph for Canada. Sound banks (thanks more to Paul Martin's refusal to relax restrictions than to anything the Conservatives had done), an effective stimulus program, a solid debt-to-GDP ratio, and declining unemployment made Canada an exemplar of how to manage a national economy. It didn't hurt to have oil and other natural resources to feed the maw of the fast-developing nations such as China, India, and Brazil. But the fact remained that one strength of Canadian foreign policy in recent years has been our ability to stand before the world as a paragon of sound political and economic management.

While Canada–U.S. relations are merely correct, thanks to the Harper–Obama chill, the situation with China is much better. After the full-court press that the Harper government launched in 2009, relations steadily improved. By June 2010, when President Hu Jintao came to Canada for the Toronto G20, things were back on an even keel. In his 2014 book on Sino-Canadian relations, University of British Columbia political scientist Paul Evans concluded, "In many respects, the high policy of engagement was back where the Martin government had left it in 2005."[24] There would be good days and bad days on the Canada–China front in the latter years of the Harper decade, but the relationship would never regress to where it had been prior to 2009. And no one mentions Huseyincan Celil anymore.

The Harper government's suspicion of the United Nations turned to outright hostility after Canada lost its bid for a Security Council seat. Harper pointedly didn't bother to address the General Assembly twice at its annual fall sessions, even though he was in New York both times. John Baird said Canadian diplomats would no longer participate in the UN's interminable "preoccupation with procedure and process."[25] But it wasn't just the UN. There were off-the-record rumblings that Canada was pulling back from its commitments to NATO. Harper boycotted the 2013 Commonwealth summit in Sri Lanka, citing human rights abuses by the Sri Lankan government, and a year later withdrew funding for the Commonwealth Secretariat. And so on, and so on. Wherever two or three nations were gathered together in the name of diplomacy, Canada was absent.

But Harper committed to the Liberal-initiated mission in Afghanistan, transitioning to a training force in 2011 and withdrawing fully in 2014. Canadian fatalities, at 158, were third highest after the United States and United Kingdom. A Canadian general led the mission in Libya in the effort to unseat strongman Muammar Gadhafi and Canadian CF-18s flew more than their share of sorties. Canada offered the French logistical support in Mali and committed special forces to train troops and CF-18s to take part in strikes against the Islamic State. In March 2015, they expanded that mission into Syria, even as Canada increased its NATO commitment to protect Eastern Europe from Russian aggression. On the humanitarian front, apart from the signature maternal health initiative, Canada was among the first and largest responders to the devastating earthquake in Haiti. And Canadians did more than their share in the fight to contain the Ebola outbreak in West Africa in 2014.

Critics maintain that, under the Harper government, Canada is missing from the forums of nations. "Where has Canada gone?" they ask. It's a fair question. A fair reply is, "We were on the front lines. Where were you?"

As for Canada's purported hate-on for the United Nations, under the Harper government Canada continues to be the seventh most generous contributor to the UN budget. And in February 2015, former Australian prime minister Kevin Rudd asked then foreign minister John Baird to join him as co-chair of a commission on how to reform the UN's World Health Organization, in the wake of its inadequate and politics-ridden response to the 2014 Ebola epidemic. Rudd called Baird "a pragmatic internationalist," adding: "He speaks with a high degree of credibility from a realist perspective; he wants to see the UN function and function effectively."[26]

The allegation that the Harper government panders to diasporas also needs to be salted. First off, every government in Canadian history has pandered, to some extent. When Canada was mostly made up of people of English, French, Scots, and Irish stock, Canadian foreign policy was diaspora-based with a vengeance. But the Conservatives' actions in the Middle East and Ukraine are rooted in Conservative principles more than electoral calculation. Joe Harper's influence had more to do with the Harper government's approach to Israel than any stratagem to win away Eglinton–Lawrence (a Toronto riding with a large Jewish population) from the Liberals, although the Conservatives were happy to reap the rewards of a pro-Israel policy at home. (Eglinton–Lawrence switched from Liberal to Conservative in 2011.) If the question is: Is Stephen Harper's foreign policy motivated by principle or by electoral calculation, the answer is: Yes.

The most important aspect of Canadian foreign policy arguably centres on trade. Where Canada stands on the Middle East question is of interest to specialists in the Middle East; the Harper government's strong support for the new Ukrainian government is important to, at the least, 1.3 million Ukrainian Canadians. Harper's decision to boycott the Commonwealth summit in Sri Lanka over the government's treatment of Tamils heartened Tamil Canadians. But how Canada trades matters to all of us, and to our pocketbooks. Our jobs and our children's future depend on it. We are a trading nation. How much we trade and with whom dictates how well we do. We'll look at this issue in greater depth later, but it's worth noting here that on Harper's watch, Canada has signed trade agreements with Peru, Colombia, Panama, and Honduras, European nations outside the European Union, European nations inside the European Union, Jordan (suggesting the Arabs aren't *that* angry at Canada over Israel), and South Korea. All in all, Canada has signed trade agreements with thirty-eight countries during the Harper decade, by far the largest number of trade agreements negotiated by any Canadian government. The Chrétien government, apart from NAFTA (which the Mulroney government was mostly responsible for), managed three.

Kyoto, of course, was the lowest ebb for the Conservatives – the first time Canada ever withdrew from an international treaty. A Liberal government would have withdrawn as well – the country could never live up to the obligations that Jean Chrétien had agreed to. The problem was with the choice of language – it always is with Stephen Harper. Whether he sends John Baird to publicly berate the UN, or excitedly claims that Canadian jets beat back Russian planes threatening to cross into Canadian airspace,* or describes environmentalists as "foreign radicals," or promises Israel it has

---

* The Russian ambassador later recounted to the author, "I told your prime minister, 'Stephen, relax, they were Tupolevs. They could only reach Edmonton. And Stephen, I *like* Edmonton.'"

no greater friend, or, or, or . . . the Harper government's bluster, ill-tempered ranting, and chip-on-the-shoulder sidelining of the foreign affairs bureaucracy has left it unpopular and often offside, having to scramble back from positions it should never have taken, or regretting language it should never have used.

But to recast Harold Macmillan, what matters is results, dear boy, results. The Harper government prosecuted a war it had inherited in Afghanistan and joined international missions in Libya and Iraq. Canada's response to the South Asian tsunami in 2004 was an embarrassment; its response to the Haitian earthquake in 2010 was an inspiration. Canada diversified its trading relationship, strengthened the world's most generous and enlightened immigration system (as we'll see later), and earned the gratitude of the crowds in Kiev and the ire of the strongman in Moscow. And if we slackened our ties with the Commonwealth and the UN, we strengthened them with La Francophonie, where Canada successfully lobbied in 2014 to have former governor general Michaëlle Jean elected as secretary general.

In February 2015, John Baird stepped down. He was tired after twenty years in public life, and wanted to transition to the private sector while he was at the top of his game. Rumours that he was annoyed with the micro-managing coming out of the Prime Minister's Office were exaggerated, though not entirely unfounded. Baird and Harper could look back with some pride at their transformation of Canada's foreign policy. Yes, the Pearsonians weren't happy – but then they never would be. The more conservative face that Canada now presented to the world reflected global realities and the realities of a changing, more conservative, Canada. And the truth was that, however much the opposition parties berated the government's rhetoric, they usually went along with its actions. Acquiescence is the highest form of flattery.

EIGHTEEN

Hubris

The 2011 victory revealed more than the deep structural weakness of the Liberal Party, the unpopularity of its leader, Michael Ignatieff, and the surprise embrace by Quebeckers of "le bon Jack" Layton. The Conservatives had achieved something unmatched by any other conservative party anywhere in the world. They had become a conservative party that attracted the support of large numbers of immigrants. This was a remarkable, though precarious, achievement. Precarious, because to sustain its popularity, the new seemingly natural governing party needed to preserve and deepen that bond, which is no easy feat.

There's a tension on the right over immigrants. Some of the *pure laine* Reformers didn't much like seeing the country transformed from white to brown, which led to the early anti-immigrant stance of the party. But people like Stephen Harper had chafed against this strand of conservatism from the get-go. As far back as the 1980s, he was warning Preston Manning that Reform had to appeal to suburban voters, and that meant appealing to immigrants. Personally, he has always been colour blind. In 1987, he introduced John Weissenberger to Angela Tu, a Vietnamese Canadian, a fellow graduate student with whom Harper shared an office. Harper thought the two might hit it off, if only because he knew they both shared a fondness for classical music. The Weissenbergers have been married for twenty-five years.

As leader of the Conservative Party, Harper realized that Canada, uniquely among nations, is so heavily immigrant that no federal party could hope to come to power without winning a plurality of the immigrant vote. In Canada, more than any other democracy, immigrant voters elect the government. Brian Mulroney deserves much of the credit for that. His government opened the immigration floodgates in 1990, increasing Canada's annual intake to 250,000 a year. Once the Liberals returned to power, and especially after the books were balanced, Jean Chrétien kept them open. As a result, by 2011, Canada had imported the population equivalent of two new Torontos, almost all of them from China, the Philippines, and India (the top three intake countries) or other parts of the developing world. Many of these immigrants settled in and around Toronto and Vancouver, and over time, they came to have an enormous influence on elections.

Consider the GTA. In 2011, there were fifty-three ridings in the Greater Toronto Area, representing just under 20 per cent of the seats in the House of Commons. Apart from the downtown Toronto ridings, which have almost always gone to the Liberals or NDP, these GTA seats are the political equivalent of the American swing states. In the United States, the Northeast and Pacific coasts are reliably Democrat, while the South and Plains states are reliably Republican, making Ohio, Indiana, Iowa, and other Midwestern states, along with Florida (a southern exception to the Republican rule), Pennsylvania, Virginia, Colorado (two former Republican bastions that are trending Democrat), and a few others the true battleground in any presidential election.

The same is true in Canada. Since the 1960s, Quebeckers have voted mostly for progressives, of either the sovereigntist or federalist variety. Atlantic Canadians have tended to vote either for conservative progressives or for progressive conservatives. Rural English Canada, and voters on the Prairies generally, have voted for one conservative party or another. Downtown Toronto and downtown Vancouver have voted progressive. That makes the suburban ridings around Toronto the Canadian equivalent of Ohio or Florida: their votes – along with those of mirror-image voters in the Lower Mainland outside downtown Vancouver – tip the balance and decide the government. They are home to the Persuadables. In every election going back to Pierre Trudeau's first landslide victory, the ridings surrounding Toronto have reflected the outcome of the election. The sole exception was 2006, when the Conservatives formed a weak minority government despite having little support in the 905. But in the next two elections, the 905 increasingly, and then emphatically, backed the Conservatives. In Canada, the 905 elects the government. And by 2011, the 905 had become quite brown.

"Eighteen of the 53 ridings that overlap with the Toronto, Hamilton, and Oshawa CMAs [Census Metropolitan Areas] have majority immigrant populations and immigrants make up between 30 and 50 per cent in another 20 ridings," one study concluded, based on data from the 2011 Canadian Election survey.[1] "The political geography of Canadian immigration, which features high concentrations of politically efficacious immigrants in electorally salient regions, in combination with a very efficient citizenship regime and Canada's SMP electoral system, creates incentives for all parties to court new Canadian voters." Translated into English, the authors were saying that any party that wanted to win a federal election needed to court immigrants in the GTA ridings, because they have tremendous voting power, and use it. Liberals had always been able to count on these voters, because the Liberal Party was the party of immigrants, and had been since the time of Laurier, while the Conservatives were the party of nativist farmers and WASPs, and therefore anti-immigrant. But Harper knew this had to change, and that's where Jason Kenney came in.

Like Harper, Kenney is an Ontarian who was transplanted to the Prairies – in Kenney's case with his family, as a child. Like Harper, he is an apostate Liberal, having served as executive assistant to Ralph Goodale back in the eighties, when the future finance minister was Saskatchewan's Liberal leader. Like Harper, Kenney underwent a Damascene conversion to Christianity and conservatism. Like Harper, he worked for a conservative pressure group – in Kenney's case, as head of the Canadian Taxpayer's Federation. Unlike Harper, he is a Christian conservative who advocates celibacy outside of marriage and who fiercely opposes abortion. Unlike Harper, he was a strong supporter of Stockwell Day.

Jason Kenney arrived in Parliament as a Reform MP in 1997 – just as Harper was leaving – convinced that the party was missing an opportunity to attract immigrant voters from Asia and the Pacific, who, he believed, were more economically and socially conservative than the European variety that had come before. Although Harper was personally receptive when the two first talked about it in an Ottawa pub back in 1994,[2] the party was not. Neither were the immigrants. In the 2000 election, with Kenney running under Stockwell Day as a member of the new Canadian Alliance, fully 70 per cent of immigrants voted for the Liberal Party, with the rest splitting among the Alliance, the Progressive Conservatives, the NDP, and the Bloc Québécois. For all we know, some of them might have voted Green.

When the Conservatives came to power, Harper had no cabinet post available for yet another Calgary MP. As well, Kenney's close ties to Day rendered him suspect in the leader's eyes. Instead, Harper made Kenney his parliamentary secretary, with a mandate to forge connections with the immigrant community. Kenney attacked the file with such gusto – he would attend six or seven events a day in his outreach to visible minority communities – that a year later Harper appointed him secretary of state for multiculturalism and Canadian identity. A year later, Kenney was minister of citizenship and immigration, where he launched the Harper government's Fourth Big Thing: a complete overhaul of Canada's immigration and refugee policy.

Kenney believed that the Conservatives could win over immigrants by stressing a combination of smaller government and tougher law-and-order measures. As a devout Catholic, he knew that churches were increasingly filled with immigrants from developing countries who embraced a socially conservative approach to faith and family. And he was convinced that the conventional notion that any efforts to curb abuses within the immigration system would be perceived as anti-immigrant was wrong. Immigrants themselves were least tolerant of abuse of the system, he reasoned, since they had entered the country legally, not by jumping the queue. He reasoned as well that, provided the overall annual intake remained at its now traditional level of 250,000 new arrivals a year, existing immigrants would understand if the system cut back on family-class immigration (immigrants who sponsored their parents and grandparents to come over) while increasing the intake of those with skills to match emerging job shortages.

Events conspired to prove him right. The Israeli invasion of Lebanon in 2006 revealed that thousands of Canadian citizens were living there, desperate to get out. Harper diverted his government plane as it returned from the G8 summit in St. Petersburg to pick up refugee citizens in Cyprus. But as the crisis eased, the questions arose: Why were there so many Canadian citizens in Lebanon? Were they merely citizens of convenience, Lebanese who had picked up Canadian citizenship and its accompanying passport – and pension benefits – while never actually intending to live in and commit to Canada? And who were the immigration consultants who had made that possible?

The arrival of a shipload of Tamil refugee claimants off the coast of British Columbia in August 2010 highlighted both the deep tensions between the Sri Lankan government and its Tamil minority and the unscrupulous trafficking in people willing to risk life and fortune to reach Canada. But letting in anyone who reaches Canadian soil by land, air, or sea and who then claims asylum is an ill-considered refugee policy, and the arrival of the MV *Sun Sea* further discredited that policy. Furthermore, Canadian refugee procedures seemed to take forever to reject claimants, who invariably found a way to stay through appeals, even though they had in some cases been convicted of a crime. Kenney changed the refugee rules by designating safe third countries, such as the United States or France. Anyone applying from such countries would have their applications swiftly rejected, since clearly those countries did not persecute people on their soil. With claims being settled and claimants deported in a matter of weeks, word soon circulated overseas that Canada was no longer a soft touch. Though the overall number of refugees admitted to Canada remained constant at around twelve thousand – an exceptionally generous figure, by international standards – almost all now arrive through United Nations programs or private sponsorship. Applications from people arriving unannounced from designated safe countries to claim refugee status has dropped by 80 per cent.[3]

High-profile honour killings – such as Muhammad Shafia's murder (aided by his son and second wife) of his first wife and three daughters in 2009 – provided cover for new laws condemning and banning cultural practices that clashed with Canadian values. And a new guide that immigrants who wished to become citizens were required to master replaced the themes of peacekeeping and multiculturalism with pride in Canada's martial past and strict adherence to the country's founding Judeo-Christian values and British and French legal and legislative heritage.

The reforms culminated in an entirely new system of admissions, launched in 2015, that radically altered the selection process for new arrivals. Instead of joining a queue and waiting to reach the top of it, applicants could be recruited immediately or never, depending on where they ranked in an application process that graded their language skills, education, and likelihood of finding work.

At their worst, the reforms appeared cruel and punitive, especially the rule that stripped failed refugee claimants of access to public health care. (The courts struck the rule down, as well they should have.) And when Kenney decided to relax the rules for letting in temporary foreign workers, the numbers spiralled out of control, as employers resorted to cheap off-shore hires rather than recruiting workers from nearby, forcing Kenney to impose strict new conditions in 2014. But at their best, the reforms made the refugee system more effective and credible, and they better matched immigrant applicants to economic needs. They gave Canadians greater confidence in their ability to remain the world's most generous importer of talent, without worrying that clever operators were gaming the system.

And while on its face, all of this might have seemed likely to deter immigrants from voting Conservative, the "Minister of Curry in a Hurry," as Kenney was dubbed, personally attended every mosque, temple, church, community centre, celebration, commemoration, or pot luck supper thrown by every ethnic community in the land, delivering the message that immigrant values were Conservative values. He successfully convinced the government to halve the hated thousand-dollar landing fee for immigrants, led the successful campaign to offer a government apology for the historic abuse of the Chinese head tax, and pushed annual quotas higher than the Liberals had ever allowed them. In 2010, the intake of more than 280,000 immigrants was the highest number in half a century. And in 2014, the government increased the overall quota for new arrivals from 250,000 to 280,000, making the world's most generous immigration program more generous still.[4]

The political payoff was sweet. Just as Kenney had predicted, immigrants could be brought over to the Conservatives if they believed the party had the right policies and genuinely welcomed them. They were prepared to accept strict limits on refugee claimants, whom they viewed as queue-jumpers. They accepted limits on bringing in parents and grandparents as immigrants in exchange for super-visas that allowed them to stay in the country for up to ten years. The Tories advertised relentlessly in the ethnic media. Harper was far more willing to grant a one-on-one interview with a television station or newspaper that appealed to Sikhs or Chinese or Ukrainians than he was to sit down with the *Globe and Mail* or *National Post*. During the 2011 election campaign, Harper appeared repeatedly, with Kenney by his side, in Greater Toronto ridings that contained large numbers of immigrant voters.

The result? In the GTA, virtually every riding outside Toronto that had a large immigrant population went Conservative. And in Toronto itself, just as voters cleaved between downtown and the suburbs over Rob Ford, so too they cleaved over Stephen Harper. The Conservative Party became the only conservative party in the developed world that counted on a large immigrant vote. This represented a landmark shift in voting patterns. "The growth of Conservatism in Canada, our electoral support, has been largely [driven] by our penetration of immigrant voters," Harper declared in an interview with the *Wall Street Journal*. "Fifteen years ago, like many Conservative parties in other parts of the world, we had a very small share of that vote. Today, we win most of those communities."[5]

Immigrants in the 905, it turned out, were willing to ally with Westerners and with rural folk in Ontario in support of an economically and socially conservative party. Such a coalition, if it could be maintained, might make the Tories the natural governing party of the twenty-first century. That's how much the party, and Harper, owed Jason Kenney.

———————

Majority government offered Harper the opportunity to implement those parts of his conservative agenda that he could never get through minority parliaments. It also allowed him to ignore Parliament altogether, and the media and any other tormentors who, to his mind, sought to obstruct for the sake of obstruction.

For that reason, the real Speech from the Throne that laid out the government's agenda, as opposed to the one that Governor General David Johnston read out on June 3, 2011, was delivered in Davos, Switzerland, seven months later, with Harper himself reading it. In an address to the World Economic Forum, Harper chastised other leaders – really, he was chastising the opposition parties at home – for becoming "complacent about our prosperity, taking our wealth as a given, assuming it is somehow the natural order of things, leaving us instead to focus primarily on our services and entitlements."[6] He then outlined his government's economic agenda for the next four years: pursuing new trade agreements and pushing through new pipelines, reforming immigration while retaining the existing high quotas, reforming as well the pension system, to keep it sustainable.

It pleased Harper to lay out this agenda in Davos rather than in Ottawa, to a gathering of mostly like-minded politicians and business leaders, and devoid of opposition MPs or pesky reporters. He would make it a habit: the biggest headlines based on announcements from the prime minister increasingly took place offshore, in front of friendly crowds, hosted by the editor-in-chief of the *Wall Street Journal* or some equally pliant interrogator who was unconcerned with domestic squabbles, and who lobbed softball questions that Harper was happy to knock out of the park.

This lack of respect for Parliament, which tradition dictates should be the scene of major legislative announcements, was proof positive for critics of "the clear and present danger that the Harper government's approach presented to Canada's democracy."[7] Peter Milliken, former long-serving Speaker of the House of Commons, told author Michael Harris, "Parliament can hardly be weakened any more than it already is. . . . It will have to be returned to its former state by someone if we are to have a democracy."[8] He was referring to the Conservative penchant for limiting debate on parliamentary committees; manipulating the Access to Information Act to delay and defeat requests; routinely imposing closure to limit debate on legislation; and subverting the ability of committees to examine public servants or political staff.

The omnibus bills were the worst of all, and Bill C-38 may have been the worst of the worst. Dressed up as a bill to implement Jim Flaherty's 2012 budget, C-38 raised the retirement age for those receiving Old Age

Security and the Guaranteed Income Supplement from sixty-five to sixty-seven, as foreshadowed by Harper's speech in Davos. It also tightened eligibility requirements for Employment Insurance. Harper was finally tackling the "culture of defeat" by requiring workers on the dole to take a job that paid up to 30 per cent less than their previous job even if it was located up to an hour from home, or lose benefits.

Both measures were sound; both would have benefited from robust parliamentary scrutiny. Both might even, arguably, have belonged inside the same bill. But they were only two of seventy legislative changes, many of them major, crammed into the mammoth, four-hundred-page document. The bill streamlined ("gutted" was the word critics preferred) environmental reviews of pipeline proposals and other infrastructure projects. It loosened protection of the fisheries, scuppered the Fair Wages and Hours of Labour Act (which required contractors bidding on federal contracts to meet certain standards in wages and overtime), shut down the controversy-plagued Rights and Democracy agency, formally withdrew Canada from the Kyoto Protocol, transferred responsibility for inspecting seed crops to the private sector, scrapped the requirement of contractors doing business with the federal government to abide by employment equity guidelines, and on and on.

It was followed mere months later by the 443-page Bill C-45, the Jobs and Growth Act, which further watered down environmental protections, limited land rights on reserves, reduced MP pension benefits, required public servants to contribute more to their health care plans, and raised the retirement age for new hires. Before these two bills, in autumn 2011 came C-10, which introduced a host of changes to the criminal justice system. These included imposing new mandatory minimum sentences for drug and sex offences, limiting judicial discretion in imposing house arrest, increasing the likelihood of adult sentences for young offenders convicted of violent crimes, replacing pardons with "record suspensions," and making it harder for Canadians convicted of crimes overseas to return to Canada to serve out their sentences.

Again, all or most of the measures in these three bills were defensible, though some would have benefited from sober second thought. But they didn't receive it, because the bills were pushed through parliamentary committees overwhelmed by what they were looking at and pressured to report the bills back to Parliament with a minimum of revision or debate.

Do such shenanigans represent a clear and present danger to Canadian democracy, as Milliken argues? Might Canada no longer be a democracy at all? Of course not. The Charter of Rights and Freedoms remains intact. The courts work – so well that they have become a serious brake on parts of the Conservatives' agenda. The premiers continue to stand watch over their provinces' interests. But the omnibus bills were bad bills. They abused the parliamentary process. With proper scrutiny, much of what was in them could have been made better. Is Stephen Harper, with his all-controlling, suspicious, polarizing approach to politics, government, and life, to blame? Absolutely. Except . . .

Historian and author Allan Levine wrote in the *Winnipeg Free Press* in 2014 about a 1930s editorial cartoon featuring R.B. Bennett holding a cabinet meeting. Every minister at the table is R.B. Bennett, and so are the waiter and messenger. There was a joke back then that had Bennett walking down the street talking to himself. What's that all about? a visitor asked. The prime minister is having a cabinet meeting, his friend replied. Bennett had a reputation for being an autocrat, but he was hardly the first or last. Stephen Harper "follows in a long line of, if not control freaks, then certainly dictatorial prime ministers," Levine observed in 2014. "It has always been the nature of the job – particularly if you want to succeed at it."[9]

Macdonald and Laurier bent cabinet and caucus to their will, through flattery or intimidation as required; King destroyed cabinet ministers who crossed him and had no time for disrespectful journalists; Pearson's cabinet leaked like a sieve and he could never manage more than minority governments. Clark, Turner, and Martin failed as leaders in part because they couldn't control their caucus. Mulroney's caucus eventually dissolved into three separate parties. But Trudeau, Chrétien, and Harper exercised dictatorial control over their governments, and all were strong and successful prime ministers. Michael Harris's book *Party of One*, and many similar indictments of the Harper government, reflect a tradition of protest that recalls Jeffrey Simpson's *The Friendly Dictatorship* (about Chrétien) and Richard Gwyn's *The Northern Magus* (about Trudeau).

As previously observed, opposition parties have done their part in undermining the legitimacy of Parliament. In 1981, Joe Clark used a procedural trick to let the bells ring for days, calling members to a vote that never occurred. He wanted to draw attention to the Trudeau government's ham-fisted approach in forcing the patriation of the Constitution. All very noble, but it undermined a tradition of trust and good-sportsmanship on which parliamentary conventions are based. The rules were changed to prevent parliamentary paralysis through bell-ringing, and a pattern was set: the opposition exploits a good-faith convention to frustrate a majority government bent on exercising its will; the government closes the loophole; the opposition finds another; trust erodes; things go downhill.

Had the Harper government respectfully, even deferentially, placed each of the legislative measures in the omnibus bills before Parliament as stand-alone legislation, can anyone doubt what would have followed? Each bill would have been treated as a *cause célèbre* by the opposition and parts of the media. Each would have been hung up in committee as Liberals and New Democrats sought sweeping amendments. Ultimately, the government would have been forced to impose closure, to cries of "Tyranny!" from the other side; so much time would have been wasted that much of the legislation might never have been passed.

This mutual erosion of trust and responsibility lay behind the government's decision to provide no oversight mechanisms in Bill C-51, the government's 2015 anti-terrorism legislation that conferred sweeping new powers on CSIS, the national security service. Even Conservative supporters worried that the legislation failed to provide proper checks and balances. But the Conservatives refused to create a parliamentary committee to keep a watch on CSIS, arguing off the record that the opposition parties couldn't be trusted to protect state secrets.

If Parliament is to matter in the twenty-first century, it must move into the twenty-first century, becoming more responsive and responsible. We are never going back to an Elysian agora that never really existed in the first place. The real question is whether anyone outside Parliament even cares. Harper thinks they don't; he thinks voters expect their government to get the job done and aren't fussy about how it gets done.

One thing we can predict. The next prime minister will be little different, whoever that prime minister might be. The system requires it. The NDP chose

Thomas Mulcair because they know he's as tough and mean as Harper, with a track record in Quebec politics to prove it. As for Justin Trudeau, "opponents who deride Harper's dictatorial rule should not kid themselves," Levine concludes. "Justin Trudeau – he who has blocked a candidate from running in a riding, when he said he would never do so, and decreed that all Liberal party candidates must be pro-choice – also has control-freak tendencies and no doubt would as prime minister, too. It's in his genes."[10]

Jack Layton wanted to be prime minister. He took over the leadership of the NDP in 2002 determined to bring it to power. In each election, he grew the party's support. In 2011, he campaigned with vigour despite his bad hip, using his cane as a campaign prop, wowing the audience on Radio-Canada's incredibly influential TV program *Tout le monde en parle*. Everything he had dreamed of was coming true: the country cleaving into a two-party system with the NDP the party of the left. The Liberals were in danger of vanishing and he had personally vanquished Gilles Duceppe's Bloc Québécois so thoroughly that it was unlikely ever to rise again. Jack Layton was the leader of the official opposition, the prime minister in waiting.

A month later, as an NDP filibuster over back-to-work legislation for postal workers was wrapping up, Layton turned to his House leader, Thomas Mulcair, and asked: "Tom, will you be able to give the wrap-up speech? I'm feeling a little discomfort."[11]

"Of course," Mulcair replied, putting his hand on his leader's back. The jacket was soaked in sweat.

In July, Layton appeared at a news conference gaunt and hoarse, shocking the nation. He was stepping aside from the leadership temporarily to fight "a new form of cancer." A month later, he was dead.

Harper had known something was very wrong when he chatted with Layton on the floor of the House during the filibuster. Layton and Harper had each outlasted four Liberal leaders: Chrétien, Martin, Dion, and Ignatieff. Harper played the piano; Layton played the guitar. They should have jammed together.

Harper offered a state funeral for the late leader of Her Majesty's Loyal

Opposition, channelling a national outpouring of grief. Or so it seemed. For the blanket coverage given to Jack Layton's funeral was in its way a reflection of Pierre Trudeau's state funeral. It was really the Laurentian elite in mourning. Others, who liked Layton personally but did not share his political world view, simply remained silent.

Pollster Darrell Bricker has observed that "progressive voters need leaders that inspire them. The left needs to love."[12] Conservative politicians are, at best, in office to get a job done. But the deep Whiggish strain that runs through the Western narrative celebrates progress toward a fairer, more equal, more enlightened humanity, and celebrates the icons who have led the way. In Canada, those icons were Tommy Douglas, Pierre Trudeau, and, latterly, Jack Layton, even though he never served in government or greatly influenced the national agenda. Shut out of power, facing years of Conservative majority-government rule, Laurentian Canada turned Jack Layton's funeral into a requiem for everything that it had lost.

These were grey days. The world had narrowly avoided a second Great Depression, but the giddy years of housing bubbles and tech booms had given way to high unemployment, little growth, and cascading shocks – Greece, Portugal, Italy, Spain, Greece again – that threatened to snuff out a weak and sluggish recovery. A generation of young adults graduating from school began to realize that secure jobs and pensions were never going to be part of their life. One study after another painted a picture of growing inequality, lowered expectations, shuttered factories, offshoring and outsourcing, and less of everything. Southwestern Ontario took the worst of it. Three hundred and seventy thousand manufacturing jobs lost. Complacent affluence converted to struggle and decline and empty storefronts on Main Street. The oil sands of Alberta drove what little growth there was, but at what cost to the environment? Thank God Apple had invented the iPhone as a distraction. Except that the phone virtually destroyed BlackBerry, taking with it thousands more Canadian jobs.

For going on six years, Stephen Harper had dominated the federal scene. He had consistently led all of his rivals in the polls. An aura of inevitability had grown up around him. Neither Stéphane Dion nor Michael Ignatieff had succeeded in presenting themselves as credible contenders for the post of prime minister. Jack Layton might have risen to the challenge, had he lived, but now he was gone – and in any event it is hard to imagine that the nation, no matter how much people liked "le bon Jack," would have voted in an NDP government. In any case, both the Liberals and the NDP were leaderless. Books hit the stores arguing for the merger of the two parties as the only hope for a Canada free of Stephen Harper.[13] John Reynolds, long retired from the House of Commons, predicted: "I think one of the achievements he'd like to have is to be the longest-serving Conservative prime minister – if not the longest serving prime minister" of all.[14]

At his best, Harper offered managerially competent, fiscally conservative government that was tough on crime and reliable on security. This is what voters around the world always turned to when the dreams of the progressives foundered on the shoals of economic reality. Voters in Canada had endorsed that approach through three elections. But not only the left needs to love. The whole nation craved inspiration after a near-miss depression. Instead, a grey, dour prime minister, having conquered all opposition, presided over grey, dour times. Yes, he steered the ship with a steady hand. But was there nothing more?

Roosevelt, Kennedy, Trudeau, Thatcher, Reagan, Clinton, Blair, Obama, Layton. Some politicians could inspire the people to think beyond the next tax cut. They could offer hope for a more perfect union rather than simply a less imperfect one. "Love is better than anger," Layton had written in his farewell letter to Canadians. "Hope is better than fear. Optimism is better than despair. So let us be loving, hopeful and optimistic. And we'll change the world."[15]

The letter. The funeral. The longing. But all that was on offer was a "strong, stable, national, majority Conservative government." All we had were fights over the real cost of the F-35, and accusations of contempt for democracy and the promise of a balanced budget and more tax cuts down the road. Was there no one who could dream Canada, rather than just manage it? Was there no one who could inspire us to be greater than ourselves?

As a matter of fact, there might be.

NINETEEN

Nemesis

Without question, Justin Trudeau saved the Liberal Party, which was broke, broken, and on the brink when he took over as leader. The party was in such awful shape that at first Trudeau refused even to run for the leadership, declaring after the 2011 election that he wanted to focus on raising his two children. After all, he had watched his parents' marriage come apart when he was a child; it was not an experience he wanted to inflict on Xavier and Ella-Grace. Besides, interim leader Bob Rae, who had run unsuccessfully for leader in 2006 and 2008, was likely going to take a third shot at the job, and would almost certainly succeed this time, though there wasn't much of a Liberal Party left to inherit. (According to one internal report, as many as a third of the riding associations across the country were moribund – effectively non-existent.) But Rae announced in June 2012 that he didn't want the job. It was the right call; Rae was sixty-three, a former NDP leader, and part of the party's disastrously faction-ridden past. The party needed renewal. Rae was wise enough and honest enough with himself to realize he could not renew it.

Trudeau was inundated by a "tsunami" of phone calls, as he put it, urging him to reconsider. He took the summer off, to mull things over with his wife, Sophie Grégoire – or so he said. But as it turned out, a leadership team was already in place and organizing a campaign, and he had quietly warned Rae in the spring that he planned to run (another, and perhaps the most important, reason that Rae decided to call it quits). Trudeau was now considered the prohibitive favourite. After all, he had knocked down Patrick Brazeau back in March.

Trudeau had decided that he should go three rounds with a Conservative before he turned forty. Peter MacKay and Rob Anders both turned him down, but Senator Brazeau was happy to take up the challenge. Brazeau had a black belt in karate, was bigger and heavier than the lithe Liberal MP, and should have beaten him senseless. But Trudeau trained and Brazeau didn't – at least, not enough – and stamina prevailed over brute force. Trudeau won the match, which was sufficient for the commentariat to declare that he was the natural choice to bring the once-natural-governing Liberal Party back from the abyss. And they were right. No one was surprised when Trudeau declared that autumn that he would run for leader. No one was surprised when he won the leadership in a walk, or when the polls put the Liberals in first place. And no one was surprised when the Conservative attack ads that had devastated Stéphane Dion and Michael Ignatieff bounced harmlessly off the new leader's Teflon reputation. In politics, either you have it or you don't. Trudeau has it.

But what if Trudeau had been knocked senseless in the first round? Would he still have run and would he still have won? Who knows? It's impossible to speculate on how different the political landscape would look if New Brunswick MP Dominic LeBlanc or Quebec MP and former astronaut Marc Garneau were leading the Liberals. It is, however, entirely reasonable to surmise that, whoever was leading the third party, Stephen Harper's government was eventually going to get into trouble. In politics, as in some marriages, there truly is such a thing as the seven-year itch.

Presidents and prime ministers almost always have lousy second (or sometimes third) terms. With Truman, it was Korea; with St. Laurent, it was the pipeline; with Eisenhower, it was *Sputnik* and the U-2; with Diefenbaker, it was the Bomarc missile crisis (among many other things); with Johnson, it was Vietnam; with Nixon, it was Watergate; with Trudeau, it was stagflation and René Lévesque; with Reagan, it was Iran–Contra; with Clinton, it was Lewinsky; with Chrétien, it was sponsorship and Paul Martin; with Bush, it was Iraq.

By 2013, Stephen Harper had been in power for seven years – just the point when you might expect a president or prime minister to get into trouble. As a wise mind who prefers not to be identified observed, the characteristic that brings down a politician is usually the same characteristic that brought him or her to power in the first place. Harper defeated Paul Martin and Stéphane Dion and Michael Ignatieff because he was seen as a strong leader and they were seen as weak. By the end of 2013, he was in mortal peril because he was seen as a strongman – as in dictator. And he had only himself to blame.

The bad news began in Guelph. The campaign in the mid-sized city just west of Toronto had been particularly vicious in 2011. The riding had gone Conservative under Brian Mulroney, and Liberal under Jean Chrétien. It stayed Liberal after Stephen Harper came to power; in 2008, Liberal candidate Frank Valeriote squeaked in by fewer than two thousand votes, even as Southwestern Ontario swung from red to blue. In 2011, the Tories were determined to take the riding away from the Liberals; the Liberals were grimly determined to hang on.

Many campaign workers are young, passionate, and partisan beyond reason. Many of them are on leave from jobs in Ottawa – the "future prime ministers" that Harper had so despised during his first stint in Ottawa back in 1985. It is not unheard of during election campaigns for workers to deface or steal the other team's election signs. More serious is the misuse of "robocalls" – phone messages dialled and delivered by computers. One dirty trick, for example, is to call people in the middle of the night claiming to be from the other candidate's party and asking for the voter's support.

In Guelph, both the Liberals and the Conservatives used robocalls illegally. The Liberals used them to tell voters that the Conservative candidate, Marty Burke, opposed abortion. But the calls failed to identify the local Liberal campaign as the source of the calls, and the Canadian Radio-television and Telecommunications Commission found Frank Valeriote's campaign guilty of violating the Telecommunications Act, fining it $4,900.

The Conservatives' sins were far worse. Thousands of robocalls went out on Election Day to voters, alerting them to changes in the location of the polling stations. Except the polling stations hadn't been changed. The calls claimed to be from Elections Canada, but weren't. That's clearly electoral fraud, a serious crime. Obviously, someone or some group of persons on the Conservative side had sent out these fraudulent calls. And whoever ordered up the robocalls must have had access to CIMS, the Conservative Party's by then very sophisticated database. That database would have the names and numbers of people in Guelph who had been identified as Liberals. Most or all of the robocalls appeared to have gone out to Liberal supporters. The good news, as far as the Conservatives were concerned, was that they lost the riding. Guelph was one of only two Ontario ridings outside the GTA and Ottawa (Kingston and the Islands was the other) that went Liberal in 2011. So any electoral fraud in Guelph had been for naught.

But what if the fraud wasn't limited to Guelph? After Stephen Maher of Postmedia and Glen McGregor of the *Ottawa Citizen* broke the story in February 2012 of Elections Canada investigating the Guelph robocalls, people in other ridings started phoning newspapers, networks, and Elections Canada with complaints that they had received similar calls. As the weeks passed, and the Elections Canada investigation dragged on, thousands of complaints in scores of ridings flooded in. "McMaher," as the journalists were dubbed in honour of their Woodward and Bernstein ("Woodstein") forebears, revealed that the calls in Guelph had been traced to an Edmonton-based company called RackNine that the Conservatives had hired to do robocalling – of the strictly legal variety. Had the party also used the company's services (without the company's knowledge) to send out misleading or fraudulent robocalls in ridings across the country? If so, this would be a scandal worthy of Watergate: an illegal, fraudulent campaign to mislead voters and to rig the 2011 election. If that were true, then the only other question that mattered would be, What did the prime minister know, and when did he know it? If Stephen Harper had authorized or even been aware of electoral fraud carried out by his campaign team, he would have to resign, and might well end up in jail.

To Harper's fiercest critics, it only made sense that he was guilty. Many people don't believe Harper is legitimately prime minister. He is the intolerable contradiction of a syllogism: Canada is a progressive country; conservatives are, by definition, not progressive; therefore conservatives cannot win elections in Canada. And yet there Stephen Harper was, refuting the proposition. How to explain it? Maybe it was all the result of an incredible run of luck, "not just one or two turns of happenstance. More like six or seven," as Lawrence Martin put it. ". . . Most of the breaks that catapulted him to power were from out of the blue."[1] Or maybe it was something more nefarious. Maybe the Tories had rigged the election.

It didn't matter that Harper had stood in the House of Commons and declared, without qualification, "The Conservative Party can say absolutely, definitively, it has no role in any of this,"[2] or that Guy Giorno, who had served as campaign co-chair, declared, "nobody in his right mind running a campaign would have done that" and that "suppressing the vote is a despicable, reprehensible practice, and everybody ought to condemn it."[3] Both men were obviously lying through their teeth.

Not only voter suppression was involved, according to this particularly febrile interpretation of events. In Etobicoke Centre, which the Conservatives won by only twenty-six votes, the Liberal challenger alleged voter irregularities, and though the Supreme Court ruled otherwise, others remained convinced there had been widespread fraud. "It has become clear to many Canadians that our democracy was tested and perhaps undermined during the last election," interim Liberal leader Bob Rae declared. "Reports and allegations of election fraud are widespread and there are many cases still under investigation. This has cast serious doubts on the integrity of our electoral system."[4]

In the end, Elections Canada investigated all the complaints and concluded there was no basis for any charges outside the riding of Guelph, where Michael Sona, a Conservative campaign worker, was convicted of election fraud in August 2014. In his decision, Justice Gary Hearn stated that he strongly suspected that someone else on the campaign team might also have been in on the scheme, but there was nothing to suggest an orchestrated, national campaign to suppress the vote. And RackNine was fully exonerated from any wrongdoing.

Nonetheless, Harper paid a political price for the robocalls affair, as he deserved to. His own secretive, suspicious nature and his relentless determination to do everything within the legal limit to discredit and defeat his opponents created the win-at-all-costs culture that convinced Sona, and possibly others, to cross the line. And Harper's lack of remorse – he is a man who simply doesn't do remorse – meant that the same no-holds-barred culture he created would remain in place for the 2015 campaign.

As it turned out, the robocalls affair was mere prelude. The real crisis came from something that Harper had hated his entire adult life: the Senate.

———————

On November 20, 2013, Corporal Greg Horton of the RCMP applied for a warrant to obtain government records. He was searching for further evidence in support of what he believed was criminal fraud involving Senator Mike Duffy and Nigel Wright, former chief of staff to Stephen Harper. It was the lowest moment in Stephen Harper's life as a politician.

Harper had long sought Wright for chief of staff. When Ian Brodie stepped down, he made his first pitch, but Wright declined. After Guy Giorno decided to leave in autumn 2010, he made his pitch again, this time successfully. Inside and outside Tory circles, landing Nigel Wright was seen as a major coup, though the new chief of staff was an odd pick, in a way. Wright had gone to Trinity College, Harper's bane, where he earned the unbridled admiration of fellow students such as Jim Balsillie, who would go on to co-found Research In Motion (developer of the BlackBerry); Andrew Coyne, the future columnist; John Duffy, who would become a Liberal strategist; and the future writer Malcolm Gladwell. Relentlessly even-tempered, far too well dressed for a university student, dedicated to his studies and far beyond merely smart, even as a college student, "the question was: 'Will Nigel be on the Supreme Court or be prime minister?'" Duffy remembered.[5]

Wright was a partisan Conservative from the get-go, unlike Harper, who had repented of his Liberalism only after he moved to Alberta. He campaigned to unseat Joe Clark and replace him with Brian Mulroney; Harper would get his political start defending Jim Hawkes, a Clark supporter. Wright worked in Brian Muloney's office after he became prime minister, a government that Harper ultimately rejected. After law degrees at the

University of Toronto and Harvard, he went into law and then business, making his money on Bay Street, where he mingled comfortably with the business side of the Laurentian elite, a group Harper has never trusted. He publicly supported the Meech Lake Accord, which Stephen Harper opposed. Most important, he was never going to be the kind of aide who deferred to Harper's wisdom, who cowered at his passions, who watched helplessly, too frightened to speak up, whenever the boss lurched toward a bad decision. The two should not have been a good fit. But they were. As far back as the early nineties, Wright was praising Stephen Harper to people like Tom Long – the political strategist who would help bring Mike Harris to power – as someone who could unite the right and bring it to power. He even helped fundraise for Harper during his bid for the Alliance leadership and for the Conservative Party.

Apart from being prescient, Wright was also supremely talented. He helped land the deal that got the Confederation Bridge built, linking Prince Edward Island to the mainland. At Onex Corporation, where he was managing director, he capably handled business deals, especially in aviation, worth hundreds of millions of dollars, amassing a respectable personal fortune along the way. Soft-spoken, obsessively dedicated, he is up at 4 a.m. and runs for an hour and a half – twenty kilometres – every morning. According to one friend, only three things have mattered to Nigel Wright throughout his life: "work, his mother, and honouring his God."[6] He had, in spades, the one quality Harper prizes more than any other in his staff or cabinet: the ability to get the job done.

As chief of staff, he personally handled complex trade negotiations involving the European Union and the Trans-Pacific Partnership. He worked intimately with Harper on the CNOOC/Nexen file. He developed a reputation inside the Langevin Block for being able to synthesize seemingly conflicting points of view, or to bring others around to his own. Quiet, capable, charming, he was able to offer Harper his advice more frankly than any chief of staff before or since, without offending or angering the boss. People inside the office called him the deputy prime minister – though never, of course, to his face.

And so Harper's shock was genuine on May 14, 2013, when he was told that Robert Fife of CTV had reported the night before that Wright had written a personal cheque for ninety thousand dollars to Senator Mike Duffy, and that the report was true. Senior staff had debated whether to tell Harper that evening, but the consensus was to work on preparing a response and present the whole package to the prime minister in the morning. (There was little danger of Harper finding out on his own, since he never listens to the evening news.) At first, the strategy was to weather the storm: the cheque was probably a mistake, but one made in good faith. But within four days, Wright was out: he had resigned or Harper had fired him, depending on which version of events you believed. Harper himself started out saying Wright had resigned, but by the autumn, under relentless attack by Thomas Mulcair in the House of Commons, he had changed his story, saying he had fired Wright as soon as he learned of his transgression.

Harper was beyond angry at Wright. It went deeper than that. He spoke to those closest to him of betrayal. His most trusted aide had betrayed him. He hadn't meant to, of course. Wright was simply doing what he thought was best for his boss, by keeping him in the dark about the cheque. Plausible deniability, they call it. But Harper raged against the term. It was *his* government; how could Wright have kept this from him? More than any prime minister who had sat in the chair, Harper wanted to know everything that was going on; if he was going to answer for a government decision in the House of Commons, then he would be the one to make the decision. Wright knew this, and yet he had made this huge commitment, taken this enormous risk, without even consulting him. How could he have done such a thing?

Although Duffy would later claim that the whole affair was cooked up by Wright, with Harper's knowledge and against Duffy's own wishes, Corporal Horton's Information to Obtain affidavit describes an entirely different situation. Here is how the police decided it went down: Back in the autumn of 2012, alerted by press reports and the auditor general, a Senate committee chaired by Tory senator David Tkachuk began looking at the expenses of Tory senators Mike Duffy, Pamela Wallin, and Patrick Brazeau, along with those of Liberal senator Mac Harb. In the case of Duffy, Brazeau, and Harb, the question was whether they had properly claimed living expenses and travel expenses between Ottawa and what they claimed were their principal residences: in PEI for Duffy; Maniwaki, Quebec, for Brazeau;

and a house near Pembroke, Ontario, for Harb. For Wallin, the question was whether she had properly claimed travel expenses. By February 2013, the whole thing seemed sufficiently suspicious for the committee to call in auditors. By March 2013, the RCMP was getting ready to launch its own investigation. Duffy had already announced that he might have mistakenly, though in good faith, claimed about ninety thousand dollars in expenses that he shouldn't have. He promised to pay it back, and the Senate later reported that he had kept his word.

Behind the scenes, both Wright and Harper had ordered Duffy to pay up. The prime minister was frustrated with the oleaginous senator. Harper had never worried much about accumulating wealth. Before Stornoway, the family had lived modestly; neither Stephen nor Laureen had expensive tastes, and neither judged nor envied anyone based on wealth. Power was Harper's coin; he had chased it his whole life, and by that measure he was a rich man. But to compromise yourself in order to pad your lifestyle or feed your habits – it not only infuriated Harper, it left him mystified.

Duffy claimed he didn't have the money to pay back the expenses, and in any case he had done nothing wrong. At first, when it appeared he owed only around thirty thousand dollars, the Conservative Party agreed to pay the money in his stead. But when the amount ballooned to more than ninety thousand dollars, the party backed out. Wright is the sort of person who, when confronted with a problem, searches for the quickest and cleanest way to fix it. By now, the Senate expenses affair was consuming the government – the media were reporting on little else. If Duffy needed ninety thousand dollars, then in Wright's mind the quickest, cleanest solution was for the chief of staff to give him the money. For a man of his wealth, such a sum was the equivalent of petty cash. But for Horton, this on its face constituted a bribe: Wright had paid a senator money in order to get that senator to do something. There was more to the affair, but the questions that mattered were these: Had Wright committed bribery and/or fraud by secretly helping Duffy to pay off his expenses? And had Harper known anything about the cheque before it became public knowledge?

Horton believed that Wright and Duffy "did commit breach of trust in connection with the duties of their offices."[7] In other words, Wright offered and Duffy accepted a bribe. But that was only one way to interpret the facts. One element of a crime is what is called *mens rea*: criminal intent. To commit a crime, you must or should know that what you are doing is a crime. Horton states in the document that Wright said he was simply doing what he felt was right – paying back the money that Duffy owed the taxpayers. Also, both Duffy's lawyer and a lawyer inside the Prime Minister's Office knew about and had approved the payment. They obviously didn't think they were aiding and abetting a crime. In the end, Wright was never charged. And as Horton affirmed in the Information to Obtain, there was never any evidence that Harper knew about the payment before it became public knowledge.

None of that mattered. Corrupt senators. A secret cheque. The Harper government may have been autocratic, secretive, and cruel, but at least it had been clean, or so it claimed. Now even that no longer appeared to be true.

Bad news sticks to governments in trouble. And bad news was all the Conservatives seemed able to attract in 2013. Part of the problem was that Harper could be a remarkably poor judge of horseflesh. Bruce Carson, his former aide, was charged with influence peddling after he left the PMO. Police claimed he improperly lobbied on behalf of First Nations and others. As this book went to press, those charges had not been tested in court. Harper appointed Arthur Porter, once director general of the McGill University Health Centre, to the board of the Security Intelligence Review Committee, and then made him chair. Porter was arrested in Panama in May 2013 on charges related to the Quebec corruption scandal. In 2002, Harper hired Dimitri Soudas as a press aide. Soudas rose through the ranks to become director of communications in 2010, developing a reputation along the way as one of the most bare-knuckle partisans in Harper's office. By 2013, he was executive director of the Conservative Party. In 2014, he was fired for using his office to advance the efforts of his girlfriend, Mississauga MP Eve Adams, to secure a riding nomination. By February 2015, Adams had crossed the floor, and Soudas was now working to get her elected as a Liberal – though he insisted he was only helping her, not the Liberal Party as a whole.

Harper liked to choose as his parliamentary secretaries MPs who didn't mind flouting parliamentary tradition or even common courtesy to bait the opposition during Question Period. Pierre Poilievre served as Harper's muscle in the Commons for several years, before being sent to his reward in cabinet. He was replaced by Peterborough MP Dean Del Mastro, who defended the government during the robocalls scandal, accusing Elections Canada of leaking information to the press. But Del Mastro was soon in trouble of his own; Elections Canada charged him with overspending during the 2011 election, and he went from being an attack dog to being expelled from caucus. He was found guilty in October 2014 and resigned his seat.

Del Mastro was replaced by Paul Calandra, who had the admittedly difficult task of defending the government during the Senate expenses scandal. He did it so ineptly that even those who thought the House of Commons could sink no lower were shocked. Calandra's answers were so non sequitur, and so obviously the product of talking points generated by the so-called kids in short pants in the Prime Minister's Office, that Tory MPs angrily complained to Harper himself. Ultimately, a tearful Calandra apologized to the House, taking all the blame.

But those short-panted kids were another part of the government's problem. Harper had replaced Nigel Wright with Ray Novak, born in 1977, who had started out literally carrying Harper's luggage. Alykhan Velshi, born in 1984, was in charge of issues management. Jenni Byrne, born in 1977, had left party headquarters to work as co-deputy chief of staff. It's a myth that governments become sclerotic because the same people cling to their jobs year after year. The problem is exactly the opposite. The life of a political aide is gruelling. Twelve-hour days are the norm, weekends are often non-existent, the price for making a mistake can involve public humiliation and instant dismissal, and the pay is lousy compared with what's available on the outside. Staff burn out and are replaced with people who are younger, less experienced, and more prone to bad judgment. Stephen Harper's biggest problem during the Senate expenses scandal was that there were few people in his office he could trust to advise him well – not that he was wont to take advice in the first place. He was alone, and it showed.

Nothing roils the Conservative caucus like the issue of abortion. For the social-conservative wing of the caucus – typically, MPs from the West or from rural Ontario – Harper's unwillingness even to permit some discussion of when life begins is disappointing and frustrating. He at least offered them a sop back in 2010, when the government prohibited the funding of abortion services as part of its maternal health initiative. But Harper ultimately abandoned even such token gestures. Instead, during the 2011 election campaign, he vowed: "As long as I'm prime minister, we are not reopening the abortion debate. The government will not bring forward any such legislation, and any such legislation that is brought forward will be defeated."[8]

Some backbenchers tried to get the issue raised through the back door. Stephen Woodworth of Kitchener proposed a motion that, if adopted, would have struck a committee to consider when a newborn can legally be considered a human being under the criminal code. Harper voted against the motion, but ten cabinet ministers and much of his caucus voted for it. He was more than annoyed. In the early years of his leadership, Harper had taken special care to listen to caucus and attend to the needs of backbenchers as much as possible. But after seven years in government, his determination to exercise control over the caucus and the party had trumped any desire to placate the so-con MPs. Besides, he had made a pledge during the election that caucus was ignoring. He vowed not to let it happen again.

When Tory MP Mark Warawa of Langley, British Columbia, introduced a motion during the winter 2013 session condemning sex-selective abortion, trained-seal MPs on the committee that examines private members' business deemed it non-votable. Frustrated, Warawa decided to speak to the issue in the House during Members' Statements. But Gordon O'Connor, now the party whip, refused to put him on the roster. That was a big mistake. Warawa appealed to Speaker Andrew Scheer on a point of privilege. About twenty Tory MPs in all appeared to be publicly on Warawa's side. Others no doubt were so privately. Harper had a full-fledged caucus rebellion on his hands.

As governments age, and certain backbenchers realize they are never going to make cabinet, they become harder to control. Paul Martin's coup against Jean Chrétien was as much a backbench rebellion as anything else. In that context, Harper's increasingly restive caucus was simply a typical symptom of a government that was getting on in years. But this all came amid the Senate expenses scandal, adding to the growing impression that the Tory ship was starting to list.

———————

CTV broke the story about Nigel Wright's cheque in May; by autumn, Senate shenanigans were still the only thing anyone was talking about on the Hill. An independent audit concluded Pamela Wallin had improperly charged $121,348 in travel expenses. She paid the money back, through gritted teeth, accusing the media and her fellow senators of a "lynch mob mentality."[9] A Senate committee also concluded that Patrick Brazeau owed $51,482. Mac Harb was on the hook for $231,649.07. He paid the money back, resigned from the Senate, and was later charged with fraud. But all the attention focused on the Conservative senators. Duffy, Wallin, and Brazeau were expelled from the Conservative caucus and then suspended from the Senate.

They did not go quietly. The government writhed in agony as the senators took to the floor to condemn their former colleagues. "You cannot concoct false charges on a whim," Wallin protested. ". . . Throwing a member of this Senate under the bus, finding her guilty without a fair hearing . . . is a fundamental affront to Canadian democracy, and makes a mockery of this chamber."[10] Mike Duffy accused the government of railroading him into accepting Nigel Wright's cheque. "I allowed myself to be intimidated into doing what I knew in my heart was wrong, out of a fear of losing my job, and a misguided sense of loyalty."[11]

Meanwhile, in the Commons, Thomas Mulcair revealed that his true calling might have been Crown attorney, as he grilled the prime minister relentlessly, day after day, week upon week. "Did the Prime Minister offer Mike Duffy a guarantee that, in turn for going along with the repayment scheme, the Conservative-controlled Senate would let him off the hook?" was one typical question, asked on October 30.[12]

"Mr. Speaker, I am not quite sure what the question is there," Harper replied. But many days, he looked so weary and defeated that he seemed barely able to rise to his feet.

He'd been down in the dumps before: during the coalition crisis, when it appeared his government was headed for defeat; after he lost an election he could have won in 2004; when he was running for leader of the Alliance and discovered he had no money or organization, despite weeks of effort. It's easy to imagine him at home in 1993, discouraged by his confrontations with Preston Manning and ready to give up even running for Parliament in the upcoming election. (And he would have quit, if his father Joe hadn't talked him out of it.) He might have felt like this as he sat in Strachan Hall, eating Trinity's execrable food and surrounded by men of college who had no idea who he was, and who didn't care.

Paralyzed. Defeated. Weary. Pessimistic. Depressed.

At times like this, Harper's instinct is to withdraw – into himself and from public view. He goes into a funk and he stays in a funk until the situation changes or someone talks him out of it. But he couldn't, this time. This time he couldn't go to ground. People who work for him have often been surprised at the sophistication of his grasp of communications strategy. He may loathe the media for what he perceives as their superficial, sensationalist, and intel- lectually lazy approach to their jobs, but he knows what makes them tick. More important in October 2013, he knew what would and wouldn't work with the public, what could be sold and what could not be sold, better than those hired to advise him on such things. In this darkest hour, he knew he had to keep his face in front of the public. Prorogation was out; handing the affair off to a minister or parliamentary secretary was out. The press and the public wanted to see this government whipped for the sins of the Senate. Only if he accepted the punishment did he have a chance of survival. So he stood there, and let Tom Mulcair have at him, day after day after day. This was penance. And in that penance lay his only hope of redemption.

Governments, as they reach the end, begin to smell of rot. Even some of Harper's closest advisors noticed something strange and unpleasant in the air. If Harper lost his will to power, if he sulked and moped and yelled and disengaged, then the rot would truly set in. He knew this better than anyone. He knew that, throughout this public whipping, he had to keep the government going, keep the agenda moving forward. They were all watching. The staff in the PMO were watching, to see if he was staying interested in, and on top of, his files. The senior mandarins were watching, for signs of a government that was checking out, in which case they would down tools and wait for the next crew to take over. His colleagues on the Priorities and Planning Committee were watching. He chaired that committee, which set the governing agenda. If he lost control there, then it was over.

But it wasn't over. Through sheer force of will, Harper got himself through the fall of 2013 and winter of 2014. He stayed on the job. He kept his temper under control (at least by his standards). He kept busy, and kept his staff and cabinet busy. No rot. Not this time. Not yet. Stephen Harper's performance in the teeth of the Senate expenses scandal may be his most impressive achievement as a leader. He single-handedly kept himself and his government together when both were at their greatest danger of falling apart. But Lord, the days were long. He struggled against surrendering to his own despair. His staff repeatedly warned him not to look down at his shoes while giving answers in Question Period. There were bad days – days when people wondered whether the PM would be able to carry on, days when he must have wondered it himself.

On October 31, 2013 – yet another Halloween gathering – the Conservative Party met in convention in Calgary. It was a grim affair. Efforts to force Duffy, Wallin, and Brazeau out of the Senate had been stymied by Tory senators concerned about the arbitrary dismissal of their own. They delayed the vote, giving Duffy a second chance to harangue the Senate and prolonging the government's agony. (Duffy, Wallin, and Brazeau would finally be turfed, with their pay suspended, on November 5.) Stephen Harper's speech to the convention was defiant, painting a government in its third term as an underdog insurgency with a widening circle of enemies. He railed against the "lobbyists, academics and bureaucrats" arrayed against him. He reminded the crowd that he and Laureen "didn't go to Ottawa to join private clubs or become part of some elite."[13]

But in the corridors, and in the bars, the mood was bleak. Peter MacKay and Jason Kenney had both come to the defence of Nigel Wright, of whom Harper was speaking in increasingly harsh terms in the House. The party was running third in some polls, with Justin Trudeau sailing high. The consensus among Harper's closest friends and supporters was that he had six months to turn things around. Otherwise, it would be better for someone else to lead the party into the next election. And Harper knew the truth of that himself.

Stephen Harper's government was at rock bottom.

TWENTY

Catharsis

Jim Flaherty had become the literal embodiment of the Harper government's ills. He had gained weight, become puffy. Behind the scenes, people talked of him tiring easily, sometimes losing track of what was happening. The rumour mill churned; to calm it, Flaherty told the *Globe and Mail* in January 2013 that he was battling bullous pemphigoid, a painful but non-life-threatening autoimmune disease that is treated with steroids, which he said caused the weight gain. The disease was curable, and he planned to carry on with his work until the budget was balanced in 2015. Harper had no choice but to let him.

The prime minister had actually planned to move Flaherty out of Finance back in 2007 as part of a cabinet shuffle that would have seen Jim Prentice moved from Indian and Northern Affairs to Finance, and Flaherty from Finance to Industry. The goal was to beef up the economic clout of cabinet (and to get the underperforming Maxime Bernier out of Industry). But Flaherty refused to move. If he couldn't have Finance, then he'd move to the backbench, he told Harper when he first proposed the move. Then Flaherty walked out of the PM's office, got in his car, and drove to Whitby. To avoid a cabinet crisis, Harper left Flaherty where he was and put Prentice into Industry.[1] (Had Jim Prentice become finance minister, provincial politics in Alberta might be quite different today.)

Jim Flaherty had always hoped to be the first great Conservative finance minister, the right's answer to Paul Martin or Walter Gordon. The quick-tempered, quick-humoured pint-sized pugilist wanted to be known as the finance minister who ended the fiscal imbalance and presided over the broadest and deepest tax cuts of modern times, while forging a national securities regulator to replace the patchwork quilt of provincial commissions.

Lehman Brothers put an end to that. Though Flaherty was disastrously unwilling to admit publicly he was going to have to run up deficits, he was in the room with U.S. Treasury Secretary Hank Paulson and Ben Bernanke, chair of the U.S. Federal Reserve, when the two crafted together the five-point plan to rescue failing American banks in order to prevent a global depression.[2] When he realized he had to take the budget back into deficit, he did it without making that deficit permanent. Though the Supreme Court scotched his proposed national securities regulator, and he went back on his own word by taxing income trusts, in the main Flaherty managed the nation's finances well through a difficult time. "He was a man of principle who believed in fixing banks when they were broken, sound money and balanced budgets," was how Mark Carney put it, after he had left his job as governor of the Bank of Canada to take up the same post at the Bank of England.[3]

In March 2014, with the budget on track to be balanced within a year, with a provincially run national securities regulator approved and gaining traction with the provinces, with the most important tax cuts in place, and with federal finances as a share of GDP lower than they had been in decades, Flaherty stepped down. Harper appointed Natural Resources Minister Joe Oliver to replace him. And then, on April 10, Jim Flaherty collapsed at his condominium with a massive heart attack. By the time paramedics arrived, he was gone. Harper was devastated when he heard the news. Those who have watched him closely note that Harper gets very upset by the unexpected death of someone he knows well. The mask comes off, and he can become quite emotional. This was one of those times. Flaherty's condition wasn't supposed to have been fatal. Harper liked Flaherty personally, and had come to count on him as a steady hand in the government's most important portfolio.

To be sure, Flaherty had an independent streak that grated on Harper. The finance minister had publicly ruminated after the 2013 budget that the government's 2011 election promise of introducing income splitting – which would allow couples with uneven incomes to combine them for tax purposes, resulting in a lower bill – might not be a good idea. Only a small minority of tax filers – essentially, families where the husband worked and the wife stayed home to raise the kids, *Leave It to Beaver* style – would benefit. Flaherty's successor, Joe Oliver, brought a modest version of the program in anyway. But overall, the partnership between the prime minister and his finance minister, the most important relationship in any government, had worked well.

It was a shaken Stephen Harper who formally announced Flaherty's passing. Laureen stood beside him, wiping away tears, as he told reporters what everyone already knew, that "our colleague, my partner and my friend" had passed away.[4] The prime minister offered, and the family accepted, a state funeral. It was the least he could do for his long-serving finance minister and friend.

It seemed as if the bad news would never end. Harper was getting nowhere with either the Keystone XL or Northern Gateway pipeline, thanks to opposition from environmentalists and First Nations, and a dithering American president. The government got into a public shouting match with both the chief electoral officer, Mark Maynard, and the former auditor general, Sheila Fraser, over the Fair Elections Act. (The act limited the investigatory ambit of Elections Canada, though the government eventually withdrew requirements for voter ID.) In March, the Supreme Court threw out Harper's choice of Marc Nadon as a Supreme Court judge, ruling his appointment unconstitutional (we will return to this later), and it seemed impossible to nail down the final text of a landmark free trade agreement with the European Union. Stephen Harper's prime ministership had become one damn thing after another.

And then, on May 2, Shawn Atleo quit.

––––––––––

The failure of the First Nations Control of First Nations Education Act in spring 2014 only warranted a few days' headlines, but in fact it was a tragedy, a road not taken that could have brought fundamental change to the lives of tens of thousands of young Aboriginal Canadians living on reserve. In the coming months, political, civic, and Aboriginal leaders would excoriate Harper for refusing to launch a public inquiry into missing and murdered Aboriginal women. But if they had really wanted change, rather than a scapegoat, these leaders would have gotten behind the act.

Relations between the Conservatives and Aboriginal Canadians had deteriorated steadily since Harper had offered his moving apology for residential schools in June 2008. The reason was simple: the government rejected and obstructed all of the key demands of the First Nations leadership. First Nations leaders rightly claim that their people were dispossessed of their land by European settlers. They seek redress in the form of increased federal transfers, treaties (where they exist) that are generously interpreted and fully honoured, and land claims that are swiftly settled on their terms. This would include the right of veto over the use of Crown land, and a share in the revenues from any resources extracted from those lands. Given the chronic poverty in which so many Aboriginal Canadians live, why have successive federal governments refused to honour these demands?

The answer is that a large portion of the Canadian economy depends on cutting down trees and taking things out of the earth. There are only 330,000 First Nations people living on reserves. Settling claims on their terms would deprive Ottawa of revenue to look after the needs of the other 35.2 million Canadians. There are more than 630 separate First Nations represented on reserves, with a plethora of different languages and cultures, all of these groups aspiring to some version of complete self-government – to some version of sovereignty. Securing the consent of each and every First Nation involved in order to, say, run a pipeline from Alberta to the Pacific, can prove virtually impossible. So governments past and present have stalled, prevaricated, taken half measures, and generally made things worse, while tens of thousands of men, women, and children have languished in poverty. (Though it's important to note as well that First Nations people on reserves in southern, urban areas often enjoy living standards close or equal to those of non–First Nations.)

The Martin government believed that a five-billion-dollar injection of federal funds would break the cycle of poverty, disease, despair, violence, and abuse. But the Harper government cancelled the Kelowna Accord. For Harper, such a solution would mean pouring good money after bad. Instead, he and successive Aboriginal affairs ministers – Jim Prentice, Chuck Strahl, John Duncan, and Bernard Valcourt – sought to improve on-reserve governance. Despite widespread opposition from the chiefs, they extended Charter rights to women living on reserves; they required reserve governments to publicly declare what chiefs and band members were earning. They strengthened private property rights on reserve, at the expense of collective rights. And they targeted education.

The Conservatives believed that unless and until First Nations youth received the same quality of education that other young Canadians received, they would never possess the job skills to participate in the local economy or the freedom to move elsewhere in pursuit of higher education and better jobs. But on-reserve high school graduation rates are a dismal 40 per cent, compared to 90 per cent for the general population. What's more, that figure hadn't improved in a generation, despite a plethora of new programs. Seventy per cent of First Nations children who leave the reserve graduate from high school, so clearly the problem is with the schools on reserves.[5]

The reasons are many, as are the culprits. Respecting the principle of self-government, federal education funding flows to reserves in the form of block grants. Some chiefs use the money wisely and well. Others decide that the money should be spent on improving health care, or delivering potable water. A few simply squander it. In some cases, providing an education system for a remote reserve that is even vaguely equivalent to the nearest public school is simply impossible. And then there is the residual fear of assimilation – that teaching a curriculum steeped in Western history, culture, and values will divorce Aboriginal children from their own history, culture, and values. Why, goes the argument, should First Nations leaders impose the modern equivalent of residential schools on their own children? All of these reasons, separately and in combination, conspire to limit the quality of education on many reserves. Unimpressed with the efforts of the chiefs, federal governments have starved the system of funding. So even those reserves that do want to give their children the best education possible find themselves struggling with a per-child grant that's only a fraction of what children in the public education system receive.

In 2010, Stephen Harper and Shawn Atleo decided to place Aboriginal education at the top of the list of priorities, and to tackle the problem together. Atleo was the young, new national chief of the Assembly of First Nations. The AFN and the federal government had never worked together as partners on a single file before. But they jointly sponsored a task force that recommended a wholesale restructuring of education on reserves. Individual First Nations would pool their education funding to create regional or provincial boards of Aboriginal education, controlled by First Nations leaders, with an emphasis on Aboriginal cultures and languages, but operating at the provincial standard. The boards would set curriculum, allocate capital funding, hire and fire principals and teachers, and maintain standards. Ottawa would fund the boards directly, rather than the individual reserves, and would increase funding so that the boards would have a fighting chance of making the new system work. Those bands that preferred to control education on their reserves could opt out and would be funded directly at the old level.

It took years for the task force to report and for Ottawa to craft Bill C-33, the First Nations Control of First Nations Education Act. It never stood a chance. Some chiefs complained they hadn't been properly consulted; others worried that involving the provinces would dilute the nation-to-nation relationship between the First Nations and the Crown. Others believed that Atleo, who supported the bill, was a weak leader who was being co-opted by the Conservatives. And the education act, whatever its own merit, was the victim of the deteriorating relationship between the Conservatives and the chiefs, a condition that had led to Theresa Spence's Idle No More hunger strike in the winter of 2012–2013.

Besieged, and with the AFN at risk of disintegrating, Atleo resigned as national chief on May 2, 2014. The government suspended passage of the bill. Everything had been for naught. Instead, attention focused on murdered Aboriginal women, and on Stephen Harper's refusal to call a public inquiry. Harper dislikes public inquiries: they are expensive to hold and their recommendations are invariably expensive to implement. And anyway, the Conservatives had their own answer to the crisis: improve the education of young women (and young men, who also are murdered and go missing) so that they can escape environments that put them at risk. But the chiefs were having none of that. And so another generation of young women and men living on reserve are at risk of being lost.

Stephen Harper has never been able to reconcile his contradictory views on First Nations Canadians. On the one hand, he shares with his former mentor and later aide, Tom Flanagan, the belief that reserves, and the indigenous cultures sheltered on them, are anachronisms that have no hope for long-term survival in a globalized, digital world of ever-accelerating change. He seethes with frustration at the chiefs who seek to block economic development of natural resources, and the courts that side with them. And so his government pushed through legislation to force reserve governments to operate more like typical municipal governments and, as much as possible, to hold the reserves accountable under Canadian laws.

But there is another side to him as well. The thought of children suffering bothers him deeply, even emotionally. It helped spur the maternal health initiative overseas and prompted him to offer the apology for residential schools in the House. It lay behind his support for the First Nations education act. But in the end, the contradictions of the government's approach to First Nations, and divisions among the First Nations leadership, undermined Stephen Harper's best efforts to rescue vulnerable First Nations students desperately in need of the only thing that could rescue them from poverty and dependency: a good education.

The loss is incalculable. Actually, that's not true; it's quite calculable. The figure is 25 percentage points. That's the difference between the national high school graduation rate for students on reserve, 40 per cent, and British Columbia's high school graduation rate for students on reserve, 65 per cent. B.C. implemented reforms similar to those in the First Nations Control of First Nations Education Act fifteen years ago. That's what the act could have achieved. That's what has been lost.

———

The nadir of Stephen Harper's prime ministership came not during the Senate expenses scandal, but in spring 2014, when he got himself into a very public dust-up with Beverley McLachlin, chief justice of the Supreme

Court. Not only did he lose the fight; he tarnished his reputation and damaged what should be the sacrosanct separation of powers between executive and judiciary.

Conservatives lamented the advent of the Charter of Rights and Freedoms, fearing that courts would use its provisions to override Parliament and generally act like a third legislature whose commands are not subject to review. And the Supreme Court obliged their worst fears. Over the past thirty years, the Court has moved to limit the rights of police in criminal investigations; struck down the law that made abortion illegal; extended civil rights to gays, lesbians, and other sexual minorities; protected French language rights outside Quebec; and strengthened the right of Aboriginal Canadians to a say in lands they claim as their own and to use those lands for traditional purposes. But the most important change, as Rainer Knopff, a member of the Calgary School, observed, was in the relationship between the courts and Parliament, with judges accruing to themselves new powers they would not have claimed before the Charter came into force.[6]

For Stephen Harper, this was simply another way in which liberal urban elites in Toronto and Ottawa and Montreal imposed their agenda on the rest of the country. It was another way in which those elites rendered their critics not merely wrong, but illegitimate. To criticize the Court was to criticize the Charter, which was to criticize civil liberties, which made you stupid at best and racist or sexist or homophobic at worst.

Liberal governments for the most part accepted the new judicial activism of the courts. After all, the Charter was their invention, and almost every Liberal prime minister has been a lawyer. But Harper had seethed against the smug, stifling certainty of these elites all his adult life. That is why, once he came to power, he set out to radically reform the justice system. And he succeeded. In fact the imposition of a tough new law-and-order agenda marks the Fifth Big Thing that Stephen Harper has accomplished in his decade in power. It might also be the most controversial of the lot.

From the 1960s to the early 1990s, crime rates worsened throughout the developed world. Every year, on average, there were more killings, more assaults, more robberies. The situation was worst in the United States, which struggled with racial tensions and a wide-open gun culture, but it was bad elsewhere, too. Then the picture started to improve. New policing methods might have had something to do with it, but the biggest factor was the end of the baby boom, as women decided they wanted fewer babies. Fewer babies in the 1970s meant fewer young men in the 1990s, which meant less crime, for young men are more likely to commit crimes than men of any other age or women of any age at all. As the birth rate continued to drop, crime continued to drop with it. The homicide rate in Canada today is about where it was in 1960.

Nonetheless, many people worry about crime in their community. Everyone knows someone who has had their bicycle stolen or their home broken into. Everyone sees the graffiti on the community post-office box. Gang members shoot at each other in broad daylight without caring who might get killed in the crossfire. Immigrant Canadians arrive from countries with corrupt courts and police, and bring with them fears for their safety. And conservatives hold to the belief that the justice system should place less emphasis on rehabilitating offenders and more on punishing them.

The Tories pushed part of their law-and-order agenda through minority Parliaments, and then imposed the rest when they achieved a majority government. That agenda is bold. Stephen Harper has transformed the justice system. There are new mandatory minimum sentences for crimes involving guns, drugs, and sexual assaults. Convicts enjoy less credit than in the past for time served before their conviction. It's hard to obtain a pardon and easier for non-citizens to be deported for committing a crime. And the government moved to eliminate any real hope of parole for those found guilty of some forms of first-degree murder. The idea is out there that the courts have neutered this agenda. That idea is false. Since 2005, the number of Canadians in custody has increased by 17.5 per cent, even though overall crime rates have fallen steadily. The overall cost of the federal corrections system has almost doubled, from $1.6 billion in 2006 to just under $3 billion in 2012. Under the Tories, a lot more people are doing the time, even though a lot fewer people are doing the crime.[7]

But the Supreme Court has imposed some limits on Harper's law-and-order ambitions, and may impose more. The Court softened the restrictions on credit for time served and quashed the mandatory minimum sentence law for gun crimes. Another ruling declared that Internet service providers can no longer routinely hand over information about customers to police without a warrant. The Court has also moved to strike down laws that have been on the books for decades, including laws against prostitution and assisted suicide. Harper has repeatedly complained to his inner circle that, under Chief Justice Beverley McLachlin, the Court has become a sociology seminar, with the judges/professors able to turn their theories into laws, and Parliament unable to stop them.

One solution, of course, would be to appoint more conservative judges to the Court. But such judges are nowhere to be found. Harper has appointed seven of the nine judges currently on the Court, without any apparent influence on their decisions. In Canada, the consensus within the legal community on how the justice system, and society in general, should operate is broad, deep, and unshakable. It has left Harper fuming at this ultimate, and most successful, gesture of defiance from the urban elites he despises, and who despise him.

The breaking point came with the Nadon affair. On September 30, 2013, Harper appointed Marc Nadon to the Supreme Court. Nadon, while sitting on the Federal Court of Appeal, had written a dissent arguing that the majority on the court was wrong when it ordered the patriation of Omar Khadr, the Canadian who had been held in legal limbo at Guantanamo for years after killing an American in Afghanistan. The court, Nadon argued, was interfering in the conduct of the federal government's foreign policy, which was outside its jurisdiction.

This was just the sort of judicial deference that Harper wanted to see on the Supreme Court. The problem was that Nadon was semi-retired. Even more important, because he sat on the Federal Court of Appeal, he had no real ties to the Quebec bar, and the vacancy belonged to one of the Supreme Court seats reserved under the Constitution for Quebec. A lawyer affronted by Harper's presumption launched a legal complaint, which the Quebec government soon joined. The Supremes were now tasked with deciding whether Nadon should be allowed to join them.

The government had already produced opinions from former Supreme Court judges Louise Charron and Ian Binnie, along with constitutional scholar Peter Hogg, all declaring that there was no constitutional bar to Nadon's appointment. As a failsafe, Justice Minister Peter MacKay had introduced legislation specifically permitting federal court judges to sit as Quebec judges on the Supreme Court. It too went to the Supreme Court for review. On March 21, 2014, the Court delivered the judicial equivalent of a punch in the nose. Nadon, as a federal court judge, was ineligible to sit on the Supreme Court as a Quebec judge. Furthermore, any legislative attempt to alter the rules for appointment to the Court required a constitutional amendment approved by the legislatures of all ten provinces.

Harper was furious with the ruling. The Court had set itself up as the unofficial opposition to his prime ministership. To make matters even worse, the Court had separately decided that his efforts to reform the Senate were also unconstitutional. As far as Harper was concerned, the Court under McLachlin had resolved to dismantle as much of his government's agenda as it could get away with, and was immune to criticism for doing so. Not only that, he was convinced McLachlin had opposed Nadon's appointment to the Court and had meddled in the selection process in order to frustrate his appointment. Staff talked the prime minister down from launching a full, public assault on the impartiality of the Court, but he still went pretty far.

On May 1, John Ivison of the *National Post* reported, "Rumours about Beverley McLachlin, the Chief Justice, are being shared with journalists, alleging she lobbied against the appointment of Marc Nadon to the court. . . . It is also being suggested she has told people the Harper government has caused more damage to the court as an institution than any government in Canadian history."[8] McLachlin's office immediately released a statement saying she had said and done no such things. The Tories upped the ante, saying in an official statement that McLachlin had made an "inadvisable and inappropriate" attempt to contact Stephen Harper directly to warn about the Nadon appointment, but that Harper had refused to take the call, because "neither the Prime Minister nor the Minister of Justice would ever call a sitting judge on a matter that is or may be before their court."[9]

McLachlin decided the time had come to speak to the issue directly. Yes, she had flagged the potential problem with Nadon's appointment, she said in a statement. "Given the potential impact on the Court, I wished to ensure that the government was aware of the eligibility issue. At no time did I express any opinion as to the merits of the eligibility issue. It is customary for Chief Justices to be consulted during the appointment process and there is nothing inappropriate in raising a potential issue affecting a future appointment."[10] The legal community was in an uproar. Never, ever had a prime minister openly criticized a chief justice, forcing her to publicly defend her good name. More than 650 lawyers, including 11 former presidents of the Canadian Bar Association and the Council of Canadian Law Deans, along with anyone who could convince a newspaper to offer space, wrote in protest of this flagrant abuse of the division of powers.

Of course Harper didn't apologize. For him, the outrage over his criticism of McLachlin was on par with the outrage over the long-form census: the white wine set was railing against someone who refused to bend to their will. Eventually, the whole thing died down. But the prime minister had set a dangerous precedent, undermining the separation of executive and judiciary powers on which the whole democratic system of government is based. Looking back, with passions cooled, Harper was right to equate the furor over his attack on the chief justice with the furor over his decision to kill the census. They rank as his two most discreditable acts as prime minister.

———————

In June 2014, with the Supreme Court furore finally fading, Ray Novak went to visit the boss in Harrington Lake. The chief of staff had a tough message. It was time for Harper to decide whether to stay on or step down. If Harper still had the will to win, then he should make it clear he intended to lead. If he didn't want to face the trial ahead, now was the time to signal to the party that it was time to choose a new leader. When Harper is presented with unwelcome news that requires a difficult decision, he typically leans back, purses his lips, stares steadily at the messenger, then nods, which means "Go away." Then he thinks for as long as he needs to think, before he decides.

Things could have looked worse. First, and perhaps foremost, it was clear that the base had stayed faithful. The Senate expenses scandal offered the ultimate test of loyalty among conservatives toward the Conservatives. Identifying and holding a political base is vital to any political party's long-term survival. The NDP went into crisis in the 1990s, when it lost its traditional base of support from unionized workers and urban activists. The Liberal Party went into crisis the following decade, when it lost its base of federalist Quebeckers, urban Ontarians, and Catholics and immigrants generally. Since its founding, the Conservative Party had counted on the support of Westerners and rural and suburban voters in Ontario. They represented about 30 per cent of the population, and up until the Senate scandal, they had stayed with the party come what may. But that scandal was a pretty drastic "what may." It undermined the core Conservative message of honest and frugal government. Would the base abandon Stephen Harper? No, the answer came back. Though a few polls showed support for the Tories slipping below 30 per cent, by spring the general consensus was that the base had stayed with the party, which meant the prime minister was still in the game.

Even the most seasoned political operative, or journalist, can be blinded by a scandal. When the drama is at its peak, it becomes all-consuming, like a fire engulfing a warehouse. But unlike that warehouse, once a scandal subsides, the political structure may still be intact. To torture the metaphor, unless a scandal is constantly fed, it burns itself out, or at least becomes a bank of smouldering embers, waiting for fresh fuel.

What saved the Conservatives from destruction over the Senate scandal was time. Once Duffy, Wallin, and Brazeau had been expelled from the Senate, they lost their public forum. Justin Trudeau kept the story alive by expelling all Liberal senators from caucus – a bold and politically dexterous move. It meant the party would be immunized from any revelations that abuse of living and travel allowances was widespread. After all, the auditor general was now looking at everyone's books.

But as winter 2013 reluctantly gave way to spring 2014 in Ottawa, no one could find any fresh revelations of senatorial shenanigans, or leaked word of widespread abuse of taxpayers' money. Whatever the former Tory and Liberal senators may or may not have been guilty of, ethically or criminally, most other senators appeared to have kept within the lines when filing expenses.

Then came word in April 2014 that the RCMP would not lay charges against Nigel Wright, which was no surprise. Wright clearly had not intended to bribe Duffy – he had just wanted to help him, and the party, out. There had been no back-channel payments to Wright in compensation. If Wright were charged, would the lawyers for the party and for Duffy, who had signed off on the agreement, be charged as well? Duffy was, however, charged on July 17 with bribery, fraud, and twenty-nine other counts. The scandal-monger mill cranked back into action, with the pundits predicting that Harper would step down rather than face the damning revelations certain to come out at trial. But by then, Harper had already made up his mind to stay.

Novak was right to force the issue. It takes tremendous will to lead a party into an election. The path ahead for Harper would be difficult, and he might not like the destination. The Liberals were still well ahead in the polls, Trudeau was resonating with the public, and there would be the Duffy trial. Whether Harper gave Novak an answer only Harper and Novak know. For everyone else who was watching, the answer was clear when the PM returned from his summer holiday. He was going to fight. Indeed, by early autumn the people around the prime minister had begun to notice a bit of a spring in his shuffle. Almost imperceptibly, bit by bit, things were once again starting to go his way, partly thanks to fate and partly because he was able and willing to give fate a good shove, by cementing the Sixth Big Thing that Stephen Harper achieved in his first three terms: trade agreements.

Harper came to power determined to restore both trading and diplomatic relations with the United States. Latent Liberal anti-Americanism lay behind the increasingly clogged border, he was convinced. With good will and hard work, a Conservative government could restore the world's most successful bilateral relationship.

But Canada had nothing to do with the thickening border, with passport requirements, with the Recovery Act's Buy American provisions, with tighter security and longer waits. The trauma of September 11 had left the Americans angry and afraid. The trauma of the 2009 financial crisis only left them more angry and afraid. By then, Stephen Harper's foreign policy education was complete, and it convinced him he had placed far too many eggs in one trade basket. "The markets in the United States and in Europe that have been our more traditional market will probably experience slower growth for some time to come," he told reporters in Seoul, after back-to-back trips that had taken him to Singapore, India, China, and Korea. "So the greater opportunity is obviously in the Asia-Pacific region," where markets were new and expanding, and to which millions of immigrant Canadians still had ties, giving Canada a natural competitive advantage over other Western nations.[11]

He was learning on the job. In the early years, Harper was uncertain about trade, as he struggled to preserve a weak minority government. Textile interests, agricultural interests, shipbuilding interests, auto-sector interests – it didn't take much to get the Conservatives to walk away from a trading table. A tentative push to increase trade ties with Latin America was foiled by Brazil's determination to create and dominate its own trade sphere. But gradually, as the Conservatives became more confident and their Parliamentary hand strengthened, they also became better trade negotiators. Even though Brazil rebuffed Canada's efforts to be part of a North and South America free trade zone, the Harper government was able to approve trade agreements with a clutch of small Latin American countries, and had launched Canada into talks with the European Union. Negotiations with India, Thailand, Japan, and South Korea would follow.

They didn't all bear fruit: internal paralysis in Delhi made it difficult to get anywhere with the Indians, for example. But the European talks went better, in part because Harper needed a big trade win, and in part because the Europeans needed one even more, to counter the impression that the zone had become sclerotic and unable to cope with economic challenges. By October 2014, an agreement was in place, which was already being talked about as the template for a European–American free trade agreement. And it took little imagination to realize that the American and Canadian agreements with Europe might one day be harmonized, creating a new and powerful Atlantic trading area.

And in December, after far too many years of talks, Canada and South Korea announced that they had also negotiated a trade agreement, the first Canada had signed with an Asian nation. The much-talked-about reorientation of Canadian trade from north–south to east–west (with Europe in one direction and Asia and the Pacific in the other) was finally starting to emerge. And signs increasingly pointed to an eventual conclusion to the Trans-Pacific

Partnership talks. Final ratification of that agreement was still uncertain; even under the best of circumstances it could take years, but the potential was obvious: if you reconciled a Trans-Pacific Partnership agreement with a North American–European Union agreement, you would create a vast free trade zone stretching from Tallinn in Estonia to Perth in Australia. The BRICs – Brazil, Russia, India, and China – would inevitably join, along with any other state that wanted to belong to the future rather than the past. Globalization would be complete, and Canada would be able to claim no small share of the credit for helping it happen.

And Stephen Harper would be able to say he was present at the creation.

———————

The Harper government had long been suspicious of the rebel alliance that sought to topple Syrian president Bashar al-Assad. There were too many radical elements within it for Foreign Affairs Minister John Baird's taste. While the United States and Europe took halting steps to aid the insurgents, Canada limited itself to offering humanitarian aid to refugees displaced by the civil war. Canadian suspicions were borne out when an ultra-radical Islamist faction emerged that called itself the Islamic State of Iraq and the Levant (ISIL) or the Islamic State of Iraq and Syria (ISIS), and, after June 2014, simply the Islamic State, having now declared itself a caliphate. Soon, these new militants were sweeping through Iraq in a murderous rampage that Western nations agreed had to be checked. Canada contributed special forces to train Kurdish fighters in the north and a squadron of CF-18s to the air campaign against the Islamic State. Both the NDP and the Liberals opposed the mission, on the grounds that Canada had become embroiled in enough Middle Eastern quagmires since the Arab Spring first swept through the region, toppling and destabilizing regimes. But Justin Trudeau made his first serious mistake as leader when he derided the mission, asking, "Why aren't we talking more about the kind of humanitarian aid that Canada can and must be engaged in, rather than, you know, trying to whip out our CF-18s and show them how big they are?"[12] Such flippancy put him at odds with a public growing increasingly concerned about rising extreme Islamist violence.

Things got better for Harper on the foreign affairs file. His "I guess I'll shake your hand . . ." jibe at Vladimir Putin earned favourable press coverage throughout the Western world. And in December, Barack Obama revealed that Ottawa had hosted talks between his government and the Cuban regime, thanking Canada for its role in negotiations that led to the United States restoring diplomatic relations with the Communist regime. Although Canada took no part in the talks, simply providing a discreet venue where the two sides could meet, the act of playing host at least revealed that the Harper government and the Obama administration were still talking to each other. "It's a good development and probably an overdue development," Harper said in a year-end interview with the CBC. ". . . Change is coming to Cuba. . . . I think that's an economy and a society just overdue for entry into the 21st century."[13] He was displaying a nuanced appreciation of *realpolitik* that had eluded him in his earlier, more ideological days as prime minister.

And there was other good news that fall – splendid news, actually, to Harper's mind. As we know, he had long been obsessed by the mystery surrounding the Franklin expedition. Various groups had spent years in a fruitless search for the ships. In 2012, Harper personally launched a new research vessel, complete with state-of-the-art equipment, to continue the search. "The modern age abhors a mystery; mysteries must be solved," he declared.[14] The hunt appealed to his love of both history and the Arctic. On September 1, a helicopter pilot walking along the shore of an island near the search site found what looked like a tuning fork. The survey ship *Investigator* began trolling the bottom, where cutting-edge sonar equipment soon detected the hull of a ship. It was *Erebus*. The Franklin mystery was solved, and the Harper government would get some well-earned credit for helping to solve it. It didn't hurt, either, that Canada was asserting its presence in, and control over, the disputed waters of the High Arctic.

Each Wednesday morning, the three political parties represented in the House of Commons meet in caucus: the government in the Parliamentary Reading Room, located on the west side of the corridor known as the Hall of Honour in Centre Block, and the opposition in the Railway Committee Room (as it is informally called) across the hall. On the morning of October 22, 2014, Harper was addressing caucus when MPs heard what one of them described as the sound of a tray dropping on the stone floor outside. Harper continued talking. Then came a volley of gunfire – dozens of shots. Parliament was under attack.

Harper's first thought was that a group of armed men had shot their way into Centre Block. If so, the logical conclusion was that this was an assassination attempt, and he was the target. "You're in the caucus room there, all you hear is a whole lot of shooting coming towards you," he recalled later. "And you don't know whether that's a fire fight or whether that's just a bunch of guys with automatic weapons wiping everybody out in their path."[15] He also knew that his RCMP protective detail was outside the Parliament buildings, and his House of Commons security team was outside the room. There was gunfire in the hallway and the prime minister was unprotected. Harper had received training from his protective detail on what to do in certain situations, including a situation in which the protective detail is absent. The first priority is to get away from the danger. If that's not possible, then search for a place to hide. If that's not possible, then fight back with whatever you have.

In accordance with that training, Harper headed for the back entrance of the room to get away. But his executive assistant, Myles Atwood, blocked him. You have no idea what is going on out there, he told the PM. Atwood pushed Harper into a closet and closed the door, which was what the situation and their training called for. This led later to accusations of cowardice. "My father raised us to step towards trouble rather than step away from it," Justin Trudeau observed, when asked what he would have done in such a situation, "but, again, I won't speculate on that."[16] But in fact, stepping toward the danger would have been incredibly irresponsible for Harper. He was the head of government, at a moment of national crisis. His single greatest priority was to keep himself safe and to get to a place where he could resume governing. At that moment of controlled panic, as MPs barricaded the door and grabbed flagpoles to use as spears, the closet was the safest place for Harper to be. Minutes later, the security detail whisked him out the back door and his motorcade sped to 24 Sussex Drive, where

Harper fumed at the lack of available information and the fact that his public safety, defence, and justice ministers were still locked down in the caucus room.

The attack, as we all know, was the work of a single gunman, Michael Zehaf-Bibeau, who had already killed Corporal Nathan Cirillo at the National War Memorial and wounded a Commons security guard before being brought down in a hail of bullets, the fatal shot coming from Sergeant-at-Arms Kevin Vickers. That attack, along with the killing two days before of Warrant Officer Patrice Vincent by Martin Couture-Rouleau, who told a 911 operator he did it in the name of Allah,[17] brought home the reality to all Canadians that this country is involved in the fight against Islamist terrorism, and that an attack on the home front could happen anywhere, any time.

For once, everyone mourned together. The day after the shootings, the Commons erupted in ovation as Vickers entered the Chamber carrying the ceremonial mace. Harper crossed the floor and embraced both Mulcair and Trudeau. It was an extraordinary gesture from a man of such partisan convictions – not to mention from someone so disinclined to hug.

Was it the shooting on the Hill that caused the Conservatives' numbers to improve as 2014 gave way to 2015? Was it the fact that Stephen Harper had committed forces to the fight against the Islamic State, which Thomas Mulcair and Justin Trudeau opposed? Did the killings of the journalists at *Charlie Hebdo* in Paris in January contribute to the sense of a crisis, to the growing realization that "the international jihadist movement has declared war" on Canada and its allies, as Harper put it?[18] Was it simply that the world's longest political honeymoon was finally coming to an end for Trudeau? The Conservatives' uptick in the polls could have been the result of any and all of those things. It is probably true that the Tories' situation was never as bleak as it appeared in the depths of the Senate expenses scandal. Nor was a Conservative victory assured simply because the governing party had drawn more or less even with the Liberals in the spring of 2015.

All anyone could say for sure was that, a year after *Götterdämmerung*, Stephen Harper was back in the fight.

Afterword

They have bought a piece of land at Bragg Creek, in the foothills of the Rocky Mountains, about half an hour west of Calgary. Laureen dreams of something airy, light-filled, a place where they can live together, where she can walk in the hills, where they can entertain their children's children, a place where two empty nesters can enjoy their semi-retirement.

Ben is at Queen's University studying commerce. He is so much like his mother: tall, good looking, outgoing, athletic, and of course smart. He's good in school and passionate about volleyball. He loves to play the guitar, and jams with his father. (Harper, the ultimate music geek, once proudly confided to the owner of an Ottawa music store, "You know, I've been to Abbey Road.")[1] Rachel will finish high school soon. She is so much like her father: quiet, intense, studious, and smart as all get-out. Neither of them is showing any interest in following in their father's footsteps. According to the Harpers' friends, they're great kids, who have survived being raised in the fishbowl of 24 Sussex Drive with remarkably few scars. They can thank their parents for that. (They could probably also have a good talk with Justin Trudeau about what it's like.)

And what will Stephen Harper do, once he is no longer prime minister and he and Laureen are living in their foothills retreat? Teach, maybe. Maybe write his memoirs. (He has that journal to draw from.) His friends talk, half-jokingly, half-wistfully, of what a fine commissioner of the National Hockey League he'd make. Whatever it is, he won't be part of a team. He doesn't do team. He has to be in charge. In any case, the question is not what he'll do after politics, but when "after politics" will begin.

In the summer of 2015, as he prepared to enter his fifth campaign as national party leader, Harper knew the odds were against him. Only Laurier and Macdonald had succeeded in winning four consecutive terms. He knew the weight of the baggage he dragged along after ten years in government. He knew that Thomas Mulcair was a tough and seasoned political scrapper who would never cede an inch of turf without leaving blood on the ground. And he knew that Justin Trudeau was a mortal foe, whose sunny ways and promise of a kinder, more peaceful, more environmentally responsible government resonated after a decade of Harperism.

Still, Harper thought he would win. He had a solid record, an experienced team. The Conservatives had way more money in the bank than the other parties, and they had CIMS. Trudeau was offside on national security – opposing the widely supported mission in Iraq and then Syria while supporting the much more dubious anti-terrorism bill – and fuzzy on economic issues. The base had stayed loyal, and all that was needed was to persuade enough of the Persuadables. On all the key issues, internal research suggested that suburban Ontario voters' values aligned with Conservative values, which was why the Liberal and NDP platforms looked so remarkably similar to the Conservatives'. Immigrant voters in the 905 hadn't abandoned him – though his opposition to the niqab and complaints about an anti-women bias in Muslim culture flirted dangerously with nativism. Winning conditions were within reach if he campaigned well and a couple of the breaks came his way. He thought he could land a solid minority government, maybe even a slim majority. Either way, he wasn't planning on staying around much longer, those close to him believe. Obviously, if he lost he'd be gone. If he formed a minority government, he'd govern for a year, and then hand off to a new leader and prime minister. If he won a majority, he'd govern for two years or so and then signal his intention to depart, so the next leader would have time to establish a governing agenda.

Truth be told, there wasn't much left to do. He had created a large and stable conservative coalition with room to grow. The West and suburban

Ontario: they were a beautiful friendship. It had required enormous political skill to make them friends, and a weak leader could drive them apart. But the conservative coalition made sense; he had proven it time and time and time again. Ralph Klein used to say that the secret to his political success was finding out where the parade was going and then getting in front of it.[2] And in a sense, that's what Stephen Harper had done. The West had been growing in power and population and influence for years, and it tended to divide politically between Conservatives and the NDP, with the Conservatives winning most of the seats most of the time. And the millions of immigrants who filled the burgeoning suburbs and exurbs outside Toronto came from societies with more conservative economic and social values than native-born Canadians were used to. They were making Canada more conservative. All Harper had done was nurture and lead this emerging conservative coalition – he had gotten to the head of their parade.

But once he led it, he led it. A more conservative Canada made Stephen Harper, and Stephen Harper made Canada more conservative. He cut taxes by the score, and neither the Liberals nor the NDP plan to raise them again, except here and there at the margins. He reshaped federal–provincial relations, and no future leader will ever try to impose a top-down, Toronto-inspired national vision on the provinces ever again. No one is going to dismantle his law-and-order agenda. ("If elected, I promise to make it easier for sex offenders to get out of prison!") No one is going to dismantle the Tories' landmark immigration reforms. ("If elected, I promise to welcome boatloads of refugee claimants and open Canada's doors to elderly grandparents!") The east–west trade ties he forged will only strengthen in the years ahead. And the leader who vows to withdraw Canada from foreign commitments lest they increase the risk of reprisals at home will be labelled a coward and shown the door.

There were still a few things left to do, such as reducing internal barriers to the economic union. Jim Flaherty had established a voluntary and provincially run national securities regulator. Maybe that could become a template in other fields of regulation. Maybe Ottawa could nudge the provinces into accepting a national certificate for teaching, say, or a single means of accrediting lawyers (in the common-law provinces at least). Maybe it could become as easy for Ontario to trade with B.C. as it will be for Ontario to trade with France under the terms of the new European Union trade agreement. But that would require a lot of negotiating, maybe even a first ministers' conference, and he hated those.

He failed at some things. He never really cared much about global warming, and Canada lags behind others in responding to that threat. He did care about improving the education of children on reserve, but he didn't try hard enough, or compromise enough, to get his First Nations education act through. Some paragraphs of his foreign policy remain incoherent: how did he manage to get so offside with the American president? These challenges are for the next prime minister, and sooner or later that prime minister will belong to another party.

Remarkably, that prime minister might be NDP. But the Liberals are also contenders. Harper had so wanted to destroy the Liberal Party, to reshape Canadian politics along American or British or Australian lines, with a dominant party of the centre right – his – and a dominant party of the centre left – the NDP, or the Liberal New Democrats, or whatever emerged; he really didn't care. He might have pulled it off, had Patrick Brazeau landed a lucky knockout punch against Trudeau in the first round. But though the NDP was resurgent, the Liberals were still in the game. Oh well. Some day, maybe. At least he got to watch the Annex and the Glebe and Outremont and the Queen's faculty club and everyone at the *Toronto Star* and the CBC rage against him for ten long years in absolute futility. He enjoyed that. That was fun.

He wasn't any better liked by the general public a decade after being in power than he was after the first day. That didn't bother him. He was never in it to be loved, and a good thing, too. Some people hated him. He is such a polarizing figure that his opponents don't just attack his policies, they attack him. They don't believe he is wrong; they believe he is evil. More books have been written about Stephen Harper by far than about any other prime minister still in office. Almost all of them are highly critical. Several of them claim he is a tyrant and that Canada is no longer a democracy.

This is rot. Canada remains one of the freest and most blessed places on earth. And there is nothing in Stephen Harper's life story, from growing up in Leaside to studying at the University of Calgary to his years in Parliament, his years at the National Citizens Coalition, his years as Alliance and then

Conservative leader and prime minister, to suggest he is disillusioned with democracy. He dislikes the Charter, that's for sure, and he's a political street fighter, that's for sure too. And for sure he likes to be completely in control of everything all the time, and he's suspicious of strangers, and everyone's a stranger. And yes, on his watch, ancient institutions that increasingly ill fit the times – the parliamentary committee, the Senate, the newspaper – continued their long, sad decline. But then new forums emerged: Facebook. Twitter. Instagram. Crowdsourcing. Occupy. Idle No More.

After ten years of the Conservatives allegedly attempting to destroy democracy, democracy seems pretty robust. But we have never had a politician who divides people the way Harper has divided us. Partly it's the times; partly it's the man.

———————————

Though politicians can be weak and vain and greedy, most of them seek office hoping to leave things in better shape than they found them. Stephen Harper can be weak and vain and greedy, but I believe that he sought office hoping to leave things in better shape than he found them and that he has, in the main, succeeded. I believe he has governed well. But he has also, at times, governed badly: undermining the census; getting offside with the Americans; attacking the judiciary; eroding the powers of Parliament. Someone's going to have to fix that.

Above all, he governed as a conservative, as best he could. He made government mean less in your life. That's all he really wanted to do.

As for the man: well, he is who he is. Perhaps now we know better why.

Sources

Note: In cases where page numbers are not provided, source material was retrieved from the Internet. No URL has been provided, because such addresses can change and are in any case of little use to those who read the print edition of the book. Readers seeking to consult an online source can do so by copying material from the text or from the citation into a search engine. In rare instances, a URL has been provided where employing the above method might prove insufficient.

BOOK ONE: RISE

ONE: Suburbs

1. http://leaside100.ca. This is a history of Leaside prepared by a committee charged with commemorating the hundredth anniversary of the community's incorporation in 1913. The following paragraphs draw from this history.
2. Taken from: William Johnson, *Stephen Harper and the Future of Canada* (Toronto: Douglas Gibson, 2005). See also: Ernest Clarke, *The Siege of Fort Cumberland, 1776: An Episode in the American Revolution* (Montreal: McGill-Queen's University Press, 1999).
3. Lawrence Martin, "A Family Tragedy That Stephen Harper Has Not Forgotten," *Globe and Mail*, 8 July 2009.
4. Mark Kennedy, *Rebel to Realist: How Politics Changed Stephen Harper and How He Is Changing Canada* (Toronto: Postmedia), Ch. 1.
5. Johnson, *Stephen Harper*, 5.
6. Interview with Robert Harper.
7. The two monographs were: Francis Dunbar and Joseph Harper, *Old Colours Never Die: A Record on Colours and Military Flags in Canada* (Toronto:

F.J. Dunbar and Associates, 1992) and Joseph Harper, *A Source of Pride: Regiment Badges and Titles in the Canadian Expeditionary Force, 1914–1919* (Ottawa: Service Publications, 1999).

8. Interview with Gordon Shaw.

9. John Michailidis, "Glimpses of East York," *East Yorker*, January 2013.

10. Gordon Shaw interview.

11. Michael Ignatieff, "I Wish Someone Had Told Me This before I Became a Politician: A Letter to a Young Liberal," *New Republic*, 22 November 2014.

12. Linda Diebel, "Stephen Harper: Double-Edged Sword," *Toronto Star*, 12 October 2008, ID01.

13. Robert Harper interview.

14. Ibid.

15. Kennedy, *Rebel to Realist*, Ch. 1.

16. Andrew Matte, "Stephen Harper Talks about His Days as a Leasider," *Town Crier*, 15 July 2003.

17. Johnson, *Stephen Harper*, 6.

18. Robert Harper interview.

19. Paul Watson, *Where War Lives: A Journey into the Heart of War* (Toronto: McClelland & Stewart, 2007), 72.

20. Andrew Duffy, "Stephen Harper: A Political Life in Three Movements," *Ottawa Citizen*, 28 January 2006, B2.

21. Ibid.

22. Michelle Mandel, "No Dirt Sticks to Steve," *Toronto Sun*, 20 September 2008.

23. Robert Harper interview.

24. Gordon Shaw interview.

TWO: Lost

1. Interview with George Koch.

2. Robert Harper interview.

3. George Koch interview.

4. David Staples, "Memories of a Younger – and Liberal – PM," *Edmonton Journal*, 14 December 2011, A5.

5. Ibid.

6. Ibid.

7. Howard Palmer and Tamara Jeppson Palmer, *Peoples of Alberta: Portraits of Cultural Diversity* (Regina: Western Producer Prairie Books, 1985).

8. Stephen Harper, "On Second Thought," *National Post*, 5 October 2000, A18.

9. Marci McDonald, "The Man Behind Stephen Harper," *The Walrus*, October 2004.

10. Anthony Hall, "Flanagan's Last Stand?" *Veterans Today*, 23 March 2013.

11. McDonald, "The Man Behind Stephen Harper."

12. John Ibbitson, "Educating Stephen," *Globe and Mail*, 26 June 2004, F4.

13. McDonald, "The Man Behind Stephen Harper."

14. Ibid.

15. Interview with Cynthia Williams.

THREE: Epiphany

1. Interview with Jim Hawkes.

2. Johnson, *Stephen Harper*, 26.

3. Jim Hawkes interview.

4. Darrell Bricker and John Ibbitson, *The Big Shift: The Seismic Change in Canadian Politics, Business and Culture and What It Means for Our Future* (Toronto: HarperCollins, 2013).

5. Robert Harper interview.

6. Cynthia Williams interview.

7. Interview with John Weissenberger.

8. Peter Brimelow, *The Patriot Game: National Dreams and Political Realities* (Toronto: Key Porter, 1986).

9. Brimelow, *Patriot Game*, 3.

10. Mia Rabson, "Brian Really Was Lyin': Memos Prove Mulroney Was Totally Involved in CF-18 Debacle," *Winnipeg Free Press*, 14 August 2010.

11. Preston Manning, *Think Big: My Adventures in Life and Democracy* (Toronto: McClelland & Stewart), 23.

12. Ibid., 26.

13. Ibid., 27.

14. Stephen Joseph Harper, *The Political Business Cycle and Fiscal Policy in Canada* (Calgary: University of Calgary, 1991).

15. Interview with Robert Mansell.

16. Lorne Gunther, "Preston Manning," *National Post*, 10 November 2005.

17. Preston Manning, *Choosing a Political Vehicle to Represent the West: A Presentation to the Western Assembly on Canada's Political and Economic Future* (Calgary: University of Calgary Archives, 1987).

18. Tom Flanagan, *Waiting for the Wave: The Reform Party and the Conservative Movement* (Montreal/Kingston: McGill-Queen's University Press), Ch. 3.

19. Stephen Harper and John Weissenberger, "A Taxpayers Reform Agenda," 1987.

FOUR: Refooorrrm!

1. Johnson, *Stephen Harper*, 74.
2. *Constitution of Reform Party of Canada* (Calgary: University of Calgary Archives, 1987). http://contentdm.ucalgary.ca/cdm4/document.php? CISOROOT=/reform&CISOPTR=237&REC=7
3. Stephen Harper, *Achieving Economic Justice in Confederation* (Reform Association of Canada, 1987).
4. Johnson, *Stephen Harper*, 85.
5. Preston Manning, *The New Canada* (Toronto: Macmillan Canada, 1992), 149.
6. John Weissenberger interview.
7. Johnson, *Stephen Harper*, 88.
8. Ibid.
9. *Platform and Statement of Principles of the Reform Party of Canada* (Calgary: Reform Party, 1988), 23.
10. Interview with Preston Manning.
11. John Duffy, *Fights of Our Lives: Elections, Leadership and the Making of Canada* (Toronto: HarperCollins, 2002), 322.
12. Margaret Thatcher, *The Downing Street Years* (New York: HarperCollins, 1993), 321.
13. Duffy, *Fights of Our Lives*, 352.
14. "Mordecai Richler and Rick Salutin on Free Trade," *The Journal*, first broadcast November 19, 1987. *CBC Digital Archives*, www.cbc.ca/archives /categories/economy-business/trade-agreements/canada-us-free-trade-agreement/how-much-should-one-drink-for-ones-country.html.
15. Jim Hawkes interview.
16. Johnson, *Stephen Harper*, 94.
17. Cynthia Williams interview.
18. Johnson, *Stephen Harper*, 98.
19. *Platform*, 1988.

FIVE: Stephen

1. Deborah Grey, *Never Retreat, Never Explain, Never Apologize: My Life, My Politics* (Toronto: Key Porter, 2004), 90.
2. Manning, *Think Big*, 36.
3. Flanagan, *Waiting for the Wave*, Ch. 3.

4. Interview with Deborah Grey.

5. Johnson, *Stephen Harper*, 132.

6. Ibid.

7. Ibid., 133.

8. Deborah Grey interview.

9. Pierre Trudeau, "P.E. Trudeau: 'Say Goodbye to the Dream' of One Canada," *Toronto Star*, 27 May 1987.

10. Canada, *House of Commons Debates*, 3 April 1989.

11. George Koch interview.

12. Stephen Harper, *Memorandum to Preston Manning*, 10 March 1989.

13. Preston Manning, *Leadership for Changing Times. An Address to the October 27–29 Assembly of the Reform Party of Canada* (Calgary: University of Calgary Archives).

14. Bob Plamondon, *Full Circle: Death and Resurrection in Canadian Conservative Politics* (Toronto: Key Porter, 2006), 440.

15. George Koch interview.

16. Preston Manning interview.

17. Leo Ryan, "Canadians Expected to Vote Down Constitutional Reform Proposal," *JOC.com*, 22 October 1992.

18. Preston Manning interview.

19. Manning, *Think Big*, 74.

20. Tom Flanagan interview.

21. Johnson, *Stephen Harper*, 163.

22. Ibid.

23. Cynthia Williams interview.

24. Anne Kingston, "Wife of the Party," *Maclean's*, 13 August 2007.

25. Gordon Shaw interview.

26. Kingston, "Wife of the Party."

27. Ibid.

28. Warren Kinsella, *The War Room* (Toronto: Dundurn, 2007), 176.

29. Jim Hawkes interview.

30. Johnson, *Stephen Harper*, 198.

SIX: Temper

1. Tom Flanagan, *Harper's Team: Behind the Scenes in the Conservative Rise to Power, Second Edition* (Montreal and Kingston: McGill-Queen's University Press, 2009), 15.

2. Tom Flanagan interview.

3. Confidential source.

4. Tom Flanagan interview.

5. Jason Fekete, "Stephen Harper Prone to Fits of Rage and Growing Increasingly Isolated, Former Aide Bruce Carson Says," *National Post*, 28 May 2014.

6. Tom Flanagan interview.

7. Tom Flanagan, *Persona Non Grata: The Death of Free Speech in the Internet Age* (Toronto: Signal, 2014), 29.

8. Chris Selley, "L'affaire Flanagan, Revisited," *National Post*, 28 March 2014.

9. Chris Purdy, "University of Calgary Announces Tom Flanagan's Retirement after Condemned Child Pornography Remarks," *National Post*, 28 February 2013.

10. Preston Manning interview.

11. Tom Flanagan interview.

12. Gordon Shaw interview.

13. George Koch interview.

14. Ibid.

15. John Weissenberger interview.

16. Tom Flanagan interview.

17. Flanagan, *Waiting for the Wave*, 177.

18. Ibid.

19. Johnson, *Stephen Harper*, 203.

20. Canada, *House of Commons Debates*, 19 October 1994.

21. Canada, *House of Commons Debates*, 30 October 1996.

22. Manning, *Think Big*, 74.

23. Stephen Harper, "Where Does the Reform Party Go from Here?" *Globe and Mail*, 21 March 1995, A23.

24. Johnson, *Stephen Harper*, 221.

25. Preston Manning interview.

26. Randall Palmer and Louise Egan, "Insight: Lessons for U.S. from Canada's 'Basket Case' Moment," *Reuters*, 21 November 2011.

SEVEN: Exile

1. Flanagan, *Harper's Team*, 17.

2. Taken from a speech Harper gave in 1998 announcing he would not be a candidate for the Progressive Conservative leadership. The text as quoted

can be found at this link: http://members2.boardhost.com/CanConCluTruPat/ msg/958.html

3. Interview with Gerry Nicholls.

4. Susan Delacourt, *Shopping for Votes: How Politicians Choose Us and We Choose Them* (Toronto: Douglas & McIntyre, 2013), 160.

5. Ibid., 207.

6. Gerry Nicholls interview.

7. Interview with Mark Kihn.

8. George Koch interview.

9. Johnson, *Stephen Harper*, 259.

10. Interview with Don Newman.

11. Stephen Harper and Tom Flanagan, "Our Benign Dictatorship," *Next City*, Winter 1996/97.

12. Ibid.

13. Stephen Harper, "Canada's Not a Bilingual Country," *Calgary Sun*, 15 July 2001.

14. Stephen Harper, *Speech to the Council for National Policy*, June 1997.

15. Bruce Carson, *14 Days: Making the Conservative Movement in Canada* (Montreal/Kingston: McGill-Queen's University Press, 2014), 26.

16. Gerry Nicholls, *Loyal to the Core: Stephen Harper, Me and the NCC* (Freedom Press Canada, 2009).

17. John Ibbitson, "Alliance Hopefuls Split on Abortion in Final Debate," *Globe and Mail*, 14 June 2000, A4.

18. Taken from a *Canadian Encyclopedia* reprint of a *Maclean's* magazine profile of Stockwell Day published 12 April 1999.

19. Canada, *House of Commons Debates*, 25 September 2000. Intervening exchanges have been edited out.

20. Brian Laghi, "Second Day, Second Gaffe," *Globe and Mail*, 24 October 2000.

21. Chantal Hébert, *French Kiss: Stephen Harper's Blind Date with Quebec* (Toronto: Vintage, 2007), 168.

22. Les Whittington, "Chrétien Fighting 'Dark Forces,'" *Toronto Star*, 29 October 2000.

23. "Liberal Immigration Minister Launches Attack at Alliance Supporters," Canadian Press, 15 November 2000.

24. Ibid.

25. Brian Laghi, "Chrétien and Day Get Nasty," *Globe and Mail*, 11 November 2000, A1.

26. Gerry Nicholls interview.

27. Stephen Harper, "Separation, Alberta-Style: It Is Time to Seek a New Relationship with Canada," *National Post*, 8 December 2000, A18.

28. Stephen Harper, Tom Flanagan, Ted Morton, Rainer Knopff, Andrew Crooks, and Ken Boessenkool, "An Open Letter to Ralph Klein," *National Post*, 26 January 2001, A14.

29. George Koch interview.

EIGHT: Faith

1. Gerry Nicholls interview.

2. Lloyd Mackey, *The Pilgrimage of Stephen Harper* (Toronto: ECW Press, 2005).

3. Cynthia Williams interview.

4. John Weissenberger interview.

5. Lloyd Mackey, "Latest Evangelinks in the CA World," *Canadian Christianity*, 2001.

6. Preston Manning interview.

7. Marci McDonald, *The Armageddon Factor: The Rise of Christian Nationalism in Canada* (Toronto: Random House Canada, 2010), 12.

8. Scott Anderson, "Stockwell Day Ruined My Life," *Now*, 16–23 November 2000.

9. Grey, *Never Retreat*, 192.

10. Manning, *Think Big*, 370.

11. Jeffrey Simpson, "Message to Stephen Harper: Don't Do It!" *Globe and Mail*, 20 July 2001.

12. Robert Harper interview.

13. Johnson, *Stephen Harper*, 292.

14. Flanagan, *Harper's Team*, 27.

15. Johnson, *Stephen Harper*, 295.

16. Flanagan, *Harper's Team*, 39.

17. Norma Greenaway, "Leadership Race Too Close to Call," *Calgary Herald*, 20 March 2002, A11.

18. Johnson, *Stephen Harper*, 296.

NINE: Frustration

1. Grey, *Never Retreat*, 237.

2. Kingston, "Wife of the Party."

3. Edward Greenspon, "Stephen Harper: A Neo-Con in a Land of Liberals," *Globe and Mail*, 23 March 2002, A17.

4. Stephen Harper, *Getting It RIGHT: Strong and Principled Leadership* (2002 Canadian Alliance leadership campaign pamphlet). http://hfnn.ca /articles.php?showArticle=21887&offset=60

5. Johnson, *Stephen Harper*, 302.

6. "New Alliance Leader Says 'Defeatist' Attitude on East Coast Needs Changing," *Canadian Press*, 28 May 2001.

7. Johnson, *Stephen Harper*, 3.

8. "New Alliance Leader," *Canadian Press*, 28 May 2001.

9. Mark Kihn interview.

10. Canada, *House of Commons Debates*, 21 May 2002.

11. Susan Delacourt, *Juggernaut: Paul Martin's Campaign for Chrétien's Crown* (Toronto: McClelland & Stewart, 2003).

12. Mark Blanchard, "Clark to Step Down as Conservative Leader," *UPI*, 6 August 2002.

13. Hugh Segal, *The Long Road Back: Creating Canada's New Conservative Party* (Toronto: HarperCollins, 2006), 120.

14. Don Martin, "Why Is Peter MacKay's Love Life So Fascinating to Us?" *National Post*, 10 June 2010.

15. *The Orchard–MacKay Agreement*, www.davidorchard.com/online/ campaign-2003/orchard-mckay.html.

16. Flanagan, *Harper's Team*, 90.

17. Plamondon, *Full Circle*, 290.

TEN: Union

1. Segal, *The Long Road Back*, 249.

2. Norma Greenaway, "MacKay 'Open' to Talks with Alliance," *Ottawa Citizen*, 20 June 2013, A5.

3. *Agreement-in-Principle on the Establishment of the Conservative Party of Canada.*

4. "Secret Talks Held to Unite the Right," *CBC News*, 18 September 2003.

5. Paul Samyn, "Alliance, Tories, Call Off Merger," *Winnipeg Free Press*, 30 September 2003, A11.

6. "Harper, MacKay Unwrap New Conservative Party," *CBC News*, 16 October 2003.

7. Darren Yourk, "MacKay Betrayed Tories: Orchard," *Globe and Mail*, 17 October 2003.

8. Ibid.

9. Jim Brown, "Clark, Two Others, Walk Out on New Conservative Party," *Hamilton Spectator*, 9 December 2003, A9.

10. Bruce Cheadle, "Stronach Leaves Mixed Impression in First Foray into Political Spotlight," *Canadian Press*, 20 January 2004.

11. Flanagan, *Harper's Team*, 104.

12. Flanagan, *Harper's Team*, 126.

13. Canadian Press, "Bono Endorses Martin, Canada in Helping Third World," *Globe and Mail*, 16 November 2003.

14. "The Paul Martin Era Begins," *The National*, first broadcast 14 November 2003. *CBC Digital Archives*.

15. Paul Wells, *Right Side Up: The Fall of Paul Martin and the Rise of Stephen Harper's New Conservatism* (Toronto: McClelland & Stewart, 2006), 76.

16. Canadian Press, "I Believe What Occurred Is Inexcusable," *Winnipeg Free Press*, 13 February 2004.

17. Canada, *House of Commons Debates*, 20 March 2003.

18. Flanagan, *Harper's Team*, 160.

19. John H. Pammett and Christopher Dornan, eds., *The Canadian General Election of 2004* (Toronto: Dundurn, 2004), 261.

20. "The Truth – Liberal Party of Canada Ad," YouTube video, 0:32, posted by "llehman84," 21 May 2008.

21. Tonda MacCharles, "The World According to Harper," *Toronto Star*, 22 March 2004, A7.

22. Jonathan Rose, "Television Attack Ads: Planting the Seeds of Doubt," *Policy Options*, September 2004.

23. Flanagan, *Harper's Team*, 183.

24. "Harper's Campaign Mistake," *CBC News*, 20 June 2004.

25. Flanagan, *Harper's Team*, 179.

26. Ibid.

27. Flanagan, *Harper's Team*, 180.

28. Tom Flanagan interview.

29. Sue Bailey, "Harper Ducks Future Plans," *Winnipeg Free Press*, 30 June 2004.

ELEVEN: Winning

1. Flanagan, *Harper's Team*, 195.
2. Bill Curry, "NDP Studies Its Options in Familiar Landscape," *Globe and Mail*, 25 June 2006.
3. Stephen Harper, Gilles Duceppe, and Jack Layton, *Letter to the Governor General*, 9 September 2004.
4. "PM Promises More Money for Healthcare," *CBC News*, 26 March 2004.
5. John Ibbitson, "A Stark Reflection on the Two Halves of Canada," *Globe and Mail*, 17 September 2003.
6. "Delegates Reject Controversial Riding Changes," *Globe and Mail*, 19 March 2005.
7. Wells, *Right Side Up*, 145.
8. "Text of Prime Minister Paul Martin's Speech," *CBC News*, 21 April 2005.
9. Carson, *14 Days*, 104.
10. Robert Benzie and Sean Gordon, "Harper 'Read Her the Riot Act,' Sources Say," *Toronto Star*, 18 May 2005, A6.
11. Flanagan, *Harper's Team*, 217.
12. Plamondon, *Full Circle*, 294–295.
13. Johnson, *Stephen Harper*, 432.
14. Julie Van Dusen, "Dissident Quebec Conservatives Slam Harper's Leadership," *Hill Times*, 19 September 2005.
15. Johnson, *Stephen Harper*, 455.
16. Shannon Montgomery, "Teen Killed, Six Injured after Shots Fired in Downtown Toronto on Boxing Day," *Canadian Press*, 27 December 2005.
17. "Unfortunate Choice of Words," *Calgary Herald*, 30 December 2005, A22.
18. Lyrics from the song "Gee, Officer Krupke."
19. "2006 Liberal Attack Ad," YouTube video, 0:29, posted by "fakestephenharper," 9 October 2007.
20. Gloria Galloway, "Tory Ottawa Would Be Moderated by Liberal Influences: Harper," *Globe and Mail*, 17 January 2006.
21. "Stephen Harper's Victory Speech," *Canada.com*, 24 January 2006. www.canada.com/ottawacitizen/story.html?id=8a636173-8ff2-4cc2-89fe-280960bcbb0b&k=51207
22. George Koch interview.

BOOK TWO: POWER

TWELVE: 24

1. Brian Mulroney, *Memoirs* (Toronto: McClelland & Stewart, 2007), 505.
2. Interview with Derek Burney.
3. Carson, *14 Days*, 154.
4. Ibid.
5. "Global Corporate Tax Rates from Lowest to Highest," *Forbes.com*.
6. "Harper's Big Game Hunter Look a Fashion Faux Pas, Expert Says," *Ottawa Citizen*, 31 March 2006.
7. Carson, *14 Days*, 170.
8. Canada, *Hansard*, 11 June 2008.

THIRTEEN: Control

1. Interview with Derek Burney.
2. Ralph Surette, "Attention Voters! Send Tories Packing." *Halifax Chronicle Herald*, 23 January 2015.
3. Mark Bourrie, *Kill the Messenger: Stephen Harper's Assault on Your Right to Know* (Toronto: HarperCollins, 2015), Ch. 1.
4. Lawrence Martin, "Is This Still a Democracy? You Be the Judge," *iPolitics*, 12 April 2012. The list of government abuses recited in this chapter was inspired by the "march of audacities" that Martin chronicled in *Harperland: The Politics of Control* (Toronto: Viking, 2010), 272.
5. John Ralston Saul, *The Comeback* (Toronto: Viking 2014).
6. "Democracy Index 2013: Democracy in Limbo," *The Economist Intelligence Unit*.
7. Reporters Without Borders, *World Press Freedom Index 2014*.
8. Michael Babad, "Provinces to Snatch Back the Bulk of Ottawa's Tax Breaks: BMO," *Globe and Mail*, 30 March 2015.
9. Bill Curry, "By 2015, Harper Will Have Shrunk Government to Smallest Size in 50 Years," *Globe and Mail*, 18 November 2013.
10. Ian Bailey and Bill Curry, "In a Surprise Move, Flaherty Lays Out Health Care Plans Till 2024," *Globe and Mail*, 19 December 2011.
11. Chris Simpson, *Inaugural Address of Incoming President Chris Simpson* as delivered to the annual general meeting of the Canadian Medical Association, 21 August 2014.

12. "The Tories' Neater, Less Effective Federalism," *Toronto Star*, 29 December 2014.

FOURTEEN: Crisis

1. Rob Gillies, "Sliding in Polls, Canada's PM Unveils Platform," *USA Today*, 7 October 2008.
2. Bruce Cheadle, "Gala Crowd, 'Ivory Towers' Earn Harper Scorn," *Canadian Press*, 23 September 2008.
3. Canadian Broadcast Standards Council Decision, Atlantic Regional Panel, decided 6 April 2009.
4. Tonda MacCharles, "Tories Pounce on Dion Tape," *Toronto Star*, 10 October 2008.
5. Canadian Broadcast Standards Council decision, 6 April 2009.
6. "The Conservative Party Is Canada's Party," YouTube video, 7:56, posted by "Canuck Politics," 15 November 2008.
7. APEC stands for Asia-Pacific Economic Cooperation, a forum of twenty-one Pacific Rim countries that seeks to promote economic cooperation throughout the Asia-Pacific region.
8. *Protecting Canada's Future: Economic and Fiscal Statement 2008* (Ottawa: Department of Finance Canada, 2008).
9. This meeting was first reported in Paul Wells, *The Longer I'm Prime Minister: Stephen Harper and Canada, 2006–* (Toronto: Random House Canada, 2013). I have confirmed it independently.
10. Brian Topp, *How We Almost Gave the Tories the Boot: The Inside Story Behind the Coalition* (Toronto: Lorimer, 2010), 145.
11. Thomas Joseph, *8 Days of Crisis on the Hill: Political Blip or Stephen Harper's Revolution Derailed?* (Bloomington, IN: iUniverse, 2009), 107.
12. See, for example, Peter Russell and Lorne Swain, eds., *Parliamentary Democracy in Crisis* (Toronto: Lorimer, 2009).
13. Michael Ignatieff, *Fire and Ashes: Success and Failure in Politics* (Toronto: Random House Canada, 2013), 109.

FIFTEEN: Prorogue

1. Joan Bryden and Jim Brown, "Liberals Ditch Dion Exit Plan," *Toronto Star*, 7 December 2008.
2. Ignatieff, *Fire and Ashes*, 109.

3. John Wiersema, *2011 Fall Report of the Auditor General* (Ottawa: Government of Canada, 2011).

4. Steven Chase et al., "Stimulus Program Favours Tory Ridings," *Globe and Mail*, 21 October 2009.

5. Ignatieff, *Fire and Ashes*, 112.

6. Carson, *14 Days*, 249.

7. Ibid., 185.

8. Don Martin, "Conservatives Too Eager to Wage War with Diplomat," *Calgary Herald*, 20 November 2009, A6.

9. Military Police Complaints Commission, *Commission's Final Report – MPCC 2008-042 – Concerning a Complaint by Amnesty International Canada and British Columbia Civil Liberties Association in June 2008* (Ottawa, 27 June 2012).

10. Interview with Ted Morton.

SIXTEEN: Fulfillment

1. Jessica Leeder and Jane Taber, "Harper Performed with a Little Help from His Wife," *Globe and Mail*, 24 October 2009.

2. Stephen Harper, *A Great Game: The Forgotten Leafs and the Rise of Professional Hockey* (Toronto: Simon & Schuster, 2013), 287.

3. Harper, *A Great Game*, 17.

4. Tonda MacCharles, "Prime Minister Stephen Harper's Bodyguard, Mountie Bruno Saccomani, Faces Workplace Harassment Probe," *Toronto Star*, 30 May 2013.

5. Elections Canada, *Registered Party Financial Returns*, 2011.

6. Wells, *The Longer I'm Prime Minister*, Ch. 9.

7. Jane Taber, "NDP Makes Hay of Ignatieff Truancy as 'Serene' Liberals Lash Out," *Globe and Mail*, 25 April 2011.

8. "PM Harper May 2011 Election Night behind the Scenes," YouTube video, 5:13, posted by "Steve Harper," 11 June 2013.

9. "Harper Wins Conservative Majority," YouTube video, 14:53, posted by "Canuck Politics," 3 May 2001.

SEVENTEEN: Foreigners

1. Much of the material in this chapter is drawn from John Ibbitson, *The Big Break: The Conservative Transformation of Canada's Foreign Policy* (Waterloo: Centre for International Governance Innovation, 2014).

2. Louis St. Laurent, "The Foundations of Canadian Policy in World Affairs," *Statements and Speeches* (Ottawa: Department of External Affairs, 1947).

3. *Platform and Statement of Principles of the Reform Party of Canada*, 25.

4. "Won't Sell Out on Rights Despite China Snub: PM," *CBC News*, 15 November 2006.

5. Ibbitson, *The Big Break*, 7.

6. Bruce Cheadle, "Harper Sides Firmly with Israel," *Canadian Press*, 13 July 2006.

7. Geoff Dyer, "Harper Clashes with China on Human Rights," *Financial Times*, 4 December 2009.

8. Steve Rennie, "After Harper's Comments, Putin Cast as Pariah at G8 Summit," *Canadian Press*, 17 June 2013.

9. "Stephen Harper at G20 Tells Vladimir Putin to 'Get Out of Ukraine,'" *Canadian Press*, 15 November 2014.

10. Confidential source.

11. John Ibbitson, "Justin Trudeau Can't Ignore Domestic Concerns in Foreign Policy," *Globe and Mail*, 22 May 2014.

12. Edward Greenspon et al., "How Obama Shocked Harper as Keystone's Frustrator in Chief," *Bloomberg News*, 26 April 2014.

13. Taken from John Ibbitson, *Open and Shut: Why America Has Barack Obama, and Canada Has Stephen Harper* (Toronto: McClelland & Stewart, 2009).

14. John Ibbitson, "Harper Unbound: An Analysis of His First Year as Majority PM," *Globe and Mail*, 28 April 2012.

15. Shawn McCarthy, "Keystone Pipeline Approval 'Complete No Brainer,' Harper Says," *Globe and Mail*, 21 September 2011.

16. Greenspon et al., "How Obama Shocked Harper."

17. Joe Oliver, *An Open Letter from The Honourable Joe Oliver, Minister of Natural Resources, on Canada's Commitment to Diversify Our Energy Markets and the Need to Further Streamline the Regulatory Process in Order to Advance Canada's National Economic Interest* (Ottawa: Natural Resources Canada, 9 January 2012).

18. Jennifer Campbell, "Whither Canada's Foreign Policy?" *Ottawa Citizen*, 10 December 2013.

19. Joe Clark, *How We Lead* (Toronto: Random House Canada, 2013).

20. Paul Heinbecker, *Getting Back in the Game* (Toronto: Key Porter, 2010).

21. Susana Mas, "Stephen Harper Tells UN Maternal and Child Health Close to His Heart," *CBC News*, 25 September 2014.

22. Mike Blanchfield, "PM Harper Pledges \$3.5 Billion to Extend Maternal, Child Health Initiative to 2020," *Hamilton Spectator*, 9 May 2014.

23. Confidential source.

24. Paul Evans, *Engaging China: Myth, Aspiration and Strategy in Canadian Policy from Trudeau to Harper* (Toronto: University of Toronto Press, 2014), 75.

25. John Baird, *Address by Minister Baird to the United Nations General Assembly* (Ottawa: Foreign Affairs, Trade and Development Canada, 1 October 2012).

26. Mike Blanchfield, "John Baird Touted by Ex-Australian PM to Help Reform WHO," *Toronto Star*, 1 February 2015.

EIGHTEEN: Hubris

1. Zack Taylor, Phil Triadafilopoulos, and Christopher Cochrane, *On the Backs of Immigrants? Conservative Politics and New Canadian Voters.* Unpublished study, 2012.

2. Marci McDonald, "True Blue," *The Walrus*, May 2014.

3. Citizenship and Immigration Canada, *Report on Plans and Priorities 2014–2015* (Ottawa: Government of Canada, 2014).

4. John Ibbitson, *Bootstrap Immigrants: Assessing the Conservative Transformation of Canada's Immigration Policy* (Waterloo: Centre for International Governance Innovation, 2014).

5. Quoted in Susan Delacourt, "Immigrants a Key Bloc for All Parties in Next Election," *Toronto Star*, 26 December 2014.

6. *Statement by the Prime Minister at the World Economic Forum* (Ottawa: Office of the Prime Minister, Government of Canada), 26 January 2012. http://pm.gc.ca/eng/news/2012/01/26/statement-prime-minister-canada-world-economic-forum

7. Michael Harris, *Party of One: Stephen Harper and Canada's Radical Makeover* (Toronto: Penguin, 2014), 421.

8. Ibid., 430.

9. Allan Levine, "Control Freaks and Dictators: Successful Prime Ministers Tend to Have Autocratic Personalities," *Winnipeg Free Press*, 3 November 2014.

10. Ibid.

11. Brad Lavigne, *Building the Orange Wave* (Toronto: Douglas & McIntyre, 2013), 244.

12. Darrell Bricker, *Progressive Voters Need Leaders That Inspire Them. The*

Left Needs to Love. Trudeau Has It, Mulcair Needs to Find It, Twitter post, 26 August 2014, 5:59 a.m., http://twitter.com/darrellbricker.

13. See Warren Kinsella, *Fight the Right: A Manual for Surviving the Coming Conservative Apocalypse* (Toronto: Random House Canada, 2012), and Paul Adams, *Power Trap: How Fear and Loathing between New Democrats and Liberals Keep Stephen Harper in Power – And What Can Be Done about It* (Toronto: Lorimer, 2012).

14. John Ibbitson, "Harper Unbound: An Analysis of His First Year as Majority PM," *Globe and Mail*, 28 April 2012.

15. Jack Layton, *A Letter to Canadians from the Honourable Jack Layton*, 20 August 2011.

NINETEEN: Nemesis

1. Martin, *Harperland*, 13, 18.

2. Steve Rennie, "Harper Says Tories Not Behind Robocalls," *Winnipeg Free Press*, 29 February 2012.

3. John Ibbitson, "The Case against a Conspiracy," *Globe and Mail*, 5 March 2012.

4. John Ibbitson, "What's Really at Stake in Etobicoke Hearing?" *Globe and Mail*, 11 July 2012.

5. Steven Chase, "Nigel Wright, the Man Who Bailed Out Mike Duffy," *Globe and Mail*, 13 May 2013.

6. Confidential source.

7. Greg Horton, "In the Matter of an Application for Production Orders Pursuant to Section 487.012 of the *Criminal Code*."

8. Andrew Mayeda and Althia Raj, "Harper Vows Not to Reopen Abortion Debate as Prime Minister," *Postmedia News*, 21 April 2011.

9. Pamela Wallin, "Pamela Wallin's 3,000-Word Speech to the Senate: Full Text," *National Post*, 23 October 2013.

10. Ibid.

11. "Mike Duffy's 1,750-Word Speech to the Senate: The Full Text," *National Post*, 23 October 2013.

12. Rosemary Barton, "Thomas Mulcair Shows Off His Legal Skills in Question Period," *CBC News*, 14 November 2013.

13. "Full Speech: Harper Addresses the Conservative Convention," *Global News*, 1 November 2013.

TWENTY: Catharsis

1. Taken from Carson, *14 Days*, 207, and independently confirmed.
2. John Ivison, "Why Jim Flaherty Will Go Down as One of Canada's Best Finance Ministers," *National Post*, 11 April 2014.
3. Ibid.
4. Bill Curry, "Flaherty's Death Comes as a 'Terrible Shock,' Harper Says," *Globe and Mail*, 10 April 2014.
5. Josh Dehaas, "First Nations Dropout Rate Falls, But Less So on Reserves," *Maclean's*, 2 May 2014.
6. "Six Big Changes the Charter of Rights Has Brought," *CBC News*, 17 April 2012.
7. The above paragraphs draw from John Ibbitson, "How Harper Created a More Conservative Canada," *Globe and Mail*, 6 February 2015.
8. John Ivison, "Tories Incensed with Top Court; Some Allege Chief Justice Lobbied Against Nadon as Tensions Mount," *National Post*, 1 May 2014.
9. Mark Kennedy, "PMO Says Harper Avoided 'Inappropriate' Call from Chief Justice on Nadon," *Ottawa Citizen*, 2 May 2014.
10. *News Release* (Ottawa: Supreme Court of Canada, 2 May 2014).
11. John Ibbitson, "A New Era for Canada Rises in the East," *Globe and Mail*, 8 December 2014.
12. Kady O'Malley, "Justin Trudeau Says PM 'Hasn't Even Tried' to Make Case for Expanded Iraq Role," *CBC News*, 2 October 2014.
13. "Full Text of Peter Mansbridge's Interview with Stephen Harper," *CBC News*, 17 December 2014.
14. Kat Long, "Stephen Harper's Franklin Fever," *National Post*, 12 May 2014.
15. Mansbridge interview with Stephen Harper, 17 December 2014.
16. Ryan Maloney, "Trudeau Won't 'Second Guess' Harper for Ducking into Closet During Shooting," *Huffington Post*, 5 January 2015.
17. Allan Woods, "Canadian Solder Killed in Suspected Terror Attack Identified," *Toronto Star*, 21 October 2014.
18. Steven Chase and Darryl Hol, "New Anti-Terror Laws Coming as Jihadis 'Declare War,' Harper Says," *Globe and Mail*, 8 January 2015.

Afterword

1. Dean Beeby, "Behold Stephen Harper's Little-Known Guitar Collection," *CBC News*, 18 January 2015.
2. Joan Crockett, "Ralph Klein: Joker, Smoker . . . Trailblazer," *Maclean's*, 30 March 2013.

Index

Note: The initials SH in a subheading refer to Stephen Harper. The letter *n* following a page number indicates that the information is in a footnote.